SIDE BY SIDE
A Multicultural Reader

HANDBOOK FOR WRITERS

Harvey S. Wiener *Adelphi University*

Charles Bazerman

Houghton Mifflin Company   **Boston**   **Toronto**

Geneva, Illinois   Palo Alto   Princeton, New Jersey

CREDITS

Maya Angelou: From *I Know Why The Caged Bird Sings* by Maya Angelou. Copyright © 1969 by Maya Angelou. Reprinted by permission of Random House, Inc.

James Baldwin: "If Black English Isn't a Language, Then Tell Me What Is?" *The New York Times*, July 29, 1979. Copyright © 1979 by the New York Times Company. Reprinted by permission.

Albert Camarillo: "Zoot Suit Riots" from Chicanos in California: A History of Mexican Americans in California. Copyright © 1984 by Boyd & Fraser Publishing Company, San Francisco, CA 94118. Reprinted by permission.

Stephen L. Carter: "I Am an Affirmative Action Baby," *Op-Ed, The New York Times*, August 5, 1991. Copyright © 1991 by the New York Times Company. Reprinted by permission.

Janice Castro: "Spanglish Spoken Here," *Time*, July 11, 1988. © 1988 Time Inc. Reprinted by permission.

Humberto Cintron: "Across Third Avenue: Freedom," *Puerto Rico Perspectives*, ed. Edwin Mapp, The Scarecrow Press, Inc., 1974, pp. 18–162. Reprinted by permission of the publisher.

Athlone G. Clarke: "Crossing a Boundary," from *Newsweek*, May 13, 1991. Reprinted by permission of the author.

Jesus Colon: "Easy Job, Good Wages," *A Puerto Rican in New York* (New York: Mainstream, 1961). Reprinted by permission of International Publishers, New York.

Ellen Tashie Frisina: "See Spot Run: Teaching My Grandmother to Read." Reprinted by permission of the author.

David Gelman: "Of Mice and Men—and Morality," from *Newsweek*, July 18, 1988. © 1988 Newsweek, Inc. All rights reserved. Reprinted by permission.

Credits continued on p. 550.

Sponsoring Editor: *Renée Deljon*
Editorial Assistant: *Jennifer Huber*
Senior Project Editor: *Susan Westendorf*
Production Editorial Assistant: *Gabrielle Stone*
Associate Production/Design Coordinator: *Jennifer Waddell*
Senior Manufacturing Coordinator: *Priscilla Bailey*

Printed in the U.S.A.

ISBN: 0-395-71925-9

Examination copy ISBN: 0-395-76574-9

Library of Congress Catalog Card Number: 95-76998

456789-QF-00 99 98

Contents

CHAPTER 6

Side by Side: The Sum of the Parts   375

UNIT TWO

Mechanics   505

Rhetorical Contents*

*Most selections are listed under more than one rhetorical strategy.

DESCRIPTION

EXAMPLE AND ILLUSTRATION

NARRATION

PROCESS ANALYSIS

Preface

Side by Side is a multicultural reader for writers devoted to a curriculum of inclusion; its aim is to capture the varieties of American experience, drawn from diverse ethnic, social, and cultural groups, and to present a range of readings that help define our country and enrich its written legacy. Our collection of readings reflects the unprecedented mix of writers now speaking to American readers and students now filling college classrooms across the country. In this Second Edition of *Side by Side* we continue our emphasis on content-rich selections and extensive apparatus to lead students to analyze what they read, apply their own experiences and knowledge of the topic of the selection, and then justify and develop their responses in writing. In our wish to provide a comprehensive reading and writing program for beginning college students, we have included in this new edition a "Handbook for Writers," which addresses students' questions about sentences, word choice, grammar and mechanics.

THEMATIC ORGANIZATION ▬▬▬▬▬▬

Part I, Readings, begins with an essential discussion on "Writing and Reading." We explore the writing-reading connection, critical thinking through writing, prewriting activities, limiting and developing topics, selecting rhetorical strategies, and drafting. In the rest of Part I, we have divided the fiction and non-fiction readings into six chapters, each organized around a theme that links the readings:

> *Childhood: Born in the U.S.A.* presents the common experience of growing up from the perspectives of children with different culture backgrounds.

Selves: True Colors focuses on individuals searching for their identities through their culture and heritage.

Language: Our Words, Our Voices explores language and its effect on our culture and behavior.

Jobs: Dollars and Dreams shows how Americans of all backgrounds can struggle in their pursuit of the "American Dream."

Prejudice: Tears in the Rainbow Fabric looks at the damaging effects of racism and discrimination.

Side by Side: The Sum of the Parts celebrates the individuality and diversity of the people of our nation.

We have updated each chapter by adding lively new selections that explore the themes and engage readers' attention. Taken together, these themes, we believe, represent the dreams and aspirations, the joys and disappointments, the aches and longings of the men, women, and children who people our nation.

APPARATUS

To guide study and to focus conversation, we offer a rich set of apparatus. A brief overview focuses on the issues that emerge from the selections in each unit.

- *Prereading Journal* questions ask students to explore their background knowledge and opinions of the ideas presented in the unit.
- An *explanatory headnote* provides context for the selection that follows.
- *Key vocabulary* gives definitions for difficult words in the reading.
- *Details and Their Meanings* asks students to explore their comprehension of the details and ideas of the readings.
- *Reading and Critical Thinking* leads students to examine inferential meanings and judge the writer's ideas.
- *The Writer's Strategies* require students to analyze the rhetorical techniques that advance the writer's meaning in the selection.
- *Thinking Together* encourages students to draw on collaborative learning techniques to discuss and apply an essential issue related to the reading selection.

- A *vocabulary* exercise helps students integrate unfamiliar words and phrases into the student's linguistic resources.
- *Writing Workshop* offers varied opportunities for students' writing. First, "Critical Thinking in Writing" provides challenging tasks to stimulate short essays on the ideas expressed in the readings. Next, "Connecting Ideas" guides students to link issues raised in one selection with related issues from other readings throughout the text. This activity encourages multiple perspectives on major topics in the text.
- At the end of each chapter, *Side by Side* prompts students to reflect in writing about the units' themes. Students can return to their prereading journal entries and consider how the chapter essays provided new insights or confirmed old ones.
- The new "Handbook for Writers" will guide students to consider the conventions of edited American English as students advance through drafts to final copy. A handy reference chart and correction symbols on the inside back cover will allow students to check the comments and marks on a paper against appropriate sections in the Handbook.

ACKNOWLEDGEMENTS

Many people helped us with this book by providing valuable comments in early stages of the manuscript. We would like to thank the following reviewers:

Norma Cruz-Gonzales, San Antonio College, TX
Jane Maher, Nassau Community College, NY
Elisabeth B. Leyson, Fullerton College, CA
E. Jane Melendez, East Tennessee State University, TN
Gail Mooney, Middlesex Community College, MA
Patricia Patterson, Community College of Allegheny County, PA
Peggy R. Porter, Northwest College—Westchester Campus, TX
Mary Tower, Atlantic Community College, NJ
Amy Ulmer, Pasadena City College, CA
Linda Weeks, Dyersburg State Community College, TN

PART ONE

Reading Selections

Writing and Reading

Each of us has a mental picture of the complex world we live in. Everyday experiences contribute to our world view and to our understanding of the peoples and cultures that occupy our planet, our country, our city, our neighborhood. Certainly, all the reading we do, both formal and informal, plays a major role in shaping how we think; reading brings detail, focus, and specificity to our mental picture. Indeed, the selections in *Side by Side* will sharpen and expand your concept of the world community. But only by sharing information with others—by speaking and by writing—can you be sure that your conclusions about issues are sound and that your mental picture takes into account the thoughts and experiences of other people.

THE WRITING-READING CONNECTION

The writing-reading connection helps us to develop an informed vision of the world. Reading places before our eyes a range of thoughts and ideas that we otherwise might never encounter. Writing helps us share our understanding so that others see how we think and can react to our ideas. Writing helps us sharpen our thoughts on a subject because clear writing demands thinking about an idea in a rigorous way.

In this book, we examine readings not only to explore their multicultural content and their perspectives on the American experience but also to analyze how writers write, what effects they achieve, and how they achieve those effects. This plan enables us to evaluate how the experience of reading affects our thoughts about a subject and can shape our written responses to what we have read.

All through your education, you have explored different kinds of readings. In your earliest schooldays, you read for facts or for entertainment. As you advanced through the grades, your teachers assigned material that required you to interact with the ideas and information. Some selections pleased and entertained more than others, but probably the common thread that connected the readings was that each one helped to focus your picture of the world. Readings of value add to your information base, expand your point of view about a topic, help you to analyze or evaluate your situations, introduce fresh perspectives on issues, and challenge you to develop and justify your own beliefs.

Reading for meaning is different from reading for pleasure or even reading for facts. To know that you understand a selection, you need to apply the material in some way, to incorporate it into your thinking and to use it to help you understand the world. The most constructive way to use the material is to write about it.

CRITICAL THINKING THROUGH WRITING ──

Writing helps you think critically about what you read. The first step in critical thinking is comparing or applying your own experience or prior thoughts about a subject to the selection you have just read. Your own experience is a valuable tool because it is the resource that you have most readily at hand. Even though many of the selections in this book deal with topics far removed from your everyday experience, your thoughts and emotions are good guides to whether a writer is presenting ideas sincerely and accurately.

The activities in *Side by Side* ask you to write regularly about the issues emerging from the selections. Generally, we make specific assignments that highlight a focused and dynamic issue from the selection, one that may require a particular rhetorical strategy for appropriate essay development.

In the writing assignments, we have provided a variety of tasks. The most basic kind of writing that we encourage is summary writing. In a summary, you need to reproduce the information of a selection in your own words in order to state what a reading means. You identify the main idea, the essential support that the writer provides, and the conclusion (if any) that the writer draws. In a summary, you don't have to worry about whether you agree with the writer or whether the selection seems logical or true. Those critical judgments come later.

In other places, we ask you to react informally to what you have read—that is, to provide an initial emotional or intellectual response to one or more key issues that emerge from the selection. We suggest that you write a journal entry or a letter to stimulate a flow of ideas independent of any formal essay requirements. But we do not neglect the formal essay: many of the assignments you will do here require some command of essay conventions—for example, introduction, thesis, body, rhetorical strategies, transitions, convincing details, and conclusions. We encourage library research when a topic takes you into areas about which you have limited knowledge or information from your own experience. Many of the questions we ask about the selections reflect these concerns, so you should be primed to apply to your own writing what we have highlighted about essay form and technique for each piece in *Side by Side*.

Another approach we take to stimulate writing about your reading is to ask you in "Connecting Ideas" to compare and contrast various selections that you have read. In some instances, you can create a *synthesis* of two or more pieces by combining the information into a picture of the subject that is larger and more coherent than the picture you had after reading only one of the selections. However, you may find that writers offer opposing views about the same topic or that they present a problem similarly but disagree about the course of action to follow. In those situations, you will need to weigh carefully the support a writer uses to back up an argument. You can start by asking what is the writer's *warrant* for making a particular assertion. A warrant is the authority, justification, or grounds that support a particular claim. Direct experience is usually a good warrant for some issues, but not always. Ask yourself how much experience the writer has with the topic, whether he or she has any ideological or personal stake in advancing a certain claim, whether he or she is presenting information fairly or slanting it. Once you have evaluated the writer's support, you can render a reasoned judgment of your own about the topic.

PRE-WRITING

As you try to frame a written response to your reading, look carefully at the questions we have provided. Wherever you can, use them or questions your instructor gives you to help you start to think about a topic that interests you. Narrow the topic, if necessary, to suit your own concerns. Talk with your friends, roommates, and teachers about the issues that prod your thoughts.

A number of informal techniques can help you get started in formulating a written reaction to a selection.

Freewriting

An easy, enjoyable kind of writing to stimulate thought is called *freewriting*. When you freewrite, you write nonstop on a topic for a set amount of time (fifteen minutes, for example) without worrying about where your thoughts are going or how your writing will look. Nobody will ever judge what you freewrite, so you need not slow down to make sure that your grammar and spelling are correct. Your ideas don't even have to follow any logical order. Freewriting is exactly like talking to yourself about something.

The point of talking to yourself on paper is to help you identify feelings, clarify responses, and develop ideas that you will be able to use later in a formal assignment. Committing ideas to paper in this way can be useful even months later to remind you of your reaction to a particular topic or selection.

Journal Writing

Because writing, like any other activity, usually becomes easier the more you do it, a good place to gather your responses is in a *writing journal* that you update regularly. All the units in *Side by Side* begin with some suggestions for journal assignments, and the more writing you do in your journal, the deeper and richer your writing will become. Journal writing is closer to freewriting than to the formal essay writing process. In some of the journal entries that we recommend, you will freewrite your ideas and feelings about a subject; in others, you will set down your thoughts and observations. Because journals are portable, you can add to an entry whenever an idea occurs to you. Because journals are also private, you can write what you wish and pay little attention to grammar and spelling. Concentrate only on getting your unedited thoughts down on paper.

Brainstorming

Another technique for getting started is *brainstorming*. It is usually a group activity in which a few people or even a whole class verbalizes ideas without worrying about how good those ideas are. Maybe you'll have a terrible idea that will make the next person think of something that will help you improve your own idea, which in turn can stimulate another person to say something really profound. Brainstorming is an excellent strategy to follow in the various group activities we encourage throughout *Side by Side*. Once you get started with this process of free-associating, the ideas are likely to grow better and better.

Asking Reporters' Questions

A useful start-up technique that many investigative reporters use is asking *who, what, when, where, why*, and *how* questions. These questions help clarify and focus a topic, generate specific details, and even highlight aspects of a thought that may need special attention. Reporters' questions enable you to limit and focus a topic. The five *w* and one *h* questions can be used again at any time in the writing process when you get stuck on a point.

Making a List

To stimulate ideas in responses to an essay question, you can simply make a list of everything that comes to mind about a subject. Do not worry about the connections between ideas that you generate or whether the ideas flow logically from one to the other. Later you can connect related thoughts and eliminate anything that seems inappropriate. Your initial goal is to fill a page with random thoughts that, when expanded, can yield fruitful essay responses.

Making Rough Outlines

As a topic stimulates their thinking, some writers jot information down in a *rough outline.* Major areas of thought appear in headings; possible supporting thoughts, in subheadings. Rough outlines allow you to develop ideas and loosely organize them at the same time. Don't fuss about using roman and arabic numerals or capital and lowercase letters to list your ideas in a rough outline. Simply indicate broad areas suggested by the topic, and place under them any supporting or related ideas.

Whether you are working from a freewriting paragraph, a list, or a rough outline, once you finish you will have a tangible document in your hands, something concrete that marks the beginning of the writing process. You are now approaching the point at which you can begin your formal writing.

LIMITING AND DEVELOPING YOUR TOPIC ——

Limiting Your Topic

Before you begin to produce a draft, start to limit your topic by eliminating and grouping information from your prewriting exercise. Doing so will make writing a formal essay easier and more precise. Grouping related ideas together in an informal outline creates a basis for paragraphs. If you find one idea that doesn't go anywhere or fit in with your other ideas, you might want to leave it out of your essay. If you produced a rough outline during prewriting, flesh it out. If you used some other pre-writing strategy, grouping or outlining will help you to limit your topic and organize your initial responses.

Besides grouping, there are several helpful guidelines for limiting a topic. You need to ask yourself, "Who will read this paper—who is my *audience?*" In just the same way that you speak to your grandparents differently from the way you speak to your classmates, knowing who will read your essay will help you decide how elaborate your explanations should be, how formally you need to approach a topic, and how much detail and support you should provide. How much do your readers already know about a topic? With what terms and concepts will they already be familiar? Which ones will you need to explain?

Another important question that will help you limit your topic is "What is the *purpose* of this paper?"—that is, what response are you looking for from your reader? If you are telling a funny story, then the response you want is laughter. If you are giving instructions for loading a disk into a computer, then you want your reader to be able to perform that task successfully. If you are writing about the benefits of recycling, then you want your reader to agree that recycling is a good idea. With your audience and purpose in mind, you can make appropriate word choices and construct sentences designed to achieve your goals.

Generating a Thesis

Once you finish your outline and other efforts to limit your topic, the next essential step is to generate a *thesis*. Every piece of writing you do should have at its heart a main point, an assertion, a belief, a discovery. The thesis is a one-sentence statement of what you want to communicate to your reader. It informs the reader about the topic, and it indicates your attitude toward, or opinion about, the topic. A good thesis tells the reader exactly what you want to assert in the essay and what the reader will understand if he or she reads what you have written. Often you can construct an effective thesis from the language in the assignment that you have been given, so read the writing task statement carefully. Suppose that the assignment is this:

> Do you personally identify more with your roots or with some newer version of evolving American culture? Write an essay describing the culture that you feel part of or want to be part of.

You can construct a thesis like this, which draws on the words from the task:

> As the American daughter of Korean immigrant parents, I always identified with a newer born-in-America version of our evolving culture until my shocking adventures on a trip to Seoul, home of my mother's parents.

In other cases, as with a broadly stated assignment, you'll have to construct the thesis exclusively from your own language resources. For example, if your announced topic is simply *affirmative action*, you might propose one of these sentences as your thesis:

> Affirmative action policies have allowed many minority women to move upward on the career ladder in high-level academic jobs.
>
> The attacks on affirmative action policies by some government leaders have had devastating effects on how white America views job opportunities for black men and women.

In the early stages of your writing, you should view your thesis as tentative: it will change as you continue thinking about the ideas and details of your essay. Experienced writers often tinker with their thesis statements right up to the final draft. But in all the examples given above, notice how the writer states a limited topic and makes an assertion about it.

SELECTING RHETORICAL STRATEGIES ━━━━

After you have written a tentative thesis and have weighed your audience and purpose, consider the various rhetorical strategies available to you as you develop your essay. Most college writing is expository—designed to inform and explain something about a topic. You will find it helpful to consider some of the subgroups under the writing category "exposition" as ways of developing an idea clearly and thoughtfully. The following list identifies and defines these subgroups and shows how a writer might develop an essay response to a typical topic by using various rhetorical techniques.

Topic: Affirmative Action

Technique	Example
Description: Provide a picture.	Describe a scene at McDonald's in which members of a multi-ethnic work force, created through affirmative action, work together harmoniously.

Technique	Example
Narration: Tell a story.	Tell a story about how a relative was accepted for a job-training program because of affirmative action guidelines.
Illustration: Explain by giving examples.	Illustrate three cases of how affirmative action policies helped people turn their lives around.
Comparison and Contrast: Explain by showing similarities and differences.	Indicate what an office was like before and after the employer established affirmative action guidelines.
Process Analysis: Explain by showing how to do or make something.	Identify the steps to be taken to make affirmative action policies work on your campus.
Causal Analysis: Explain the cause and effects of some issue or event.	Analyze the reasons why affirmative action policies were developed, or analyze the consequences of those policies on the job.
Classification: Explain an idea by setting up categories.	Classify the kinds of responses that communities can make to affirmative action policies.
Definition: Explain by giving an expanded meaning.	Define affirmative action in the twenty-first century.
Argumentation: Take sides on a controversial point.	Argue for (or against) continuing affirmative action policies in government employment.

The writing assignments in *Side by Side* sometimes specify the rhetorical task—"Write a narrative essay to show how you moved beyond some restrictions of your childhood to discover a bigger world," for example. Other assignments are more open-ended, and you should choose a method or combination of methods of development on your own. Your thesis, audience, and purpose all will affect your selection of the most appropriate developmental mode.

DRAFTING

When the preliminary tasks are out of the way, you can concentrate on crafting your essay. Your first attempt is called the *first draft*. Sometimes—when you are doing an in-class test, for instance—the first draft is all you have time to write. Don't worry. If you have followed the steps described above, you will be able to do a good, though somewhat rough, job of presenting your ideas even when you have time only for one draft. Despite the press of time in an in-class essay exam, do not sacrifice pre-writing, even if you can give only a few minutes to it.

In most college writing courses, however, the first draft is just a rough draft. You will have time to go over your work several times, making each draft better and a little more polished. Try to make the rough draft a relaxed effort. Don't censor yourself or inhibit the flow of ideas. The main purpose of a rough draft is to write consecutive sentences on paper about a topic that you've thought about carefully.

After you get through your essay once, let it sit for a while. Do something else. You will produce a better revision if you get a fresh perspective. Taking a break between drafts helps clear your mind and makes you more objective.

This is often a good stage at which to let someone else take a look at your work. Another reader is often useful for clarifying for you the kind of revision that is needed. But whether there is another reader or you are the only person reading your rough draft, the same issues should guide you toward a revised draft.

Two essential issues are unity and coherence, and any revision must address them carefully. *Unity* refers to the idea that all sentences in an essay must relate to the thesis as well as to each other. *Coherence* refers to the idea that all written thoughts must connect to each other logically, clearly, and smoothly. Unity and coherence are the writer's and reader's guarantee that the piece makes sense.

In your revision efforts, pay attention to how you have ordered the details in your paper. Especially in a narrative or process essay, you may want to organize information chronologically, that is according to a clear time sequence. In a descriptive paper, you may wish to present details spatially—top to bottom, front to back, or side to side, for example. Or you might wish to consider arranging details in order of importance, where you build to an essential point by presenting the less important information before you tell the reader the most important details.

As you revise, you need to ask questions such as these: "Does the writing make sense?" "Did I leave anything out?" "Could the essay be clearer if I changed the order of ideas?" "Do I need more examples or more specific details?" "Are there some things I should leave out?" "Can the beginning or ending be stronger?" "Have I presented my ideas in a grammatically fluent way without too many spelling, punctuation, or other kinds of errors?"

If you handwrite or type your paper, you might use a different colored pencil or pen at this stage to cross out or draw lines indicating where to move words and sentences. Insert new pages with changes. Write notes to yourself in the margins; put arrows or stars where you want to add material. Don't worry about the mess. The key aim of revision is to produce a guide for the next draft. As long as you produce a useful document, you are revising correctly. If you use a computer, your revisions will be much easier to accomplish; move words around and insert phrases using the various options of your word-processing program.

Start with a fresh sheet of paper for the second draft. Work slowly to make sure you integrate all the changes from the first draft. Make sure you proofread for both content and grammar. Make sure you copy everything exactly as you want it to be, without missing anything or copying something incorrectly.

When you are finished with the second draft, put it aside for a while before you come back to it. When you reread it, be strict with yourself. Can you rewrite any sentences to make them clearer? Are your most important statements in the most important places in your paragraphs? Could your language be more precise, livelier, more direct? One of your main concerns at this stage should be *editing,* that is correcting all errors that you may have ignored (appropriately) in early drafts as you worked toward clearer, fuller sentences and logical paragraphs. Are there mistakes in grammar, spelling, sentence structure, or punctuation? If you are satisfied with your responses to each question, you may decide it is time to hand the essay in. If you are not satisfied, writing another draft is a good idea.

You'll have lots of opportunity to read and write from the selections in *Side by Side.* Enjoy—and learn.

ONE

Childhood:
Born in the U.S.A.

INTRODUCTION ━━━━━━━━━━━━━━━━━━━━

America is a country of many contrasts—between the future and the past, tradition and change, poverty and wealth, glaciers and rain forests, high-tech cities and simple country towns, and children and adults. Sometimes it isn't easy to cope with the sharp divisions and contradictions of American life. All Americans are constantly pulled in many directions, between the need to fit in and the need to be themselves, between the desire to preserve the past and the desire to embrace the future, between their ethnic identities and the dominant American culture.

Children only gradually discover that growing up in America can be a difficult challenge. In this unit, you will read about children past and present, from many parts of the country, who are of different classes and ethnic groups. You will discover what they learned about America and how they struggled to make difficult decisions. In "An American Dream," by Rosemary Santini, you will read about the struggle between heritage and change. In "The Struggle to Be an All-American Girl," by Elizabeth Wong, there is the struggle between American and ethnic cultures.

Parents and other relatives are often important teachers, easing the road to maturity—or making it more complex. In "Moon on a Silver Spoon," Eudora Welty tells how she learned an important lesson from her mother. Yet sometimes parents can be a source of conflict, as Langston Hughes recalls in "Salvation," a moving portrayal of a religious experience in his youth. Sometimes the conflicts between parents and children are the result of cultural clashes, as in "America's New Wave of Runaways," a report on conflicts in values between Southeast Asian immigrant children and their more traditional parents, and "Growing Up in Black and White," an essay on the difficulties encountered by African American children as they grow up in the United States. There are even times when a child must reject his or her parents' world completely, as Sam Moses points out dramatically in "A New Dawn," an account of a teenager's daring escape from Cuba.

What binds these essays from many cultural perspectives is the intensely realized efforts of the writers to understand the ways of childhood in an increasingly complicated world.

16

PREREADING   JOURNAL

Before you go to the selections in Unit One, write about one of the following topics in your journal.

1. Compare your experiences of growing up with what you know or imagine were your parents' experiences. What do you think was especially easy or hard about growing up then? How do the challenges and opportunities faced by your parents differ from the challenges and opportunities facing you? How was America a different place for them than it is for you?

2. What was the most important lesson you learned in growing up? How did you learn it? Who taught it to you? Write about the events surrounding this experience.

3. Write about a time in your childhood when you were in conflict about being a member of your family and part of the world at large. The reason for the conflict might be something you wanted to do despite your parents' opposition, or there might have been a conflict between the identity you wanted for yourself and the identity your parents wanted for you, or the conflict could have been between your family and outsiders, such as your friends.

America's New Wave of Runaways

Michelle Ingrassia

In this essay Michelle Ingrassia describes the pressures that have led to an increasing number of runaways among Southeast Asian immigrant teenagers.

KEY WORDS

Hmong (par. 2)   members of Laotian hill tribes, many of whom fled to the United States after the Vietnam War

monosyllabic (par. 3)   referring to short words, having only one syllable

Pol Pot (par. 4)   dictator under whom millions of Cambodians were murdered

cadence (par. 6)   speech rhythm

ramshackle (par. 8)   run-down, deteriorated

ethnographer (par. 10)   a researcher who describes social groups and events

SOME NIGHTS, KHAMHOM KEODARA is so worried about her son, Khampheth, that she wanders the streets of south Seattle looking for him. Her 11-year-old boy disappears for days at a time—he has skipped classes so often that his school doesn't want him back. And though he always returns home, Khampheth refuses to say where he's been. His parents, Laotian refugees who arrived in the United States six years ago, are at a loss to understand the American culture that seduces him. They've urged him to give up his mod haircut, his baggy pants, his plump down jacket. And they've changed their phone number time and again, desperate to cut Khampheth off from the crowd he hangs with. Nothing works. "Unless you've got good control, you cannot bring your child up," says his father, Khamseaen, 68. "It seems like I have lost control."

2   They're lumped in with all the whiz kids, the "miracle" immigrants with unlimited futures and unassailable family ties. But for
many Southeast Asian teenagers, American life has not been the
snap experts predicted. The first cracks appeared in the 1980s, in
the stunning rise of Asian youth gangs. Now, in a widening rift
between generations and cultures, a growing number of Southeast
Asian children are running away, vanishing for days or months
into a loose, nationwide network of "safe houses." No one knows
how many Vietnamese, Cambodian, Laotian, and Hmong youths
are on the run. But counselors in Seattle estimate that one-third of
all refugee families in the area have had at least one child run away
from home. "It is a big, big problem in the community," says Wins-
low Khamkeo, a Laotian counselor for the Refugee Federation Service Center. Just last month Milwaukee police discovered a hang-
out on the city's south side that was sheltering Asian runaways,
including three Hmong teens from California and two from Minnesota, all missing for months. In other cities, Asian runaways as
young as 11 or 12 are commonplace. "If you look at who become
National Merit scholars, valedictorians, and winners of national
music contests, a lot of them are Southeast Asians," says Northwestern University professor Paul Friesema. "But clearly that
masks the problem."

3   Why do so many who don't succeed run? The stress of assimilation often divides children eager to be embraced by their new
world and parents terrified by it. Khampheth has perfected the
adolescent leave-me-alone shrug. But even his monosyllabic answers hint at his alienation. Asked if kids would make fun of him
if he wore the clothes his father wants him to, he nods, "Yes."
Asked how they tease him, the young Laotian says: "They call
you Chinese."

4   Many parents find it difficult to understand the new pressures
their kids feel. The adults are an isolated, "highly traumatized"
group, especially those who lived through the 1970s regime of
Cambodian dictator Pol Pot, says San Francisco social worker Eve-
lyn Lee, who works with Asian immigrants. "These families spend
a lot of time just coping with the past," she says. Many are doomed
to menial jobs or welfare. Unlike the wealthy, educated elite who
fled Vietnam in the mid-1970s, the second and third waves rarely
have the resources to make it in urban America.

5   Families reach the breaking point as children hit adolescence
and rebel against Old World mores, and adults are powerless to

stop them. "The only thing the parents offered them was food and a roof over their heads. But if a friend can offer those things, the kids don't need them any more," says Tom Nakao, a Seattle youth outreach worker, which has one of the largest concentrations of Asian refugees in the country.

6   Noc, a 15-year-old Cambodian refugee, fled his Seattle home last summer after a fight with his mother, who didn't want him to get an earring. In defiance, he got two. "The reason my mom and I don't get along is because, like, she won't let me do whatever I want to," says Noc, who's assumed the homeboy cadence of the projects. "I told her, 'Hey, it's *my* ear, you know?'" To some degree, Noc's struggle parallels the battles played out by every generation of immigrants. But there are differences. The Southeast Asians face a greater cultural gap than most European immigrants did. Worse, being tossed into the "miracle generation" upped the pressure on them to succeed.

7   Unlike many runaways, though, these teens rarely hide under bridges and down alleys. They sack out instead in "crash pads," small apartments or houses rented by large numbers of teens, that become hangouts for runaways. These "couch surfers" drift from house to house until they run out of places to stay. When they're caught—or bored—they go home, for a while.

8   On a recent night in a ramshackle section of Seattle's Rainier Valley neighborhood, a small, sparsely furnished apartment is crowded with a dozen young Asians speaking Vietnamese to each other and halting English to a visitor. At the center is Tony, a 27-year-old Vietnamese American. Though he opens his home to many young drifters, Tony is reluctant to talk about it, except to say he's been on his own since he was 11. The young crashers offer a torrent of complaints about the police, echoing the familiar concerns of young African Americans. "They think all Asians are gangsters," says one. A friend adds: "They want you to tell them who did things. They try to scare us, tell us they'll send us to prison or back to Vietnam."

9   **Organized gangs?**   Police say they are increasingly suspicious of the Southeast Asian street kids because many of them have turned from hiding out to committing crimes. Lee, a 13-year-old Laotian from Milwaukee, ran away last summer to stay with older friends in the Twin Cities. For two weeks, they hopped from dance clubs to bars. "It was really fun being in the fast lane," brags Lee. But

the $80 Lee left home with quickly disappeared, so he and his friends turned to petty theft. Lee believes many runaways are involved in bigger things: "What's really going on is violence and gangs and stealing and robbing and guns." Police and counselors agree. In Seattle, police say crack is appearing among runaways; so are guns. And gangs once content with looting cars are turning to drive-by shootings.

10   At least one expert believes that the phenomenon is actually rooted in some aspects of Southeast Asian culture. Northwestern University ethnographer Dwight Conquergood says that in Hmong communities in Asia, villagers commonly take off for a few days during times of trouble: "It's a natural conflict-resolution mechanism in Hmong society to go off to the next village or town for a period of time when there's tension at home."

11   **New pressures:**   Whatever the cause, parents seem unable to stop their children from running. Few call police or even have the language skills to communicate. Of the six runaways found on Milwaukee's south side last month, only one had been reported missing. "I don't think they [Asian parents] trust the authorities. I don't think they feel we can help," says Milwaukee Police Officer Kay Hanna, who investigates reports of missing children. "I think they are confused about what they should be doing."

12   So are their communities. Although shelters and drop-in centers for teenage runaways abound, many agencies aren't equipped to handle Asian kids who don't speak much English. Similarly, many Asian-American institutions—Buddhist temples, the Vietnamese Catholic Church—are set up for traditional families, not runaway kids. In Minnesota, state Representative Dave Bishop has submitted a bill that would make it a felony to transport minors across state lines, arguing that many runaways are lured by older teens. It's a start, but counselors say the real solution is getting parents to bend their Old World rules.

13   That won't be easy. Speaking through a translator, Kham, the father of the young Milwaukee runaway named Lee, explains that Southeast Asians come to the United States for the same reasons all immigrants do: to find a better future for their children. And they're heartbroken when it doesn't work out. Kham mourns for his young son, who has become a stranger. "They learn the new lifestyle and they don't really believe in or respect the old traditions," he says. "It is very difficult for us to understand each other." The pain only deepens when a child runs away. "The hope we had

is lost, and we feel like it was not worth coming," he says. What he doesn't know is whether he can reclaim the spark, or his son.

EXERCISES

Details and Their Meanings

1. Who are the "new wave of runaways" described in the selection? How old are they? Why are they running away from home? Where do they go? What do they do when they are away from home?
2. Who is Khampheth Keodara? What has happened between him and his parents? In what way is he typical of other youths described in this story?
3. According to estimates, how many refugee families in Seattle have had children run away? What other facts indicate the extent of the runaway problem?
4. Who is Noc? Who is Tony? How does each fit into the pattern of runaways? Who is Lee? How does he represent another aspect of the runaway problem?
5. What features of Southeast Asian culture seem to support young people's running away from their families? How have parents and communities reacted to the runaways? What obstacles prevent families and institutions from responding to this situation?

Reading and Critical Thinking

1. In what way is the recent increase of Southeast Asian immigrant runaways surprising? How does it contradict the stereotype of Asian youth? How does the success of other Southeast Asians hide the problem of the children discussed in this essay?
2. How do the children feel about the clothes and the way of life their parents want them to have? What do the youth want that their parents seem to be keeping from them? How do you interpret Khampheth's reaction to being called "Chinese"?
3. What difficulties do Southeast Asian immigrant parents have

in understanding their children? How do they react to their children's attitudes? How might the parents' own problems interfere with their ability to relate to their children? Do you think the parents' reactions increase or decrease the problem? Why or why not?

4. What problems does this generation of Southeast Asians face that are different than those experienced by European immigrants? How do the patterns of runaway living differ from previous generations of runaways? What might account for these differences?

5. What solutions to the problem does the writer offer? How effective do you think they are likely to be? What solutions would you offer? What strategies would you suggest to help Southeast Asian immigrant parents stop their children from running away?

The Writer's Strategies

1. What is the main point of this selection? What sentence or sentences come closest to stating the writer's thesis? How does the title contribute to your understanding of the thesis?

2. What question does the essay try to answer? Where is this question asked directly? Which sentence gives the most direct answer?

3. In what ways does the writer use narrative? cause and effect? comparison and contrast?

4. List all the personal narratives told. What is the point of each one? In what way does each of the narratives connect with the cause-and-effect structure of the selection?

5. Where does Ingrassia introduce the words of experts? What is the purpose of these expert statements?

6. What is the tone of the final paragraph? How does the writer convey it? What effect does this final paragraph have on the reader?

Thinking Together

Discuss in small groups the issue of runaway youth in the United States. Explore the problem as you understand it from newspaper and media reports, as well as from individual cases you may know personally. Where do you think the problem lies—in behavior of the youth, in parent attitudes, in troubled families, in social pressures, in temptations offered by society, in economic conditions? After you have explored the problem, develop a statement about what can or should be done about it.

Summarize your findings for the class.

Vocabulary

In this selection, the writer uses quotation marks to set off the following phrases. In your own words, define each phrase and explain why she put quotation marks around it.

1. "safe houses" (par. 2)
2. "highly traumatized" (par. 4)
3. "miracle generation" (par. 6)
4. "crash pads" (par. 7)
5. "couch surfers" (par. 7)

The essay draws on sociological terms to identify the experiences of Southeast Asian immigrants in the United States. Define each term.

6. assimilation (par. 3)
7. mores (par. 5)
8. Old World (par. 5, 12)
9. cultural gap (par. 6)
10. conflict-resolution mechanism (par. 10)

WRITER'S WORKSHOP ━━━━━━━━━━━━

Critical Thinking in Writing

1. Have you or anyone you know ever run away from home (even for a short time)—or wanted to but didn't? Write an essay exploring your firsthand experience (how you felt, your reasons for feeling this way) with the runaway situation.
2. As you were growing up, did your values ever conflict with the values of your parents? Describe one such conflict, and write a causal analysis of it; that is, describe the causes that you believe

led up to this conflict. Try to understand what led you and your parents to act as you did in this situation.

3. Imagine that you are a community leader attempting to help resolve the problem of Southeast Asian immigrant runaways. Consider its various causes, and write a plan to resolve it.

Connecting Ideas

Read "The Jacket" by Gary Soto (page 64). Compare Soto's feelings about his jacket to the conflicts over clothing described in this selection. Why are clothing and physical appearance so important to Soto and to the young runaways interviewed in this selection?

Salvation

Langston Hughes

Langston Hughes is best remembered as a poet, but he was also an accomplished essayist, journalist, and playwright, as well as one of the major figures in the growth of African-American culture during the Harlem Renaissance of the 1920s. In this piece from his autobiography The Big Sea *(1940), Hughes offers an irreverent account of how his conversion "saved" him.*

KEY WORDS

dire (par. 3)   frightening, dreadful
gnarled (par. 4)   bent and twisted, like knots in a tree
rounder (par. 6)   usually someone who walks on rounds like a police officer but here probably a drifter
deacons (par. 6)   members of a congregation who assist the minister
serenely (par. 7)   very peacefully
knickerbockered (par. 11)   wearing loose, knee-length pants, called *knickers* for short

---

I WAS SAVED FROM sin when I was going on thirteen. But not really saved. It happened like this. There was a big revival at my Auntie Reed's church. Every night for weeks there had been much preaching, singing, praying, and shouting, and some very hardened sinners had been brought to Christ, and the membership of the church had grown by leaps and bounds. Then just before the revival ended, they held a special meeting for children, "to bring the young lambs to the fold." My aunt spoke of it for days ahead. That night I was escorted to the front row and placed on the mourners' bench with all the other young sinners, who had not yet been brought to Jesus.

2   My aunt told me that when you were saved you saw a light, and something happened to you inside! And Jesus came into your

life! And God was with you from then on! She said you could see and hear and feel Jesus in your soul. I believed her. I had heard a great many old people say the same thing and it seemed to me they ought to know. So I sat there calmly in the hot, crowded church, waiting for Jesus to come to me.

3   The preacher preached a wonderful rhythmical sermon, all moans and shouts and lonely cries and dire pictures of hell, and then he sang a song about the ninety and nine safe in the fold, but one little lamb was left out in the cold. Then he said: "Won't you come? Won't you come to Jesus? Young lambs, won't you come?" And he held out his arms to all us young sinners there on the mourners' bench. And the little girls cried. And some of them jumped up and went to Jesus right away. But most of us just sat there.

4   A great many old people came and knelt around us and prayed, old women with jet-black faces and braided hair, old men with work-gnarled hands. And the church sang a song about the lower lights are burning, some poor sinners to be saved. And the whole building rocked with prayer and song.

5   Still I kept waiting to *see* Jesus.

6   Finally all the young people had gone to the altar and were saved, but one boy and me. He was a rounder's son named West-ley. Westley and I were surrounded by sisters and deacons praying. It was very hot in the church, and getting late now. Finally Westley said to me in a whisper: "God damn! I'm tired o' sitting here. Let's get up and be saved." So he got up and was saved.

7   Then I was left all alone on the mourners' bench. My aunt came and knelt at my knees and cried, while prayers and songs swirled all around me in the little church. The whole congregation prayed for me alone, in a mighty wail of moans and voices. And I kept waiting serenely for Jesus, waiting, waiting—but he didn't come. I wanted to see him, but nothing happened to me. Nothing! I wanted something to happen to me, but nothing happened.

8   I heard the songs and the minister saying: "Why don't you come? My dear child, why don't you come to Jesus? Jesus is waiting for you. He wants you. Why don't you come? Sister Reed, what is this child's name?"

9   "Langston," my aunt sobbed.

10   "Langston, why don't you come? Why don't you come and be saved? Oh, Lamb of God! Why don't you come?"

11   Now it was really getting late. I began to be ashamed of myself, holding everything up so long. I began to wonder what God thought about Westley, who certainly hadn't seen Jesus either, but

who was now sitting proudly on the platform, swinging his knick-erbockered legs and grinning down at me, surrounded by deacons and old women on their knees praying. God had not struck West-ley dead for taking his name in vain or for lying in the temple. So I decided that maybe to save further trouble, I'd better lie, too, and say that Jesus had come, and get up and be saved.

12   So I got up.

13   Suddenly the whole room broke into a sea of shouting, as they saw me rise. Waves of rejoicing swept the place. Women leaped in the air. My aunt threw her arms around me. The minister took me by the hand and led me to the platform.

14   When things quieted down, in a hushed silence, punctuated by a few ecstatic "Amens," all the new young lambs were blessed in the name of God. Then joyous singing filled the room.

15   That night, for the last time in my life but one—for I was a big boy twelve years old—I cried. I cried, in bed alone, and couldn't stop. I buried my head under the quilts, but my aunt heard me. She woke up and told my uncle I was crying because the Holy Ghost had come into my life and because I had seen Jesus. But I was really crying because I couldn't bear to tell her that I had lied, that I had deceived everybody in the church, that I hadn't seen Jesus, and that now I didn't believe there was a Jesus any more, since he didn't come to help me.

EXERCISES

Details and Their Meanings

1. Where and when do the events take place?
2. Who is responsible for bringing young Hughes to church?
3. What has Hughes been told to expect will happen in church?
4. Where do the children sit while they are waiting to be saved? What is the significance of the name of the area?
5. Who is Westley? Why is he important?
6. What emotion motivates Hughes to get up? How does the congregation react when he gets up?
7. What does Hughes do when he is alone in his room?

Reading and Critical Thinking

1. What point is Langston Hughes making about his experience at the revival?
2. Why is the title of this piece ironic—that is, suggesting the opposite of what it appears to be saying?
3. How does the writer describe the people at the revival?
4. Why does Hughes expect that Westley will be punished?
5. Why does Hughes cry at the end of the story? What does Aunt Reed think is the reason for his tears?
6. In the last paragraph, the writer says he cried for the last time in his life but one. What other event do you think might have made him cry?
7. What do you think would have happened to Hughes if he had not come forward to declare his faith?

The Writer's Strategies

1. How old is the narrator? From what perspective is this narrative written?
2. Which paragraphs serve as the introduction?
3. What ordering strategy does the writer use?
4. Paragraphs 5 and 12 are each one sentence long. Why does the writer use such short paragraphs?
5. Which paragraph serves as an epilogue? (An epilogue is additional material describing events that take place after the ending of a narrative.)

Thinking Together

The narrator in "Salvation" finally gives in to the pressures from his surroundings, despite a struggle with his conscience. What other circumstances cause young people to go against what they know and believe is right? How do peer pressures influence a person's behavior? Working in groups, make a list of the elements that influence young people to challenge what they believe is right. Share your list with other groups in the class. At your instructor's suggestion, after your discussion write a short essay sharing your thoughts on this issue.

Vocabulary

The following terms from the selection are associated with religion. Write a short definition of each.

1. revival (par. 1)
2. preacher (par. 3)
3. sermon (par. 3)
4. altar (par. 6)
5. deacons (par. 6)
6. congregation (par. 7)

WRITER'S WORKSHOP ━━━━━━━━

Critical Thinking in Writing

1. Religion is a very personal experience for most people. Write about your own faith or the faith of someone close to you. What is it based on? Did you ever attend a revival meeting? If you did, was your experience different from Langston Hughes's? Write a brief description of the revival and your reaction to it.
2. Should children be expected to embrace the religion of their parents and guardians, or should they be allowed to make up their own minds about faith? What conflicting issues are raised by this question? What ideas can you think of to support each position? Write a brief paper to explore these issues.
3. Write a narrative about a pivotal experience that you believe helped you grow up.

Connecting Ideas

Read James Baldwin's piece on black English on page 208. In paragraph 7, Baldwin says that it was the genius of the black church to create a unique black speech and culture. What kind of culture do you see at work in "Salvation"? How is Hughes participating in something larger than a personal religious experience? What would Baldwin say that Hughes isn't getting about the church experience?

A New Dawn

Sam Moses

Journalist Sam Moses has written for a number of periodicals, among them Sports Illustrated. *In this piece, he introduces us to Lester Moreno Perez, a young Cuban American with a remarkable story.*

KEY WORDS

annals (par. 1)   recorded histories
counterrevolutionary (par. 3)   moving against radical changes in government—in this case, opposing Fidel Castro
infrared (par. 12)   a kind of radiation below visible light, given off by objects that radiate heat
wishbone (par. 16)   a *y*-shaped bone
odyssey (par. 17)   an epic journey
blitz (par. 19)   an all-out, sudden attack

IN THE ANNALS OF great escapes, the flight by seventeen-year-old Lester Moreno Perez from Cuba to the United States surely must rank as one of the most imaginative. At 8:30 on the night of Thursday, March 1, Lester crept along the beach in Varadero, a resort town on the north coast of Cuba, and launched his sailboard into the shark-haunted waters of the Straits of Florida. Guided first by the stars and then by the hazy glow from concentrations of electric lights in towns beyond the horizon, Lester sailed with 20-knot winds, heading for the Florida Keys, 90 miles away.

2   Two hours past daybreak on Friday, Lester was sighted by the Korean crew of the *Tina D*, a Bahamian-registered freighter. The boom on his craft was broken, and he was just barely making headway, 30 miles south of Key West. The astonished crew pulled Lester aboard, fed him spicy chicken and white rice, and then radioed the U.S. Coast Guard, which sent the patrol boat *Fitkinak* to take him into custody. After five days in the Krome Detention Center

in Miami while paperwork was being processed, he was issued a visa by U.S. immigration officials and released into the welcoming arms of his relatives.

3   Except for his rich imagination and broad streak of courage, Lester could be any seventeen-year-old who decides to leave home. He was raised in the shoreside town of Varadero, the second-oldest of five children in his family. "As soon as I started thinking a little bit—when I was seven or eight years old—I wanted to come to America," he says. Independent thinking ran in the family; his grandfather, Urbino, had been imprisoned for attending a counter-revolutionary meeting early in Fidel Castro's regime and spent nearly five years in jail. Furthermore, Lester's sister Leslie, who had been on the national swim team and had traveled to several foreign countries, had told intriguing tales of life outside Cuba. Lester also did not like the idea of serving three years in the Cuban army and then facing the possibility of having his career chosen for him by the Communist Party. There was also trouble at home; he and his stepfather, Roberto, were at odds, mostly over politics. So Lester decided he wanted to go to America, not Angola.

4   When he was ten years old, Lester taught himself to windsurf by hanging around the European and Canadian tourists who rented boards on the beach at Varadero. "If you made friends with them, they would sometimes let you use their equipment," he says. As he grew older and got better at the sport, he found he liked the isolation and freedom of the sea. "Sometimes I would sail for eight hours without stopping and go very far out," he says. His wind-surfing to freedom seemed destined.

5   Recently, Lester sat in a big easy-chair in the Hialeah, Florida, apartment of Ana and Isidro Perez, the great-aunt and great-uncle who took him in. Lester is so skinny—5'6", 130 pounds—that it seems there is room for two or three more of him in the chair. On his head he wears Walkman earphones, which he politely removes when a visitor enters the room. He has been in America only a few weeks, but he has already been interviewed several times and has been chauffeured all over Miami in a limo on a radio station-sponsored shopping spree. The tops of his feet are still covered with scabs, the result of the hours he spent in the sailboard's foot-straps; but his hands show no blisters, only hard, white calluses.

6   As he waits for a translator to arrive, Lester rocks back and forth in the chair like a hyperactive child. He clicks the television on with the remote control, passes a Spanish-language station and stops at a morning show on which a man is explaining, in English,

how to prevent snoring by placing a Ping-Pong ball between your shoulder blades, a move that forces one to sleep facedown. When a visitor demonstrates this to Lester through gestures and snores, the young man rolls his dark eyes, smiles, and says in perfect English, "People are all crazy here."

7   A few minutes later, the translator, who owns a windsurfing shop in Miami, arrives, and Lester begins to tell his story through him.

8   "I had only been thinking of making the trip on a sailboard for about a month," he says. "Before that, I'd been thinking of leaving the country by marrying a Canadian girl—every couple of months a few would come that were pretty nice-looking. But I decided to sail because I was training hard and was confident I would be able to make the trip easily. I had windsurfed in bad weather and even surfed during Hurricane Gilbert, so I was already out in really rough conditions and wasn't worried about it.

9   "Right before I left, I was watching the wind patterns. A cold front had passed by and it was pretty strong, so I waited until it subsided a little. Usually after a cold front passes, the wind shifts to the east, and it's just a straight reach to the U.S., so I waited for that. Then I told two of my friends, who said they would help me. I wasn't hungry, but I ate a lot—three or four fried eggs, some rice, and half a liter of milk—so I would be strong for the journey." His friends also persuaded him to take along some water, a can of condensed milk, and a knife.

10   At 7:00 on the evening of March 1, Lester, who had said nothing to his family, slipped out of his house and went down to the Varadero beach, where he worked at a windsurfing rental booth by day while attending high school at night. Earlier that day, he had carefully rigged the best mast and strongest boom he could find with a big 5.0-square-meter sail. Then he had lashed the sail rig in the sand with the rental boards. Under cover of darkness, he unlocked the shed where the privately owned boards were kept and removed his sleek and durable Alpha model. It had been a gift to him from a man who sympathized with his plight—a generous East German whom Lester called Rambo for the camouflage hat he always wore. Lester fastened the sail rig to the board and carried it to the water. He waded into the ocean until he was knee-deep, glanced over his shoulder to make sure he hadn't been seen, and stepped onto the board. His ride on the wind to freedom had begun.

11   "I wasn't nervous," he says. "I had to be very clear minded once I decided to go; otherwise they would catch me and I would be in a lot of trouble. It would have meant three or four years in prison if I had been caught. No lie about what I was doing was possible."

12   About one and a half blocks away from the beach was a tower usually manned by guards with infrared binoculars. Lester, who was sailing without lights, also had to keep an eye out for freighters and pleasure boats that would be cruising in the busy Straits of Florida.

13   "At first I wasn't able to get my feet in the footstraps," he says, "because there wasn't enough wind for my sail. But as I got farther out and was able to get fully powered up, I began feeling more confident. The swells were very steep, maybe four or five meters, and I was going so fast I had no choice but to jump them."

14   As he recalls the moment, Lester rises from his chair, plants his bare feet on the tile floor and extends his thin arms, grasping an imaginary boom. He begins in English, "Wind coming, coming, coming . . . out, out, out . . . is very strong." He's hanging in his invisible harness now, arms stretched wide, eyes lit up, flying over the waves. "Whoosh!" he cries. "Is good!"

15   For ten hours he rode the wind, never once fearing failure, or drowning. He thought of his family and how worried they would be when they discovered he was missing. But he wasn't alone out there. "Ever since I left, I could see the sharks coming out and in, coming up on the board. I was hoping and thinking they were dolphins, but when the sun came up, I could see there was no way they were dolphins."

16   Around daybreak, the aluminum boom broke, separating the connection to the mast like pieces of a wishbone. He tried fixing the boom with his knife but couldn't, so he sailed on, clutching the pieces of the broken wishbone. This made control of the board extremely difficult, and he couldn't rest in the harness he had rigged. "My arms and hands were getting really tired, but by then I could already see the big kites of the fishermen, so I wasn't really worried. When I saw the freighter, I tried to point [into the wind] as much as I could and sail toward it."

17   A similar crossing was made in January 1984 by Arnaud de Rosnay, a Frenchman who boardsailed from Key West to Cuba as a personal challenge and a publicity stunt. De Rosnay, one of the best boardsailors in the world, had sailed in daylight with a chase

boat. His trip included two stops for repairs and two stops to rest, and he completed the crossing in about seven hours. (In November of the same year, de Rosnay vanished while trying to cross the Straits of Formosa.) But only a month before Lester's odyssey, another young Cuban had perished attempting to reach the Keys in a raft.

18   Not surprisingly, Hollywood has come knocking on Lester's door. "The story is a natural," says Paul Madden, the president of Madden Movies. "It's *Rocky* and *The Old Man and the Sea* in one. If this picture is done right, by the end of it the audience will be standing up in the theater and cheering." Madden might not be one of those doing the cheering; he was outbid for the rights to Lester's story by Ron Howard's Imagine Films.

19   Lester has handled the movie offers—assumed to have reached six figures—and the media blitz with uncommon courtesy and self-assurance. A new acquaintance has even invited him to spend the summer at Hood River, Oregon, where he will be able to jump the formidable swells of the Columbia River. This sounds good to Lester. But right now, one of his teenage friends has invited him to go sailing off Miami Beach. That sounds like the most fun of all.

EXERCISES

Details and Their Meanings

1. Who is Lester Moreno Perez? How old is he? Where did he grow up? How did he learn to windsurf? Who helped him?
2. What members of Lester's family influenced his decision to leave Cuba?
3. What convinced Lester that the time had come to leave Cuba?
4. What means of escape from Cuba presented themselves? Which method did Lester choose? Why did he reject the others?
5. What would have happened to Lester if he had been caught?
6. How did Lester know the weather would be good for a crossing? How did he know he was heading in the right direction?
7. What difficulties did Lester face crossing to Florida? Who eventually rescued him?

Reading and Critical Thinking

1. What can we infer about life in Cuba from Lester's actions?
2. Why did Lester choose to risk his life when other means of escape presented themselves? What choice do you think other people would make in the same situation?
3. Why do armed guards occupy watch towers on the coast of Cuba? What are they guarding against? What does their presence tell you about Cuba?
4. Why didn't Lester tell his parents what he was doing? What might have happened if he had confided in them? Do you think he made the right decision? Why or why not?
5. What makes Lester Moreno Perez's story appealing to movie producers? Which actor would you cast as Lester? Why?
6. What evidence does the writer give about how well Lester is adjusting to life in America? How would you react to life in a new culture without your immediate family to support you?

The Writer's Strategies

1. What is the meaning of the title, "A New Dawn"?
2. How does Sam Moses use narration? How does he use description?
3. What is the writer's attitude toward his subject? Why did he write about Lester Perez? Why doesn't he discuss negative aspects of life in Cuba?
4. In which paragraphs does the writer cite secondhand information? How reliable is it?
5. Why does the writer tell about Arnaud de Rosnay in paragraph 17? What is his purpose in doing so?

Thinking Together

Imagine that you are living in a politically repressive country like Cuba. Do you have a responsibility to stay and work for change, or should you run away and make a better life for yourself elsewhere? Brainstorm with your classmates to develop a list of reasons for each option, and then discuss which reasons you think are the strongest.

Vocabulary

The following nautical terms are used in the selection. Write a definition for each term.

1. Straits (par. 1)
2. knot (par. 1)
3. freighter (par. 2)
4. windsurf (par. 4)
5. boom (par. 10)
6. swells (par. 13)
7. mast (par. 16)

WRITER'S WORKSHOP ━━━━━━━━━━━━━━━

Critical Thinking in Writing

1. Assume that you are Lester Perez. Write a journal entry describing your thoughts and feelings during key periods of your escape.
2. Write an essay explaining the decision you made in "Thinking Together" about whether it is better to flee oppression or to stay and fight against it.
3. Assume that you are in Lester Perez's situation. Write a letter to your parents to explain why you are leaving the country of your birth.

Connecting Ideas

Read Armando Rendón's "Kiss of Death" (p. 125) and Gary Soto's "Looking for Work" (p. 243). How would Lester Perez respond to these authors, who are critical about life in America? What could Perez remind them about?

The Struggle to Be an All-American Girl

Elizabeth Wong

The writer looks back on her childhood and on the way the culture she was born into interfered with her attempts to be an American. Notice how Elizabeth Wong's attitudes about the culture of her birth may have changed since she was a child.

KEY WORDS

stoically (par. 1)   in a manner unaffected by joy, grief, pleasure, or pain
kowtow (par. 6)   to show respect by bowing deeply
phonetic (par. 6)   speech sounds represented by symbols, each of which stands for a separate and distinct sound
pidgin (par. 10)   speech that is a mixture of two or more languages
Cinco de Mayo (par. 13)   the Fifth of May, Mexican Independence Day

IT'S STILL THERE, THE Chinese school on Yale Street where my brother and I used to go. Despite the new coat of paint and the high wire fence, the school I knew ten years ago remains remarkably, stoically the same.

2   Every day at 5 P.M., instead of playing with our fourth- and fifth-grade friends or sneaking out to the empty lot to hunt ghosts and animal bones, my brother and I had to go to Chinese school. No amount of kicking, screaming, or pleading could dissuade my mother, who was solidly determined to have us learn the language of our heritage.

3   Forcibly, she walked us the seven long, hilly blocks from our home to school, depositing our defiant tearful faces before the stern principal. My only memory of him is that he swayed on his heels

like a palm tree, and he always clasped his impatient twitching hands behind his back. I recognized him as a repressed maniacal child killer, and knew that if we ever saw his hands we'd be in big trouble.

4   We all sat in little chairs in an empty auditorium. The room smelled like Chinese medicine, an imported faraway mustiness. Like ancient mothballs or dirty closets. I hated that smell. I favored crisp new scents. Like the soft French perfume that my American teacher wore in public school.

5   There was a stage far to the right, flanked by an American flag and the flag of the Nationalist Republic of China, which was also red, white, and blue but not as pretty.

6   Although the emphasis at the school was mainly language— speaking, reading, writing—the lessons always began with an exercise in politeness. With the entrance of the teacher, the best student would tap a bell and everyone would get up, kowtow, and chant, "Sing san ho," the phonetic for "How are you, teacher?"

7   Being ten years old, I had better things to learn than ideographs copied painstakingly in lines that ran right to left from the tip of a *moc but*, a real ink pen that had to be held in an awkward way if blotches were to be avoided. After all, I could do the multiplication tables, name the satellites of Mars, and write reports on *Little Women* and *Black Beauty*. Nancy Drew, my favorite book heroine, never spoke Chinese.

8   The language was a source of embarrassment. More times than not, I had tried to disassociate myself from the nagging loud voice that followed me wherever I wandered in the nearby American supermarket outside Chinatown. The voice belonged to my grandmother, a fragile woman in her seventies who could outshout the best of the street vendors. Her humor was raunchy, her Chinese rhythmless, patternless. It was quick, it was loud, it was unbeautiful. It was not like the quiet, lilting romance of French or the gentle refinement of the American South. Chinese sounded pedestrian. Public.

9   In Chinatown, the comings and goings of hundreds of Chinese on their daily tasks sounded chaotic and frenzied. I did not want to be thought of as mad, as talking gibberish. When I spoke English, people nodded at me, smiled sweetly, said encouraging words. Even the people in my culture would cluck and say that I'd do well in life. "My, doesn't she move her lips fast," they would say, meaning that I'd be able to keep up with the world outside Chinatown.

10   My brother was even more fanatical than I about speaking English. He was especially hard on my mother, criticizing her, often cruelly, for her pidgin speech—smatterings of Chinese scattered like chop suey in her conversation. "It's not 'What it is,' Mom," he'd say in exasperation. "It's 'What *is* it, what *is* it, what *is* it'!" Sometimes Mom might leave out an occasional *the* or *a* or perhaps a verb of being. He would stop her in midsentence: "Say it again, Mom. Say it right." When he tripped over his own tongue, he'd blame it on her: "See, Mom, it's all your fault. You set a bad example."

11   What infuriated my mother most was when my brother cornered her on her consonants, especially *r*. My father had played a cruel joke on Mom by assigning her an American name that her tongue wouldn't allow her to say. No matter how hard she tried, "Ruth" always ended up "Luth" or "Roof."

12   After two years of writing with a *moc but* and reciting words with multiples of meanings, I finally was granted a cultural divorce. I was permitted to stop Chinese school.

13   I thought of myself as multicultural. I preferred tacos to egg rolls; I enjoyed Cinco de Mayo more than Chinese New Year.

14   At last, I was one of you; I wasn't one of them.

15   Sadly, I still am.

EXERCISES

Details and Their Meanings

1. When it was time to go to Chinese school, how did Elizabeth Wong and her brother behave? What attitude toward the school did their behavior reveal? How did the children's behavior contrast with the attitude of their mother? How did the children's behavior contrast with the appearance of the school and the principal?
2. How did the auditorium smell? How did the American teacher smell? Which smell did young Elizabeth prefer? Which flag did she prefer, the flag of the Nationalist Republic of China or the flag of the United States? Which language, Chinese or English,

did she prefer? What attitude do you think these preferences expressed?

3. What politeness exercises did the students have to do each day? What can you infer about Wong's attitude toward these exercises?

4. What kind of work did Wong do in Chinese school? in American school? In which school was she more advanced? In which was the work more interesting to her? What were the rewards and penalties for her accomplishments in each school?

5. When did Wong see people speak Chinese? Who were the people? What was her impression of spoken Chinese?

6. How did Chinese people react to Wong's skill in English? How did other people react to it?

7. What mistakes did Wong's mother make in English? How did Wong's brother respond to his mother's errors? What attitude about language did the children's feelings toward their mother's and grandmother's use of language show?

8. When and how did Wong's experience with Chinese school end? What attitude did she seem to have toward Chinese school when she stopped attending? What foods and holidays did she prefer at that time? Did those foods and holidays represent the dominant American culture or something else?

Reading and Critical Thinking

1. What seems to be Elizabeth Wong's general attitude toward her cultural background and the training she received in it? Why do you think she feels that way? Is that feeling warranted? How do you think that attitude may have influenced her behavior?

2. Overall, how do you characterize the experience the writer and her brother had in Chinese school? Do you believe their experience is typical of the experiences of many children who receive some kind of cultural training? Why or why not? Do you believe such training has value? in what ways?

3. How did the writer and her brother generally feel about the traditional Chinese language and culture of their family? Is it typical for children to feel embarrassed by or even hostile toward the traditional culture and language of their family? Is the problem worse for children of immigrants or for other

groups? Is the embarrassment inevitable? Is there anything parents can do to avoid the problem? Are there any positive aspects to this cultural discomfort?

4. What is the significance of Elizabeth Wong's interest in French perfume and language and Mexican food and holidays? What does she mean about being an "All-American girl"? What does America represent to her? Do you agree with her view of what it means to be all-American? Do you think all Americans share her view?

5. What do the closing paragraphs of the essay indicate about the way Elizabeth Wong now views her experiences at Chinese school? Has her attitude changed? Do you think the change in attitude reflects a deep change in the goals she will pursue in her life or just reflects some passing feelings? What could she now do to act on those feelings? Would those actions be likely to lead her to adopt a totally Chinese way of life?

The Writer's Strategies

1. What are the opening three words of the essay? In the opening paragraph, what impression is the writer trying to give of the Chinese school? Why? How does the opening set up the issues discussed in the rest of the essay? What is the significance of the school's solidity and endurance for the young children and for Wong as an adult?

2. What is Wong's thesis? In paragraphs 2 through 5, what story does Wong tell? What points does she make by this story? Why does she use a narrative to make these points? Why does she use a generalized narrative about "every day" instead of a specific narrative about "one day"?

3. In which paragraphs can you find comparisons? What are the items being compared? What is the point of the comparisons? How do the various comparisons support the overall conflict of this essay? What is that conflict?

4. What associations does the writer make with various smells? What kinds of evaluative words does she associate with the use of different languages? How do these associations help develop the themes of this essay?

5. In the last four paragraphs, several rapid changes in attitude are expressed. What are the attitudes? What time in the writer's

life does each of the attitudes express? How does the inclusion of these changing statements of attitude change the meaning or interpretation of the essay?

6. The last two sentences, which are the last two paragraphs, are very short and repeat words and sentence patterns. Describe these repeated patterns, and discuss how they achieve a special effect.

Thinking Together

As a class, brainstorm about the various ways in which you are formally and informally taught about the cultures of your birth— including parochial or ethnic schooling, community cultural celebrations, and family experiences and discussions. Then, in small groups, compare your experiences of this kind, and describe your feelings about them.

Do you feel that these experiences were totally positive? Do you ever feel that they were unpleasant or something you did not want to do? Have you ever felt that aspects of your birth culture were standing in the way of your being part of the dominant American culture or any other group? Do you feel differently about these issues now from the way you felt as a child?

Vocabulary

The following words from the selection contain one or more small words or roots. The meaning of each small word or root is related to the meaning of the larger word in which it is embedded. Identify the small word or root; then define the larger word and explain its relation to the smaller units.

1. forcibly (par. 3)
2. repressed (par. 3)
3. maniacal (par. 3)
4. mustiness (par. 4)
5. painstakingly (par. 7)
6. ideograph (par. 7)
7. lilting (par. 8)
8. pedestrian (par. 8)
9. chaotic (par. 9)
10. fanatical (par. 10)

WRITER'S WORKSHOP ━━━━━━━━━━━━

Critical Thinking in Writing

1. Does growing up in America make children feel proud and happy or uncomfortable and embarrassed about their family, ethnic, or cultural background? How does this feeling affect how children learn and develop? Write an essay exploring your ideas about the effect of ethnic identity on children growing up in America.

2. Write an essay describing your curiosity about cultures other than your own as you were growing up. Did you ever feel that other cultures were more interesting than or preferable to your own? What cultures were you curious about? Did you ever try to act in accordance with that other culture? Was your curiosity or behavior encouraged or discouraged? Did it create any tension within your family?

3. Write a narrative about how you learned or were introduced to some cultural practice or belief that was part of your family's background. Reveal directly or indirectly how you felt about that experience then and how you feel about it now.

Connecting Ideas

Look ahead to the essay "Minority Student" by Richard Rodriguez (p. 144). What similar issues do Rodriguez and Wong raise? How are their perspectives different? How do their separate cultures influence those perspectives, do you think? Write a one-page essay comparing and contrasting the two selections.

Boys Only: Separate But Equal?

Janny Scott

Janny Scott reports on the current debate over whether placing African American boys in separate classes helps them do better in school.

KEY WORDS

skirting (par. 3)   evading
inconclusive (par. 7)   uncertain
promontory (par. 13)   bluff, high place
scourge (par. 13)   plague, destruction
conceived (par. 24)   designed, created
accommodate (par. 26)   meet the specific needs of
disproportionate (par. 27)   greater than average
mandatory (par. 28)   required
curricula (par. 28)   plans of study for educational courses
methodological (par. 32)   concerning the way research is
   carried out
coeducational (par. 35)   male and female students attending
   school together
subsidized (par. 38)   financially supported
bromide (par. 44)   patent medicine
subsequent (par. 50)   later

MICHAEL HUNT IS A roly-poly fifth grader who wants to become a minister—or maybe a singer. He suddenly has found himself at the center of a bitterly controversial educational and social experiment.

2   Michael is enrolled at an all-black inner-city elementary school where the principal and teachers have decided that their pupils may learn better if segregated by sex.

3   The school is one of at least two dozen throughout the country, mostly in heavily African American districts in the East, that in the

past five years have been quietly skirting the law by separating boys from girls.

4   The practice, now something of a grass-roots movement, is aimed at improving the academic performance of black boys, who in many districts have lower achievement and higher dropout rates than other groups.

5   Proponents believe—more from gut feeling than hard proof—that all-male classes might help provide boys with black, male role models and an education more tailored to their needs.

6   But federal education officials say the classes are illegal. And civil libertarians, feminists, and some prominent black educators say they represent a retreat from equality and a return to the discredited notion of "separate but equal."

7   Furthermore, research on the benefits of single-gender education is inconclusive at best, experts say. If such programs help anyone, they say, it is girls, not boys.

8   Though support for boys-only classes does not divide along racial lines, the debate has placed largely white organizations such as the American Civil Liberties Union and the NOW Legal Defense and Education Fund in the awkward position of opposing black educators and parents on what is best for their children.

9   "The ultimate question is who's going to determine what's in the best interests of African American children," said Jawanza Kunjufu, a well-known black writer who has advocated all-boys schools and other radical educational reforms.

10   "The ACLU and the NOW organization think they can decide that," said Kunjufu, president of African-American Images, a consulting company in Chicago. "I think black parents need to make that decision."

11   Some say they should decide against single-gender schooling. "They're doing the wrong thing for the right reasons," said Hugh J. Scott, the first black superintendent of the Washington, D.C., school system who now is dean of education programs at Hunter College in New York. "What these students need, and the heart of the problem, is good teachers," he said.

12   The biggest experiment in single-gender classes is in Baltimore, where boys and girls attend separate classes in more than a dozen schools and where district administrators not only know about the practice but, for now, support it.

13   The most elaborate example is the Robert W. Coleman Elementary School, crouched on a wind-swept promontory in the crumbling neighborhood of Coppin Hill, where crack cocaine became

such a scourge a few years back that a grand jury visited the school to see how the children were holding up.

14   At Coleman, Principal Addie Johnson started the first all-male class four years ago after learning that certain boys were falling behind. Now, almost all classes are single-gender. Girls and boys mix for music class and meals and on the playground.

15   "I had been doing reading about how boys learn differently from girls," Johnson recalled recently, referring to controversial theories that boys have shorter attention spans and are more energetic and physical. "I thought, let's test this. . . . We did it kind of quietly."

16   In Rochester, New York, Principal Anita Boggs took a similar approach five years ago at the Dr. Martin Luther King Jr. School—a large elementary school whose student body is 97 percent minority and mostly low-income, evenly divided between blacks and Latinos.

17   "It was extremely upsetting to me to look at my fresh-faced, exuberant, happy children and know that 10 years from now, they might be dead," she said in an interview. "I could see that they were hungry for a significant male role model in their lives, for something to be proud of."

18   So when two teachers asked Boggs whether they should move more girls into a boy-heavy second-grade class, Boggs suggested they just move the girls out. To teach the boys, she assigned a young male teacher who was born in Latin America.

19   "To be frank with you, I kept a real low profile," said Boggs, who ran the single-gender classes for four years until the district and state stopped the practice and transferred her to another school.

20   In Philadelphia, where a lawsuit forced the city a decade ago to admit girls to Central High School, the principal of Robert Fulton Elementary School, in a lower-income, racially mixed neighborhood, has set up a second-grade class this year for boys only.

21   "Really, I guess it's against the law. But I wasn't trying to break the law," said Principal Dietra Spence, who organized the class at a teacher's request. "I'm sure once this gets out, someone will come and disband it."

22   Some districts have toyed with the idea but decided against it for fear of litigation. They have turned instead to "heritage immersion" programs that emphasize the accomplishments of African Americans. The Savannah-Chatham County, Georgia, district is be-

ginning such a program this month because its lawyers advised against boys-only classes.

23   The Detroit district, which is 89 percent African American, has opened three so-called African-centered schools. The ACLU and the NOW Legal Defense and Education Fund had sued in 1991 and blocked plans for all-male academies.

24   The heritage immersion programs also were conceived to help African American boys, whose rates of suspension, absenteeism, and delinquency were the highest in those school systems. In some districts, administrators say the boys have the lowest course-passage rate and are the most likely to be held back a grade.

25   Experts disagree on the reasons behind such statistics. But some black theorists believe they stem in part from a clash between the male culture of young black boys and what some describe as the female-dominated culture the boys encounter at home and in school.

26   Kunjufu, whose controversial writings inspired Johnson, has found that boys' test scores begin to drop during the third and fourth grades. He believes the heavily female ranks of elementary schoolteachers have failed to accommodate what he describes as black male learning styles—a notion that is vigorously disputed by some feminists, among others.

27   Teachers have measured boys against female standards of behavior, Kunjufu argues, faulting them for their failure to be quiet and eager to please. Naturally energetic, boys have wrongly been labeled *hyperactive* and forced into special education classes in disproportionate numbers, he says.

28   Kunjufu, who is best known for a three-volume work called *Countering the Conspiracy to Destroy Black Boys*, wants mandatory training for teachers, especially white women, in what he describes as black, male learning styles—their shorter attention spans, higher energy levels, competitiveness, and stronger motor skills. He would also like curricula modified.

29   Those views are partially shared by Spencer Holland, an educational psychologist at Morgan State University in Baltimore and another prime advocate of boys-only classes. He and others say these programs may be needed only to get through the crucial elementary school years.

30   Holland believes that African American boys who grow up in households headed by women develop attitudes toward girls and women that inhibit learning. For example, they may refuse to imi-

tate a female teacher, when imitation and modeling are crucial to elementary school learning.

31   So in the late 1980s, Holland began advocating single-gender classes—taught by men who understand "boy behavior" from personal experience. "It caused a furor," he recalled recently. "I was accused of sexism: 'You can't do this in public school! Where's the research?'"

32   The research, as it turns out, is not clear-cut and does not explicitly examine the merits of special schooling for black boys. Studies of the single-gender education are few, relatively recent, and plagued by methodological questions. What's more, they have focused on secular private academies and Catholic schools.

33   One of the best-known researchers is Valerie Lee, an associate professor of education at the University of Michigan. Lee found some favorable effects of single-gender Catholic schools, mostly in girls; she found few positive, and some negative, effects of single-gender, independent schools.

34   Students at girls' Catholic schools seem to have higher educational aspirations and achievement, and less tendency to engage in sexual stereotyping. But in private boys' schools, Lee found examples of girls and women being treated as sex objects.

35   Slightly different conclusions were reached by Cornelius Riordan, a professor of sociology at Providence College in Rhode Island, who has found that female and minority students do better in single-gender Catholic schools, whereas white boys do better in coeducational schools.

36   Although single-gender schools are not necessarily more effective than others, they tend to have certain positive attributes, Riordan said. Those include a greater degree of order, a "pro-academic culture," and fewer anti-intellectual values.

37   They also offer more successful "same-sex role models" among the students, Riordan said, and greater leadership opportunities. If there are indeed gender differences in learning, as some people argue, Riordan said single-gender schools might cater to those differences.

38   On the issue of legality, a report released last month by the U.S. Department of Education stated that federally funded, single-gender classrooms are illegal under Title IX, which prohibits discrimination on the basis of sex in federally subsidized school programs. The only exceptions are classes in human sexuality and contact sports, and classes for pregnant girls, on grounds of privacy or safety.

39   As for single-sex schools, the report said they are allowed only if comparable schools exist for both genders. But Norma V. Cantu, assistant secretary for civil rights, said in an interview that the education department is reconsidering that policy.

40   Cantu attributed any rise in interest in single-gender schooling to "the lack of enforcement of the civil rights laws." As soon as the government comes out clearly against "certain types of groupings, then you'll see administrators cease to experiment," she said.

41   Others see a worrisome philosophical shift behind the interest in boys-only classes and single-race schools—as well as in girls science and math classes, such as those offered at Ventura High School.

42   Included among those critics are such prominent black intellectuals as Kenneth B. Clark, a key figure in persuading the U.S. Supreme Court to rule that "separate but equal" schools violate the Constitution. Clark has argued that the ruling should apply no less to gender than to race.

43   Some sense a growing preoccupation with the differences, rather than similarities, between races and between genders, and a loss of enthusiasm for the traditional liberal ideal of integration as the route to equality.

44   "I think a lot of people committed to integration have been so disappointed for so long that when the new medicine man comes to town and has a new bromide in the bottle, people are in such pain they'll try anything," said Norman Siegel, executive director of the New York Civil Liberties Union.

45   Among other things, critics fear that single-gender classes reinforce ideas about gender differences—for example, that the opposite sex is a distraction and that boys cannot learn with girls.

46   On a recent morning, a group of ten- and eleven-year-olds at Baltimore's Coleman school talked animatedly about the advantages and drawbacks of single-gender classes. Both boys and girls agreed that they found it easier to concentrate and that they had learned something about self-respect and self-control, in part because they felt more comfortable airing personal issues.

47   Administrators said test scores and achievement levels have also improved significantly. They were also struck by how much the girls seemed to flourish and how many more were now taking math.

48   Parents, too, are pleased with the experiment. Boys and girls both "are able to focus on the correct kind of competition," said Sidney Matthews, a Baltimore father who teaches at Coleman and

whose daughter is in an all-girls class there. Matthews said boys no longer fear appearing to be "sissies" and girls do not hesitate to use their intelligence.

49   In Rochester, too, attendance improved, suspensions dropped, and achievement levels rose, according to Boggs.

50   After four years, the principal says, state and district officials discontinued the classes. A lawyer for the district said they were stopped as soon as the district learned of them. The lawyer said Boggs's subsequent transfer had nothing to do with the single-gender classes.

51   Looking back, Boggs still believes single-gender classes should exist as an option.

52   In Baltimore, fifth grader Michael Hunt agrees. He says life at his school is more harmonious. Parents have become more involved in the school—and no longer simply to gripe about fights among their children.

53   "From what I see, the parents are not coming up that much [to complain]," he said. "They're coming up to help."

_____

EXERCISES

Details and Their Meanings

1. How many public schools in the United States have been practicing single-gender education in the last five years? What is the aim of these programs? Who are they designed to help and how? Why haven't more schools set up separate classes for boys and girls?
2. What groups of people oppose boys-only classes? What reasons do they give for their opposition?
3. What theories about the ways boys learn (in particular African-American boys) do supporters of single-gender education use to strengthen their argument? What makes these theories "controversial"?
4. What alternatives to single-gender education do analysts propose? How do these alternatives attempt to address the needs of African-American boys? Why have these alternatives been proposed?

5. What examples of single-sex classes does the writer present in the essay? How did each of these programs develop? What has been the experience in each of the cases?
6. What do students say about the advantages and disadvantages of single-gender classes? What do parents say? According to the writer, how important are these views?

Reading and Critical Thinking

1. Jawanza Kunjufu claims that "the ultimate question" involved in the debate over single-gender education is "Who's going to decide what's in the best interest of African-American children?" Who does he think should decide? Do you agree or disagree with his position? Why or why not? Do you think programs of the kind described in this article should be permitted and publicly funded? Why? Should you, in fact, have a voice in the issue?
2. What problems in public education do educators, parents, and students face today? To what degree does single-gender education address these problems?
3. Opponents claim that single-gender education is a step backward toward segregation and a challenge to integration as the best means to achieve equality. Do you think that establishing "separate but equal" classes for African American males is a step backward? Why or why not?
4. Supporters of boys-only classes have been accused of sexism. Do you think that this accusation is valid? Why or why not?
5. What does research show about the positive and negative effects of single-gender education? How significant are these findings for the issues presented here? Which side of the debate, if any, do the results of recent research support?

The Writer's Strategies

1. What technique does the writer use to begin the selection? What is the effect of opening the piece in this way? How do paragraphs 1 and 2 make you feel about the debate over single-gender education?
2. In which paragraphs does the writer summarize the two posi-

tions in the debate? How does the language she uses in these paragraphs reveal her own position?

3. What would you say is the thesis of this selection?

4. How much space does the writer devote to each side of the argument? Does she give equal space to each, or does she give more space to one side or the other? Are you satisfied with her presentation? Why or why not?

5. What kinds of "authorities" does the writer cite? Which authorities seem more "authoritative"? Which seem less "authoritative"? Why?

6. Comment on the paragraph length throughout the essay. Why does the writer use so many one- and two-sentence paragraphs?

7. How does the writer end the selection? Is it effective? Why or why not?

Thinking Together

In small groups, discuss your experiences in elementary school with regard to gender and race. Were your teachers the same gender and race as you? How did these factors contribute to the way you think your teachers treated you? How did these factors contribute to your relation with the teacher? Were you in single-sex or coeducational classrooms? Were your classmates predominantly of a single race or ethnic group similar to or different than your own? How did the makeup of the class affect your behavior and learning? Would you have preferred to go to school with a different group of students? Why?

Vocabulary

The following terms from this selection reflect the legal aspects of the debate over single-gender education. Find each word, and write a brief definition of how it is used in the context of the essay. If necessary, consult a dictionary or an encyclopedia.

1. segregated (par. 2)
2. grass-roots (par. 4)
3. civil libertarians (par. 6)
4. feminists (par. 6)
5. advocated (par. 9)

6. ACLU (par. 10)
7. NOW (par. 10)
8. grand jury (par. 13)
9. litigation (par. 22)
10. special education (par. 27)
11. sexism (par. 31)
12. enforcement (par. 40)
13. civil rights laws (par. 40)
14. "separate but equal" (par. 42)
15. liberal ideal (par. 43)
16. integration (par. 44)

WRITER'S WORKSHOP ━━━━━━━━━

Critical Thinking in Writing

1. Write a one-page summary of the argument for single-sex education presented here. Then write a one-page summary of the argument against single-sex education presented here.
2. Write an informal journal entry describing an incident in elementary or secondary school in which you felt being separated by sex was an advantage or being part of a coeducational group was a disadvantage.
3. Are boys-only classes a good idea? Do the advantages outweigh the disadvantages? Write a brief essay of a page or two in which you present your own position on single-gender education.

Connecting Ideas

Read Felicia R. Lee's "Model Minority" (page 96). Then write an essay comparing the experiences of Asian-American students and African-American male students. How are the problems faced by the two groups different? In what ways are these problems similar? Would segregated classes help to resolve the problems faced by Asian-American students? Why or why not?

An American Dream

Rosemarie Santini

Rosemarie Santini has published articles in many publications, and her books include The Secret Fire, Abracadabra, A Swell Style of Murder, *and* The Disenchanted Diva. *This account, which first appeared in the magazine section of a Sunday newspaper, tells how life has changed over the years for a family of three generations of Italian Americans who live together in the Queens section of New York City. Santini suggests that reaching for the American Dream has resulted in a gradual forgetting of the rich traditions of the past.*

KEY WORDS

tenements (par. 1)   inexpensive, crowded apartment houses occupied by working-class people
affluent (par. 19)   well-to-do
reiterates (par. 22)   repeats
melodramatic (par. 24)   extremely emotional and overacted
tumultuous (par. 27)   full of turmoil
oblivious (par. 29)   not aware

"WHERE ARE THE CHILDREN?" Ida Rinaldi asks as she breaks one egg after another into a large mound of flour, first breaking each egg into a glass and inspecting it for any discoloration. It is a process learned in the old days, in the tenements on Thompson St., when the eggs were often bad and destroyed whatever they were put into. "My mother taught me how to do this," she says.

2   Resting on the tablecloth that covers her kitchen table is a large, wooden board on which she begins to knead the mixture. On the counter nearby, other necessities for her Italian cuisine are in evidence: tomatoes, canned, of course, in Italia, tomato paste from the same country—very expensive—beef meats, and stale bread mixed in milk, all ready to be rolled into large meatballs. She enjoys her chores, part of a process which will take hours. She is preparing

fettucine as her Neapolitan mother taught her. "Let's see, eight people, eight eggs," she counts with peasant logic.

3   It is hot in the kitchen this August day, and she puts her hand to her forehead, smearing her tanned complexion with white flour. "Where are the children?" she asks again, although there is no one to answer.

4   At 67, Mrs. Rinaldi does not fit the popular picture of an Italian Mama. She is chic, petite, and slender. She wears the tight pants of the seventies, a shell blouse, and tiny gypsy earrings. On the left finger of her right hand are a diamond engagement ring and a wedding band in an antique setting. They are not the original ones. In 1931 when she married, she was given no engagement ring, and her wedding band was of plain silver.

5   Other things were different then, too. Now her house is a three-story brick, attached house in a lovely section in Queens. A backyard, a porch, a lawn are her proud possessions. Her apartment on the second floor could be featured in *The Sunday News* interior decorating pages. It is modern and sleek, and the only signs of her Italian heritage are tiny Botticelli angels in antique gold, which liven up the living room.

6   In 1931, her wedding home was an unheated, three-room tenement apartment in the Italian section of Greenwich Village. There, while working as a dressmaker, she raised her family, keeping the small apartment spotless, cooking on an old stove, cooling her groceries in an ice box; a living-room couch was her children's bed. Enduring these hardships, Ida Rinaldi and her husband worked and saved for the fulfillment of their American Dream, a house of their own. Finally, when their daughter Kathleen married and had a family, the Rinaldi–DeGiovanni clan moved from the tenements to the suburban splendor of Queens.

7   Here the brick houses all stand in a row, attached but separated by fence lines announcing ownership in this working-class neighborhood. Most owners, like the Rinaldi family, spent their entire life savings on the down payments. Only the electrical wires, hanging like kite lines over the pretty streets, mar the vista of this lovely neighborhood, an effect which the homeowners add to by stringing up clothesline in the backyards, probably a hangover from tenement days. Although most houses have washer-dryers, old habits die hard, and the Italians prefer their clothes bleached and dried in the sun, a custom inherited from ancestors who washed clothes in the village brooks of Italy.

8   Other neighbors have planted tomatoes in their gardens, but

not this family. In the Rinaldi house, there is a *House Beautiful* quality of floors polished almost too clean, of furniture oiled, of dustlessness, and in the duplex below, where the DeGiovannis live, the same cleanliness dominates all.

9   The other dominating interest in this household is "What's for dinner?" Today, it is the egg fettucine specialty, hand rolled, to be served with a thick meat sauce. Mrs. Rinaldi explains that she is spending so much time on this delicacy as a treat for the children, her two grandsons, teenagers Paul and John, who were, of course, a major reason for the Rinaldi–DeGiovanni move from Greenwich Village. But where are the children?

10   Kathleen DeGiovanni brings her mother the news. Her two sons have baseball games to play. After that, they are going to the DeGiovanni beach club for a swim and a party.

11   Mrs. Rinaldi's eyes look sad. "What about the egg noodles?" she asks.

12   "Can we keep them?" her tall, brunette daughter suggests.

13   Sighing, the older woman cuts the dough carefully in strips, then carries the long, thin pasta into the extra bedroom. "Well, no one's using the extra bedroom. We can lay them out here," she says, laying the pasta carefully on the bed.

14   Afterwards, she pours a cup of espresso. "It's all changed," she says. "When we first came here, our life was more centered in this house. It was the sixties, and we were so glad to get out of the tenements. This seemed like a good place for our grandchildren to play and grow up. Now, everyone is going this way and that. I guess that's life."

15   She spoons three sugars into her tiny demitasse cup. "I hope it doesn't get damp. Noodles are impossible to keep separate when it gets damp." As she sits, her hands move with infinite patience and care, a habit from another era when hands were important for darning, sewing, crocheting, knitting, making pasta.

16   Does she miss the old style of living in the Italian section of Greenwich Village? "I loved it, but now everyone has either died or moved away. When I walk down the streets, I don't know anyone." But weekly, she does walk down the streets, riding the bus and subway into the city to have her hair done, buying ricotta and mozzarella in the old cheese store across the street from the church, the same store where she shopped as a young bride whenever she could afford it. Once in a while, she runs into an old neighbor or friend who tells her how terrible living in the Village is nowadays.

17   Sometimes she wonders whether her life has really improved,

although they have more room and more conveniences. Later, her daughter Kathleen comments on this: "I grew up sleeping on a living-room couch. Here, my sons have a bedroom to themselves. We moved into a brand-new area where everyone was mostly Italian and mostly friendly. When the kids were small, I could leave them on the front lawn and not worry about them."

18   But the kids were no longer small, and Kathleen and her husband spend most of their time working in the city, going to church and school meetings, chauffeuring the boys to baseball games, grabbing a moment or two at the beach club, where a swim, a game of tennis give them much pleasure, not returning home until it is time to sleep.

19   The boys do not even mow the lawn nowadays, even though their weekly allowance from their grandfather should influence them to do so. Their major interests are sports, dancing, music, visiting more-affluent neighborhoods, attending rock concerts, meeting new girls. John and Paul, fifteen and seventeen, are tall, solid, muscular young men who say they want to live farther out on Long Island, near the sea, in a house complete with a boat moored at a dock, an office nearby in town, and lots and lots of privacy.

20   Dark-haired, studious Felix DeGiovanni agrees with his sons. "My parents were immigrants, born in Europe. They didn't have any choice on how to live when they arrived here. I had to compromise, too, and live in Queens, instead of farther out, because I work in the city."

21   Although Mr. DeGiovanni likes suburban living, he feels that his boys have been too much sheltered. "I learned all about life very young, on the city streets. I was working in the neighborhood pasta store after school when I was thirteen. My kids will be put through college without having to work. They have everything they need. They don't know how to take care of themselves, and I'm not sure that's good for them."

22   Mr. DeGiovanni earned his M.A. in engineering by going to night school and working as a draftsman during the day. Because his children do not have to struggle, he feels they are not as mature as he was at their age. Also, he reiterates a familiar parental theme, questioning whether his sons have any respect for authority.

23   Grandfather Rinaldi agrees that life is very, very different from the time he came over on a boat from Italy. "Then we worked hard and respected our parents and our family." White-haired, retired from the U.S. Post Office, Mr. Rinaldi sits on the porch in his rocking chair, pensively smoking his pipe as he watches the comings

and goings in the neighborhood, talking about how different his life would have been if his parents were not immigrants.

24   If he had stayed in Italy, he might wander down to the town's square where he would find the other older men sitting and pondering the past and would argue with them, raising his voice in melodramatic splendor. If he had remained in Greenwich Village, he might walk over to the private men's club where Italian men play bocce and pinochle and talk about politics. But in Queens there are only a few senior-citizen centers for this kind of social interchange, and Mr. Rinaldi says the people there are too old.

25   Still, he is happy that he has at last attained his idea of a successful life: a house he owns out of what he considers the city, a safe place far removed from tenement living. Yet, there is a bittersweet element to his satisfaction, as if now he has everything, what does he really have?

26   "When we lived in Italy, I felt superior," he explains. "My parents were respected. We lost all that when we came to America. For years, I couldn't speak the language properly. Other kids from the neighborhoods called me names. I had to fight a lot, and I didn't understand the ways of living here. It took me a long time to get accustomed to America. That's why I worked so hard to better myself. To get what I had dreamed of all these years."

27   What is this dream anyhow, and has it worked for these former city dwellers in their effort for a better life? There is a lack of primitiveness here on these residential streets, so far from the tumultuous streets of their youth in the city . . . a sterility, almost a disease of cleanliness, where a speck of trash spills over onto their private thoughts and peaceful existence. Yet the neighborhood concepts which most of these former tenement dwellers grew up with are still in evidence. There are eyes in every second-story window, observing any stranger on the streets in minute detail, and visitors are associated with this house and that. There are pleasantries on the street, greetings of neighbors and friends.

28   Then, suddenly, the streets are empty. It is 5:30, dinner time in an Italian working-class neighborhood. The men have walked or driven home from their jobs. The children have stopped playing. In the Rinaldi–DeGiovanni home, the beautiful homemade noodles lie on the bed in the guest bedroom, uncooked, waiting for the meat sauce and imported, expensive cheese.

29   In the kitchen of the top-floor apartment, the Rinaldi grandparents are eating vegetables in garlic oil with fresh Italian bread, waiting for the third generation of the family to be available from their busy life. This third generation is swimming in the beach-club pool,

clowning with friends, listening to rock music, drinking soda pop, eating frankfurters, oblivious to the lifetime of dedication and hardship represented by the plates of rare and delicious fettucine in marvelous sauce that await them.

EXERCISES

Details and Their Meanings

1. Where does the piece take place? Where is the Rinaldi–DeGiovanni house? In what room does the action occur? In what ways is the setting significant?
2. Where did Ida Rinaldi learn to inspect eggs? Where else in the essay is that place mentioned? How many times is it mentioned? In what ways does that place contrast with Ida's current location?
3. What details indicate the way Ida cooks? What details indicate the way she dresses? How does the way she cooks contrast with the way she dresses? What does the contrast indicate?
4. What is significant about the order in which the family members appear? Where are the grandsons when the piece begins and later in the afternoon? Where are they when the piece ends? What is the significance of where they are and where they are not?
5. Where did DeGiovanni grow up? What did his childhood teach him that he is afraid his boys aren't learning? How do the boys spend their time, and what are their ambitions?
6. What sacrifices did Grandfather Rinaldi make and for what purpose? What were the results of his sacrifice? Did he get something of the sort he had hoped for? Does he miss anything he may have left behind in his struggle?

Reading and Critical Thinking

1. What values are important for the grandfather? for the father? for the children? How have these values changed from one generation to the next? Do you agree that the grandsons are not learning important values? Why or why not?

2. In what ways is the boys' life better than the childhoods of their parents and grandparents? In what way might the boys' childhood be less satisfactory than their parents' and grandparents'?
3. How does the old life in the Greenwich Village neighborhood compare with current life in Queens? Which do you feel is preferable?
4. How much are the grandsons aware of the Italian traditions? Ought they be more aware? Is their lack of knowledge a natural part of becoming an American?

The Writer's Strategies

1. Look at the opening sentence. How does the question help set up the thesis of the selection?
2. How many places and ways of life are contrasted in this piece? List all the contrasts you can find, and identify the main point established by each.
3. How does the topic of conversation switch when each new person enters the room? How do these multiple perspectives enrich the main point?
4. How many references to food and cooking can you find? In what ways does food establish the ethnic culture of the selection? What does the concern about food tell you about the family's way of life? What is the significance of the dinner's having to be postponed until the children return?

Thinking Together

In discussion groups of three or four students, share the story of how your parents and grandparents lived and how your lives may be different from theirs. Compare where they lived, the houses they lived in, the food they ate, and the amusements they had with those you experience.

Vocabulary

The following italicized words refer to details of Italian culture mentioned in the essay. From the context in which the words appear and from your knowledge of Italian culture, identify the meaning of each term.

1. other necessities for her Italian *cuisine* (par. 2)
2. tomatoes, canned, of course, *in Italia* (par. 2)
3. She is preparing *fettucine* (par. 2)
4. as her *Neapolitan* mother taught her (par. 2)
5. tiny *Botticelli* angels in antique gold (par. 5)
6. pours a cup of *espresso* (par. 14)
7. into her tiny *demitasse* cup (par. 15)
8. buying *ricotta* and *mozzarella* in the old cheese store (par. 16)
9. working in the neighborhood *pasta* store after school (par. 21)
10. where Italian men play *bocce* and *pinochle* (par. 24)

WRITER'S WORKSHOP ━━━━━━━━━━━━

Critical Thinking in Writing

1. Do you think modern American youth have it "too easy"? What does having it "too easy" mean, and what are the consequences of it? State your position about the current generation in three or four paragraphs.
2. What values did your parents hope you would develop? Did you in fact develop those values? Do your values come from what your parents told you or from the challenges you have faced? Write several paragraphs describing your parents' efforts to transmit values to you and the results of those efforts.
3. Do you believe that becoming affluent and leading a comfortable life necessarily means losing contact with one's ethnic identity? Write an essay of about a page stating your position and giving reasons for your beliefs.

Connecting Ideas

Compare the view in this selection with the process of becoming American in Elizabeth Wong's "The Struggle to Be an All-American Girl" (page 39). Do you think the boys in "An American Dream" and the girl in "The Struggle" would have the same or different attitudes toward their ethnic heritage? In what ways might the Rinaldis' and DeGiovannis' feeling about the boys be similar to the regrets Elizabeth Wong feels as an adult? Write an essay of three or four paragraphs exploring these connections.

The Jacket

Gary Soto

Gary Soto describes his feelings about growing up by telling a story about an article of clothing that seems to sum up his social failures. This selection may make you think about the old saying, "The clothes make the man."

KEY WORDS

guacamole (par. 2)   a yellow-green spread made from
   mashed avocados

MY CLOTHES HAVE FAILED me. I remember the green coat that I wore in fifth and sixth grades when you either danced like a champ or pressed yourself against a greasy wall, bitter as a penny toward the happy couples.

2   When I needed a new jacket and my mother asked what kind I wanted, I described something like bikers wear: black leather and silver studs with enough belts to hold down a small town. We were in the kitchen, steam on the windows from her cooking. She listened so long while stirring dinner that I thought she understood for sure the kind I wanted. The next day when I got home from school, I discovered draped on my bedpost a jacket the color of day-old guacamole. I threw my books on the bed and approached the jacket slowly, as if it were a stranger whose hand I had to shake. I touched the vinyl sleeve, the collar, and peeked at the mustard-colored lining.

3   From the kitchen, mother yelled that my jacket was in the closet. I closed the door to her voice and pulled at the rack of clothes in the closet, hoping the jacket on the bedpost wasn't for me but my mean brother. No luck. I gave up. From my bed, I stared at the jacket. I wanted to cry because it was so ugly and so big that I knew I'd have to wear it a long time. I was a small kid, thin as a young tree, and it would be years before I'd have a new one. I

64

stared at the jacket, like an enemy, thinking bad things before I took off my old jacket whose sleeves climbed halfway to my elbow.

4   I put the big jacket on. I zipped it up and down several times, and rolled the cuffs up so they didn't cover my hands. I put my hands in the pockets and flapped the jacket like a bird's wings. I stood in front of the mirror, full face, then profile, and then looked over my shoulder as if someone had called me. I sat on the bed, stood against the bed, and combed my hair to see what I would look like doing something natural. I looked ugly. I threw it on my brother's bed and looked at it for a long time before I slipped it on and went out to the backyard, smiling a "thank you" to my mom as I passed her in the kitchen. With my hands in my pockets, I kicked a ball against the fence and then climbed it to sit looking into the alley. I hurled orange peels at the mouth of an open garbage can, and when the peels were gone, I watched the white puffs of my breath thin to nothing.

5   I jumped down, hands in my pockets, and in the backyard on my knees I teased my dog, Brownie, by swooping my arms while making bird calls. He jumped at me and missed. He jumped again and again, until a tooth sunk deep, ripping an L-shaped tear on my left sleeve. I pushed Brownie away to study the tear as I would a cut on my arm. There was no blood, only a few loose pieces of fuzz. Damn dog, I thought, and pushed him away hard when he tried to bite again. I got up from my knees and went to my bedroom to sit with my jacket on my lap, with the lights out.

6   That was the first afternoon with my new jacket. The next day I wore it to sixth grade and got a D on a math quiz. During the morning recess Frankie T., the playground terrorist, pushed me to the ground and told me to stay there until recess was over. My best friend, Steve Negrete, ate an apple while looking at me, and the girls turned away to whisper on the monkey bars. The teachers were no help: they looked my way and talked about how foolish I looked in my new jacket. I saw their heads bob with laughter, their hands half-covering their mouths.

7   Even though it was cold, I took off the jacket during lunch and played kickball in a thin shirt, my arms feeling like braille from goose bumps. But when I returned to class, I slipped the jacket on and shivered until I was warm. I sat on my hands, heating them up, while my teeth chattered like a cup of crooked dice. Finally warm, I slid out of the jacket but a few minutes later put it back on when the fire bell rang. We paraded out into the yard where we, the sixth graders, walked past all the other grades to stand

against the back fence. Everybody saw me. Although they didn't say out loud, "Man, that's ugly," I heard the buzz-buzz of gossip and even laughter that I knew was meant for me.

8   And so I went, in my guacamole jacket. So embarrassed, so hurt, I couldn't even do my homework. I received Cs on quizzes, and forgot the state capitals and the rivers of South America, our friendly neighbor. Even the girls who had been friendly blew away like loose flowers to follow the boys in neat jackets.

9   I wore that thing for three years until the sleeves grew short and my forearms stuck out like the necks of turtles. All during that time no love came to me—no little dark girl in a Sunday dress she wore on Monday. At lunchtime I stayed with the ugly boys who leaned against the chainlink fence and looked around with propellers of grass spinning in our mouths. We saw girls walk by alone, saw couples, hand in hand, their heads like bookends pressing air together. We saw them and spun our propellers so fast our faces were blurs.

10   I blame that jacket for those bad years. I blame my mother for her bad taste and her cheap ways. It was a sad time for the heart. With a friend I spent my sixth-grade year in a tree in the alley waiting for something good to happen to me in that jacket, which had become the ugly brother who tagged along wherever I went. And it was about that time that I began to grow. My chest puffed up with muscle and, strangely, a few more ribs. Even my hands, those fleshy hammers, showed bravely through the cuffs, the fingers already hardening for the coming fights. But that L-shaped rip on the left sleeve got bigger; bits of stuffing coughed out from its wound after a hard day of play. I finally Scotch-taped it closed, but in rain or cold weather the tape peeled off like a scab, and more stuffing fell out until that sleeve shriveled into a palsied arm. That winter the elbows began to crack and whole chunks of green began to fall off. I showed the cracks to my mother, who always seemed to be at the stove with steamed-up glasses, and she said that there were children in Mexico who would love that jacket. I told her that this was America and yelled that Debbie, my sister, didn't have a jacket like mine. I ran outside, ready to cry, and climbed the tree by the alley to think bad thoughts and watch my breath puff white and disappear.

11   But whole pieces still casually flew off my jacket when I played hard, read quietly, or took vicious spelling tests at school. When it became so spotted that my brother began to call me *camouflage*, I flung it over the fence into the alley. Later, however, I swiped the

jacket off the ground and went inside to drape it across my lap and mope.

12   I was called to dinner: steam silvered my mother's glasses as she said grace; my brother and sister with their heads bowed made ugly faces at their glasses of powdered milk. I gagged too but eagerly ate big rips of buttered tortilla that held scooped up beans. Finished, I went outside with my jacket across my arm. It was a cold sky. The faces of clouds were piled up, hurting. I climbed the fence, jumping down with a grunt. I started up the alley and soon slipped into my jacket, that green ugly brother who breathed over my shoulder that day and ever since.

_____

EXERCISES

Details and Their Meanings

1. What did Gary Soto want his new jacket to look like? Why do you think he wanted that kind of jacket? How would such a jacket make him appear among his schoolmates? Did his mother understand what he wanted?
2. What was Soto's reaction to the jacket his mother got him? Why was the size important? Why do you think his mother got him this kind of jacket? In what ways did he accept his mother's choice? In what ways did he not accept it?
3. What happened the first time Soto wore the jacket? Why do you think he did not repair the jacket immediately? What attempts did he make to repair it? What happened to the rip over time? What did that rip seem to signify?
4. How did Soto's classmates and friends react to his jacket? Was their reaction temporary or long lasting?
5. What happened to Soto's grades? to his social standing? to his friendships with girls? Why did he believe these events were caused by the jacket?
6. In what ways did Soto try to hide the jacket, not wear it, or otherwise try not to make it conspicuous? Why couldn't he get rid of it altogether? Why did his brother start to call him *camouflage*? How did his effort to avoid appearing in public because

of the jacket reflect on his social presence and confidence during those years?

7. How did the jacket come to look over time? How did that appearance seem to reflect Soto's attitude toward his life?

Reading and Critical Thinking

1. To what extent do you think Gary Soto exaggerates the effect of the jacket? Do these exaggerations reflect the thinking of the young boy or the adult writer?

2. What was the psychological impact of the jacket and people's reaction to it on the young boy? Do you believe clothes can have such a psychological impact?

3. In what ways does Soto blame his misfortunes on his mother for purchasing the jacket? What does his attitude toward his mother's purchase of the jacket reveal about his relationship with her?

4. Were Soto's teenage years happy or unhappy? What do you think were the causes of those feelings? To what extent were those feelings caused by either the jacket or the mother?

5. What does this piece tell you about growing up? Does it in any way reflect on the particular experience of Hispanic youths, or are youths in all groups likely to go through something similar?

The Writer's Strategies

1. What is the opening sentence? How does that sentence relate to the narrative that follows? Is that sentence an accurate portrayal of the causes of the boy's difficulties? If it is not, why do you think the writer insists on blaming the jacket?

2. Why does the writer state in the opening paragraph that "in fifth and sixth grades . . . you either danced like a champ or pressed yourself against a greasy wall"? How does this choice set up the problem of the selection?

3. The writer presents a number of similes (comparisons using *like* or *as*), such as "bitter as a penny" and "arms feeling like braille." Find other similes. For both of the similes presented here and for others that you find, explain the meaning that is conveyed and tell how the simile supports the ideas and mood of the selection.

4. In how many places is it mentioned that the mother's glasses were steamed up as she cooked? What is happening between the mother and Soto at each of those times? What is the writer trying to show by this repeated imagery of the mother's glasses fogged by cooking?

5. In what order are the events told? What is the general progress of the writer's life over that period? What is the condition of the jacket over that period? How do these three elements fit together in a single pattern?

6. What parts of the piece seem exaggerated? Why does the writer exaggerate? What impression is the writer trying to give? Does the exaggeration strengthen or weaken the selection?

7. The writer ends by comparing the jacket to a "green ugly brother." Where does he make that comparison earlier? What does the writer mean by it? Why does he end the piece with that comparison? Why does he say that the "green ugly brother . . . breathed over my shoulder that day and ever since"?

Thinking Together

In small groups, compare the kinds of clothes you had as you grew up, particularly as you entered your teen years. Discuss which clothes you hated and why and which clothes you liked. Discuss which clothes your parents picked for you and when you were allowed to choose your own clothes. Which clothes made you feel part of a group. Which made you stand out in a positive way, and which made you appear to be an outsider? Then each group should write a description of the most excellent and most awful outfits for both male and female teenagers. Be prepared to consider in a general class discussion why each outfit would result in social acceptance or rejection.

Vocabulary

The following words appear in the selection. Define each one in terms that fit its context.

1. braille (par. 7)
2. scab (par. 10)
3. vicious (par. 11)

4. camouflage (par. 11)
5. tortilla (par. 12)

WRITER'S WORKSHOP ⎯⎯⎯⎯⎯⎯⎯⎯⎯⎯

Critical Thinking in Writing

1. Clothes and external appearances are very important to children entering their teen years. What does this preoccupation say about children at that age and about the nature of their relations with others? Write an essay about the importance of appearance to preteens and teenagers.
2. To what extent does Gary Soto blame other people or external events for his own misfortunes? Is he correct to do so? Have you ever done this? Write a short essay exploring how you focus your discontents by blaming someone or something outside yourself.
3. Have you ever had a conflict with your parents over the clothes you wear? How did the conflict turn out? What were the consequences? Write a biographical narrative recalling the incident and its implications.

Connecting Ideas

Read "'Those Loud Black Girls,'" by Joan Morgan (page 104). Compare the problems those young women face in trying to develop an identity they are happy with to the problems faced by Gary Soto. What are the different strategies they choose to solve the problem? What are the consequences of their different strategies?

Growing Up in Black and White

Jack E. White

Jack E. White uses personal experience to start an investigation of how we still transmit racial stereotypes to children despite increasing integration and tolerance in our society.

KEY WORDS

proliferation (par. 5)   rapid increase in number
espouse (par. 6)   support
mainstream (par. 7)   prevailing direction or group
subtexts (par. 9)   underlying messages
susceptibility (par. 10)   likeliness to be affected
inoculate (par. 12)   give protective exposure against a
   disease

"MOMMY, I WANT TO be white."

2   Imagine my wife's anguish and alarm when our beautiful brown-skinned three-year-old daughter made that declaration. We thought we were doing everything right to develop her self-esteem and positive racial identity. We overloaded her toy box with black dolls. We carefully monitored the racial content of TV shows and videos, ruling out *Song of the South* and *Dumbo,* two classic Disney movies marred by demeaning black stereotypes. But we saw no harm in *Pinocchio,* which seemed as racially benign as *Sesame Street* or *Barney* and a good deal more engaging. Yet now our daughter was saying she wanted to be white, to be like the puppet who becomes a real boy in the movie. How had she got that potentially soul-destroying idea and, even more important, what should we do about it?

3   That episode was an unsettling reminder of the unique burden that haunts black parents in America: helping their children come

71

to terms with being black in a country where the message too often seems to be that being white is better. Developing a healthy self-image would be difficult enough for black children with all the real-life reminders that blacks and whites are still treated differently. But it is made even harder by the seductive racial bias in TV, movies, and children's books, which seem to link everything beautiful and alluring with whiteness while often treating blacks as afterthoughts. Growing up in this all pervading world of whiteness can be psychologically exhausting for black children just as they begin to figure out who they are. As a four-year-old boy told his father after spending another day in the overwhelmingly white environment of his Connecticut day-care facility, "Dad, I'm tired of being black."

4   In theory it should now be easier for children to develop a healthy sense of black pride than it was during segregation. In 1947 psychologists Kenneth and Mamie Clark conducted a famous experiment that demonstrated just how much black children had internalized the hatred that society directed at their race. They asked 253 black children to choose between four dolls, two black and two white. The result: two-thirds of the children preferred white dolls.

5   The conventional wisdom had been that black self-hatred was a by-product of discrimination that would wither away as society became more tolerant. Despite the civil rights movement of the 1960s, the black-is-beautiful movement of the seventies, the proliferation of black characters on television shows during the eighties, and the renascent black nationalist movement of the nineties, the prowhite message has not lost its power. In 1985 psychologist Darlene Powell–Hopson updated the Clarks' experiment using black and white Cabbage Patch dolls and got a virtually identical result: 65 percent of the black children preferred white dolls. "Black is dirty," one youngster explained. Powell–Hopson thinks the result would be the same if the test were repeated today.

6   Black mental-health workers say the trouble is that virtually all the progress the United States has made toward racial fairness has been in one direction. To be accepted by whites, blacks have to become more like them, whereas many whites have not changed their attitudes at all. Study after study has shown that the majority of whites, for all the commitment to equality they espouse, still consider blacks to be inferior, undesirable, and dangerous. "Even though race relations have changed for the better, people maintain those old stereotypes," says Powell–Hopson. "The same racial dy-

namics occur in an integrated environment as occurred in segregation; it's just more covert."

7   Psychiatrists say children as young as two can pick up these damaging messages, often from subtle signals of black inferiority unwittingly embedded in children's books, toys, and TV programs designed for the white mainstream. "There are many more positive images about black people in the media than there used to be, but there's still a lot that says that white is more beautiful and powerful than black, that white is good and black is bad," says James P. Comer, a Yale University psychiatrist who collaborated with fellow black psychiatrist Alvin F. Poussaint on *Raising Black Children* (Plume).

8   The bigotry is not usually as blatant as it was in Roald Dahl's *Charlie and the Chocolate Factory*. When the book was published in 1964, *The New York Times* called it "a richly inventive and humorous tale." Blacks didn't see anything funny about having the factory staffed by "Oompa-Loompas," pygmy workers imported in shipping cartons from the jungle where they had been living in the trees.

9   Today white-controlled companies are doing a better job of erasing racially loaded subtexts from children's books and movies. Yet those messages still get through, in part because they are at times so subtle even a specialist like Powell–Hopson misses them. She recently bought a book about a cat for her six-year-old daughter, who has a love of felines. Only when Powell–Hopson got home did she discover that the beautiful white cat in the story turns black when it starts to behave badly. Moreover, when the products are not objectionable, they are sometimes promoted in ways that unintentionally drive home the theme of black inferiority. Powell–Hopson cites a TV ad for dolls that displayed a black version in the background behind the white model "as though it were a second-class citizen."

10   Sadly, black self-hatred can also begin at home. Even today, says Powell–Hopson, "many of us perpetuate negative messages, showing preference for lighter complexions, saying nappy hair is bad and straight hair is good, calling other black people 'niggers,' that sort of thing." This danger can be greater than the one posed by TV and the other media because children learn so much by simple imitation of the adults they are closest to. Once implanted in a toddler's mind, teachers and psychologists say, such misconceptions can blossom into a full-blown racial identity crisis during adolescence, affecting everything from performance in the classroom

to a youngster's susceptibility to crime and drug abuse. But they can be neutralized if parents react properly.

11   In their book, Comer and Poussaint emphasize a calm and straightforward approach. They point out that even black children from affluent homes in integrated neighborhoods need reassurance about racial issues because from their earliest days they sense that their lives are "viewed cheaply by white society." If, for example, a black little girl says she wishes she had straight blond hair, they advise parents to point out "in a relaxed and unemotional manner . . . that she is black and that most black people have nice curly black hair, and that most white people have straight hair, brown, blond, black. At this age what you convey in your voice and manner will either make it O.K. or make it a problem."

12   Powell–Hopson, who along with her psychologist husband Derek has written *Different and Wonderful: Raising Black Children in a Race-Conscious Society* (Fireside), takes a more aggressive approach, urging black parents in effect to inoculate their children against negative messages at an early age. For example, the authors suggest that African-American parents whose children display a preference for white dolls or action figures should encourage them to play with a black one by "dressing it in the best clothes, or having it sit next to you, or doing anything you can think of to make your child sense that you prefer that doll." After that, the Hopsons say, the child can be offered a chance to play with the toy, on the condition that "you promise to take the very best care of it. You know it is my favorite." By doing so, the Hopsons claim, "most children will jump at a chance to hold the toy even for a second."

13   White children are no less vulnerable to racial messages. Their reactions can range from a false sense of superiority over blacks to an identification with sports superstars like Michael Jordan so complete that they want to become black. But if white parents look for guidance from popular child-care manuals, they won't find any. "I haven't included it because I don't feel like an expert in that area," says T. Berry Brazelton, author of *Infants and Mothers* and other child-care books. "I think it's a very, very serious issue that this country hasn't faced up to." Unless it does, the United States runs the risk of rearing another generation of white children crippled by the belief that they are better than blacks and black children who agree.

14   As for my daughter, we're concerned but confident. As Comer says, "In the long run what children learn from their parents is more powerful than anything they get from any other source." When my little girl expressed the wish to be white, my wife put aside her anguish and smilingly replied that she is bright and black

and beautiful, a very special child. We'll keep telling her that until we're sure she loves herself as much as we love her.

———————

EXERCISES

Details and Their Meanings

1. Which shows and videos did the author and his wife let their daughter see? Which did they exclude? Why did they choose the ones they did? Why did they seem to make a bad choice?
2. According to White, which social movements have affected discrimination? How have these movements affected children's self-image?
3. According to White, what is the youngest age children can pick up racial stereotypes? How are these stereotype "signals" transmitted? What is the specific message sent?
4. When *Charlie and the Chocolate Factory* first appeared, who considered it offensive and who didn't? When was it published? What, according to the essay, would be different about it if it were published today? What are examples of racially loaded messages that still get through today?
5. How are white children affected by current racial stereotypes? Do the stereotypes have a simple, single effect on white children? To what extent does this reflect some changes in American society?

Reading and Critical Thinking

1. What conclusions do you draw from the comparison of the experiment conducted by the Clarks in 1947 and the updated version of this experiment conducted by Darlene Powell–Hopson in 1985? How does that conclusion contradict common wisdom? Is the conclusion surprising? Why or why not?
2. Why, according to African-American mental-health workers, have racial stereotypes remained? In order for these stereotypes to change, who would have to change what ideas?
3. What kinds of messages from parents can increase African-American children's self-hatred? Why are these comments

strong influences on children? When children grow to adolescence, what is the effect of these comments?

4. What practical advice does the writer offer to parents in paragraphs 11 and 12? What are the differences between the two sets of advice? Which advice do you think is best? Why?

5. What is the consequence of child-care manuals not offering guidance on racial stereotypes? What predictions does the writer make about not revising these manuals? Do you think the predictions are likely to become real? Why or why not?

6. In general, does the author feel that children should be exposed to or shielded from a wide range of racial images? Why? Do you agree with him?

The Writer's Strategies

1. What is the writer's central idea or thesis? Where do you find it? How does he use the opinion of experts to develop his argument?

2. Consider the title of this selection. Why does the author use the terms *black* and *white* instead of *African-American* and *Caucasian*? How do the words *black* and *white* (or the phrase *black and white*) reinforce the writer's main point? Does the title have more than one meaning? What do you think the title means?

3. Which personal experiences does White use? How do these personal experiences support the main idea of the selection? How does the experience of the author and his family define a problem addressed by the essay?

4. How does the conclusion help unify the essay? How does it reflect the thesis?

5. What is the tone of the selection? Is the writer remote, angry, confused, resigned, frightened? Support your view with specific references to the text.

Thinking Together

Throughout the selection, the writer uses specific examples of television, film, and books to illustrate how the media subtly sends the message that white is good and black is bad. Brainstorm in small groups about the subtle and not-so-subtle messages about race conveyed in the media surrounding you: in television, films, news reports, music videos, books, or games. List specific examples and then discuss whether the messages are positive, negative, or both at once.

Vocabulary

Write definitions for each of the adjectives taken from the selection. Check the paragraphs indicated for context clues to the meaning.

1. benign (par. 2)
2. alluring (par. 3)
3. seductive (par. 3)
4. pervading (par. 3)
5. covert (par. 6)
6. blatant (par. 8)
7. nappy (par. 10)

WRITER'S WORKSHOP ━━━━━━━━━━

Critical Thinking in Writing

1. How can parents rear children not to have negative stereotypes about themselves and others? Write an essay expressing your beliefs about the subject and stating how you might help your children in this area.
2. Choose a television show or movie that presents people of several races. Then write an essay on the meaning of race and racial identities as explored in what you have viewed.
3. What messages did you receive about race from your parents and your peers as you grew up? How have those messages influenced or affected you? Write an essay explaining the effect on you of the racial ideas of people around you.

Connecting Ideas

Read the selection entitled "America's New Wave of Runaways" by Michelle Ingrassia (p. 19). How does the pressure to assimilate into white, mainstream American culture affect the children in that selection? How are the experiences of those Asian-American children similar to or different from the experiences of African-American children described in this selection?

Moon on a
Silver Spoon

Eudora Welty

Eudora Welty is one of America's foremost writers. Her work includes fiction, poetry, and criticism, much of it concerned with the South. In this selection from One Writer's Beginnings *(1984), her autobiography, she discusses her family's love of reading.*

KEY WORDS

initiating (par. 10)   introducing
keystone (par. 10)   the stone in an arch that holds everything together
acute (par. 13)   sharp
opulence (par. 15)   showy richness
reposing (par. 15)   reclining, lying down
insatiability (par. 16)   the condition of not being able to be satisfied
cadence (par. 18)   beat or rhythm; in this case, the rhythm of words in a text

ON A VISIT TO my grandmother's in West Virginia, I stood inside the house where my mother had been born and where she grew up.

2 "Here's where I first began to read my Dickens," Mother said, pointing. "Under that very bed. Hiding my candle. To keep them from knowing I was up all night."

3 "But where did it all *come* from?" I asked her at last. "All that Dickens?"

4 "Why, Papa gave me that set of Dickens for agreeing to let them cut off my hair," she said. "In those days, they thought very long, thick hair like mine would sap a child's strength. I said *No!* I wanted my hair left the very way it was. They offered me gold earrings first. I said *No!* I'd rather keep my hair. Then Papa said,

'What about books? I'll have them send a whole set of Charles Dickens to you, right up the river from Baltimore, in a barrel.' I agreed."

5   My mother had brought that set of Dickens to our house in Jackson, Mississippi; those books had been through fire and water before I was born, she told me, and there they were, lined up—as I later realized, waiting for *me*.

6   I learned from the age of two or three that any room in our house, at any time of day, was there to read in, or to be read to. My mother read to me. She'd read to me in the big bedroom in the mornings, when we were in her rocker together, which ticked in rhythm as we rocked, as though we had a cricket accompanying the story. She'd read to me in the dining room on winter afternoons in front of the coal fire, with our cuckoo clock ending the story with "Cuckoo," and at night when I'd get in my own bed. I must have given her no peace.

7   It had been startling and disappointing to me to find out that storybooks had been written by *people,* that books were not natural wonders, coming up of themselves like grass. Yet regardless of where they came from, I cannot remember a time when I was not in love with them—with the books themselves, cover and binding and the paper they were printed on, with their smell and their weight and with their possession in my arms, captured and carried off to myself.

8   Neither of my parents had come from homes that could afford to buy many books, but though it must have been something of a strain on his salary, my father was all the while carefully selecting and ordering away for what he and Mother thought we children should grow up with.

9   Besides the bookcase in the living room, which was always called the library, there were the encyclopedia tables and dictionary stand under windows in our dining room. There was a full set of Mark Twain and a short set of Ring Lardner in our bookcase, and those were the volumes that in time united us as parents and children.

10   I live in gratitude to my parents for initiating me—and as early as I begged for it, without keeping me waiting—into knowledge of the word, into reading and spelling, by way of the alphabet. They taught it to me at home in time for me to begin to read before starting school. I believe the alphabet is no longer considered an essential piece of equipment for traveling through life. In my day it was the keystone to knowledge. You learned the alphabet as you

learned "Now I lay me" and the Lord's Prayer and your father's and mother's name and address and telephone number, all in case you were lost.

11   My love for the alphabet, which endures, grew out of reciting it, but before that, out of seeing the letters on the page. In my own storybooks, before I could read them for myself, I fell in love with various winding, enchanted-looking initials at the heads of fairy tales. In "Once upon a time," an *O* had a rabbit running it as a treadmill, his feet upon flowers. When the day came, years later, for me to see the Book of Kells, Gospels from the ninth century, all the wizardry of letter, initial, and word swept over me, a thousand times over, and the illumination, the gold, seemed a part of the word's beauty and holiness that had been there from the start.

12   In my sensory education I include my physical awareness of the word. Of a certain word, that is; the connection it has with what it stands for. Around age six, perhaps, I was standing by myself in our front yard waiting for supper, just at that hour in a late summer day when the sun is already below the horizon and the risen full moon in the visible sky stops being chalky and begins to take on light. There comes the moment, and I saw it then, when the moon goes from flat to round. For the first time it met my eyes as a globe. The word *moon* came into my mouth as though fed to me out of a silver spoon. Held in my mouth the moon became a word. It had the roundness of a Concord grape that Grandpa took off his vine and gave me to suck out of its skin and swallow whole, in Ohio.

13   Long before I wrote stories, I listened for stories. Listening *for* them is something more acute than listening *to* them. I suppose it's an early form of participation in what goes on. Listening children know stories are *there*. When their elders sit and begin, children are just waiting and hoping for one to come out, like a mouse from its hole.

14   When I was six or seven, I was taken out of school and put to bed for several months for an ailment the doctor described as "fast-beating heart." I never dreamed I could learn away from the schoolroom, and that bits of enlightenment far-reaching in my life went on as ever in their own good time.

15   An opulence of storybooks covered my bed. As I read away, I was Rapunzel, or the Goose Girl, or the princess in one of the *Thousand and One Nights* who mounted the roof of her palace every night and of her own radiance faithfully lighted the whole city just by reposing there.

16   My mother was very sharing of this feeling of insatiability. Now, I think of her as reading so much of the time while doing something else. In my mind's eye *The Origin of Species* is lying on the shelf in the pantry under a light dusting of flour—my mother was a bread maker; she'd pick it up, sit by the kitchen window, and find her place, with one eye on the oven.

17   I'm grateful, too, that from my mother's example, I found the base for worship—that I found a love of sitting and reading the Bible for myself and looking up things in it.

18   How many of us, the Southern writers-to-be of my generation, were blessed in one way or another, if not blessed alike, in not having gone deprived of the King James Version of the Bible. Its cadence entered into our ears and our memories for good. The evidence, or the ghost of it, lingers in all our books.

19   "In the beginning was the Word."

EXERCISES

Details and Their Meanings

1. Where did Eudora Welty's mother grow up? Where did Welty grow up?
2. Why did Welty's mother receive a complete set of Dickens? Why did the mother carry her books from one place to another?
3. What is the first word the narrator associates with an object in the world?
4. Which authors did the family read?
5. What book was most important in shaping Welty's ear as a writer?
6. How did Welty learn the alphabet?

Reading and Critical Thinking

1. Why did Welty's mother read Dickens under the covers at night? What does this tell you about her?
2. What can you infer from the fact that the collection of Dickens

survived "fire and flood"? What books would you protect from damage?

3. Why did the father feel that buying books was a priority? How much of a priority is buying books for families today? Explain your answer.
4. Why does Welty associate words with religion?
5. Why does Welty decide to become a writer? What critical facility does she possess that her mother did not?
6. Where does Welty criticize modern culture? What is her criticism? Is this criticism justified? Why or why not?

The Writer's Strategies

1. How many different age periods does Welty refer to? Where is this account told from an adult's perspective? Where is it told from a child's perspective?
2. How do narration and description serve in developing the essay?
3. Where does the writer use sensory details? What are some of the most vivid?
4. What is the significance of the title?
5. What is the conclusion of this selection? What new idea is introduced in the conclusion?

Thinking Together

Evidently, Welty's parents believed that providing their daughter with a love of reading was important to her future. If you have children, what important skills or enthusiasms will you try to encourage in them? Develop a list in small groups; then compare your answers as a class.

Vocabulary

The following items mentioned in the selection are likely to be familiar to you. Write a brief description of each. If necessary, consult a dictionary or an encyclopedia.

1. Charles Dickens (par. 4)
2. Mark Twain (par. 9)

3. Ring Lardner (par. 9)
4. Book of Kells (par. 11)
5. Rapunzel (par. 15)
6. Goose Girl (par. 15)
7. *A Thousand and One Nights* (par. 15)
8. *The Origin of Species* (par. 16)
9. King James Bible (par. 18)

WRITER'S WORKSHOP ━━━━━━━━━━

Critical Thinking in Writing

1. Which books were important to you as you grew up? Describe some of the books that you loved the most as a child.
2. In many households, television and videocassettes have replaced books as the primary source of entertainment for children. Is there anything wrong with that? Can television and videocassettes convey the wonder and mystery that Welty got from books?
3. What should be the role of parents in influencing their children's activities such as reading? Should parents leave children to develop their own interests and tastes, or should parents take a strong hand in guiding their children—to books and away from television, for example? Write an essay discussing your views on the matter.

Connecting Ideas

Read "See Spot Run," by Ellen Tashie Frisina (page 173). How does the experience of reading presented in that selection differ from Welty's account? What principal differences between the Welty and Frisina households can you discover? What is the reason for their different attitudes toward books?

SIDE BY SIDE

1. Which of the selections in this unit was closest to your own experience of childhood? With which character or situation did you identify most closely? Explain what you identified with in the piece. In what ways is your own experience different from what you read?

2. Write a definition paper in which you discuss the phrase "Born in the U.S.A." What does this phrase mean to you? How do the selections in this unit help you to understand its meaning?

3. Imagine that you are going to write a letter to a child from another country about what to expect from growing up in the United States. From your own experiences and what you have read in this unit, tell the child what to be aware of, what to look out for, and what challenges and opportunities to be prepared to face.

TWO

Selves: True Colors

INTRODUCTION ━━━━━━━━━━━━━━━━━━━

What gives us our identity? Do we fashion it ourselves from education, experience, and choice? Or is it a gift from our families, our cultures, and our ethnic heritage? How much of us belongs to the past, to the geographical locations of our ancestors, to the beliefs they held, and perhaps even to the beliefs about them developed and passed down by others over the centuries? How much of what we have become is the product of our own choices, and how much is the result of prejudices for or against members of our group?

One of the lasting myths about America is the idea that the United States is a melting pot, a vast cauldron into which people from all over the world flow and out of which streams a single culture, a single standard, a single unified and coherent way of life. Despite the popularity of this myth and its impact on our consciousness, the lives of people living side by side in the United States often challenge the melting-pot vision. The single melting pot sometimes vanishes, and several different pots bubble on the stove.

In this unit you will read about Americans who have grappled with the idea of the melting pot. Although the writers of many of the selections hope that a unified society will fulfill America's promise of liberty and justice for all, the context for many of their pleas is an American society that lacks racial harmony and that must adjust to meet the needs and talents of a multifaceted community. Steve Marsh reports on the role of the medicine man in modern Lakota life and the revival of spiritual fervor among Native Americans. Joan Morgan reports on a study that shows that we need to affirm diversity of both gender and ethnicity in order to help African-American female students succeed, and Felicia R. Lee examines the negative effect that positive stereotyping can have on Asian schoolchildren. Armando Rendón and Patricia Raybon remind us of the need to hold on to our separate identities and to take pride in our ancestors and their cultures. Stephen Carter asks us to reconsider our assumptions about the present as we work toward a new harmony. Richard Rodriguez points toward a future that promises a synthesis of cultures.

Throughout these selections, interesting writers explore the issues of self, identity, and American culture.

PREREADING JOURNAL

1. Write about what you consider to be the typical American household. What do you think of when you hear the phrase "typical American family"? How does this family live? What kind of house do they have? What is an average day like for this family? In what ways is your family a typical American one? In what ways is it not typical?

2. Write about something that reflects your ethnic heritage: a holiday celebration, a wedding ceremony, funeral rites, the foods you eat, the clothes you wear, traditional customs that you practice. Who taught you about these things? How do they help you understand your heritage?

3. Psychologists, philosophers, and religious leaders, among others, have tried to define the self. What do you think the self is? What elements contribute to your self? How do racial, cultural, and religious backgrounds influence the self? What role does physical appearance play in how we define the self?

Letting in Light

Patricia Raybon

In this selection, Patricia Raybon, a professor of journalism and mass communication, reflects on the importance of a tradition passed down by the women of her family.

KEY WORDS

interest rate (par. 1)   the charge for borrowing money
translucent (par. 7)   transmitting light, but not images

THE WINDOWS WERE A gift or maybe a bribe—or maybe a bonus—for falling in love with such a dotty old house. The place was a wreck. A showoff, too. So it tried real hard to be more. But it lacked so much—good heat, stable floors, solid walls, enough space. A low interest rate.

2   But it had windows. More glass and bays and bows than people on a budget had a right to expect. And in unlikely places—like the window inside a bedroom closet, its only view a strawberry patch planted by the children next door.

3   None of it made sense. So we bought the place. We saved up and put some money down, then toasted the original builder—no doubt some brave and gentle carpenter, blessed with a flair for the grand gesture. A romantic with a T-square.

4   We were young then and struggling. Also, we are black. We looked with irony and awe at the task now before us. But we did not faint.

5   The time had come to wash windows.

6   Yes, I do windows. Like an amateur and a dabbler, perhaps, but the old-fashioned way—one pane at a time. It is the best way to pay back something so plain for its clear and silent gifts—the light of day, the glow of moon, hard rain, soft snow, dawn's early light.

7   The Romans called them *specularia*. They glazed their windows

89

with translucent marble and shells. And thus the ancients let some light into their world.

8   In my own family, my maternal grandmother washed windows—and floors and laundry and dishes and a lot of other things that needed cleaning—while doing day work for a rich, stylish redhead in her Southern hometown.

9   To feed her five children and keep them clothed and happy, to help them walk proudly and go to church and sing hymns and have some change in their pockets—and to warm and furnish the house her dead husband had built and added onto with his own hands—my grandmother went to work.

10   She and her third daughter, my mother, put on maids' uniforms and cooked and sewed and served a family that employed my grandmother until she was nearly 80. She called them Mister and Missus—yes, ma'am and yes, sir—although she was by many years their elder. They called her Laura. Her surname never crossed their lips.

11   But her daughter, my mother, took her earnings from the cooking and serving and window washing and clothes ironing and went to college, forging a life with a young husband—my father—that granted me, their daughter, a lifetime of relative comfort.

12   I owe these women everything.

13   They taught me hope and kindness and how to say thank you.

14   They taught me how to brew tea and pour it. They taught me how to iron creases and whiten linen and cut hair ribbon on the bias so it doesn't unravel. They taught me to carve fowl, make butter molds, and cook a good cream sauce. They taught me "women's work"—secrets of home, they said, that now are looked on mostly with disdain: how to sweep, dust, polish, and wax. How to mow, prune, scrub, scour, and purify.

15   They taught me how to wash windows.

16   Not many women do anymore, of course. There's no time. Life has us all on the run. It's easier to call a "window man," quicker to pay and, in the bargain, forget about the secret that my mother and her mother learned many years before they finally taught it to me:

17   Washing windows clears the cobwebs from the corners. It's plain people's therapy, good for troubles and muddles and other consternations. It's real work, I venture—honest work—and it's a sound thing to pass on. Mother to daughter. Daughter to child. Woman to woman.

18   This is heresy, of course. Teaching a girl to wash windows is

now an act of bravery—or else defiance. If she's black, it's an act of denial, a gesture that dares history and heritage to make something of it.

19   But when my youngest was 5 or 6, I tempted fate and ancestry and I handed her a wooden bucket. Together we would wash the outdoor panes. The moment sits in my mind:

20   She works a low row. I work the top. Silently we toil, soaping and polishing, each at her own pace—the only sounds the squeak of glass, some noisy birds, our own breathing.

21   Then, quietly at first, this little girl begins to hum. It's a nonsense melody, created for the moment. Soft at first, soon it gets louder. And louder. Then a recognizable tune emerges. Then she is really singing. With every swish of the towel, she croons louder and higher in her little-girl voice with her little-girl song. "This little light of mine—I'm gonna let it shine! Oh, this little light of mine—I'm gonna let it shine!" So, of course, I join in. And the two of us serenade the glass and the sparrows and mostly each other. And too soon our work is done.

22   "That was fun," she says. She is innocent, of course, and does this work by choice, not by necessity. But she's not too young to look at truth and understand it. And her heart, if not her arm, is resolute and strong.

23   Those years have passed. And other houses and newer windows—and other "women's jobs"—have moved through my life. I have chopped and puréed and polished and glazed. Bleached and folded and stirred. I have sung lullabies.

24   I have also marched and fought and prayed and taught and testified. Women's work covers many bases.

25   But the tradition of one simple chore remains. I do it without apology.

26   Last week, I dipped the sponge into the pail and began the gentle bath—easing off the trace of wintry snows, of dust storms and dead, brown leaves, of too much sticky tape used to steady paper pumpkins and Christmas lights and crepe-paper bows from holidays now past. While I worked, the little girl—now 12—found her way to the bucket, proving that her will and her voice are still up to the task, but mostly, I believe, to have some fun.

27   We are out of step, the two of us. She may not even know it. But we can carry a tune. The work is never done. The song is two-part harmony.

EXERCISES

Details and Their Meanings

1. How does the writer describe her house in the first three paragraphs? What does this description tell you about the writer's values? What does she care about? What matters to her and why?
2. In paragraph 3 the writer reveals her ethnic identity. How does she do this? Where else does this detail arise? How important is the writer's race to the central point she is making in this selection?
3. What did the women in the writer's family do to provide for their families? What lessons has the writer learned from them? In paragraph 12, the writer states, in reference to the women in her family, "I owe these women everything." What does she mean by this?
4. What is the secret that the writer's grandmother and mother learned from washing windows? What song does the writer's daughter sing as she washes the windows? What do the words of the song mean? How do both the secret and the song fit together?
5. How does the writer feel about teaching her daughter to wash windows? Why does she say that, by doing so, she "tempted fate and ancestry"? How does the writer's daughter feel about washing windows? How well has her daughter learned the lesson that she has tried to teach her?

Reading and Critical Thinking

1. In the third paragraph, the writer describes the original builder of the house as "A romantic with a T-square." What does this mean? What values does the writer share with this "brave and gentle carpenter"? Do you share these values? Why or why not?
2. Compare the kinds of work that the writer has done to the kinds of work done by other women in her family. For the writer and her daughter, how is the task of washing windows different from what it was for the mother and grandmother? How does the writer's attitude toward washing windows differ from that of her daughter?

3. How would you characterize the writer's attitude toward "women's work"—"liberal" or "conservative"? "modern" or "traditional"? How might feminists react to this attitude? Do you agree or disagree with this attitude? Why or why not?
4. How does the writer distinguish between the experiences of women and the experiences of African-American women? Do you think these distinctions are valid? Why or why not?
5. What conclusions about the importance of passing on traditions from one generation to the next can you draw from this selection? What makes traditions valuable?

The Writer's Strategies

1. What is the writer's thesis? State it in your own words.
2. The title of this selection, "Letting in Light," is a metaphor. What are both the literal and the metaphorical (or figurative) meanings of the title? How is the title echoed in details of the selection? How does the double meaning of the title reinforce the central idea that the writer is making?
3. What historical details does the writer state in the essay? How does she use the past in order to explain the present? How does the writer contrast the past with the present?
4. Why does the writer contrast her and her family's attitude toward washing windows and similar work?
5. In what places are singing or music mentioned in this selection? In what ways are music and singing used to add to the meaning of this selection?
6. In paragraphs 13, 14, and 15, the writer begins each of six sentences (out of a total of seven) with the word *they*. Why does she repeat sentence openings in this way? How does the word *they* serve as a transitional element? How does the word contribute to the overall coherence of the essay?

Thinking Together

1. In small groups, discuss tasks you had to do that others consider to be "unpleasant" but that you enjoyed. Who taught you to do them and why? What made these tasks enjoyable or at least worthwhile?
2. In small groups, discuss the kind of work that your mother,

grandmothers, aunts, and other women in the family have done. Would you consider this work to be "women's work" today? yesterday? Why or why not? How has our society's view of gender-based work evolved?

Vocabulary

The meanings of the following words emerge through context. Find the locations of these words in the selection, and write definitions in your own words.

1. stable (par. 1)
2. T-square (par. 3)
3. dabbler (par. 6)
4. glazed (par. 7)
5. surname (par. 10)
6. forging (par. 11)
7. bias (par. 14)
8. disdain (par. 14)
9. therapy (par. 17)
10. consternations (par. 17)
11. heresy (par. 18)
12. defiance (par. 18)
13. resolute (par. 22)

WRITER'S WORKSHOP ━━━━━━━━━━

Critical Thinking in Writing

1. Write a paragraph describing, in as much detail as possible, the work that one of the women in your family did. Consider the work itself as well as who did it and for whom it was done.
2. Describe in several paragraphs the nature of "women's work" today. How has it changed since your mother or grandmother was a little girl? How has it stayed the same?
3. Is hard work valuable in itself? Write a brief essay, using details from your own experience, to support the position you take.

Connecting Ideas

Read Jesus Sanchez's piece "Era Passes from the Landscape" (page 299). How are the attitudes expressed about the importance of tradition (and traditional work) in this selection similar to or different from the attitude expressed by Raybon? What do both pieces have to say about the inevitability of change from one generation to the next as opportunities increase and broaden?

Model Minority

Felicia R. Lee

*Felicia R. Lee examines the commonly held view of Asian school-
children as super students who effortlessly excel in all their classes,
especially math and science. She shows how even positive stereotyping sometimes puts pressure on people to live up to false expectations.*

KEY WORDS

émigrés (par. 4)   people who have left their homeland
   permanently
docile (par. 4)   peaceful and tame
harassment (par. 9)   continual annoyance
advocacy (par. 10)   arguing in favor of something
stoicism (par. 11)   a philosophy in which the ideal is to rise
   above both pleasure and pain and to accept all situations
   in the same calm way
schizophrenic (par. 31)   suffering from a mental illness

ZHE ZENG, AN 18-YEAR-OLD junior at Seward Park High School in
lower Manhattan, translates the term *model minority* to mean that
Asian Americans are terrific in math and science. Mr. Zeng is terrific in math and science, but he insists that his life is no model for
anyone.

2   "My parents give a lot of pressure on me," said Mr. Zeng, who
recently came to New York from Canton with his parents and older
brother. He has found it hard to learn English and make friends
at the large, fast-paced school. And since he is the only family
member who speaks English, he is responsible for paying bills
and handling the family's interactions with the English-speaking
world.

3   "They work hard for me," he said, "so I have to work hard for
them."

4   As New York's Asian population swells, and with many of the

new immigrants coming from poorer, less-educated families, more and more Asian students are stumbling under the burden of earlier émigrés' success—the myth of the model minority, the docile whiz kid with one foot already in the Ivy League. Even as they face the cultural dislocations shared by all immigrants, they must struggle with the inflated expectations of teachers and parents and resentment from some non-Asian classmates.

5   Some students, like Mr. Zeng, do seem to fit the academic stereotype. Many others are simply average students with average problems. But, in the view of educators and a recent Board of Education report, all are more or less victims of myth.

6   "We have a significant population of Chinese kids who are not doing well," said Archer W. Dong, principal of Dr. Sun Yat-sen Junior High School near Chinatown, which is 83 percent Chinese. "But I still deal with educators who tell me how great the Asian kids are. It puts an extra burden on the kid who just wants to be a normal kid."

7   **The Dropout Rate Rises**   Perhaps the starkest evidence of the pressures these students face is the dropout rate among Asian-American students, which has risen to 15.2 percent from 12.6 percent in just one year, though it remains well below the 30 percent rate for the entire school system. In all, there are about 68,000 Asians in the city's schools, a little more than 7 percent of the student population.

8   Behind these figures, the Board of Education panel said, lies a contrary mechanism of assumed success and frequent failure. While teachers expect talent in math and science, they often overlook quiet Asian-American students who are in trouble academically.

9   The report also said that Asian students frequently face hostility from non-Asians who resent their perceived success. And though New York's Asian population is overwhelmingly Chinese, this resentment is fed by a feeling in society that the Japanese are usurping America's position as a world economic power. Some educators said that because they are often smaller and quieter, Asian students seem to be easy targets for harassment.

10   Teresa Ying Hsu, executive director of an advocacy group called Asian-American Communications and a member of the board panel, described what she called a typical exchange at a New York City school. One student might say, "You think you're so

smart," she said, then "someone would hit a kid from behind and they would turn around and everyone would laugh."

11   Since Asian cultures dictate stoicism, she explained, students in many cases do not openly fight back against harassment or complain about academic pressures. But though they tend to keep their pain hidden, she said, it often is expressed in ailments like headaches or stomach troubles.

12   **"Acutely Sensitive"**   "We have a group of youngsters who are immigrants who are acutely sensitive to things other students take in stride, like a door slamming in their face," said John Rodgers, principal of Norman Thomas High School in Manhattan.

13   Norman Thomas, whose student body is about 3 percent Asian, had two recent incidents in which Chinese students were attacked by non-Asian students. The attackers were suspended.

14   But tensions escalated after a group of 30 Chinese parents demanded that the principal, John Rodgers, increase security, and rumors spread that "gangs of blacks" were attacking Chinese. Both incidents, however, were one-on-one conflicts and neither attacker was black. In some cases, Mr. Rodgers said, Chinese students say they are attacked by blacks but that they cannot identify their attackers because all blacks look alike to them.

15   In response to the parents' concerns, Mr. Rodgers said, he increased security and brought in a speaker on cross-cultural conflict.

16   Traditionally, Asian parents have not been that outspoken, educators say. While they often place enormous pressures on their children to do well, most Asian parents tend not to get involved with the schools.

17   Lisa Chang, a 17-year-old senior at Seward Park—which is 48 percent Asian—recalled being one of six Asians at a predominantly black intermediate school.

18   "Inside the school was no big deal," she said. "I was in special classes and everyone was smart. Then I remember one day being outside in the snow and this big black boy pushed me. He called me Chink.

19   "Then, at home, my parents didn't want me to dress a certain way, to listen to heavy metal music," Ms. Chang said. When she told her dermatologist that she liked rock and roll, the doctor accused her of "acting like a Caucasian."

20   Ms. Chang and other students say there are two routes some Asian students take: they form cliques with other Asians or they

play down their culture and even their intelligence in hopes of fitting in.

21   **Wedged Between Two Cultures**   Most Asian students are acutely aware of being wedged between two cultures. They say their parents want them to compete successfully with Americans but not become too American—they frown on dating and hard-rock music. There is also peer pressure not to assimilate completely. A traitor is a "banana"—yellow on the outside, white on the inside.

22   There is anger, too, over the perception that they are nerdy bookworms and easy targets for bullies.

23   "A lot of kids are average; they are not what the myth says," said Doris Liang, 17, a junior at Seward Park. "In math, I'm only an average student and I have to work really hard."

24   Ms. Liang said she sometimes envies the school's Hispanic students.

25   **"Not Make Any Mistakes"**   "The Hispanic kids, in a way they are more open," she said. "They're not afraid to bring their dates home. If you're Chinese and you bring your date home, they ask a lot of questions. My parents only went to junior high school in China, so when we got here they wanted us to do well in school."

26   Nicole Tran, a 15-year-old senior who spent the early part of her life in Oregon, said she believes her generation will be far more assertive.

27   "We are the minority minority," said Ms. Tran. "We are moving too fast for them," she said of the dominant white culture.

28   Dr. Jerry Chin-Li Huang, a Seward Park guidance counselor, said he believes that Asians in New York are in part experiencing the cultural transformations common to all immigrants.

29   He notes that more of the new Asian immigrants—whose numbers in New York have swelled 35 to 50 percent in the past five years to about 400,000—are coming from smaller towns and poorer, less educated families.

30   It was the early waves of educated, middle-class Asian immigrants whose children became the model minority, Dr. Huang said. Many of the students he sees have problems.

31   For one thing, Dr. Huang said many Asian parents are reluctant to admit that their children need help, even in severe cases. He said he had a schizophrenic Chinese student who began constantly wearing a coat, even on the hottest summer days. The parents were of little help.

32   "I have other children who run away from home because of the pressures," said Dr. Huang. "I had two sisters who had to go to school, then work in the factories, sewing. Their parents could not speak English so they were helping them with the bills. The girls said they barely had time to sleep."

33   Dr. Huang said many non-Asian teachers come to him for his insights because they have few Asian co-workers. Asians are 1.4 percent of all school counselors; 0.8 percent of all principals, and 1.4 percent of all teachers in New York City.

34   Among its recommendations, the task force called for more Asian counselors and teachers.

35   People like Ms. Hsu, of Asian-American Communications, are optimistic that the situation for Asian students will improve as students and educators talk openly about it.

36   "I gave a workshop and I talked about the quotas, the Chinese Exclusion Act," said Ms. Hsu. "Two black girls came up to me. One said: 'You know, I always thought the Chinese kids were snooty. Now after hearing what you went through, I feel you're my brothers and sisters.'"

EXERCISES

Details and Their Meanings

1. What are the experiences of Zhe Zeng, Lisa Chang, Doris Liang, and Teresa Hsu? What do their experiences have in common?
2. What are the dropout rates for Asian-American students in New York high schools? How have they changed? How do they compare with the rates for other students?
3. What has been happening to the immigration rate of Asians in the past few years? What does this change imply for New York schools? How do recent Asian immigrants differ from earlier immigrants? Why are the differences significant?
4. What stereotypes and standards do Asian students feel they have to live up to? What is the source of these pressures? To whom are the stereotypes positive and to whom negative? Why?

5. In what ways do the students interviewed by the writer find themselves in tension or conflict over the pressures created by the stereotypes?
6. What are the percentages of Asian-American counselors, principals, and teachers in the New York schools? How do those statistics compare to the percentage of Asian-American students? What consequences and implications does the comparison suggest?
7. What incidents have occurred in schools between Asian-American students and other students? What is the meaning of those incidents?
8. How do professionals and experts view the pressures on Asian students? Do they agree about how the future will be for Asian-American students in the New York schools?

Reading and Critical Thinking

1. In what way are parents' and teachers' expectations about Asian-American students similar to the stereotypes? What effect do these expectations have on the students? Overall, are these expectations simply good or bad? Is their effect different on different people?
2. In what ways are the expectations of and pressures on Asian students similar to or different from the expectations of and pressures on children of different ethnicities?
3. How do people of one ethnic group react to the expectations of and pressures on other groups? How do the expectations of and pressures from students of different ethnic groups create new pressures and tensions?
4. What difficulties or pressures do expectations of any kind create? Would you prefer to grow up with or without any of these kinds of expectations? How might expectations be made more individually appropriate rather than applied simply to a whole group?
5. How do different cultural characteristics influence how the Asian students react to ethnic stereotyping? To what extent do you think saying that people of a particular background share personality characteristics or social attitudes is itself a form of inappropriate stereotyping?
6. What is the special meaning of the word *banana* described in the selection? Are there other terms with similar meanings used by

members of other ethnic groups? What purposes do the terms serve? What harm do they do? What kind of behavior and thinking do the terms encourage or discourage?

The Writer's Strategies

1. In what paragraph does Felicia R. Lee present her overall idea or thesis? How do the first three paragraphs lead up to that thesis? Why does the article start in this way?
2. How do paragraphs 5 and 6 add new ideas that make the main point more complex? How are these new ideas supported and developed in the following paragraphs? What examples does the writer use to develop these ideas and how do the examples show the complexity of the issues?
3. Where does Lee use statistics? How do they support or develop her ideas? Does the writer indicate sources of the statistics? Why or why not?
4. Who are the various people interviewed for this piece, and what do their different statements contribute? Which interviewees are the Asian-American students who are Lee's subject? Which interviewees contribute background information? Which interviewees express opinions on the situations described by Lee?
5. What points does the writer make in the last few paragraphs through the comments of Dr. Huang and Ms. Hsu? How do these quotations provide a conclusion to the piece? What tone do they give the conclusion?

Thinking Together

In groups of three or four, discuss whether people expect too much or too little of you because of your membership in a particular group. How do you respond to any inappropriate expectations? Describe one specific incident in which inappropriate expectations were applied to you. Then compare the different incidents in an attempt to understand the different kinds of expectations and different kinds of responses. Next discuss more generally what role people's expectations have had in influencing your development in positive or negative ways.

Vocabulary

The following phrases appear in the selection. Define the italicized word in each one.

1. handling the family's *interactions* (par. 2)
2. face cultural *dislocations* (par. 4)
3. *inflated* expectations of teachers (par. 4)
4. resent their *perceived* success (par. 9)
5. Asian cultures *dictate* stoicism (par. 11)
6. tensions *escalated* (par. 14)
7. peer pressure not to completely *assimilate* (par. 21)
8. experiencing the cultural *transformations* (par. 28)

WRITER'S WORKSHOP ━━━━━━━━━━━

Critical Thinking in Writing

1. Write a personal essay describing how you are different from the various perceptions people have of you.
2. When have you been the victim of unrealistic expectations and perceptions? Write a narrative piece about an occasion in which people expected too much of you.
3. Can stereotypes be positive? Are positive stereotypes ever harmful? What is the effect of being stereotyped? Write an essay describing and evaluating several positive and negative stereotypes associated with young people.

Connecting Ideas

Write a one-page essay discussing how "Model Minority" relates to Elizabeth Wong's "The Struggle to Be an All-American Girl" (page 39). How are the pressures, conflicts, and difficulties of students described by Wong the same as or different from those described by Felicia R. Lee?

'Those Loud Black Girls'

Joan Morgan

In this selection, Joan Morgan reports on a recent study that examines some young African-American women.

KEY WORDS

anthropology (par. 1)   the study of human culture
the Academy (par. 2)   the system of higher education
contrariness (par. 3)   tendency to oppose others
relegation (par. 3)   being placed in an undesirable position
docile (par. 7)   quietly obedient, submissive
norms (par. 7)   standards for behavior
diversity (par. 7)   difference, variety
prestigious (par. 15)   distinguished, famous
divergent (par. 16)   sharply different
concurrently (par. 16)   at the same time, simultaneously

LOUD, BRASSY, FLASHY, DOMINANT, and strong Sapphires . . . hot-button stereotypes of the African-American woman. Dr. Signithia Fordham, professor of anthropology at Rutgers University, pushed these buttons when, in her latest research, she spoke of black females as "loud," and it became a controversial research project. The study is an extension of an earlier controversial work in which she found that both black male and female students sacrifice some aspect of their racial identity to attain academic achievement.

2   At a time when most research studies show that black females do better academically than black males, Fordham focuses on female needs. "Even though African-American girls may be doing better than African-American boys, they are paying an enormous

104

price for this," Fordham says. "And we should know what some of the costs are and that will help us to understand why . . . a larger percent of the girls are not doing as well."

3 In the study, "Those Loud Black Girls: (Black) Women, Silence and Gender 'Passing' in the Academy," Fordham says she uses loudness as a metaphor for "African-American women's contrariness, embodying their resistance to 'nothingness.'" This "nothingness" refers to the relegation to a lower status and value for women of African ancestry in our society, she explains.

4 Even with the risk of misinterpretation, Fordham says she thought loudness was the appropriate metaphor since it is the opposite of silence—which is how she describes other black females who have learned to be "silent" to succeed, especially academically. This silence is manifested in their relatively small circle of friends and low visibility in school arenas such as assemblies. And further, there are parental limitations on extrafamilial activities and the fulfillment of their female sexuality, Fordham says.

5 Fordham got the idea of using the term *loud* from a Grace Evans article called, "Those Loud Black Girls." Evans, an African-American social studies teacher in the public school system in several inner-city schools in London, saw a group of black girls who frustrated their teachers—especially female ones—with behavior that was a stubborn refusal to conform to standards of "good behavior" without breaking any rules.

6 Fordham says when she read Evans's article she thought it described exactly what she saw while doing research and it validated her personal experience growing up as an African-American female.

7 Silence, in the study, also refers to "gender passing," a form of adopting the norms of white middle-class American female behavior, says Fordham. "Those norms say that a woman is beautiful, passive, silent, docile," she says. "These norms don't allow for gender diversity, which means that not every social group has the same norms for what it means to be female.

8 "It may be appropriate for us to see the African-American community idealizing African-American females who are strong, not docile, and who have struggled to be something other than the norms of the larger society. This doesn't mean that our norms and standards are totally different."

9 Fordham points out that both black and white females engage in a certain amount of gender passing by often adopting male

behavior in order to succeed. But, she says, it means that in some ways the norms may differ.

10   One example of this gender difference in black and white females, she says, is historical experience in America. While white women are moving toward seeking careers, they are viewed as productive, as well as reproductive, entities.

11   "African-American females have never had alternatives. We were brought [to this country] as slave labor and after slavery we have had to work outside the home," Fordham says.

12   Other differences include styles of dress. "Often our style differences are viewed negatively." Fordham mentions a current fad among young black girls of wearing large hoop earrings. These earrings have become known as "whore hoops" and the negative association with black female sexuality is apparent.

13   Fordham's study took place at an inner-city high school in Washington, D.C., that she calls "Capital High"—a magnet school that draws students from all socioeconomic segments of the city. She studied both high-achieving and low-achieving black girls and discovered the high-achieving girls maintained an "academically successful" and "nice girl" persona that yielded "very little" external reward. Low-achieving girls were strikingly visible (known by everyone and did not try to hide the disruption that visibility implied) and had high standardized test scores but low grades.

14   Yet, Fordham says that she saw a similarity between both groups. "It seemed that at the base of both of these responses was the effort to avoid the notion of 'nothingness.'"

15   This is strikingly illustrated in the example of Rita (not her real name), one of the girls in the study. Rita was probably the brightest student in the study, Fordham says, but she "refused to conform to standards of 'good' behavior." She lived on the edge, self-consciously stretching legitimate school rules to help her retrieve a safe cultural space. "Though Rita got a scholarship to a prestigious university, she later returned home to a life of drug abuse."

16   So what is the point of discovering that Rita and other black females "struggle to co-mingle or fuse two divergent lives concurrently?"

17   Says Fordham: "It shouldn't have been that hard for Rita. Perhaps it would not be so hard for the 'Ritas' if we as a society could acknowledge and understand the meaning of gender diversity by embracing and celebrating it."

EXERCISES

Details and Their Meanings

1. Which group of students does Dr. Signithia Fordham's most recent study focus on? What term does she use to identify this group, and what are some of the group's characteristics? How do they contrast with those of the females she studied previously? What term does she use to characterize the earlier group studied?
2. Who is Grace Evans? What did Evans write about? How did her writing influence Fordham?
3. According to Fordham, how are the norms for women in the African-American community different from those in the white middle-class community? How does the writer account for these differences? How do these differences affect African-American females? Which women discussed in this selection adopted male gender behaviors and in what way?
5. In Fordham's recent study, how did two different groups of girls try to overcome "nothingness"? Where did each of the groups get their rewards? How do the two different strategies lead to two different ways of life?
6. Who is Rita? How does her experience reflect the issues raised in this selection?

Reading and Critical Thinking

1. Why is Fordham's use of the term *loud* controversial? What alternative terms might avoid controversy and at the same time convey the point she is trying to make?
2. In this selection, the writer assumes that a relation between gender roles (norms) and behavior exists. Do you agree with the assumption? Why or why not?
3. The writer claims that African-American females' behavior can be understood as "embodying their resistance to 'nothingness.'" What does she mean by *nothingness?* How does understanding this term help you explain the behavior of African-American females described in this selection?
4. In paragraph 13, Morgan discusses the rewards that both groups in Fordham's study receive for their behavior. In your

own experience, what kind of behavior has been rewarded? What form did these rewards take? Were they "external" or "internal"? Who rewarded you? Were the rewards satisfying?

5. What conclusions does Fordham draw from the results of her study? How can we help African-American females succeed? Do you agree with her conclusions? Do these conclusions apply to other groups of students besides African-American females?

The Writer's Strategies

1. What is the writer's thesis? Where, if anywhere, is it stated most directly? What are some of the subpoints that the writer is making in this selection? What is the main point you believe the writer is making?

2. Where does the writer use comparison and contrast? In each case, which groups are being compared and contrasted? How do the comparisons and contrasts help identify the particular issues and problems the writer considers?

3. In which paragraphs does the writer use definition to develop ideas? What kinds of terms does she define? How are these terms important for the ideas presented?

4. How does the writer Joan Morgan use the ideas of Signithia Fordham and Grace Evans? How does Signithia Fordham use the ideas of Grace Evans? How is the selection strengthened by the relation established among the three writers?

5. Identify the adjectives that the writer uses to describe the two groups of African-American females identified in this selection. What do these terms reveal about the writer's attitude toward the two groups? Is one group presented more favorably than the other?

6. Why does Morgan conclude her essay with the example of Rita? What problem does this example present? Do you think that using this example strengthens the writer's main point?

Thinking Together

1. As a class, brainstorm about the different "roles" played by students. For example, consider the class clown, the teacher's pet, and so on. In small groups, discuss whether males or fe-

males tend to play the roles more. Then discuss as a class the degree to which gender norms dictate who plays which roles.
2. Work in small groups to develop a chart comparing "good" and "bad" behavior along gender lines; that is, what characteristics make a "good girl" good? a "bad girl" bad? a "good boy" good? a "bad boy" bad? Then compare your findings with the rest of the class.

Vocabulary

The following terms appear within quotation marks in this selection and have special meanings developed in the surrounding context. Locate these terms in the selection and in your own words define their meanings in the selection.

1. "loud" (par. 1)
2. "nothingness" (par. 3)
3. "silent" (par. 4)
4. "good behavior" (par. 5)
5. "gender passing" (par. 7)
6. "whore hoops" (par. 12)
7. "academically successful" (par. 13)
8. "nice girl" (par. 13)

WRITER'S WORKSHOP ━━━━━━━━━

Critical Thinking in Writing

1. Write an informal journal entry reflecting the role you play in this and other classes. What kind of student are you? Are you quiet? silent? loud? What motivates you to behave the way you do? What do you get out of it?
2. Draw on your own experiences and observations to write a one-page description of the gender norm in schools for your own gender. If you have noticed two or more different patterns, you can focus on one after briefly identifying the others.
3. In the final paragraph, the writer quotes Fordham's solution to the problem described in the essay: "to acknowledge and understand the meaning of gender diversity by embracing and

celebrating it." Write an essay evaluating Fordham's solution. Do you think that it is a good one? Do you think it will work? Why or why not?

Connecting Ideas

In "Boys Only: Separate but Equal?" (page 46), Janny Scott reports on the controversial proposal to set up single-gender classes in order to meet the specific needs of African-American male students. In what ways might the experiences and feelings of the boys Scott describes be similar to or different from those of the girls described in this selection? Does the selection "'Those Loud Black Girls'" give you any fresh insights about the proposal of separating boys from girls? Would such a separation benefit African-American female students? Why or why not?

The Fight

Maya Angelou

Maya Angelou is an important voice in modern American literature. In this excerpt from one of her best-known books, I Know Why the Caged Bird Sings *(1968), Angelou describes a late 1930s fight between heavyweight champ Joe Louis (the "Brown Bomber") and former champ Primo Carnera, showing that Louis's fights were critical events in African-American culture and sports.*

KEY WORDS

apprehensive (par. 2)   filled with doubt or worry
cracker (par. 3)   slang word for an ignorant white person
maimed (par. 16)   crippled
hewers (par. 17)   cutters
ambrosia (par. 27)   in Greek mythology, the drink of the gods

THE LAST INCH OF space was filled, yet people continued to wedge themselves along the walls of the Store. Uncle Willie had turned the radio up to its last notch so that youngsters on the porch wouldn't miss a word. Women sat on kitchen chairs, dining-room chairs, stools, and upturned wooden boxes. Small children and babies perched on every lap available and men leaned on the shelves or on each other.

2   The apprehensive mood was shot through with shafts of gaiety, as a black sky is streaked with lightning.

3   "I ain't worried 'bout this fight. Joe's gonna whip that cracker like it's open season."

4   "He gone whip him till that white boy call him Momma."

5   At last the talking was finished and the string-along songs about razor blades were over and the fight began.

6   "A quick jab to the head." In the Store the crowd grunted. "A left to the head and a right and another left." One of the listeners cackled like a hen and was quieted.

7   "They're in a clench, Louis is trying to fight his way out."

8   Some bitter comedian on the porch said, "That white man don't mind hugging that niggah now, I betcha."

9   "The referee is moving in to break them up, but Louis finally pushed the contender away and it's an uppercut to the chin. The contender is hanging on, now he's backing away. Louis catches him with a short left to the jaw."

10   A tide of murmuring assent poured out the doors and into the yard.

11   "Another left and another left. Louis is saving that mighty right . . . " The mutter in the Store had grown into a baby roar and it was pierced by the clang of a bell and the announcer's "That's the bell for round three, ladies and gentlemen."

12   As I pushed my way into the Store I wondered if the announcer gave any thought to the fact that he was addressing as "ladies and gentlemen" all the Negroes around the world who sat sweating and praying, glued to their "master's voice."

13   There were only a few calls for R. C. colas, Dr. Peppers, and Hire's root beer. The real festivities would begin after the fight. Then even the old Christian ladies who taught their children and tried themselves to practice turning the other cheek would buy soft drinks, and if the Brown Bomber's victory was a particularly bloody one they would order peanut patties and Baby Ruths also.

14   Bailey and I lay the coins on top of the cash register. Uncle Willie didn't allow us to ring up sales during a fight. It was too noisy and might shake up the atmosphere. When the gong rang for the next round, we pushed through the near-sacred quiet to the herd of children outside.

15   "He's got Louis against the ropes and now it's a left to the body and a right to the ribs. Another right to the body, it looks like it was low. . . . Yes, ladies and gentlemen, the referee is signaling but the contender keeps raining the blows on Louis. It's another to the body, and it looks like Louis is going down."

16   My race groaned. It was our people falling. It was another lynching, yet another black man hanging on a tree. One more woman ambushed and raped. A black boy whipped and maimed. It was hounds on the trail of a man running through slimy swamps. It was a white woman slapping her maid for being forgetful.

17   The men in the Store stood away from the walls and at attention. Women greedily clutched the babes on their laps while on the porch the shufflings and smiles, flirtings and pinching of a few minutes before were gone. This might be the end of the world. If

Joe lost we were back in slavery and beyond help. It would all be true, the accusations that we were lower types of human beings. Only a little higher than the apes. True that we were stupid and ugly and lazy and dirty and, unlucky and worst of all, that God Himself hated us and ordained us to be hewers of wood and drawers of water, forever and ever, world without end.

18   We didn't breathe. We didn't hope. We waited.

19   "He's off the ropes, ladies and gentlemen. He's moving toward the center of the ring." There was no time to be relieved. The worst might still happen.

20   "And now it looks like Joe is mad. He's caught Carnera with a left hook to the head and a right to the head. It's a left jab to the body and another left to the head. There's a left cross and a right to the head. The contender's right eye is bleeding, and he can't seem to keep his block up. Louis is penetrating every block. The referee is moving in, but Louis sends a left to the body and it's the uppercut to the chin and the contender is dropping. He's on the canvas, ladies and gentlemen."

21   Babies slid to the floor as women stood up and men leaned toward the radio.

22   "Here's the referee. He's counting. One, two, three, four, five, six, seven . . . Is the contender trying to get up again?"

23   All the men in the store shouted, "NO."

24   "—eight, nine, ten." There were a few sounds from the audience, but they seemed to be holding themselves in against tremendous pressure.

25   "The fight is all over, ladies and gentlemen. Let's get the microphone over to the referee . . . Here he is. He's got the Brown Bomber's hand, he's holding it up . . . Here he is . . . "

26   Then the voice, husky and familiar, came to wash over us— "The winnah, and still heavyweight champeen of the world . . . Joe Louis."

27   Champion of the world. A black boy. Some black mother's son. He was the strongest man in the world. People drank Coca-Colas like ambrosia and ate candy bars like Christmas. Some of the men went behind the Store and poured white lightning in their soft-drink bottles, and a few of the bigger boys followed them. Those who were not chased away came back blowing their breath in front of themselves like proud smokers.

28   It would take an hour or more before the people would leave the Store and head for home. Those who lived too far had made arrangements to stay in town. It wouldn't do for a black man and

his family to be caught on a lonely country road on a night when Joe Louis had proved that we were the strongest people in the world.

———————

EXERCISES

Details and Their Meanings

1. What is the setting of this piece? What details help you to decide?
2. What brand-name products are mentioned? What do you think is the writer's purpose in making so many specific references?
3. Who is Uncle Willie? Why is he an important figure in the community?
4. How do the people in the store separate themselves by age and gender? Why do you think they separate like this?
5. Why have all the people come to hear the fight? Why do they consider it an important event?
6. Where is the fight taking place? What is the outcome? How do the people feel after the fight is over?
7. What does the outcome of the fight suggest to the people in town about themselves? Why is the outcome important to their self-esteem?

Reading and Critical Thinking

1. What can you infer about the townspeople described in the selection? What kind of people are they?
2. Why do the people place so much significance on this fight? What is Maya Angelou assuming that you understand about the 1930s? Is her assumption justified in your case?
3. What can you infer about the age and gender of the narrator? Why are these elements important to your understanding of this piece? Where does Angelou allow an adult's perspective to take over her narrative?
4. In paragraph 16, what does Angelou suggest would be the consequences of Louis's losing the fight? What is she implying?

5. When Louis wins, what does the narrator conclude about her race?
6. How much of the selection is a description of the fight?

The Writer's Strategies

1. State in your own words what you believe is the main idea.
2. Why does the writer focus on a group of ordinary townspeople when she is writing an appreciation of Joe Louis? Why does Louis remain so distant from the people in this narrative?
3. What main strategy is the writer using? Where does description play an important role?
4. The writer uses dialogue, but what is her reason for not having anyone talk to anyone else? How does this strategy heighten the effect of the piece?
5. To what primary sense does Angelou appeal—sound, smell, sight, taste, or touch? Why is this appropriate? Find the most unforgettable images of that sense.
6. Which paragraphs present the conclusion of this piece? How does the conclusion introduce a new element?

Thinking Together

Today, cable television and satellites enable people all around the world to experience major sports events in a much more direct way than was possible in the late 1930s when the Louis–Carnera fight took place. Can your class think of a recent sporting event that had a global or national impact? Why do sports events—football, baseball, soccer games, or major boxing matches—ignite such deep passions worldwide?

Vocabulary

Angelou uses a number of poetical expressions. Use your own words to explain the meaning of these expressions—that is, to explain the literal meaning lying underneath the figurative language.

1. as a black sky is streaked with lightning (par. 2)
2. cackled like a hen (par. 6)
3. a tide of murmuring assent (par. 10)

4. near-sacred quiet (par. 14)
5. raining the blows (par. 15)
6. drank Coca-Colas like ambrosia (par. 27)
7. ate candy bars like Christmas (par. 27)

WRITER'S WORKSHOP

Critical Thinking in Writing

1. Sports figures continue to be models for young people. Do you admire, look up to, or wish to emulate any athletes? If you do, discuss who and why. If you do not, discuss why not. Write an essay to present your points.
2. Joe Louis in his day was an important model for black Americans. What current figure do you think serves as a model for his or her people? Choose a particular racial, ethnic, or religious group; identify an appropriate model for that group; and defend your choice in a well-detailed essay.
3. In the 1930s and 1940s, Joe Louis's fights united the black community. Indeed, Louis's defeat of Max Schmeling, a German boxer who was a favorite of Hitler, was an important symbolic event for all Americans opposed to Nazism. What contemporary event would everybody in the United States or everyone from a particular group be likely to watch? Present your thoughts on this subject in an essay.

Connecting Ideas

Read "Salvation," by Langston Hughes (page 27). What similar elements of rural black culture can you find in Hughes's and Angelou's selections? The events in Angelou's piece take place twenty years later than the events in Hughes's. What signs can you find in Angelou's piece of changes that have occurred in Southern life and attitudes in that twenty-year period?

The Man to Send Rain Clouds

Leslie Marmon Silko

In this selection, Leslie Marmon Silko shows how Christian culture is absorbed into the beliefs and practices of the Native American people. Notice how the people give their own interpretation to the foreign Christian beliefs.

KEY WORDS

arroyo (par. 1)   dry creek bed
pueblo (par. 3)   village
Angelus (par. 12)   call to Catholic prayers

THEY FOUND HIM UNDER a big cottonwood tree. His Levi jacket and pants were faded light blue so that he had been easy to find. The big cottonwood tree stood apart from a small grove of winterbare cottonwoods which grew in the wide, sandy arroyo. He had been dead for a day or more, and the sheep had wandered and scattered up and down the arroyo. Leon and his brother-in-law, Ken, gathered the sheep and left them in the pen at the sheep camp before they returned to the cottonwood tree. Leon waited under the tree while Ken drove the truck through the deep sand to the edge of the arroyo. He squinted up at the sun and unzipped his jacket—it sure was hot for this time of year. But high and northwest the blue mountains were still in snow. Ken came sliding down the low, crumbling bank about fifty yards down, and he was bringing the red blanket.

2   Before they wrapped the old man, Leon took a piece of string out of his pocket and tied a small gray feather in the old man's long white hair. Ken gave him the paint. Across the brown wrinkled forehead he drew a streak of white and along the high cheekbones he drew a strip of blue paint. He paused and watched Ken

117

throw pinches of corn meal and pollen into the wind that fluttered the small gray feather. Then Leon painted with yellow under the old man's broad nose, and finally, when he had painted green across the chin, he smiled.

3 "Send us rain clouds, Grandfather." They laid the bundle in the back of the pickup and covered it with a heavy tarp before they started back to the pueblo.

4 They turned off the highway onto the sandy pueblo road. Not long after they passed the store and post office they saw Father Paul's car coming toward them. When he recognized their faces he slowed his car and waved for them to stop. The young priest rolled down the car window.

5 "Did you find old Teofilo?" he asked loudly.

6 Leon stopped the truck. "Good morning, Father. We were just out to the sheep camp. Everything is O.K. now."

7 "Thank God for that. Teofilo is a very old man. You really shouldn't allow him to stay at the sheep camp alone."

8 "No, he won't do that any more now."

9 "Well, I'm glad you understand. I hope I'll be seeing you at Mass this week—we missed you last Sunday. See if you can get old Teofilo to come with you." The priest smiled and waved at them as they drove away.

10 Louise and Teresa were waiting. The table was set for lunch, and the coffee was boiling on the black iron stove. Leon looked at Louise and then at Teresa.

11 "We found him under a cottonwood tree in the big arroyo near the sheep camp. I guess he sat down to rest in the shade and never got up again." Leon walked toward the old man's bed. The red plaid shawl had been shaken and spread carefully over the bed, and a new brown flannel shirt and pair of stiff new Levi's were arranged neatly beside the pillow. Louise held the screen door open while Leon and Ken carried in the red blanket. He looked small and shriveled, and after they dressed him in the new shirt and pants he seemed more shrunken.

12 It was noontime now because the church bells rang the Angelus. They ate the beans with hot bread, and nobody said anything until after Teresa poured the coffee.

13 Ken stood up and put on his jacket. "I'll see about the gravediggers. Only the top layer of soil is frozen. I think it can be ready before dark."

14 Leon nodded his head and finished his coffee. After Ken had

been gone for a while, the neighbors and clanspeople came quietly to embrace Teofilo's family and to leave food on the table because the gravediggers would come to eat when they were finished.

15   The sky in the west was full of pale yellow light. Louise stood outside with her hands in the pockets of Leon's green army jacket that was too big for her. The funeral was over, and the old men had taken their candles and medicine bags and were gone. She waited until the body was laid into the pickup before she said anything to Leon. She touched his arm, and he noticed that her hands were still dusty from the corn meal that she had sprinkled around the old man. When she spoke, Leon could not hear her.

16   "What did you say? I didn't hear you."

17   "I said that I had been thinking about something."

18   "About what?"

19   "About the priest sprinkling holy water for Grandpa. So he won't be thirsty."

20   Leon stared at the new moccasins that Teofilo had made for the ceremonial dances in the summer. They were nearly hidden by the red blanket. It was getting colder, and the wind pushed gray dust down the narrow pueblo road. The sun was approaching the long mesa where it disappeared during the winter. Louise stood there shivering and watching his face. Then he zipped up his jacket and opened the truck door. "I'll see if he's there."

21   Ken stopped the pickup at the church, and Leon got out; and then Ken drove down the hill to the graveyard where people were waiting. Leon knocked at the old carved door with its symbols of the Lamb. While he waited he looked up at the twin bells from the king of Spain with the last sunlight pouring around them in their tower.

22   The priest opened the door and smiled when he saw who it was. "Come in! What brings you here this evening?"

23   The priest walked toward the kitchen, and Leon stood with his cap in his hand, playing with the earflaps and examining the living room—the brown sofa, the green armchair, and the brass lamp that hung down from the ceiling by links of chain. The priest dragged a chair out of the kitchen and offered it to Leon.

24   "No thank you, Father. I only came to ask you if you would bring your holy water to the graveyard."

25   The priest turned away from Leon and looked out the window at the patio full of shadows and the dining-room windows of the nuns' cloister across the patio. The curtains were heavy, and the

light from within faintly penetrated; it was impossible to see the nuns inside eating supper. "Why didn't you tell me he was dead? I could have brought the Last Rites anyway."

26   Leon smiled. "It wasn't necessary, Father."

27   The priest stared down at his scuffed brown loafers and the worn hem of his cassock. "For a Christian burial it was necessary."

28   His voice was distant, and Leon thought that his blue eyes looked tired.

29   "It's O.K. Father, we just want him to have plenty of water."

30   The priest sank down into the green chair and picked up a glossy missionary magazine. He turned the colored pages full of lepers and pagans without looking at them.

31   "You know I can't do that, Leon. There should have been the Last Rites and a funeral Mass at the very least."

32   Leon put on his green cap and pulled the flaps down over his ears. "It's getting late, Father. I've got to go."

33   When Leon opened the door Father Paul stood up and said, "Wait." He left the room and came back wearing a long brown overcoat. He followed Leon out the door and across the dim churchyard to the adobe steps in front of the church. They both stooped to fit through the low adobe entrance. And when they started down the hill to the graveyard only half of the sun was visible above the mesa.

34   The priest approached the grave slowly, wondering how they had managed to dig into the frozen ground; and then he remembered that this was New Mexico, and saw the pile of cold loose sand beside the hole. The people stood close to each other with little clouds of steam puffing from their faces. The priest looked at them and saw a pile of jackets, gloves, and scarves in the yellow, dry tumbleweeds that grew in the graveyard. He looked at the red blanket, not sure that Teofilo was so small, wondering if it wasn't some perverse Indian trick—something they did in March to ensure a good harvest—wondering if maybe old Teofilo was actually at sheep camp corralling the sheep for the night. But there he was, facing into a cold dry wind and squinting at the last sunlight, ready to bury a red wool blanket while the faces of his parishioners were in shadow with the last warmth of the sun on their backs.

35   His fingers were stiff, and it took him a long time to twist the lid off the holy water. Drops of water fell on the red blanket and soaked into dark icy spots. He sprinkled the grave and the water disappeared almost before it touched the dim, cold sand; it reminded him of something—he tried to remember what it was, be-

cause he thought if he could remember he might understand this. He sprinkled more water; he shook the container until it was empty, and the water fell through the light from sundown like August rain that fell while the sun was still shining, almost evaporating before it touched the wilted squash flowers.

36   The wind pulled at the priest's brown Franciscan robe and swirled away the corn meal and pollen that had been sprinkled on the blanket. They lowered the bundle into the ground, and they didn't bother to untie the stiff pieces of new rope that were tied around the ends of the blanket. The sun was gone, and over on the highway the eastbound lane was full of headlights. The priest walked away slowly. Leon watched him climb the hill, and when he had disappeared within the tall, thick walls, Leon turned to look up at the high blue mountains in the deep snow that reflected a faint red light from the west. He felt good because it was finished, and he was happy about the sprinkling of the holy water; now the old man could send them big thunderclouds for sure.

EXERCISES

Details and Their Meanings

1. How are Ken and Leon dressed, and what are they doing at the beginning of this selection? What can you infer about who they are?
2. What do Ken and Leon do to the body of the old man? What do you think is the meaning of the various actions they take? What can you infer about the culture of all three?
3. What beliefs does Father Paul have? Is he from the same people and region as Leon, Ken, and Teofilo? What indications are there that he represents a foreign culture? Why don't Leon and Ken tell him the truth? What are the consequences of the truth being withheld? What does Father Paul say when he finds out the truth?
4. What role does Louise play in the ceremony? What does she request?
5. How does Father Paul react to the request at first? What

pictures are in the magazine that he picks up? What is the significance of the pictures and of his reactions to them? What does he think about the mixture of Catholic and local traditions? What does he finally do? Why do you think he changes his mind?

6. What is important about the sprinkling of holy water for the priest? For Leon? Do they interpret the ceremonies in the same way?

Reading and Critical Thinking

1. How did Ken, Leon, and Louise react to the body? With what desire do they associate care of the body? What does that reflect about their culture?

2. What is Ken, Leon, and Louise's relation to the Catholic priest and the church?

3. Are Ken, Leon, and Louise concerned with proper Christian burial? Why do they ask for the priest's cooperation? How do they incorporate Christian ceremony into their own? Is the final ceremony more Native American or Christian? How do they think about the priest?

4. What do you think the priest thinks about the ceremony he participates in? Why does he cooperate? Do you think he is totally satisfied with what has happened, with what effect his participation will have?

5. What does the piece suggest about the relative strengths of Christian and traditional beliefs among this group of Native Americans?

The Writer's Strategies

1. What is the main idea? Is it ever stated as a thesis? How do you come to find out the main idea?

2. In what way is not speaking directly part of the piece? What facts does the reader figure out only gradually? What does the priest figure out only gradually?

3. What order does the writer use to present events? What are the basic events of the selection? How does the external series of events represent a cultural and psychological process that reveals how the characters think and feel?

4. At the end of the piece, what has happened to Father Paul? Whose thoughts end the selection? What culture do those thoughts represent, and how do they reinterpret the meaning of the Christian ceremony? What is the significance of the ending?

Thinking Together

In groups of three or four, discuss religious or cultural customs you have observed that seemed to mix the traditions of two or more groups. Also discuss whether you know of any customs that you now think of as belonging to a single group but that historically came from a combining of cultures. After you have discussed some examples, decide which example shows the deepest mixing of cultures. Then as a group write a description and explanation of this case of cultural mixing.

Vocabulary

Some of the words in the following list bring to mind the life, surroundings, and customs of Native Americans. Others bring to mind the Catholic church. Indicate whether each reflects Native American (NA) or the Catholic (C) way of life; then define each word, using context clues from the selection.

1. cottonwood (par. 1)
2. arroyo (par. 1)
3. pickup (par. 3)
4. pueblo (par. 3)
5. Levi's (par. 11)
6. Angelus (par. 12)
7. holy water (par. 19)
8. moccasins (par. 20)
9. mesa (par. 20)
10. cloister (par. 25)
11. Last Rites (par. 25)
12. missionary (par. 30)
13. pagans (par. 30)
14. adobe (par. 33)
15. tumbleweeds (par. 34)

WRITER'S WORKSHOP ━━━━━━━━━━

Critical Thinking in Writing

1. How do religions change when they come in contact with new cultures? Write an essay about any case you know of when the religions or cultures of two different peoples met and mixed.
2. This piece describes people's resistance to Christian culture even while they are incorporating its rituals. How might this behavior be indicative of Native American reaction to Anglo culture? Write an essay describing the cultural attitudes expressed in this selection.
3. Write a few paragraphs describing a dramatic incident, such as reaction to a death, that reveals people's beliefs and attitudes.

Connecting Ideas

How does the response to white culture described by Leslie Marmon Silko differ from Armando Rendón's response, described in "Kiss of Death" (page 125)? Write one paragraph comparing the writers' responses and another paragraph discussing which response (if either) you feel is more appropriate or preferable.

Kiss of Death

Armando Rendón

Armando Rendón is a journalist, a scriptwriter, and an executive in a Chicago counseling firm. In this selection from his Chicano Manifesto *(1971), Rendón describes growing up in Texas and California and the challenges to his ethnic identity.*

KEY WORDS

factionalized (par. 9)   split into small, contending groups
gilt (par. 11)   cheap gold-colored covering meant to look like real gold
acculturized (par. 13)   became comfortable with a culture
mystique (par. 15)   a charmed air, charisma

I NEARLY FELL VICTIM to the Anglo. My childhood was spent in the West Side barrio of San Antonio. I lived in my grandmother's house on Ruiz Street just below Zarzamora Creek. I did well in the elementary grades and learned English quickly.

2   Spanish was off-limits in school anyway, and teachers and relatives taught me early that my mother tongue would be of no help in making good grades and becoming a success. Yet Spanish was the language I used in playing and arguing with friends. Spanish was the language I spoke with my *abuelita*, my dear grandmother, as I ate *atole* on those cold mornings when I used to wake at dawn to her clattering dishes in the tiny kitchen; or when I would cringe in mock horror at old folk tales she would tell me late at night.

3   But the lesson took effect anyway. When, at the age of ten, I went with my mother to California, to the San Francisco Bay Area where she found work during the war years, I had my first real opportunity to strip myself completely of my heritage. In California the schools I attended were all Anglo except for this little mexicanito. At least, I never knew anyone who admitted he was Mexican and I certainly never thought to ask. When my name was

125

accented incorrectly, Réndon instead of Rendón, that was all right; finally I must have gotten tired of correcting people or just didn't bother.

4   I remember a summertime visit home a few years after living on the West Coast. At an evening gathering of almost the whole family—uncles, aunts, nephews, nieces, my *abuelita*—we sat out-doors through the dusk until the dark had fully settled. Then the lights were turned on; someone brought out a Mexican card game, the Lotería El Diablito, similar to bingo. But instead of rows of numbers on a pasteboard, there were figures of persons, animals, and objects on cards corresponding to figures set in rows on a pasteboard. We used frijoles (pinto beans) to mark each figure on our card as the leader went through the deck one by one. The word for tree was called: *Arbol!* It completed a row; I had won. Then to check my card I had to name each figure again. When I said the word for tree, it didn't come at all as I wanted it to; AR-BOWL with the accent on the last syllable and sounding like an Anglo tourist. There was some all-around kidding of me and good-natured laughter over the incident, and it passed.

5   But if I had not been speaking much Spanish up until then, I spoke even less afterward. Even when my mother, who speaks both Spanish and English fluently, spoke to me in Spanish, I would respond in English. By the time I graduated from high school and prepared to enter college, the break was nearly complete. Seldom during college did I admit to being a Mexican-American. Only when Latin American students pressed me about my surname did I admit my Spanish descent, or when it proved an asset in meeting coeds from Latin American countries.

6   My ancestry had become a shadow, fainter and fainter about me. I felt no particular allegiance to it, drew no inspiration from it, and elected generally to let it fade away. I clicked with the Anglo mind-set in college, mastered it, you might say. I even became edi-tor of the campus biweekly newspaper as a junior, and editor of the literary magazine as a senior—not bad, now that I look back, for a tortillas-and-beans Chicano upbringing to beat the Anglo at his own game.

7   The point of my "success," of course, was that I had been as-similated; I had bought the white man's world. After getting my diploma I was set to launch out into a career in newspaper re-porting and writing. There was no thought in my mind of serving my people, telling their story, or making anything right for any-body but myself. Instead I had dreams of Pulitzer Prizes, syndi-

cated columns, foreign correspondent assignments, front-page stories—that was for me. Then something happened.

8   A Catholic weekly newspaper in Sacramento offered me a position as a reporter and feature writer. I had a job on a Bay Area
daily as a copyboy at the time, with the opportunity to become a
reporter. But I'd just been married, and there were a number of
other reasons to consider: there'd be a variety of assignments, Sacramento was the state capital, it was a good town in which to raise
a family, and the other job lacked promise for upward mobility. I
decided to take the offer.

9   My wife and I moved to Sacramento in the fall of 1961, and in
a few weeks the radicalization of this Chicano began. It wasn't a
book I read or a great leader awakening me, for we had no Chá-
vezes or Tijerinas or Gonzálezes at the time; and it was no revela-
tion from above. It was my own people who rescued me. There is
a large Chicano population in Sacramento, today one of the most
activist in northern California, but at the time factionalized and still
dependent on the social and church organizations for identity. But
together we found each other.

10   My job soon brought me into contact with many Chicanos as
well as with the recently immigrated Mexicans, located in the barrios that Sacramento had allocated to the "Mexicans." I found my
people striving to survive in an alien environment among foreign
people. One of the stories I covered concerned a phenomenon
called Cursillos de Cristiandad (Little Courses in Christianity), intense, three-day group-sensitivity sessions whose chief objective is
the re-Christianization of Catholics. To cover the story properly I
talked my editor into letting me make a Cursillo.

11   Not only was much revealed to me about the phony gilt lining
of religion which I had grown up believing was the Church, but
there was an added and highly significant side effect—cultural
shock! I rediscovered my own people, or perhaps they redeemed
me. Within the social dimension of the Cursillo, for the first time
in many years I became reimmersed in a tough, *macho ambiente* (an
entirely Mexican male environment). Only Spanish was spoken.
The effect was shattering. It was as if my tongue, after being struck
dumb as a child, had been loosened.

12   Because we were located in cramped quarters, with limited
facilities, and the cooks, lecturers, priests, and participants were
men only, the old sense of *machismo* and *camarada* was revived and
given new perspective. I was cast in a spiritual setting which was
a perfect background for reviving my Chicano soul. Reborn but

imperfectly, I still had a lot to learn about myself and my people. But my understanding deepened and renewed itself as the years went by. I visited bracero camps with teams of Chicanos; sometimes with priests taking the sacraments; sometimes only Chicanos, offering advice or assistance with badly needed food and clothing, distributed through a bingo-game technique; and on occasion, music for group singing provided by a phonograph or a guitar. Then there were barrio organization work; migrant worker programs; a rural self-help community development project; and confrontation with antipoverty agencies, with the churches, with government officials, and with cautious Chicanos, too.

13   In a little San Francisco magazine called *Way*, I wrote in a March 1966 article discussing "The Other Mexican-American":

> The Mexican-American must answer at the same time: Who am I? and Who are we? This is to pose then, not merely a dilemma of self-identity; but of self-in-group-identity. . . . Perhaps the answer to developing a total Mexican-American concept must be left in the hands of the artist, the painter, the writer, and the poet, who can abstract the essence of what it is to be Mexican in America. . . . When that understanding comes . . . the Mexican-American will not only have acculturized himself, but he will have acculturized America to him. ·

14   If anyone knew what he was talking about when he spoke of the dilemma of who he was and where he belonged, it was this Chicano. I very nearly dropped out, as so many other Mexican-Americans have, under the dragging pressure to be someone else, what most of society wants you to be before it hands out its chrome-plated trophies.

15   And that mystique—I didn't quite have it at the time, or the right word for it. But no one did until just the last few years when so many of us stopped trying to be someone else and decided that what we want to be and to be called is Chicano.

16   I owe my life to my Chicano people. They rescued me from the Anglo kiss of death, the monolingual, monocultural, and colorless Gringo society. I no longer face a dilemma of identity or direction. That identity and direction have been charted for me by the Chicano—but to think I came that close to being sucked into the vacuum of the dominant society.

EXERCISES

Details and Their Meanings

1. In what city did Armando Rendón first live? What language did he use in school? When did he use another language?
2. How did the writer's view of his heritage change as he moved from childhood to adolescence?
3. What is Lotería El Diablito?
4. In what college situations did Rendón find it an advantage to be of Spanish descent?
5. When did the writer rediscover his heritage? What organization helped him? What other experiences helped Rendón to strengthen his ties to the Chicano community?
6. What activities did Rendón embrace to help other Chicanos?

Reading and Critical Thinking

1. What was Rendón's mother's attitude toward Mexican culture? How do you know? Was her attitude appropriate? Why or why not?
2. From information in paragraph 3, you can tell that this selection begins during which decade?
3. How does Rendón describe Anglo culture? What doesn't he like about it? Do you think he is accurate in his criticism? Why or why not?
4. What was the purpose of the Cursillos de Cristiandad? Who was the target audience of these courses?
5. What are some elements of typical Mexican-American culture, according to Rendón? What does it mean to him to be Chicano?
6. What does Rendón mean when he says, "I owe my life to my Chicano people" (paragraph 16)? What does he imply would have happened had he not rediscovered his heritage?

The Writer's Strategies

1. Where does the writer state his main point? What is it?
2. Why does Rendón use Spanish words? What effect does the use of Spanish produce?
3. What phrases does the writer use to show the disparaging way people looked on Spanish culture?

4. According to the writer, what is the difference between a Chicano and a Mexican? Why is the distinction important in the selection?
5. What order does Rendón use to organize this piece?
6. Where does Rendón include a passage from another article that he wrote? What is his purpose in doing so?
7. Who is the intended audience for this piece, Anglos or Chicanos? How can you tell?

Thinking Together

Does Rendón present a balanced view of Anglo and Chicano cultures? What leads you to your conclusion? How does Rendón define *Anglo culture?* Break into groups and see if you can reach consensus on these questions. Report your findings to the rest of the class.

Vocabulary

Write definitions of the following Spanish words. Some are defined in the text, but you may need to look up others in a Spanish-English dictionary.

1. barrio (par. 1)
2. *abuelita* (par. 2)
3. *atole* (par. 2)
4. Lotería El Diablito (par. 4)
5. frijoles (par. 4)
6. *arbol* (par. 4)
7. Cursillo (par. 10)
8. *macho ambiente* (par. 11)
9. *camarada* (par. 12)
10. bracero (par. 12)

WRITER'S WORKSHOP ━━━━━━━━━

Critical Thinking in Writing

1. Is Rendón correct to say that Anglo culture is "monolingual, monocultural, and colorless"? Write an essay describing your

experience of American culture. What do you find are its strengths and weaknesses? How do your impressions conform to or challenge Rendón's?

2. Rendón has apparently rejected biculturalism in favor of an exclusively Chicano perspective. Do you think this is a valid choice? Should people try to stay exclusively within their ethnic identities? What is gained or lost as a result of locking oneself within one culture? Present your views in an essay.

3. Write an essay in which you define *ethnic identity* or *cultural identity*.

Connecting Ideas

Read "The Man to Send Rain Clouds," by Leslie Marmon Silko (page 117). How would you compare the treatment of a cultural heritage in the two essays? How do the values of majority cultures influence the cultural heritage of the minority group portrayed in each selection?

I Am an Affirmative Action Baby

Stephen Carter

Stephen Carter is a professor at Yale Law School. In this selection from his book Reflections of an Affirmative Action Baby *(1991), Carter urges people of color to put aside their differences on affirmative action and work together.*

KEY WORDS

pejoratively (par. 1)   in a negative or belittling way
moorings (par. 5)   the anchoring that holds a ship in place
corollary (par. 7)   a consequence of a proposition or a proposition that is incidentally proved by another proposition
portend (par. 9)   to indicate, forecast
nullification (par. 9)   voiding, doing away with
neoconservatism (par. 11)   modern political doctrine that advocates dismantling government programs that interfere with or take the place of individual initiative
abject (par. 12)   pitiful, miserable

I CALL US—black professionals of my generation—the affirmative action babies. I know that this term is sometimes used pejoratively, but it is my intention to invert that meaning, to embrace the term, not reject it.

2 Had I not enjoyed the benefits of a racial preference in professional school admission, I would not have accomplished what I have in my career. I was afforded the opportunity for advanced professional training at one of the finest law schools in the country, Yale, and I like to think that I have made the most of this privilege. So, yes, I *am* an affirmative action baby, and I do not apologize for that.

3   By the term *affirmative action baby,* I mean to imply only a temporal identification: that is the name, and an accurate one, of the civil rights age in which we live. My generation was in or about to start high school when a nation torn by violent racial strife and shattered by the murder of Martin Luther King Jr. decided to try preferential admission and hiring policies as a form, it was hoped, of corrective justice. We entered college around the dawn of the era of affirmative action in admission.

4   My law school classmates and I agonized as preferential policies went through their first major crisis, a partial rejection by the Supreme Court in the Bakke case. And now, as I look around the classrooms at the Yale Law School, where I have taught for almost a decade, I realize that the bright and diverse students of color I see before me have a shot, and a good one, at being the last members of the affirmative action generation—or, what is better still, the first members of the post-affirmative action generation, the professionals who will say to a doubting world, "Here are my accomplishments; take me or don't take me on my merits."

5   In recent years, however, affirmative action has slipped its moorings and started to drift. The drift has been slow, so slow that it has scarcely been noticed, but it has carried the programs a long and dangerous distance from the relatively placid waters of the provision of opportunities for developing talent. Nowadays, affirmative action is being transformed into a tool for representing the "points of view" of excluded groups.

6   The argument one now hears is that people of color have a distinctive voice, a vision of the world, that is not being represented in the places where vital decisions are made: the boardroom, the bureaucracy, the campus. In the new rhetoric of affirmative action, it seems, the reason to seek out and hire or admit people of color is that one can have faith that their opinions, their perspective, will be different from the opinions and perspectives of people who are white—who evidently have a distinctive set of views of their own.

7   The unfortunate logical corollary is that if the perspective a particular person of color can offer is *not* distinctive, if it is more like the "white" perspective than the "black" one, then that person is not speaking in an authentically black voice—an accusation that has become all too common.

8   As a black intellectual, I see my role as one of trying, if possible, to foster reconciliation, to promote the educational conversation

from which all of us who care about the future of black people will benefit. There is no reason for us to be at each other's throats when there is so much on both sides of the argument from which all can learn. Our task, I think, should be to find the common ground, to be at once realistic about the world and sensitive to each other.

9   Let us, then, be frank: there is good reason, given today's politics, to think that we are looking toward the end of most racial preferences. For those of us who have been positioned to take advantage of what it offers, the affirmative action era has been a decidedly mixed blessing. The prospect of its end should be a challenge and a chance; it does not portend disaster. We must never turn affirmative action into a crutch, and therefore we must reject the common claim that an end to preferences would be a disastrous situation, amounting to a virtual nullification of the 1954 desegregation ruling.

10   We should be concentrating on constructive dialogue about how to solve the problems of the real and continuing victims of the nation's legacy of racist oppression: the millions of struggling black Americans for whom affirmative action and entry to the professions are stunningly irrelevant.

11   Mine is not, I hope, a position that will be thought inauthentically black. It is not, I think, evidence of that most fatal of diseases (for a black intellectual), neoconservatism; my views on many other matters are sufficiently to the left that I do not imagine the conservative movement would want me. (Neither, I think, would the left—but that is fine with me, for it is best for intellectuals to be politically unpredictable.)

12   Surely the abject and sometimes desperate circumstances that confront so many of us who have not been fortunate enough to gain access to college and professional school are reason enough for us to stop sniping at one another. If not, we can be sure of two things: first, as professionals and intellectuals, we who are black and middle class will likely endure; second, as they struggle through the violent prisons that many inner cities have become, millions of other black people may not.

13   So perhaps, for a golden moment, we can pause in our quarreling and talk *to* one another, instead of continuing an endless, self-defeating argument over who is the authentic keeper of the flame.

EXERCISES

Details and Their Meanings

1. How has Stephen Carter benefited from affirmative action?
2. What subject does the writer teach? How many years has he been teaching?
3. During what time period did the writer grow up?
4. In the writer's opinion, how has affirmative action changed over the years?
5. What does the writer mean by the phrase "distinctive voice"?
6. How does the writer see his role as a black intellectual?
7. What does Carter expect for his students? How does he describe them?
8. How does Carter characterize *neoconservatism?*

Reading and Critical Thinking

1. Which groups do you think are involved in the conflict Carter describes? Are you part of either group?
2. Carter considers affirmative action "a decidedly mixed blessing," although he does not develop this point. Where in the essay can you find reasons to support his point? Do you agree with the "mixed blessing" idea? Why or why not?
3. Does Carter fault American society for the problems faced by black people? Why or why not? Which paragraph helps you to answer this question?
4. Which segments of the black community have criticized Carter? Which paragraphs help you to identify them? Do you agree or disagree with the criticism? Why?
5. In which paragraphs does Carter praise affirmative action? What does he say about it? Where does he criticize affirmative action? How would you evaluate this major social program in America?
6. What evidence does Carter give to support his conclusion that "we are looking toward the end of most racial preferences"? Do you agree with him? Why or why not?

The Writer's Strategies

1. What is Carter's purpose in titling this essay "I Am an Affirmative Action Baby"? Why does he use *baby* and not *man, person,* or some other word?

2. Which paragraphs make up the introduction?
3. What are the writer's main points? Where does he state them?
4. Where does Carter begin his conclusion? What warning does he give there?
5. What transitional words does the writer use to connect ideas?
6. Where does Carter first define *affirmative action?* Where does he describe it the second time? How does the definition change?
7. Who is the intended audience for this piece? What assumption is the writer making about his readers' knowledge of current politics? Is his assumption accurate in your case?

Thinking Together

Carter refers to the Bakke case, assuming that his readers will be familiar with the details of it. Look up the Bakke case in an encyclopedia or in some other reference work. What was the issue? What did the Supreme Court decide? Do you agree with its decision? Discuss your findings and responses in groups.

Vocabulary

Look in a dictionary of political terms or a book about politics to define the following terms.

1. left
2. right
3. conservative
4. liberal
5. neoconservative

WRITER'S WORKSHOP —————————————

Critical Thinking in Writing

1. What are your views on affirmative action? Do you believe it is necessary to continue preferential treatment of groups who have been historically ignored? Write an essay to explain your thoughts.
2. During his Supreme Court nomination hearing in 1991, Judge

Clarence Thomas, another Yale graduate, articulated the black neoconservative position that blacks did not benefit from affirmative action in any important way and that the goal of government should be to create a single standard for all Americans. How do you think Stephen Carter would respond to Thomas's argument? What merits can you find in each position? With whom do you agree? Write your response in an argumentative essay.

3. Carter asserts that the task for those who care about the future of black people "should be to find the common ground, to be at once realistic about the world and sensitive to each other." How might this statement serve as a kind of pact or creed for those who care about the future of humanity? Write an essay called "Finding the Common Ground" in which you argue how being realistic about the world and sensitive to each other will benefit the varied racial and ethnic groups of our country. Draw on your own experience and (or) your readings to provide a well-detailed argument.

Connecting Ideas

Read Jack E. White's essay "Growing Up in Black and White" (page 71). How are the experiences of White's children trying to establish identity between two worlds similar to and different from the experience described by Stephen Carter?

Family Ghosts

Maxine Hong Kingston

Maxine Hong Kingston was born in California. She is the author of several works, including the award-winning memoir The Woman Warrior *(1976), from which this excerpt is taken. In this selection, Hong Kingston relates several ghost stories that she learned as a child.*

KEY WORDS

magistrate (par. 7)   a government official who administers justice
incur (par. 9)   to provoke
morsels (par. 10)   bite-size pieces of food
anonymous (par. 11)   nameless, unknown

WHEN THE THERMOMETER IN our laundry reached one hundred and eleven degrees on summer afternoons, either my mother or my father would say that it was time to tell another ghost story so that we could get some good chills up our backs. My parents, my brothers, sisters, great-uncle, and "Third Aunt," who wasn't really our aunt but a fellow villager, someone else's third aunt, kept the presses crashing and hissing and shouted out the stories. Those were our successful days, when so much laundry came in my mother did not have to pick tomatoes. For breaks we changed from pressing to sorting.

2   "One twilight," my mother began, and already the chills traveled my back and crossed my shoulders; the hair rose at the nape and the back of the legs, "I was walking home after doctoring a sick family. To get home I had to cross a footbridge. In China the bridges are nothing like the ones in Brooklyn and San Francisco. This one was made from rope, laced and knotted as if by magpies. Actually it had been built by men who had returned after harvesting sea swallow nests in Malaya. They had had to swing over the faces of the Malayan cliffs in baskets they had woven themselves.

138

Though this bridge pitched and swayed in the updraft, no one had ever fallen into the river, which looked like a bright scratch at the bottom of the canyon, as if the Queen of Heaven had swept her great silver hairpin across the earth as well as the sky."

3   One twilight, just as my mother stepped on the bridge, two smoky columns spiraled up taller than she. Their swaying tops hovered over her head like white cobras, one at either handrail. From stillness came a wind rushing between the smoke spindles. A high sound entered her temple bones. Through the twin whirlwinds she could see the sun and the river, the river twisting in circles, the trees upside down. The bridge moved like a ship, sickening. The earth dipped. She collapsed to the wooden slats, a ladder up the sky, her fingers so weak she could not grip the rungs. The wind dragged her hair behind her, then whipped it forward across her face. Suddenly the smoke spindles disappeared. The world righted itself, and she crossed to the other side. She looked back, but there was nothing there. She used the bridge often, but she did not encounter those ghosts again.

4   "They were Sit Dom Kuei," said Great-Uncle. "Sit Dom Kuei."

5   "Yes, of course," said my mother. "Sit Dom Kuei."

6   I keep looking in dictionaries under those syllables. *Kuei* means "ghost," but I don't find any other words that make sense. I only hear my great-uncle's river-pirate voice, the voice of a big man who had killed someone in New York or Cuba, make the sounds—"Sit Dom Kuei." How do they translate?

7   When the Communists issued their papers on techniques for combating ghosts, I looked for "Sit Dom Kuei." I have not found them described anywhere, although now I see that my mother won in ghost battle because she can eat anything—quick, pluck out the carp's eyes, one for Mother and one for Father. All heroes are bold toward food. In the research against ghost fear published by the Chinese Academy of Science is the story of a magistrate's servant, Kao Chung, a capable eater who in 1683 ate five cooked chickens and drank ten bottles of wine that belonged to the sea monster with branching teeth. The monster had arranged its food around a fire on the beach and started to feed when Kao Chung attacked. The swan-feather sword he wrested from this monster can be seen in the Wentung County Armory in Shantung today.

8   Another big eater was Chou Yi-han of Changchow, who fried a ghost. It was a meaty stick when he cut it up and cooked it. But before that it had been a woman out at night.

9   Chen Luan-feng, during the Yuan Ho era of the T'ang dynasty

(A.D. 806–820), ate yellow croaker and pork together, which the thunder god had forbidden. But Chen wanted to incur thunderbolts during drought. The first time he ate, the thunder god jumped out of the sky, its legs like old trees. Chen chopped off the left one. The thunder god fell to the earth, and the villagers could see that it was a blue pig or bear with horns and fleshy wings. Chen leapt on it, prepared to chop its neck and bite its throat, but the villagers stopped him. After that, Chen lived apart as a rainmaker, neither relatives nor the monks willing to bring lightning upon themselves. He lived in a cave, and for years whenever there was drought the villagers asked him to eat yellow croaker and pork together, and he did.

10   The most fantastic eater of them all was Wei Pang, a scholar-hunter of the Ta Li era of the T'ang dynasty (A.D. 766–779). He shot and cooked rabbits and birds, but he could also eat scorpions, snakes, cockroaches, worms, slugs, beetles, and crickets. Once he spent the night in a house that had been abandoned because its inhabitants feared contamination from the dead man next door. A shining, twinkling sphere came flying through the darkness at Wei. He felled it with three true arrows—the first making the thing crackle and flame; the second dimming it; and the third putting out its lights, sputter. When his servant came running in with a lamp, Wei saw his arrows sticking in a ball of flesh entirely covered with eyes, some rolled back to show the dulling whites. He and the servant pulled out the arrows and cut up the ball into little pieces. The servant cooked the morsels in sesame oil, and the wonderful aroma made Wei laugh. They ate half, saving half to show the household, which would return now.

11   Big eaters win. When other passers-by stepped around the bundle wrapped in white silk, the anonymous scholar of Hanchow took it home. Inside were three silver ingots and a froglike evil, which sat on the ingots. The scholar laughed at it and chased it off. That night two frogs the size of year-old babies appeared in his room. He clubbed them to death, cooked them, and ate them with white wine. The next night a dozen frogs, together the size of a pair of year-old babies, jumped from the ceiling. He ate all twelve for dinner. The third night thirty small frogs were sitting on his mat and staring at him with their frog eyes. He ate them too. Every night for a month smaller but more numerous frogs came so that he always had the same amount to eat. Soon his floor was like the healthy banks of a pond in spring when the tadpoles, having just turned, sprang in the wet grass. "Get a hedgehog to help eat," cried

his family. "I'm as good as a hedgehog," the scholar said, laughing. And at the end of the month the frogs stopped coming, leaving the scholar with the white silk and silver ingots.

EXERCISES

Details and Their Meanings

1. Where does the narrator work? How are ghost stories helpful to her work?
2. What does the mother normally do for a living? What other jobs does she perform?
3. Where does the mother's encounter with ghosts take place? How many other times has she seen ghosts?
4. What is the secret to combating ghosts? What is Maxine Hong Kingston's source for this information?
5. Who is Kao Chung? When did he live? Why is he important in the piece?
6. What character does the writer describe as the "most fantastic eater of them all"? Do you believe this portrait? Why or why not?

Reading and Critical Thinking

1. Do the stories related in the selection take place in America or China? Do the writer and her family live in America or China? What clues help you to answer each question? What is the connection that emerges in this piece between China and America?
2. What does the phrase "Sit Dom Kuei" mean? How does the writer make figuring out the meaning of this phrase important to her narrative?
3. What are the physical characteristics of ghosts in Chinese stories? What different kinds of figures are considered ghosts in this selection? How do they compare with what you think of as ghosts?

4. Why is it necessary for the characters in several of the stories to eat the fantastic creatures they encounter? What do you suppose would happen if they didn't eat them?
5. What is the narrator's attitude toward ghosts? Does she believe in them? How can you tell?
6. Why do most of the ghost stories related here take place in the distant past? Why does the writer include just one recent example?
7. From the accounts of blue pigs and bears with "horns and fleshy wings," what can you say about the kind of place China is? What is the attitude of people there to fantastic creatures? How is their reaction likely to be different from that of Americans?

The Writer's Strategies

1. What is the thesis of this selection? Where does the writer state it?
2. Who is the narrator? How many narrators are there? Where does the shift take place?
3. How many different age perspectives does the writer provide? What purpose does the shift in perspective serve?
4. Where does the writer make use of sensory details? Provide examples of the most vivid and original sensory images.
5. Is the primary audience for this selection Chinese or American? How can you tell?

Thinking Together

Conduct a survey in your classroom to find out how many students or their parents, spouses, or extended families believe in ghosts. Tally the results. Then find out how many of your classmates have a firsthand ghost story to tell. How many know someone who has had a ghostly encounter? Share some of these stories with the class. How do the students who do not believe in ghosts respond to them?

Vocabulary

Maxine Hong Kingston creates memorable word pictures. Write your understanding of the following images.

1. branching teeth (par. 7)
2. froglike evil (par. 11)
3. swan-feather sword (par. 7)
4. smoke spindles (par. 3)
5. river-pirate voice (par. 6)
6. rope, laced and knotted as if by magpies (par. 2)

WRITER'S WORKSHOP

Critical Thinking in Writing

1. What was your favorite story as a child? In a narrative essay, retell this story in your own words, using as much detail as you can.
2. Most educated people in America do not believe in the existence of ghosts, supernatural phenomena, or magic. From the modern scientific perspective, they all come under the heading "superstitions." Nevertheless, belief in them persists. How can you explain the persistence of such beliefs? Write an essay in which you explain why you feel superstitions continue to play a role in modern society.
3. Ghost and horror stories often reflect cultural values. Relate a ghost or horror story that you know and analyze what information about cultural values and beliefs the story presents.

Connecting Ideas

Read "The Man to Send Rain Clouds," by Leslie Marmon Silko (page 117). How does the Chinese folk tradition presented by Maxine Hong Kingston in "Family Ghosts" compare with the Native-American tradition described in Silko's piece? What generalization can you make about the similarities and differences between these two cultures?

Minority Student

Richard Rodriguez

Richard Rodriguez is a writer and teacher in San Francisco, where he was born. In this selection from Hunger of Memory: The Educa-tion of Richard Rodriguez *(1982), his autobiography, he wrestles with the conflict between his ethnic and mainstream identities.*

KEY WORDS

juxtaposition (par. 3)   placing side by side or close together
implicated (par. 4)   connected with, mixed up in
rhetorically (par. 9)   for effect only
los pobres (par. 13)   Spanish phrase meaning "the poor wretches"
fawning (par. 17)   acting in a submissive, cringing way

MINORITY STUDENT—THAT WAS the label I bore in college at Stanford, then in graduate school at Columbia and Berkeley: a nonwhite reader of Spenser and Milton and Austen.

2   In the late 1960s nonwhite Americans clamored for access to higher education, and I became a principal beneficiary of the acade-my's response, its programs of affirmative action. My presence was noted each fall by the campus press office in its proud tally of Hispanic-American students enrolled; my progress was followed by HEW statisticians. One of the lucky ones. Rewarded. Advanced for belonging to a racial group "underrepresented" in American institutional life. When I sought admission to graduate schools, when I applied for fellowships and summer study grants, when I needed a teaching assistantship, my Spanish surname or the dark mark in the space indicating my race—"check one"—nearly al-ways got me whatever I asked for. When the time came for me to look for a college teaching job (the end of my years as a scholar-ship boy), potential employers came looking for me—a minority student.

3   Fittingly, it falls to me, as someone who so awkwardly carried the label, to question it now, its juxtaposition of terms—minority, student. For me there is no way to say it with grace. I say it rather with irony sharpened by self-pity. I say it with anger. It is a term that should never have been foisted on me. One I was wrong to accept.

4   In college one day a professor of English returned my term paper with this comment penciled just under the grade: "Maybe the reason you feel Dickens's sense of alienation so acutely is because you are a minority student." *Minority student.* It was the first time I had seen the expression; I remember sensing that it somehow referred to my race. Never before had a teacher suggested that my academic performance was linked to my racial identity. After class I reread the remark several times. Around me other students were talking and leaving. The professor remained in front of the room, collecting his papers and books. I was about to go up and question his note. But I didn't. I let the comment pass; thus became implicated in the strange reform movement that followed.

5   The year was 1967. And what I did not realize was that my life would be radically changed by deceptively distant events. In 1967, their campaign against southern segregation laws successful at last, black civil rights leaders were turning their attention to the North, a North they no longer saw in contrast to the South. What they realized was that although no official restrictions denied blacks access to northern institutions of advancement and power, for most blacks this freedom was only theoretical. (The obstacle was "institutional racism.") Activists made their case against institutions of higher education. Schools like Wisconsin and Princeton long had been open to blacks. But the tiny number of nonwhite students and faculty members at such schools suggested that there was more than the issue of access to consider. Most blacks simply couldn't afford tuition for higher education. And, because the primary and secondary schooling blacks received was usually poor, few qualified for admission. Many were so culturally alienated that they never thought to apply; they couldn't imagine themselves going to college.

6   I think—as I thought in 1967—that the black civil rights leaders were correct: Higher education was not, nor is it yet, accessible to many black Americans. I think now, however, that the activists tragically limited the impact of their movement with the reforms they proposed. Seeing the problem solely in racial terms (as a case of *de facto* segregation), they pressured universities and colleges to admit more black students and hire more black faculty members.

There were demands for financial aid programs. And tutoring help. And more aggressive student recruitment. But this was all. The aim was to integrate higher education in the North. So no one seemed troubled by the fact that those who were in the best position to benefit from such reforms were those blacks least victimized by racism or any other social oppression—those culturally, if not always economically, of the middle class.

7   The lead established, other civil rights groups followed. Soon Hispanic-American activists began to complain that there were too few Hispanics in colleges. They concluded that this was the result of racism. They offered racial solutions. They demanded that Hispanic-American professors be hired. And that students with Spanish surnames be admitted in greater numbers to colleges. Shortly after, I was "recognized" on campus: a Hispanic-American, a "Latino," a Mexican-American, a "Chicano." No longer would people ask me, as I had been asked before, if I were a foreign student. (From India? Peru?) All of a sudden everyone seemed to know—as the professor of English had known—that I was a minority student.

8   I became a highly rewarded minority student. For campus officials came first to students like me with their numerous offers of aid. And why not? Administrators met their angriest critics' demands by promoting any plausible Hispanic on hand. They were able, moreover, to use the presence of conventionally qualified nonwhite students like me to prove that they were meeting the goals of their critics.

9   In 1968, the assassination of Dr. Martin Luther King, Jr., prompted many academic officials to commit themselves publicly to the goal of integrating their institutions. One day I watched the nationally televised funeral; a week later I received invitations to teach at community colleges. There were opportunities to travel to foreign countries with contingents of "minority group scholars." And I went to the financial aid office on campus and was handed special forms for minority student applicants. I was a minority student, wasn't I? the lady behind the counter asked me rhetorically. Yes, I said. Carelessly said. I completed the application. Was later awarded.

10   In a way, it was true. I was a minority. The word, as popularly used, did describe me. In the sixties, *minority* became a synonym for socially disadvantaged Americans—but it was primarily a numerical designation. The word referred to entire races and nationalities of Americans, those numerically underrepresented in in-

stitutional life. (Thus, without contradiction, one could speak of "minority groups.") And who were they exactly? Blacks—all blacks—most obviously were minorities. And Hispanic Americans. And American Indians. And some others. (It was left to federal statisticians, using elaborate surveys and charts, to determine which others precisely.)

11   I was a minority.

12   I believed it. For the first several years, I accepted the label. I certainly supported the racial civil rights movement; supported the goal of broadening access to higher education. But there was a problem: One day I listened approvingly to a government official defend affirmative action; the next day *I* realized the benefits of the program. I was the minority student the political activists shouted about at noon-time rallies. Against their rhetoric, I stood out in relief, unrelieved. *Knowing:* I was not really more socially disadvantaged than the white graduate students in my classes. *Knowing:* I was not disadvantaged like many of the new nonwhite students who were entering college, lacking good early schooling.

13   Nineteen sixty-nine. 1970. 1971. Slowly, slowly, the term *minority* became a source of unease. It would remind me of those boyhood years when I had felt myself alienated from public (majority) society—*los gringos. Minority. Minorities. Minority groups.* The terms sounded in public to remind me in private of the truth: I was not—in a *cultural* sense— a minority, an alien from public life. (Not like *los pobres* I had encountered during my recent laboring summer.) The truth was summarized in the sense of irony I'd feel at hearing myself called a minority student: The reason I was no longer a minority was because I had become a student.

14   *Minority student!*

15   In conversations with faculty members I began to worry the issue, only to be told that my unease was unfounded. A dean said he was certain that after I graduated I would be able to work among "my people." A senior faculty member expressed in confidence that, though I was unrepresentative of lower-class Hispanics, I would serve as a role model for others of my race. Another faculty member was sure that I would be a valued counselor to incoming minority students. (He assumed that, because of my race, I retained a special capacity for communicating with nonwhite students.) I also heard academic officials say that minority students would someday form a leadership class in America. (From our probable positions of power, we would be able to lobby for reforms to benefit others of our race.)

16   In 1973 I wrote and had published two essays in which I said that I had been educated away from the culture of my mother and father. In 1974 I published an essay admitting unease over becoming the beneficiary of affirmative action. There was another article against affirmative action in 1977. One more soon after. At times, I proposed contrary ideas; consistent always was the admission that I was no longer like socially disadvantaged Hispanic-Americans. But this admission, made in national magazines, only brought me a greater degree of success. A published minority student, I won a kind of celebrity. In my mail were admiring letters from right-wing politicians. There were also invitations to address conferences of college administrators or government officials.

17   My essays served as my "authority" to speak at the Marriott Something or the Sheraton Somewhere. To stand at a ballroom podium and hear my surprised echo sound from a microphone. I spoke. I started getting angry letters from activists. One wrote to say that I was becoming the *gringos'* fawning pet. What "they" want all Hispanics to be. I remembered the remark when I was introduced to an all-white audience and heard their applause so loud. I remembered the remark when I stood in a university auditorium and saw an audience of brown and black faces watching me. I publicly wondered whether a person like me should really be termed a minority. But some members of the audience thought I was denying racial pride, trying somehow to deny my racial identity. They rose to protest. One Mexican-American said I was a minority whether I wanted to be or not. And he said that the reason I was a beneficiary of affirmative action was simple: I was a Chicano. (Wasn't I?) It was only an issue of race.

EXERCISES

Details and Their Meanings

1. What minority group does Richard Rodriguez belong to? Where in the essay does this information appear?
2. When did the writer go to college? What historical events coincided with his college years?
3. When did the writer realize that he was a minority student? When did other students realize that he is Hispanic?

4. Why did it suddenly become an advantage for Rodriguez to identify himself as a minority student? When did he begin to question his status as a minority student? What compelled him to speak out on the question of minorities?
5. How did Hispanic activists react to Rodriguez's public statements?
6. What factors other than race or ethnic group does Rodriguez feel are important in deciding who should receive affirmative action?

Reading and Critical Thinking

1. What economic class does the writer belong to? How can you tell? How do you think class influences the writer's point of view?
2. In what sense did the term *socially disadvantaged* not apply to Richard Rodriguez? Why didn't university officials care whether it applied to him or not? Do you think they should have cared? Why or why not?
3. How did the writer become an authority on affirmative action? How does this designation underscore the paradox of his situation?
4. Why do you think Rodriguez received support from right-wing groups? Why are left-wing groups unlikely to embrace his position?
5. How do you explain Rodriguez's decision to question his status as a member of a minority group?
6. In what paragraphs does Rodriguez mention black students? How does he see himself differently from them? Do you agree with his point of view? Why or why not?

The Writer's Strategies

1. Where does the writer state his main point? What is it?
2. How does Rodriguez order the information in this selection?
3. Where does he use comparison and contrast to help make his point?
4. Give an example of irony in this essay—where the writer says one thing but means the opposite.

5. Does Rodriguez advance this essay more by facts or by opinions? Provide evidence to support your answer.
6. How does Rodriguez define *minority student?* Why is the definition of this phrase crucial to understanding this selection?
7. How would you characterize the tone of this essay—that is, what is the writer's attitude toward his subject?
8. What is the conclusion of this essay? Why is the conclusion so tentative?

Thinking Together

Imagine that your class has been appointed as a government commission with the responsibility of overhauling affirmative action guidelines for college admission and financial aid. In small groups, develop definitions of *minority, socially disadvantaged, underrepresented,* and *economically deprived.* How will you ensure that the funds and assistance you set aside reach the right people?

Vocabulary

The following words and phrases have become part of the American discourse on affirmative action and equal opportunity. Write a definition of each.

1. nonwhite (par. 1)
2. Hispanic-American (par. 2)
3. institutional racism (par. 5)
4. culturally alienated (par. 5)
5. *de facto* segregation (par. 6)
6. Latino (par. 7)
7. Chicano (par. 8)

WRITER'S WORKSHOP ──────────

Critical Thinking in Writing

1. In paragraph 3 Rodriguez points out his discomfort with the label *minority student,* even though it brought him many advantages. Write an essay to explain how you feel about a label used

to describe you or your group. What advantages are there for you in using the label? What are the disadvantages?

2. According to Richard T. Schaefer's "Minority, Racial, and Ethnic Groups" (page 187), the designation "minority" is imposed on people by others. If that is so, does Rodriguez's discomfort with his status matter? Does the fact that he feels he has benefited unfairly from affirmative action mean that affirmative action is not working? Should educated, middle-class minority people like Richard Rodriguez receive the same benefits of affirmative action as socially disadvantaged minority people? Why or why not? Address these concerns in a brief essay.

3. Write your own essay definition of the term *minority student*.

Connecting Ideas

Read Stephen Carter's "I Am an Affirmative Action Baby" (page 132). In what ways do Carter's concerns parallel Rodriguez's? How do the two writers' conclusions differ? Why have they arrived at different views of affirmative action? Which writer has your support in this debate? Why?

SIDE BY SIDE

1. Drawing on the selections in this unit, write an essay in which you argue whether America should be a monocultural or a pluralistic society. What are the advantages and disadvantages of each position? What do Americans stand to gain or lose?

2. Revisit the issue of the *self*, which you considered in your pre-reading journal. Drawing on your journal entry, the essays in this chapter, and your conversations about them, write a paper in which you define the *self* and the special role that ethnic identity plays in that definition.

3. If the United States is to remain divided by race, ethnic culture, and class, what can be done to ensure that American society will be just? How can every individual be guaranteed equal opportunities for education and success, equal protection under the law, and equal access to the benefits of citizenship? Write a well-detailed proposal for maintaining a fair America, including provisions for enforcing this protection.

THREE

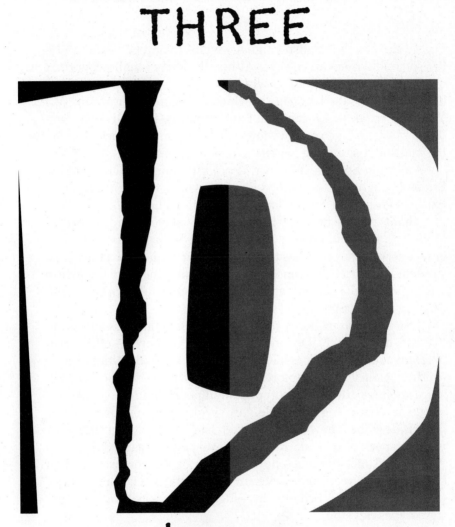

Language:
Our Words, Our Voices

INTRODUCTION

On the surface, the English language seems to be a powerful unifying force in American culture. Although only a small proportion of immigrants spoke English when they first came to this country, today English is the language in which Russian Americans in New York can speak to Chicanos in San Francisco. English is the predominant language of television, music and motion pictures, and the malls and shopping centers across the nation.

American English, however, is not the same language that the British brought to this country in the seventeenth century. James Baldwin points out in "If Black English Isn't a Language . . . What Is?" that Africans brought to America as slaves adapted British English to their own needs, creating what he argues is a separate language, one that enriches the way all Americans talk. Janice Castro details the rich influence of Spanish on American English in many parts of the country and considers the blend of Spanish and English, called "Spanglish."

This unit also explores several questions of language itself. In "What's in a Name?" Deborah P. Work reports on the effects that parental naming practices have on the individual identities of their children. Nancy Mairs explores the power of self-definition to challenge and break down stereotypes about people with physical disabilities in "On Being a Cripple." In "Women's Language," Robin Lakoff describes how English exercises control over the way women speak and relate to their world. Ellen Tashie Frisina, in "See Spot Run," discusses how the lives of women are enriched by learning to read and write. In "Minority, Racial, and Ethnic Groups," Richard T. Schaefer investigates how racial concepts and stereotypes develop.

Language is both the tie that binds us to a range of people across the nation and around the world and a key to our individual cultures and personalities. The essays in this section examine these often contradictory elements.

PREREADING JOURNAL

1. Make a list of words or phrases used in your home that come from your heritage. They can be words from another language, slang expressions, or even regional words, like *submarine, hoagie,* or *hero,* which all mean the same thing—a large sandwich made on a long roll that is split lengthwise.

2. Words are the building blocks of thoughts. Do you feel that the more words you know, the more things you can think about? Do the words you use to describe the world around you and to think about yourself help to shape how you see the world and how you feel about yourself? Write a journal entry in which you consider these questions.

3. "Sticks and stones may break my bones, but names can never hurt me." Is this old schoolyard saying true? Can the names that people call you do any harm to the way you feel about yourself or shape the kind of person you become? Write a journal entry about names you have been given—nicknames, diminutives (shortened forms, such as Mike for Michael or Sam for Samantha), pet names, and hurtful names that people directed at you because of your physical appearance, habits or personality traits, religion, or race. How did these various types of names make you feel?

Spanglish

Janice Castro, with Dan Cook and Cristina Garcia

Janice Castro and her co-authors are staff writers for Time *magazine. In this piece, they describe the growing influence of Spanish on American English.*

KEY WORDS

linguistic (par. 2)   having to do with the study of language
syntax (par. 3)   the arrangement of words into meaningful sentences
implicit (par. 5)   understood though not openly expressed
hybrids (par. 6)   mixed products of two distinct things
gaffes (par. 10)   embarrassing mistakes
mangled (par. 10)   butchered or deformed

IN MANHATTAN A FIRST-GRADER greets her visiting grandparents, happily exclaiming, "Come here, *siéntate!*" Her bemused grandfather, who does not speak Spanish, nevertheless knows she is asking him to sit down. A Miami personnel officer understands what a job applicant means when he says, "*Quiero un* part time." Nor do drivers miss a beat reading a billboard alongside a Los Angeles street advertising CERVEZA—SIX-PACK!

2   This free-form blend of Spanish and English, known as Spanglish, is common linguistic currency wherever concentrations of Hispanic Americans are found in the United States In Los Angeles, where 55 percent of the city's 3 million inhabitants speak Spanish, Spanglish is as much a part of daily life as sunglasses. Unlike the broken-English efforts of earlier immigrants from Europe, Asia, and other regions, Spanglish has become a widely accepted conversational mode used casually—even playfully—by Spanish-speaking immigrants and native-born Americans alike.

3   Consisting of one part Hispanicized English, one part Americanized Spanish, and more than a little fractured syntax, Spanglish is a bit like a Robin Williams comedy routine: a crackling line of cross-cultural patter straight from the melting pot. Often it enters Anglo homes and families through the children, who pick it up at school or at play with their young Hispanic contemporaries. In other cases, it comes from watching TV; many an Anglo child watching *Sesame Street* has learned *uno dos tres* almost as quickly as one two three.

4   Spanglish takes a variety of forms, from the Southern California Anglos who bid farewell with the utterly silly *"hasta la bye-bye"* to the Cuban-American drivers in Miami who *parquean* their *carros.* Some Spanglish sentences are mostly Spanish, with a quick detour for an English word or two. A Latino friend may cut short a conversation by glancing at his watch and excusing himself with the explanation that he must *"ir al* supermarket.*"*

5   Many of the English words transplanted in this way are simply handier than their Spanish counterparts. No matter how distasteful the subject, for example, it is still easier to say "income tax" than *impuesto sobre la renta.* At the same time, many Spanish-speaking immigrants have adopted such terms as *VCR, microwave,* and *dishwasher* for what they view as largely American phenomena. Still other English words convey a cultural context that is not implicit in the Spanish. A friend who invites you to *lonche* most likely has in mind the brisk American custom of "doing lunch" rather than the languorous afternoon break traditionally implied by *almuerzo.*

6   Mainstream Americans exposed to similar hybrids of German, Chinese, or Hindi might be mystified. But even Anglos who speak little or no Spanish are somewhat familiar with Spanglish. Living among them, for one thing, are 19 million Hispanics. In addition, more American high school and university students sign up for Spanish than for any other foreign language.

7   Only in the past ten years, though, has Spanglish begun to turn into a national slang. Its popularity has grown with the explosive increases in U.S. immigration from Latin American countries. English has increasingly collided with Spanish in retail stores, in offices and classrooms, in pop music, and on street corners. Anglos whose ancestors picked up such Spanish words as *rancho, bronco, tornado,* and *incommunicado,* for instance, now freely use such Spanish words as *gracias, bueno, amigo,* and *por favor.*

8   Among Latinos, Spanglish conversations often flow easily from Spanish into several sentences of English and back.

9   Spanglish is a sort of code for Latinos: the speakers know Spanish, but their hybrid language reflects the American culture in which they live. Many lean to shorter, clipped phrases in place of the longer, more graceful expressions their parents used. Says Leonel de la Cuesta, an assistant professor of modern languages at Florida International University in Miami: "In the United States, time is money, and that is showing up in Spanglish as an economy of language." Conversational examples: *taipiar* (type) and *winshi-wiper* (windshield wiper) replace *escribir a máquina* and *limpiaparabrisas*.

10   Major advertisers, eager to tap the estimated $134 billion in spending power wielded by Spanish-speaking Americans, have ventured into Spanglish to promote their products. In some cases, attempts to sprinkle Spanish through commercials have produced embarrassing gaffes. A Braniff airlines ad that sought to tell Spanish-speaking audiences they could settle back *en* (in) luxuriant *cuero* (leather) seats, for example, inadvertently said they could fly without clothes *(encuero)*. A fractured translation of the Miller Lite slogan told readers the beer was "Filling, and less delicious." Similar blunders are often made by Anglos trying to impress Spanish-speaking pals. But if Latinos are amused by mangled Spanglish, they also recognize these goofs as a sort of friendly acceptance. As they might put it, *no problema*.

EXERCISES

Details and Their Meanings

1. How many Hispanics are living in the United States? What American cities are centers of Hispanic culture?
2. What kinds of words do Spanish-speaking Americans borrow from English? How does Spanglish function as a kind of code? What other languages have contributed hybrids?
3. What kinds of words do English-speaking Americans borrow from Spanish?
4. Why do advertisers use Spanish to sell products? How does this strategy sometimes backfire?
5. How does Spanglish enter English-speaking households?

Reading and Critical Thinking

1. Why do you think the phenomenon of Spanglish is only about ten years old? What is a fair prediction to make about the future use of Spanglish? Do you use Spanglish? When? Where?
2. Why is the use of Spanglish mostly an urban phenomenon?
3. Is the sentence "In the United States time is money" an example of a fact or an opinion? How can you tell?
4. Why do you think English adopted Spanish words such as *bronco* and *tornado?*
5. What do the writers imply is the reason Spanish-speakers adopt English words and phrases? What is the reason English-speakers will adopt Spanish words and phrases? Do such adoptions weaken or enrich the language in your opinion?
6. Why might speakers of other hybrid forms of English be mystified by Spanglish?

The Writer's Strategies

1. Where do the writers state the main point? What is it?
2. What is the writers' purpose in writing this piece? Who is their audience?
3. In which paragraphs do the writers support their points with examples? Where do the writers make use of definition?
4. What ordering technique is used?
5. Where do the writers state the conclusion? What is it?

Thinking Together

The English language began as a hybrid of Germanic, Celtic, and French languages; Spanish began as a form of Latin. In groups of three to five, discuss whether you believe American English will someday become a hybrid form as it absorbs more and more Spanish or will remain essentially unchanged as Spanish-speaking Americans assimilate into the mainstream culture. What factors, such as the media and education, will promote or stand in the way of developing a new hybrid?

Vocabulary

The following Spanish expressions are defined in the text. Look each item up in the essay, and write a definition of it.

1. *uno dos tres* (par. 3)
2. *impuesto sobre la renta* (par. 5)
3. *almuerzo* (par. 5)
4. *escribir a máquina* (par. 9)
5. *limpiaparabrisas* (par. 9)
6. *en cuero* (par. 10)
7. *encuero* (par. 10)

WRITER'S WORKSHOP ————————————————

Critical Thinking in Writing

1. Despite vast influences on English by other languages, most Americans do not know another language well enough to speak or write it. Why is this so? Why, unlike European and Canadian children, for example, don't American schoolchildren learn well a language other than their own?
2. Look up the words *chocolate, algebra, zero, potato, television, dessert, camel, diesel, tycoon, macho, hurricane,* and *banjo* in an etymological dictionary. Where do these words come from? Write a short essay about what you think English would be like if it were not influenced by other languages.
3. Consider the influences (other than language) that Spanish culture has had on American culture—and vice versa. Write an essay providing examples of these influences and explaining whether you think they are positive or negative.

Connecting Ideas

Read James Baldwin's "If Black English Isn't a Language . . . What Is?" (page 208). Apply to Spanglish Baldwin's discussion of the reasons new dialects emerge and eventually become languages. In what sense is the use of Spanglish protective?

What's in a Name? Character, Identity, Ethnicity

Deborah P. Work

Deborah P. Work, a writer in Fort Lauderdale, Florida, reports on recent trends in naming children and what these trends tell us about contemporary values.

KEY WORDS

beckoned (par. 2)   signaled
genealogist (par. 11)   a person who traces the history of families
descent (par. 11)   ancestry, lineage
maternal grandfather (par. 11)   mother's father
Mosque (par. 36)   a building for Islamic public worship
assimilation (par. 58)   absorption into the dominant cultural tradition

LAFRANCES TROTTER WAS TALKING about how she came to name her daughter.

2   She always knew a child of hers would be given a name that was unique, a name no other child would answer to when the teacher called roll or when a friend beckoned on a crowded street.

3   In her mind's eye, she had an image of a child who would be culturally conscious and always aware of her heritage.

4   She turned to some friends from Nigeria, who helped name her baby daughter, Akija. Akija Kalembre.

5   "I've studied African literature, and have always wanted to

know more about the culture, the food, and the different celebrations. It seemed only natural that I would give my daughter an African name," says Trotter, who is African American.

6   But the name had to grow on her husband. "I don't like that," he said.

7   To help the name take root in his heart and mind, she left it around the house for him to see, spelled out in block letters on slips of paper.

8   It worked.

9   "I was determined she would have a connection to her African past," says Trotter, who lives in Sunrise, Florida. "It's like a present from her ancestors."

10   Names are important. A parent's gift, they establish identity and place, even if the name is too unusual to be found on a personalized dime-store mug.

11   Dee Cattaneo, a Palm Beach County genealogist, says today's parents have all but given up the traditional naming methods of the past. For example, many families of European descent named their eldest son after the husband's father. The next son took his maternal grandfather's name, with the same pattern used for girls. The children who followed were given names that belonged to other relatives, so the same names were recycled throughout families over and over.

12   "It would take ten children before a new name popped up," says Cattaneo, a genealogist with Palm Beach Gardens Church of Latter Day Saints.

13   But none of this is true today, she says. "The way parents name their babies has changed drastically over the years. I feel sorry for genealogists 100 years from now. They won't be able to figure anything out."

14   Unlike the sixties, which spawned a surge of children named for social and environmental causes, like Harmony and Peace, the trend today is toward names that reflect ethnic roots or economic status, like Maxwell, Winthrop, and, what else, Rich.

15   And while the Bible still remains a popular place for parents of all religions and nationalities to find a name, parents are also borrowing names from their favorite TV characters or simply making them up.

16   Daisy Camacho, who is Puerto Rican, named her son Hector, four, after his father. But her eight-year-old daughter, Christal, was named after the star of a Hispanic soap opera.

17   Camacho, of Coral Springs, Florida, says her mother-in-law didn't like the name at first because she was looking for something more traditionally Hispanic. But once she got hooked on the program, she came to love the name.

18   "Everyone is out for the unusual," Cattaneo says. "We are seeing more and more names that have no connection to family background or history."

19   In African-American communities, for example, parents are coming up with African-sounding names for their babies. Some are authentic, some are not.

20   The trend began during the Civil Rights and black power movements of the sixties, with black Americans choosing African or Islamic names, shunning the names given to slaves by European masters.

21   Today, black parents are going one step further: they are using their imaginations to coin new names.

22   This practice has been criticized for burdening children with awkward names that are difficult to pronounce, while others see it as positive.

23   Samida Jones, who works with teenage girls through a civic organization, has witnessed firsthand the movement toward non-European names.

24   For every Helen and Sandra, there is a Saqauela and a Verlisha. There is Zandra, Tamiya, Shenika, Zakia, Traveta, and Ashaunte. There is even a Lakrishaw.

25   "I said, boy, times sure have changed. Where are the Marys and Sues?" says Jones, whose own first name has Arabic roots. "Now it seems people just make them up."

26   It's not difficult to understand black parents trying to forge a new cultural identity for their children, Jones says. "The names have been called weird, but they are just weird to people who expect European names."

27   Still, made-up names lose something in the translation, she says. "Parents should consider a name's true meaning, instead of merely trying to be different."

28   Altan Erskin named her baby daughter Jamesha not because she was searching for an identity, her roots, or anything remotely resembling ethnicity.

29   She just likes the name's exotic sound.

30   "I knew I didn't want a plain name like Jane or Susan. And I wasn't trying for anything that sounded African, either," says Er-

skin, twenty-one. "I just wanted something special. So I made her name up."

31   She liked the sound *mesha,* so she started at the beginning of the alphabet: Amesha, Bamesha, Camesha.

32   "When I hit the letter J, I knew that was the one," Erskin says. "It just sounded right."

33   Neither did Joni Sabri have any reservations when she named her two sons. Since her husband Hassan Sabri is Palestinian, she gave her sons Muslim names.

34   "My husband gave me a book of Muslim names, complete with meanings. I liked that they are many generations old; they go way back," says Sabri, who lives with her family in Pompano Beach.

35   Her four-year-old is Ali, "a famous Islamic name, very simple," and the two-year-old is Khalid.

36   And Joni Sabri, raised Catholic but converted to Islam four years ago, is Fatima at home and at the Mosque.

37   Muslims are encouraged to give their children certain names, says Hassan Sabri, who has lived in this country for eight years.

38   For example, anything containing the verb *hamad,* which means 'to praise God,' is good.

39   "Mohammed is good for boys, and for girls Hamida is very popular," Hassan Sabri says.

40   One of a child's first rights is to be given a good name, Sabri says. "Islam is a full way of life, and part of that way is naming your child."

41   Genealogist Cattaneo agrees that your name is your birthright, and an important one because it follows you through life.

42   But the quest for the unforgettable name was not popular several generations back, she says. And naming was as much about family as it was about that time in history.

43   "Back then, you didn't want to appear different or ethnic. Immigrants wanted to blend in; you wanted to be a part of where you lived," Cattaneo says.

44   "My husband's parents came over from Italy. They named him Herbert, after Herbert Hoover. But they tucked in an Italian middle name—Mansuetto," she says. "Later on, they decided they didn't like (President) Hoover. So they call him Dick."

45   But today it's not as important to blend into the melting pot. People are looking for individuality. For example, libraries are being deluged with people looking for information to help

them prove they have Native-American ancestry, Cattaneo says.

46 "The number of people tracing a Native heritage has increased since the movie *Dances With Wolves*," she says.

47 Virginia Osceola, who is a Seminole Indian, named her new baby daughter Courtney. Her nine-year-old daughter Mercedes chose the name after hearing it in a local mall.

48 Osceola's other three youngsters are Tasha Kelly, Jo-Jo Dakota, and Joseph Daniel.

49 Those, however, are their Anglo names, the names they use to attend public school. But they also have Indian names.

50 What are they?

51 "They are only for Indians to know," Osceola says, taken aback that someone would ask. "They are not to be given out."

52 Seminoles are not the only people who present their children with two sets of names, one cultural.

53 In Franklin Tse's household, for example, his daughter Jennifer might answer to Tse Ying Wah, which connotes elegance and gratitude.

54 "At a Chinese gathering, I would use that name," Tse says. "Most parents, if they have hope and vision for their children, give them a name that will have impact. A dress you don't like you can throw away. But names always stick with you."

55 Many American Jews are turning back to traditional Hebrew names like Ari and Rebecca.

56 Rochelle Liederman says there is no trick to naming Jewish babies, that it's really quite basic.

57 "You want to name your first child after a deceased loved one," says Liederman.

58 Rochelle Liederman's experience illustrates how powerful a role assimilation plays in naming a child.

59 Is trying to fit in always the answer? Maybe not, she says.

60 Her husband Lee Liederman recalls being in a fistfight every day with public school kids who taunted those attending Hebrew school.

61 "It's difficult to retain your identity when there is prejudice. But it's a hurtful thing to lose your name, knowing most of your family was killed during World War II," he says. "You wonder about who you are, you try to find out."

62 "And that's why I love this movement to identify your roots. Everyone should push their children to name their offspring according to their ethnic background," says Rochelle Liederman.

"It's not to exclude others; it's because you are proud of yourself. And besides, if we don't, we will all get lost."

EXERCISES

Details and Their Meanings

1. What reasons do parents give for the names they choose for their children?
2. How do naming practices today differ from those of the 1960s? How does this selection account for these changes? What do the changes tell you about the significance of names and naming at different periods in history? What, if anything, do all of these naming practices have in common?
3. What naming practices are common in the African-American community today? When and why did this trend begin? Why do some people criticize this practice as others view it positively? How does the writer feel about it?
4. According to the writer, which groups of people give their children two sets of names? Why do they do this?
5. What similarities are there among the naming practices of different ethnic groups described in this article? what differences?

Reading and Critical Thinking

1. How do the changes in naming patterns described in this selection reflect changing attitudes toward diversity? From the information reported in this selection, what can you infer about the writer's attitude toward diversity?
2. In the title to this selection, Deborah P. Work answers the question, "What's in a name?" How does the selection elaborate on this answer? Do you agree with the answer that she gives? Why or why not?
3. According to the selection, what are the benefits and drawbacks of having an unusual name? Can you think of any other benefits or drawbacks not mentioned in the selection? Overall, do you think it is a good idea to give a child an unusual name? Why or why not?

4. How do the experiences of parents influence the names they give their children? Draw on specific examples from the essay as well as from your own experiences and observations to illustrate your response to this question.

The Writer's Strategies

1. What is the main point made by the writer in this selection? Is this point ever stated directly in a sentence? Is it stated in the title?
2. How many parents and how many children does the author interview in this article? What point is made by each of these interviews? How do the interviews help reinforce the main point of the article?
3. Which examples serve to support the main point? What do these examples have in common? What distinguishes them from each other? What is the effect of the number of examples that the writer uses?
4. What authorities does the writer cite in this selection? Do these authorities provide adequate support for the main point she is making? What is the relation in the article between information from parents and information from authorities?
5. Why does the writer end the essay with a quotation? How does the quotation contribute to the unity of the essay?

Thinking Together

In groups of four or five, discuss the naming patterns in your immediate families. How do you account for the differences and similarities within these practices? What roles do religious affiliation, ethnicity, parental values, and family history play in these practices? After you have discussed these factors, compare your findings with the rest of the class.

Vocabulary

The following groupings of adjectives refer to ethnicity, nationality, or religious affiliation. What do the terms in each grouping have in common? What distinguishes them from each other?

I
1. African (par. 5)
2. African American (par. 5)
3. black (par. 20)

II
4. European (par. 11)
5. Anglo (par. 49)

III
6. Puerto Rican (par. 16)
7. Hispanic (par. 16)

IV
8. Hebrew (par. 55)
9. Jewish (par. 56)

V
10. Native-American (par. 45)
11. Indian (par. 49)

VI
12. Muslim (par. 34)
13. Catholic (par. 36)
14. Islamic (par. 20)
15. Arabic (par. 25)

VII
16. Palestinian (par. 33)
17. Chinese (par. 54)

WRITER'S WORKSHOP

Critical Thinking in Writing

1. Write a short essay describing what you know about the origins and meaning of your own name. What effect, if any, has your name had on you?
2. Draw a "family tree" tracing your family history as far back

as you can. If necessary, call a family member to fill in details. Then write a two-page essay describing the naming practices and patterns that you discover.

3. Write a one-page journal entry answering one of the following questions: (a) Have you ever wanted to change your name? When? Why? (b) If you had to give yourself a new name, what would it be and why? (c) If you have changed your name, what did you change it to and why?

Connecting Ideas

Read the excerpt from *Roots* by Alex Haley (page 419). What role do names play in this selection? How does Haley's account of the search for his African heritage help you better understand the current naming practices of African Americans described by Deborah P. Work in this selection?

"See Spot Run"

Ellen Tashie Frisina

In this selection, Ellen Tashie Frisina recalls with affection how she as a fourteen year old helped her seventy-year-old grandmother learn to read.

KEY WORDS

differentiated (par. 1)   separated, distinguished
stealthily (par. 2)   secretly
authoritatively (par. 4)   commandingly, in an expert way
baklava (par. 13)   a dessert consisting of pastry, honey, and
 nuts

WHEN I WAS FOURTEEN years old, and very impressed with my teenage status (looking forward to all the rewards it would bring), I set for myself a very special goal—a goal that so differentiated me from my friends that I don't believe I told a single one. As a teenager, I was expected to have deep, dark secrets, but I was not supposed to keep them from my friends.

2   My secret was a project that I undertook every day after school for several months. It began when I stealthily made my way into the local elementary school—horror of horrors should I be seen; I was now in junior high. I identified myself as a *graduate* of the elementary school, and being taken under wing by a favorite fifth grade teacher, I was given a small bundle from a locked storeroom—a bundle that I quickly dropped into a bag, lest anyone see me walking home with something from the "little kids" school.

3   I brought the bundle home—proudly now, for within the confines of my home, I was proud of my project. I walked into the living room, and one by one, emptied the bag of basic reading

books. They were thin books with colorful covers and large print. The words were monosyllabic and repetitive. I sat down to the secret task at hand.

4   "All right," I said authoritatively to my seventy-year-old grandmother, "today we begin our first reading lesson."

5   For weeks afterward, my grandmother and I sat patiently side by side—roles reversed as she, with a bit of difficulty, sounded out every word, then read them again, piece by piece, until she understood the short sentences. When she slowly repeated the full sentence, we both would smile and clap our hands—I felt so proud, so grown up.

6   My grandmother was born in Kalamata, Greece, in a rocky little farming village where nothing much grew. She never had the time to go to school. As the oldest child, she was expected to take care of her brother and sister, as well as the house and meals, while her mother tended to the gardens, and her father scratched out what little he could from the soil.

7   So, for my grandmother, schooling was out. But she had big plans for herself. She had heard about America. About how rich you could be. How people on the streets would offer you a dollar just to smell the flower you were carrying. About how everyone lived in nice houses—not stone huts on the sides of mountains— and had nice clothes and time for school.

8   So my grandmother made a decision at fourteen—just a child, I realize now—to take a long and sickening thirty-day sea voyage alone to the United States. After lying about her age to the passport officials, who would shake their heads vehemently at anyone under sixteen leaving her family, and after giving her favorite gold earrings to her cousin, saying "In America, I will have all the gold I want," my young grandmother put herself on a ship. She landed in New York in 1916.

9   No need to repeat the story of how it went for years. The streets were not made of gold. People weren't interested in smelling flowers held by strangers. My grandmother was a foreigner. Alone. A young girl who worked hard doing piecework to earn enough money for meals. No leisure time, no new gold earrings—and no school.

10   She learned only enough English to help her in her daily business as she traveled about Brooklyn. Socially, the "foreigners" stayed in neighborhoods where they didn't feel like foreigners. English came slowly.

11   My grandmother had never learned to read. She could make out a menu, but not a newspaper. She could read a street sign, but not a shop directory. She could read only what she needed to read as, through the years, she married, had five daughters, and helped my grandfather with his restaurant.

12   So when I was fourteen—the same age that my grandmother was when she left her family, her country, and everything she knew—I took it upon myself to teach my grandmother something, something I already knew how to do. Something with which I could give back to her some of the things she had taught me.

13   And it was slight repayment for all she taught me. How to cover the fig tree in tar paper so it could survive the winter. How to cultivate rose bushes and magnolia trees that thrived on her little piece of property. How to make baklava, and other Greek delights, working from her memory. ("Now we add some milk." "How much?" "Until we have enough.") Best of all, she had taught me my ethnic heritage.

14   First, we phonetically sounded out the alphabet. Then, we talked about vowels—English is such a difficult language to learn. I hadn't even begun to explain the different sounds *gh* could make. We were still at the basics.

15   Every afternoon, we would sit in the living room, my grandmother with an afghan covering her knees, giving up her crocheting for her reading lesson. I, with the patience that can come only from love, slowly coached her from the basic reader to the second-grade reader, giving up my telephone gossiping.

16   Years later, my grandmother still hadn't learned quite enough to sit comfortably with a newspaper or magazine, but it felt awfully good to see her try. How we used to laugh at her pronunciation mistakes. She laughed more heartily than I. I never knew whether I should laugh. Here was this old woman slowly and carefully sounding out each word, moving her lips, not saying anything aloud until she was absolutely sure, and then, loudly, proudly, happily saying, "Look at Spot. See Spot run."

17   When my grandmother died and we faced the sad task of emptying her home, I was going through her night-table drawer and came upon the basic readers. I turned the pages slowly, remembering. I put them in a paper bag, and the next day returned them to the "little kids" school. Maybe someday, some teenager will

request them again, for the same task. It will make for a lifetime of memories.

————————

EXERCISES

Details and Their Meanings

1. How old is the narrator? How old was her grandmother when she came to the United States? Why is that information significant?
2. Where did the writer's grandmother come from? What kind of place was it? What did the grandmother believe about America? Where did she settle in the United States?
3. Where did the writer get the books to teach her grandmother? Whom did she say they were for?
4. What reading level did the grandmother achieve? How long did this accomplishment take? How successful was the narrator at teaching her grandmother?
5. What jobs did the grandmother have? Which one lasted longest?
6. What kinds of things did the narrator learn from her grandmother?

Reading and Critical Thinking

1. Why do you think the granddaughter and not one of the old woman's children tried to teach the old woman?
2. Why did the grandmother need to lie in order to be allowed into America? Was the lie justified, do you think? Why or why not? If she were coming here in the 1990s instead of 1916 would she still have had to lie? Explain your opinion.
3. What does the grandmother's decision to come to America reveal about her character?
4. What factors discouraged the grandmother from learning to read well? Why was the grandmother able to read a menu but not a newspaper?

5. What is a safe generalization to make about the grandmother's desire to learn to read?
6. What do you think was the granddaughter's motivation for teaching her grandmother to read? Are grandchildren today likely to assume the responsibility of teaching their grandparents? Why or why not?

The Writer's Strategies

1. What is the significance of the title of this piece?
2. What is the effect of the first-person narration (*I, me, my*)?
3. How does dialogue advance the narrative?
4. Why does the writer use narrative as the major organizing principle of the essay? Where do you find a narrative within the narrative? What is the effect of the writer's telling of her grandmother's life in Greece and travel to America?
5. What is the writer's main purpose? Where does the purpose become clear? What is the writer's thesis?

Thinking Together

Brainstorm to develop a list of the steps you would take if you were going to teach someone to read. What materials would you use? What homework or exercises would you assign?

Vocabulary

The following words from the selection are adverbs—that is, words that modify verbs, adjectives, or other adverbs to tell how something was done. Write a definition of each word.

1. stealthily (par. 2)
2. authoritatively (par. 4)
3. patiently (par. 5)
4. vehemently (par. 8)
5. phonetically (par. 14)
6. heartily (par. 16)

WRITER'S WORKSHOP ━━━━━━━━━━━━━

Critical Thinking in Writing

1. Obviously, coming to America alone was very hard for the grandmother. What was the hardest thing you ever decided to do? What made it difficult? How did the situation turn out? Write a narrative in which you indicate how you faced your most difficult challenge.
2. Have you ever taught someone how to do something? What was it? What was the experience of teaching like for you? What did you find agreeable about it? What was hard or frustrating? How good a job did you do? Address some of these questions in a short essay.
3. Learning to read was a profound challenge for the old woman in this selection. What other challenges face old people in America today? Write an essay in which you describe and analyze some of these challenges.

Connecting Ideas

Read "Five New Words at a Time," by Yu-Lan (Mary) Ying (page 379). Compare that account of language learning across generations of a family with the account given by Frisina. Although the two stories seem similar in many respects there are important differences. In each case, what problems motivate the language teaching and learning? Who teaches and who learns? What is the nature of the relationship between the generations in each? What are the moral and emotional lessons in each case?

Classrooms of Babel

Connie Leslie, with Daniel Glick and Jeanne Gordon

Connie Leslie and her co-authors describe how public education is meeting the challenge of increasing numbers of foreign-born and foreign-language-speaking children in almost all schools in the United States. Notice the different approaches that different communities take to the challenge.

KEY WORDS

Urdu (par. 1)   a major language of India and Pakistan
Tagalog (par. 6)   a major language of the Philippines

FOR PICTURE DAY AT New York's PS 127, a neighborhood elementary school in Brooklyn, the notice to parents was translated into five languages. That was a nice gesture, but insufficient: more than 40 percent of the children are immigrants whose families speak any one of twenty-six languages, ranging from Armenian to Urdu.

2   At the Leroy D. Feinberg Elementary School in Miami, a science teacher starts a lesson by holding up an ice cube and asking "Is it hot?" The point here is vocabulary. Only after the students who come from homes where English is not spoken learn the very basics will they move on to the question of just what an ice cube might be.

3   The first grade at Magnolia Elementary School in Lanham, Maryland, is a study in cooperation. A Korean boy who has been in the United States for almost a year quizzes two mainland Chinese girls who arrived ten days ago. Nearby, a Colombian named Julio is learning to read with the help of an American-born boy.

4   In small towns and big cities, children with names like Oswaldo, Suong, Boris, or Ngam are swelling the rolls in U.S. public schools, sitting side by side with Dick and Jane. Immigration in the 1980s brought an estimated 9 million foreign-born people to the

United States, slightly more than the great wave of 8.8 million immigrants that came between 1901 and 1910. As a consequence, at least 2 million children or 5 percent of the total kindergarten-through-12th-grade population have limited proficiency in English, according to a conservative estimate from the U.S. Department of Education. In seven states including Colorado, New Mexico, New York, and Texas, 25 percent or more of the students are not native-English speakers. And all but a handful of states have at least 1,000 foreign-born youngsters. As a result, says Eugene Garcia of the University of California, Santa Cruz, "there is no education topic of greater importance today."

5   How to teach in a Tower of Babel? Since a 1974 Supreme Court decision, immigrant children have had the right to special help in public schools. But how much? And what kind? Many districts have responded by expanding the bilingual-education programs they've been using for the past two decades. In these classes, students are taught subjects like social studies, science, and math in their native language on the theory that children must develop a firm foundation in their mother tongue before they can learn academic subjects in a new language. Proponents say that even with bilingual education it takes between four and seven years for a nonnative to reach national norms on standardized tests of most subject material.

6   In most schools, it's not economically feasible to hire bilingual teachers unless there are 20 or more students who speak the same language in the same grade. Even then, there aren't many math, chemistry, or biology teachers who can handle Vietnamese or Tagalog. In addition, critics like author and former Newton, Massachusetts, teacher Rosalie Pedalino Porter argue that the typical bilingual programs for Spanish speakers used over the last two decades haven't worked. The clearest indication of the failure, she charges, is the high dropout rate for Hispanic children—35.8 percent compared with 14.9 percent for blacks and 12.7 percent for whites.

7   Bilingual classes aren't an option in a classroom where a dozen languages are spoken. In schools such as Elsik High in Houston and New York's PS 217, all immigrant children are mixed in ESL (English as a second language) classes on their grade level. ESL teachers give all instruction in English; their special training helps them work with kids who start out not knowing a single word. Some students remain in ESL classes for three or four years. Others move into regular classes but return to an ESL room for remedial periods.

8   Still other schools such as Houston's Hearne Elementary School use the "total immersion" method. With 104 of Hearne's 970 students speaking one of 23 languages, principal Judith Miller has encouraged all of her teachers to take ESL training so that immigrant youngsters can remain in classes with their native-English-speaking peers. "The limited-English children are able to interact with their peers better and learn social skills. They also seem much happier," says Miller. Opponents see total immersion as a euphemism for "the good old days" when non-English-speaking students sank or swam in mainstream America without special treatment.

9   **Nurturing Atmosphere**   Some schools have found that immigrant parents can be a great resource, either as volunteers or hired aides. When members of New York's PS 127 Parents Association noticed that non-English-speaking families rarely made any connection with the school, they won a $10,000 grant and hired five mothers of immigrant students as outreach workers. One day each week, these women, who speak Urdu, Chinese, Russian, Haitian-Creole, or Spanish, do everything from acting as interpreters at parent-teacher conferences to helping families find city services.

10   California is experimenting with "newcomer" schools that act as a one-year stopover for foreign-born children before they move on to a neighborhood school. These centers mix children of all ages in a given classroom and offer comprehensive services such as immunizations and other health care. Bellagio Road Newcomer School for grades four through eight is one of two such schools in Los Angeles. While most classrooms are Spanish bilingual, other students are taught in English. Teaching assistants who speak a variety of languages help out with translating. Principal Juliette Thompson says the aim is to provide a nurturing atmosphere for a year while the children, many of whom carry psychological scars from living in war-torn countries like El Salvador, learn some fundamentals of English. The newcomer schools seem to be working well, but they don't reach many kids. "Unfortunately," says Laurie Olsen, a project director for an advocacy group, California Tomorrow, "the real norm is far less optimistic than what you see happening in the newcomer schools."

11   A method borrowed from Canada recognizes that the problem is not one-sided. Called "two-way immersion," the program requires students to learn subject matter in both languages. Classes in the voluntary enrichment program encourage mixed groups of

native speakers and English speakers to acquire new vocabulary.
Public schools like PS 84 in Manhattan also use two-way immersion to attract upper-middle-class parents. Lawyer Holly Hartstone
and her husband, a doctor, enrolled their nine-year-old son Adam
in PS 84, where nine of the school's twenty-five classes are involved
in voluntary Spanish two-way immersion. When Adam grows up,
his parents expect that he'll live in a global community and need
more than one language. These programs are catching on around
the country. Two-way immersion in Japanese, which began three
years ago in a Eugene, Oregon, elementary school has spread to
Portland, Anchorage, and Detroit. And the French program at Sun-
set Elementary School in Coral Gables, Florida, recently received
a grant from the French government.

12   **Young Yankees**   Being a stranger in a strange land is never
easy. "All the English-speaking kids should learn a foreign language. Then they'd know how hard it is for us sometimes," says
seventeen-year-old Sufyan Kabba, a Maryland high-school junior, who left Sierra Leone last year. But here they are, part of the
nation's future, young Yankees who in the end must rely on the
special strength of children: adaptability.

EXERCISES

Details and Their Meanings

1. Into how many languages was the notice from PS 127 translated? Why wasn't that enough? In the first three paragraphs,
   what languages are mentioned or alluded to? In paragraph 4,
   what children's names are mentioned? What continents or
   parts of the world are represented by these languages and
   names? What do these languages and places suggest about the
   backgrounds of students in American classrooms who do not
   speak English?
2. How many immigrants came to the United States during the
   1980s? What statistics indicate their impact on education? In
   how many states are more than one-fourth of the students not

native speakers of English? Are you surprised by any of the states listed? Why or why not?

3. What obligation do the public schools have to immigrant children?

4. Describe the bilingual approach to education. How does it work? How rapidly does it work for most children? How widely is it used? What are the obstacles to providing bilingual education for all students?

5. How does ESL instruction differ from bilingual education? How does the total immersion method differ from both? What are the arguments for and against total immersion?

6. How have schools and programs used immigrant parents to help? How does the use of parents suggest that the problems faced by the schools involve more than simply teaching English vocabulary and grammar?

7. What are newcomer schools? What services do they provide? What is the idea behind them? Are they succeeding? Are they widespread?

8. What is two-way immersion? What is the concept behind it? In what kinds of neighborhoods has it been used? Is it spreading to other districts?

Reading and Critical Thinking

1. How do bilingualism, ESL, and immersion differ in concept and practice? Which do you think is the best general approach? Why?

2. To what extent does each of the various programs described seem to respond to special sets of conditions or to the general problem of students whose first language is not English? Which program seems to provide the most help? Which seems most appropriate for the conditions it is addressing?

3. Why is immersion compared to "the good old days"? Do you think those days were really good? What is wrong or right with letting students sink or swim? Do you think immersion really is the same as "the good old days"? How is the idea expressed in paragraph 12, relying on children's adaptability, the same as or different from the strategy of letting them sink or swim?

4. Do you think two-way immersion is a good idea? Has it been succeeding? What goals has it served for which children? For those who are not English-speakers, does it offer the same

advantages and disadvantages as total immersion or does it work differently? Would you like to have been a participant in such a program? How does two-way immersion compare to newcomer schools in terms of goals, the children served, and the neighborhoods served? Why do you think two-way immersion is spreading and newcomer schools are not?

5. Do you think special services should be provided to immigrant children? What services (if any) would you support?

6. The United States has always been considered a land of opportunity for immigrants. In recent years, what has changed to cast a shadow on this view of America? Do you agree that a record number of immigrant children poses one of the greatest problems for American education? Why or why not?

7. Why do you think Sufyan Kabba says in paragraph 12 that English-speaking children should have to learn a foreign language? Do you agree? Why or why not?

8. Where does the final statement of the essay place responsibility for children's success in American schools? Do you agree with the point made there? Does the last sentence undermine all that has gone before? Does it free the educational system of responsibility? Or is it an accurate statement, in your view? Where do you believe the responsibility for learning should lie? How should that responsibility be divided among the system, the children, and the parents?

The Writer's Strategies

1. With what incident does the selection open? In what ways is that incident striking or memorable? How does the incident serve to introduce the issues raised in the piece? What would you say is the writers' thesis?

2. What is the main idea of the first four paragraphs? Where is it stated most directly? How does the opening sentence of paragraph 5 change the focus of the essay? How many questions are asked in paragraph 5?

3. To what extent and in what way are the questions posed in paragraph 5 answered in the rest of the selection? Are the writers concerned more with presenting the problem or with providing definite answers? What phrases or statements indicate their attitude toward providing definite answers?

4. Where do the writers provide lists of foreign names and foreign

languages? How do these lists illustrate the ideas of the essay? How are they related to its title?

5. Where, other than in the title, is Babel mentioned? What is the Tower of Babel? Why have the writers used this image? Is it fair or appropriate to use the Tower of Babel as a major image for this piece?

6. How many school programs are described? Why do the writers show so many?

7. Why does the closing paragraph turn from discussing programs to considering the attitudes of individual students? Should the writers have used this strategy earlier and more completely, or should they not have used it at all? How does the ending shift the point of the entire piece?

Thinking Together

In small groups, share your memories of classmates who did not speak English well. How did they succeed at their schoolwork? What kinds of difficulties did they seem to have? Try to put yourself in the shoes of these children. If you yourself are not a native speaker of English, describe your own memories and feelings. After group discussion, each group member should write a paragraph that describes an immigrant child's struggles and ends by saying what the school did or could have done to ease the movement of the child into the educational mainstream.

Vocabulary

Define each of the italicized words, using hints from the context in which the word appears.

1. a nice gesture, but *insufficient* (par. 1)
2. limited *proficiency* in English (par. 4)
3. *Proponents* say that even with *bilingual* education (par. 5)
4. Opponents see total *immersion* as a *euphemism* for "the good old days" (par. 8)
5. hired five mothers of immigrant students as *outreach* workers (par. 9)
6. offer *comprehensive* services such as *immunizations* (par. 10)
7. provide a *nurturing* atmosphere for a year (par. 10)
8. project director for an *advocacy* group (par. 10)

WRITER'S WORKSHOP ━━━━━━━━━

Critical Thinking in Writing

1. Write a paragraph describing what you think would be the best way to bring a student who is not a native speaker of English into the U.S. education system.
2. In a one-page essay, explain why you believe bilingual education, total immersion, or ESL instruction is the best general approach to educating immigrant children.
3. In one paragraph, describe the diversity of nationalities and language experiences of children in a school that you or someone you know attended.

Connecting Ideas

Read "Boys Only: Separate but Equal?" by Janny Scott (page 46). How do the problems of the students described there compare to the problems described in "Classrooms of Babel"? In what way are the solutions described similar and different? What do the two selections reveal about the benefits and difficulties of separating students to deal with their particular learning needs?

Minority, Racial, and Ethnic Groups

Richard T. Schaefer

Richard T. Schaefer, dean of the College of Arts and Sciences and professor of sociology at Western Illinois University, provides socio- logical definitions of minority, race, ethnicity, *and other terms.*

KEY WORDS

intermingling (par. 9)   blending together

buffoons (par. 12)   fools

deviant (par. 13)   abnormal, not in keeping with community standards

innate (par. 16)   possessed at birth

categorization (par. 20)   assignment of a place in some order

stratification (par. 20)   arrangement according to status from highest to lowest

─────────

SOCIOLOGISTS FREQUENTLY DISTINGUISH BETWEEN racial and ethnic groups. The term *racial group* is used to describe a group which is set apart from others because of obvious physical differences. Whites, blacks, and Asian Americans are all considered racial groups within the United States. Unlike racial groups, an *ethnic group* is set apart from others primarily because of its national ori- gin or distinctive cultural patterns. In the United States, Puerto Ri- cans, Jews, and Polish Americans are all categorized as ethnic groups.

Minority Groups

2   A numerical minority is a group that makes up less than half of some larger population. The population of the United States includes thousands of numerical minorities, including television actors, green-eyed people, tax lawyers, and descendants of the Pilgrims who arrived on the *Mayflower*. However, these numerical minorities are not considered to be minorities in the sociological sense; in fact, the number of people in a group does not necessarily determine its status as a social minority (or dominant group). When sociologists define a minority group, they are primarily concerned with the economic and political power, or powerlessness, of that group. A *minority group* is a subordinate group whose members have significantly less control or power over their own lives than the members of a dominant or majority group have over theirs.

3   In certain instances, a group that constitutes a numerical majority can still be a minority group in sociological terms. For example, the city of Gary, Indiana, has a majority black population (71 percent in 1980) and has had black mayors since 1968. Yet it would be incorrect to conclude that this industrial city is genuinely controlled by its black majority. Lawyer Edward Greer (1979) has convincingly shown that Gary remains ruled by outside, white-dominated organizations such as U.S. Steel, financial institutions, and chain stores. Thus, in terms of their degree of power, Gary's black citizens continue to function as a minority group.

4   Sociologists have identified five basic properties of a minority group—physical or cultural traits, unequal treatment, ascribed status, solidarity, and in-group marriage (M. Harris, 1958: 4–11):

1. Members of a minority group share physical or cultural characteristics that distinguish them from the dominant group. Each society has its own arbitrary standard for determining which characteristics are most important in defining dominant and minority groups.
2. Members of a minority experience unequal treatment and have less power over their lives than members of a dominant group have over theirs. For example, the management of an apartment complex may refuse to rent to blacks, Hispanics, or Jews. Social inequality may be created or maintained by prejudice, discrimination, segregation, or even extermination.
3. Membership in a dominant (or minority) group is not volun-

tary; people are born into the group. Thus, race and ethnicity are considered *ascribed* statuses.

4. Minority group members have a strong sense of group solidarity. William Graham Sumner, writing in 1906, noted that individuals make distinctions between members of their own group (the *in-group*) and everyone else (the *out-group*). When a group is the object of long-term prejudice and discrimination, the feeling of "us versus them" can and often does become extremely intense.

5. Members of a minority generally marry others from the same group. A member of a dominant group is often unwilling to join a supposedly inferior minority by marrying one of its members. In addition, the minority group's sense of solidarity encourages marriages within the group and discourages marriages to outsiders.

Race

5 As already suggested, the term *racial group* is reserved for those minorities (and the corresponding dominant groups) set apart from others by obvious physical differences. But what is an "obvious" physical difference? Each society determines which differences are important while ignoring other characteristics that could serve as a basis for social differentiation. In the United States, differences in both skin color and hair color are generally quite obvious. Yet Americans learn informally that differences in skin color have a dramatic social and political meaning, while differences in hair color are not nearly so socially significant.

6   When observing skin color, Americans tend to lump people rather casually into such general racial categories as "black," "white," and "Asian." More subtle differences in skin complexion often go unnoticed. However, this is not the case in other societies. In Brazil, numerous categories are used to classify and identify people on the basis of skin color. An individual can be called *branco, cabra, moreno, mulato, escuro,* and so forth (van den Berghe, 1978:71). As a result, Americans must recognize that what we see as "obvious" differences are subject to each society's social definitions.

7   The largest racial minorities in the United States are blacks, American Indians, Japanese Americans, Chinese Americans, and other Asian peoples. Information about the population and distribution of racial groups in this country is presented in Table 1.

TABLE 1   Racial and Ethnic Groups in the United States, 1980

Classification	Number in Thousands	Percent of Total Population	Geographical Distribution, %
Racial groups			
Native whites	155,844	76.7	
Blacks	26,488	11.7	South, 53
American Indians	1,418	0.6	West, 49
Chinese	806	0.4	California, 40
Filipinos	775	0.3	California, 46; Hawaii, 31
Japanese	701	0.3	California, 37; Hawaii, 34
Asian Indians	362	0.2	New York, 17; California, 16
Koreans	355	0.2	California, 29
Vietnamese	262	0.1	California, 34; Texas, 11
Hawaiians	167	0.1	Hawaii, 69
Samoans/Guamanians	74	0.01	California, 51
Ethnic groups			
White ancestry			
Germans	17,160	7.9	
British and Scottish	13,116	6.1	
Irish	9,760	4.5	
Italians	6,110	2.8	
Poles	3,498	1.6	
French	3,047	1.4	
Jews	5,925	2.6	
Hispanics	13,244	5.8	
Mexican Americans	7,932	3.5	
Puerto Ricans	1,823	0.8	
Cubans	831	0.4	
Total (all groups)	226,505		

NOTE: Percentages do not total 100 percent, and subheads do not add up to figures in major heads, since overlap between groups exists (e.g., Polish American Jews). Therefore, numbers and percentages should be considered approximations. Data on white ancestry are for 1979.
SOURCES: Bureau of the Census, 1981a, 1981b: 55–56, 1981c: 32; Himmelfarb and Singer, 1981.
Racial and ethnic groups vary in number and distribution. Some groups, such as Japanese Americans, are highly concentrated in particular regions of the United States.

8   **Biological Significance of Race**   Biologically, race has a very precise meaning. A *race* is a category of people who, through many generations of inbreeding, have developed common physical characteristics that distinguish them from other humans. Contrary to popular belief, there are no "pure races." Nor are there physical traits—whether skin color or baldness—that can be used to describe one group to the exclusion of all others. If scientists examine a smear of human blood under a microscope, they cannot tell whether it came from a Chinese or a Navajo, a Hawaiian or a black.

9   Migration, exploration, and invasion have further compromised the maintenance of pure races and led to increased racial intermingling. Scientific investigations suggest that the proportion of North American blacks with white ancestry ranges from 20 percent to as much as 75 percent (Herskovits, 1930:15; D. Roberts, 1975). Such statistics undermine a fundamental assumption of American life: that we can accurately categorize individuals as "white" or as "black."

10   Some people wish to find biological explanations that would help us to understand why certain peoples of the world have come to dominate others. Given the absence of pure racial groups, there can be no satisfactory biological answers for such social and political questions.

11   **Social Significance of Race**   One of the most crucial aspects of the relationship between dominant and subordinate groups is the ability of the dominant or majority group to define a society's values. American sociologist William I. Thomas (1923: 41–44), an early critic of theories of racial and gender differences, saw that the "definition of the situation" could mold the personality of the individual. To put it another way, Thomas, writing from the interactionist perspective, observed that people respond not only to the objective features of a situation or person but also to the meaning that situation or person has for them. Thus we can create false images or stereotypes that become real in their consequences. *Stereotypes* are unreliable generalizations about all members of a group that do not recognize individual differences within the group.

12   In the last 20 years, there has been growing awareness of the power of the mass media to introduce stereotypes into everyday life. As one result, stereotyping of racial and ethnic minorities in Hollywood films and on television has come under increasing fire. For example, Asian-American community groups in several American cities led picketing and boycotts of a 1985 film, *Year of the Dragon*, which portrayed Chinese Americans as violent killers and dope peddlers (Butterfield, 1985; Fong-Torres, 1986; Hwang, 1985). Hispanics recall that Hollywood has traditionally presented them as vicious bandits, lazy peasants, or humorous buffoons (Beale, 1984; Lichter et al., 1987). Similarly, Jack Shaheen (1984:52, 1988) is critical of prime-time television for perpetuating four myths about Arabs: "They are fabulously wealthy; they are barbaric and uncultured; they are sex maniacs with a penchant for white slavery; and they are prone to terrorist acts." While the use of stereotyping can

promote in-group solidarity, conflict theorists point out that stereotypes contribute to prejudice and thereby assist the subordination
of minority groups (Schaefer, 1988:65–68).

13   In certain situations, we may respond to stereotypes and act
on them, with the result that false definitions become accurate. This
is known as the *self-fulfilling prophecy*. A person or group is described as having particular characteristics and then begins to display the very traits that were said to exist. In assessing the impact
of self-fulfilling prophecies, we can refer back to labeling theory,
which emphasizes how a person comes to be labeled as deviant
and even to accept a self-image of deviance.

14   Self-fulfilling prophecies can be especially devastating for minority groups (see Figure 1). Such groups often find that they are
allowed to hold only low-paying jobs with little prestige or opportunity for advancement. The rationale of the dominant society is
that these members of a minority lack the ability to perform in more
important and lucrative positions. Minority group members are
then denied the training needed to become scientists, executives,
or physicians and are locked into society's inferior jobs. As a result,
the false definition has become real: in terms of employment, the
minority has become inferior because it was originally defined as
inferior and was prevented from achieving equality.

15   Because of this vicious circle, talented people from minority
groups may come to see the worlds of entertainment and professional sports as their only hope for achieving wealth and fame.
Thus, it is no accident that successive waves of Irish, Jewish, Italian,
black, and Hispanic performers and athletes have made their mark
on American society. Unfortunately, these very successes may convince the dominant group that its original stereotypes are valid—
that these are the only areas of society in which minorities can excel. Furthermore, athletics and the arts are well known in our society as highly competitive arenas. For every Fernando Valenzuela,
Bill Cosby, or Oprah Winfrey who "makes it," many, many more
will end up disappointed (Allport, 1979:189–205; Merton, 1968:
475–490; Myrdal, 1944:75–78, 1065–1970; M. Snyder, 1982).

16   Sociologist Harry Edwards (1984:8–13)—appointed in 1987 by
baseball commissioner Peter Ueberroth to assist in the hiring of
more minorities for high-level jobs—agrees that the self-fulfilling
prophecy of "innate black athletic superiority" can have damaging
consequences. Edwards points out that although this perception of
athletic prowess may cause many black Americans to be channeled
into sports, at best, only about 2,500 of them currently make a living

Self–Fulfilling Prophecy

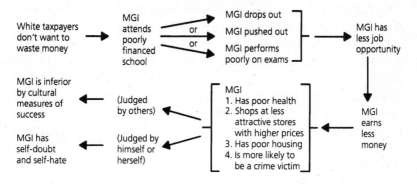

NOTE: *MGI stands for "minority group individual." Arrows represent direction of negative cumulative effect.*
SOURCE: *Schaefer, 1988: 25; see also Daniels and Kitano, 1970:21.*

FIGURE 1 *The self-validating effects of definitions made by the dominant group are shown in this figure. A minority-group person attends a poorly financed school and is left unequipped to perform jobs that offer high status and pay. He or she then gets a low-paying job and must settle for a lifestyle far short of society's standards. Since the person shares these standards, he or she may begin to feel self-doubt and self-hatred. This aspect of the cycle has been called into question in recent research.*

in professional sports as players, coaches, trainers, team doctors, and executives. In his view, blacks should no longer "put play-books ahead of textbooks," and the black community should abandon its "blind belief in sport as an extraordinary route to social and economic salvation."

17   Blacks and other minorities are not always passive victims of harmful stereotypes and self-fulfilling prophecies. In the 1960s and 1970s, many subordinate minorities in the United States rejected traditional definitions and replaced them with feelings of pride, power, and strength. "Black is beautiful" and "red power" movements among blacks and American Indians were efforts to take control of their own lives and self-images. However, although a minority can make a determined effort to redefine a situation and resist stereotypes, the definition that remains most important is the one used by a society's most powerful groups. In this sense, the historic white, Anglo-Saxon, Protestant norms of the United States still shape the definitions and stereotypes of racial and ethnic minorities (Baughman, 1971:37–55).

18   **Ethnicity**   An ethnic group, unlike a racial group, is set apart from others because of its national origin or distinctive cultural patterns. Among the ethnic groups in the United States are peoples referred

to collectively as *Hispanics,* such as Puerto Ricans, Mexican Americans, Cubans, and other Latin Americans (see Table 1). Other ethnic groups in this country include Jewish, Irish, Polish, Italian, and Norwegian Americans.

19   The distinction between racial and ethnic minorities is not always clear-cut. Some members of racial minorities, such as Asian Americans, may have significant cultural differences from other groups. At the same time, certain ethnic minorities, such as Hispanics, may have obvious physical differences that set them apart from other Americans.

20   Despite such problems of categorization, sociologists continue to feel that the distinction between racial and ethnic groups is socially significant. In most societies, including the United States, physical differences tend to be more visible than ethnic differences. Partly as a result of this fact, stratification along racial lines is less subject to change than stratification along ethnic lines. Members of an ethnic minority sometimes can, over time, become indistinguishable from the majority—though it may take generations and may never include all members of the group. By contrast, members of a racial minority find it much more difficult to blend in with the larger society and gain acceptance from the majority.

EXERCISES

Details and Their Meanings

1. According to Richard T. Schaefer, what is the key difference between racial groups and ethnic groups? Does the writer identify Hispanics as a racial or an ethnic group? Why?
2. What do sociologists mean when they use the expression *minority group?* Distinguish between a numerical minority and a minority group of interest to sociologists.
3. If Gary, Indiana, is at least 71 percent black, why aren't blacks considered the dominant group in that city? What are the major features that define a minority group?
4. Which groups are the largest racial minorities in the United States? If a scientist analyzed blood samples from different ra-

cial groups, which groups could he or she correctly identify? What makes the identification possible or stands in its way?

5. According to the writer, what defines an individual in the United States as black? How does the classification of skin color in Brazil differ from that in the United States?

6. Which groups in the United States is historically dominant? What role does the majority group serve in a nation? What roles do stereotypes play in keeping groups dominant?

7. According to the writer, why do some racial or ethnic groups seem to excel in some areas, such as sports or entertainment, but not in other areas?

Reading and Critical Thinking

1. Why does the writer suggest that prejudice and discrimination are necessary ingredients to the creation of a minority group? What do you think happens to minorities who are not discriminated against?

2. Why do people tend to marry within their own ethnic or racial groups? What happens when they do not? Do you think it is possible for society to change the way it views intermarriage? Why or why not? What view do you or your friends and relatives hold about intermarriage?

3. Why do you think there are so few skin-color categories in the United States? Why does Brazil have so many?

4. Why can't biology provide answers to the question of why some groups dominate others? Can you imagine a society without dominant groups? What would it be like?

5. In the past, what impact did Hollywood have on notions of ethnic and racial identity? In what ways (if any) has Hollywood's portrayals of racial and ethnic groups changed in recent years?

6. What advice would the writer give to a young minority man or woman who is planning a career in sports? What is misleading about the apparent domination of some sports by certain ethnic groups?

7. What is a fair conclusion about the absence of some minority groups among the ranks of scientists or business executives? If you could, would you attempt to change this situation? Why or why not?

8. Why is it reasonable to predict that some Hispanics will assimilate into the majority faster than will some members of other groups?

The Writer's Strategies

1. What is the thesis of this selection? What primary rhetorical strategy does Schaefer use to advance his point?
2. Who do you think is the audience for this selection? How can you tell?
3. What is the writer's purpose in including Table 1 (page 190)? What is his purpose in including Figure 1 (page 193)? How do the table and figure differ?
4. Why does the writer cite other authors, such as van den Berghe in paragraph 6? Where else does he cite others?
5. How much of this piece is the writer's opinion? Where do you find examples of opinion?
6. Where does Schaefer state his main purpose in writing this selection? What is his purpose? Who is the intended audience? How can you tell?
7. Where does the writer state his conclusion? What is it?

Thinking Together

Schaefer says that sometimes ethnic or racial stereotypes are adopted by minority groups in a sort of self-fulfilling prophecy. Working with two to four of your classmates, discuss whether you agree with this observation. How can stereotypes become self-fulfilling? Do you accept Schaefer's explanation that ethnic and racial stereotypes are the inventions of dominant groups and are ascribed to minorities as a means of keeping them subordinate? Discuss your group's answers with your other classmates.

Vocabulary

The following terms are used in the text. Write a definition of each.

1. dominant group (par. 2)
2. subordinate group (par. 2)
3. ascribed status (par. 4)

4. in-group (par. 4)
5. out-group (par. 4)
6. stereotype (par. 11)
7. self-fulfilling prophecy (par. 13)
8. stratification (par. 20)

WRITER'S WORKSHOP ━━━━━━━━━━━━━━━━

Critical Thinking in Writing

1. Write a summary of this selection by Schaefer. Once you have the main points clearly on paper write a short essay about the issues as if you were explaining them to elementary school children—sixth graders, say.
2. Schaefer says that replacing negative stereotypes with power, pride, and strength is a good way to overcome self-fulfilling prophecies. Write an essay in which you describe your ethnic or racial group in terms of things that you take pride in. What about your group is admirable, noble, and notable?
3. Choose a term from the vocabulary list given above—in-group, out-group, stereotype, subordinate group—or choose any other interesting term from the selection, and write your own definition paper. Draw on your own experiences or on what you have read.

Connecting Ideas

Read Marcus Mabry's "Confronting Campus Racism" (page 355). How does Schaefer's definition of prejudice apply in Mabry's essay? Who are the in-groups and out-groups in Mabry's piece? How are the in-groups trying to ascribe behavior to the out-groups? What information in the Schaefer selection might help campus groups to understand each other better?

Women's Language

Robin Lakoff

Robin Lakoff, professor of linguistics at the University of California at Berkeley, has written both scholarly and general-interest works, including Abstract Syntax, Language and Woman's Place *and* Face Value: The Politics of Beauty. *In this selection, she describes the problems imposed on women by the English language.*

KEY WORDS

elicit (par. 7)   to bring out
subliminal (par. 10)   repressed or intuitive
requisite (par. 10)   necessary, required by circumstances
idiosyncrasies (par. 12)   quirks, peculiarities
derogatory (par. 13)   belittling, insulting
denigrates (par. 20)   slanders, brings down
paramour (par. 23)   lover
consummate (par. 23)   complete, total
faux pas (par. 25)   French expression meaning a mistake,
   a false step

"WOMEN'S LANGUAGE" IS THAT pleasant (dainty?), euphemistic, never-aggressive way of talking we learned as little girls. Cultural bias was built into the language we were allowed to speak, the subjects we were allowed to speak about, and the ways we were spoken of. Having learned our linguistic lesson well, we go out in the world, only to discover that we are communicative cripples— damned if we do, and damned if we don't.

2   If we refuse to talk "like a lady," we are ridiculed and criticized for being unfeminine. ("She thinks like a man" is, at best, a left-handed compliment.) If we do learn all the fuzzy-headed, unassertive language of our sex, we are ridiculed for being unable to think clearly, unable to take part in a serious discussion, and therefore unfit to hold a position of power.

3   It doesn't take much of this for a woman to begin feeling she deserves such treatment because of inadequacies in her own intelligence and education.

4   "Women's language" shows up in all levels of English. For example, women are encouraged and allowed to make far more precise discriminations in naming colors than men do. Words like *mauve, beige, ecru, aquamarine, lavender,* and so on are unremarkable in a woman's active vocabulary, but largely absent from that of most men. I know of no evidence suggesting that women actually *see* a wider range of colors than men do. It is simply that fine discriminations of this sort are relevant to women's vocabularies, but not to men's; to men, who control most of the interesting affairs of the world, such distinctions are trivial—irrelevant.

5   In the area of syntax, we find similar gender-related peculiarities of speech. There is one construction, in particular, that women use conversationally far more than men: the tag-question. A tag is midway between an outright statement and a yes-no question; it is less assertive than the former, but more confident than the latter.

6   A *flat statement* indicates confidence in the speaker's knowledge and is fairly certain to be believed; a *question* indicates a lack of knowledge on some point and implies that the gap in the speaker's knowledge can and will be remedied by an answer. For example, if, at a Little League game, I have had my glasses off, I can legitimately ask someone else: "Was the player out at third?" A *tag-question*, being intermediate between statement and question, is used when the speaker is stating a claim, but lacks full confidence in the truth of that claim. So if I say, "Is Joan here?" I will probably not be surprised if my respondent answers "no"; but if I say, "Joan is here, isn't she?" instead, chances are I am already biased in favor of a positive answer, wanting only confirmation. I still want a response, but I have enough knowledge (or think I have) to predict that response. A tag-question, then, might be thought of as a statement that doesn't demand to be believed by anyone but the speaker, a way of giving leeway, of not forcing the addressee to go along with the views of the speaker.

7   Another common use of the tag-question is in small talk when the speaker is trying to elicit conversation: "Sure is hot here, isn't it?"

8   But in discussing personal feelings or opinions, only the speaker normally has any way of knowing the correct answer. Sentences such as "I have a headache, don't I?" are clearly ridiculous. But there are other examples where it is the speaker's opinions,

rather than perceptions, for which corroboration is sought, as in "The situation in Southeast Asia is terrible, isn't it?"

9   While there are, of course, other possible interpretations of a sentence like this, one possibility is that the speaker has a particular answer in mind—"yes" or "no"—but is reluctant to state it baldly. This sort of tag-question is much more apt to be used by women than by men in conversation. Why is this the case?

10   The tag-question allows a speaker to avoid commitment, and thereby avoid conflict with the addressee. The problem is that, by so doing, speakers may also give the impression of not really being sure of themselves, or looking to the addressee for confirmation of their views. This uncertainty is reinforced in more subliminal ways, too. There is a peculiar sentence intonation-pattern, used almost exclusively by women, as far as I know, which changes a declarative answer into a question. The effect of using the rising inflection typical of a yes–no question is to imply that the speaker is seeking confirmation, even though the speaker is clearly the only one who has the requisite information, which is why the question was put to her in the first place:

(Q) When will dinner be ready?
(A) Oh . . . around six o'clock . . . ?

11   It is as though the second speaker were saying, "Six o'clock— if that's okay with you, if you agree." The person being addressed is put in the position of having to provide confirmation. One likely consequence of this sort of speech pattern in a woman is that, often unbeknownst to herself, the speaker builds a reputation of tentativeness, and others will refrain from taking her seriously or trusting her with any real responsibilities, since she "can't make up her mind," and "isn't sure of herself."

12   Such idiosyncrasies may explain why women's language sounds much more "polite" than men's. It is polite to leave a decision open, not impose your mind, or views, or claims, on anyone else. So a tag-question is a kind of polite statement, in that it does not force agreement or belief on the addressee. In the same way a request is a polite command, in that it does not force obedience on the addressee, but rather suggests something be done as a favor to the speaker. A clearly stated order implies a threat of certain consequences if it is not followed, and—even more impolite—implies that the speaker is in a superior position and able to enforce the order. By couching wishes in the form of a request, on the other hand, a speaker implies that if the request is not carried out, only

the speaker will suffer; noncompliance cannot harm the addressee. So the decision is really left up to the addressee. The distinction becomes clear in these examples:

Close the door.
Please close the door.
Will you close the door?
Will you please close the door?
Won't you close the door?

13   In the same ways as words and speech patterns used *by* women undermine their image, those used *to describe* women make matters even worse. Often a word may be used of both men and women (and perhaps of things as well); but when it is applied to women, it assumes a special meaning that, by implications rather than outright assertion, is derogatory to women as a group.

14   The use of euphemisms has this effect. A *euphemism* is a substitute for a word that has acquired a bad connotation by association with something unpleasant or embarrassing. But almost as soon as the new word comes into common usage, it takes on the same old bad connotations, since feelings about the things or people referred to are not altered by a change of name; thus new euphemisms must be constantly found.

15   There is one euphemism for *woman* still very much alive. The word, of course, is *lady*. *Lady* has a masculine counterpart, namely *gentleman*, occasionally shortened to *gent*. But for some reason *lady* is very much commoner than *gent(leman)*.

16   The decision to use *lady* rather than *woman*, or vice versa, may considerably alter the sense of a sentence, as the following examples show:

(a) A woman (lady) I know is a dean at Berkeley.
(b) A woman (lady) I know makes amazing things out of shoelaces and old boxes.

17   The use of *lady* in (a) imparts a frivolous, or nonserious, tone to the sentence: the matter under discussion is not one of great moment. Similarly, in (b), using *lady* here would suggest that the speaker considered the "amazing things" not to be serious art, but merely a hobby or an aberration. If *woman* is used, she might be a serious sculptor. To say *lady doctor* is very condescending, since no one ever says *gentleman doctor* or even *man doctor*. For example, mention in the San Francisco *Chronicle* of January 31, 1972, of Madalyn Murray O'Hair as the *lady atheist* reduces her position

to that of scatterbrained eccentric. Even *woman atheist* is scarcely defensible: sex is irrelevant to her philosophical position.

18   Many women argue that, on the other hand, *lady* carries with it overtones recalling the age of chivalry: conferring exalted stature on the person so referred to. This makes the term seem polite at first, but we must also remember that these implications are perilous: they suggest that a "lady" is helpless and cannot do things by herself.

19   *Lady* can also be used to infer frivolousness, as in titles of organizations. Those that have a serious purpose (not merely that of enabling "the ladies" to spend time with one another) cannot use the word *lady* in their titles, but less serious ones may. Compare the *Ladies' Auxiliary* of a men's group, or the *Thursday Evening Ladies' Browning and Garden Society* with *Ladies' Liberation* or *Ladies' Strike for Peace.*

20   What is curious about this split is that *lady* is in origin a euphemism—a substitute that puts a better face on something people find uncomfortable—for *woman*. What kind of euphemism is it that subtly denigrates the people to whom it refers? Perhaps *lady* functions as a euphemism for *woman* because it does not contain the sexual implications present in *woman*: it is not "embarrassing" in that way. If this is so, we may expect that, in the future, *lady* will replace *woman* as the primary word for the human female, since *woman* will have become too blatantly sexual. That this distinction is already made in some contexts at least is shown in the following examples, where you can try replacing *woman* with *lady*:

(a) She's only twelve, but she's already a woman.
(b) After ten years in jail, Harry wanted to find a woman.
(c) She's my woman, see, so don't mess around with her.

21   Another common substitute for *woman* is *girl*. One seldom hears a man past the age of adolescence referred to as a boy, save in expressions like "going out with the boys," which are meant to suggest an air of adolescent frivolity and irresponsibility. But women of all ages are "girls": one can have a man—not a boy— Friday, but only a girl—never a woman or even a lady—Friday; women have girlfriends, but men do not—in a nonsexual sense— have boyfriends. It may be that this use of *girl* is euphemistic in the same way the use of *lady* is: in stressing the idea of immaturity, it removes the sexual connotations lurking in *woman*. *Girl* brings to mind irresponsibility: you don't send a girl to do a woman's errand (or even, for that matter, a boy's errand). She is a person

who is both too immature and too far from real life to be entrusted with responsibilities or with decisions of any serious or important nature.

22   Now let's take a pair of words which, in terms of the possible relationships in an earlier society, were simple male-female equivalents, analogous to *bull:cow*. Suppose we find that, for independent reasons, society has changed in such a way that the original meanings now are irrelevant. Yet the words have not been discarded, but have acquired new meanings, metaphorically related to their original senses. But suppose these new metaphorical uses are no longer parallel to each other. By seeing where the parallelism breaks down, we discover something about the different roles played by men and women in this culture. One good example of such a divergence through time is found in the pair, *master:mistress*. Once used with reference to one's power over servants, these words have become unusable today in their original master-servant sense as the relationship has become less prevalent in our society. But the words are still common.

23   Unless used with reference to animals, *master* now generally refers to a man who has acquired consummate ability in some field, normally nonsexual. But its feminine counterpart cannot be used this way. It is practically restricted to its sexual sense of "paramour." We start out with two terms, both roughly paraphrasable as "one who has power over another." But the masculine form, once one person is no longer able to have absolute power over another, becomes usable metaphorically in the sense of "having power over *something*." *Master* requires as its object only the name of some activity, something inanimate and abstract. But *mistress* requires a masculine noun in the possessive to precede it. One cannot say: "Rhonda is a mistress." One must be *someone's* mistress. A man is defined by what he does, a woman by her sexuality, that is, in terms of one particular aspect of her relationship to men. It is one thing to be an *old master* like Hans Holbein, and another to be an *old mistress*.

24   The same is true of the words *spinster* and *bachelor*—gender words for "one who is not married." The resemblance ends with the definition. While *bachelor* is a neuter term, often used as a compliment, *spinster* normally is used pejoratively, with connotations of prissiness, fussiness, and so on. To be a bachelor implies that one has the choice of marrying or not, and this is what makes the idea of a bachelor existence attractive, in the popular literature. He has been pursued and has successfully eluded his pursuers. But a

spinster is one who has not been pursued, or at least not seriously. She is old, unwanted goods. The metaphorical connotations of *bachelor* generally suggest sexual freedom; of *spinster*, puritanism or celibacy.

25   These examples could be multiplied. It is generally considered a *faux pas*, in society, to congratulate a woman on her engagement, while it is correct to congratulate her fiancé. Why is this? The reason seems to be that it is impolite to remind people of things that may be uncomfortable to them. To congratulate a woman on her engagement is really to say, "Thank goodness! You had a close call." For the man, on the other hand, there was no such danger. His choosing to marry is viewed as a good thing, but not something essential.

26   The linguistic double standard holds throughout the life of the relationship. After marriage, bachelor and spinster become man and wife, not man and woman. The woman whose husband dies remains "John's widow"; John, however, is never "Mary's widower."

27   Finally, why is it that salesclerks and others are so quick to call woman customers "dear," "honey," and other terms of endearment they really have no business using? A male customer would never put up with it. But women, like children, are supposed to enjoy these endearments, rather than being offended by them.

28   In more ways than one, it's time to speak up.

EXERCISES

Details and Their Meanings

1. At what age do women begin to learn a distinct form of speech?
2. What kinds of sentences are women most likely to use? What impression are these sentences likely to give?
3. According to Robin Lakoff, what is the purpose of euphemisms in forms of address for women? Why are new euphemisms constantly needed?
4. According to the writer, why have originally parallel words

like *master* and *mistress* or *spinster* and *bachelor* evolved into distinct, gender-specific words? How do they now convey different meanings?

5. In polite society, which sex is to be congratulated for getting engaged? What is the reasoning behind this distinction?

6. What does the writer mean by the phrase "linguistic double standard"?

Reading and Critical Thinking

1. Who is responsible for teaching women the rules of speaking "like a lady"? Where does the writer give you this information?

2. According to the writer, how does "women's language" reinforce negative images of women? What do women conclude about themselves on the basis of language? What aspects of "men's language" that you have heard reinforce negative images of women?

3. What reason can you give for "women's language" sounding more "polite" than men's. Is politeness more necessary for women than for men? Why or why not?

4. How does the use of the word *girl* deprive women of status? What other words also reduce a woman's power? Are there similar words that reduce men's power? What are they?

5. According to the writer, why is it inappropriate to call Sandra Day O'Connor "a woman Supreme Court justice"? Why is that use of *woman* condescending?

The Writer's Strategies

1. What is the thesis of this selection? Where is it stated?

2. What is Lakoff's attitude toward her topic? How can you tell?

3. Why does the writer list sample sentences in paragraphs 12, 16, and 20?

4. Where does the writer give examples of euphemisms?

5. Where does Lakoff state facts? Where does she express conclusions?

6. What is the conclusion of this essay? What new idea is introduced in the conclusion?

Thinking Together

Go to a place in which you can overhear men and women speaking. Likely places are your school's cafeteria, hallways, or quad, but any social situation will do. Listen to differences in the ways men and women speak. Make a list of how often you hear tag-questions and flat statements; also list the forms of address men and women use when speaking to each other. Then in class compare your results. What valid conclusions can you draw from your observations? Which of your conclusions support Lakoff's?

Vocabulary

The following terms from the selection relate to speech. Some are defined in the text, but others you may need to look up. Write a definition of each.

1. euphemistic (par. 1)
2. left-handed compliment (par. 2)
3. tag-question (par. 5)
4. flat statement (par. 6)
5. intonation-pattern (par. 10)
6. declarative answer (par. 10)
7. overtones (par. 18)
8. metaphorical (par. 22)
9. neuter (par. 24)
10. pejoratively (par. 24)

WRITER'S WORKSHOP ━━━━━━━━━

Critical Thinking in Writing

1. Do you feel that words like *dear, girl,* and *lady* really have a negative impact on women, or is their use harmless? Write a letter to Robin Lakoff in which you present your ideas on terms of address and the ways in which they influence how men and women think about themselves and each other.
2. The current generation of college students has been called "the post-feminist generation," by which is meant that young women today no longer feel a pressing need to assert their

equality. Does that label imply that women have given up the fight for equal rights or that the major battles for equality have been won? Defend your answer in a well-detailed essay.

3. Write a narrative essay about an occasion in which you were called an offensive name. How did this experience affect the way you thought about yourself?

Connecting Ideas

Read Elizabeth Wong's "The Struggle to Be an All-American Girl" (page 39). How are the issues of language that Wong raises similar to or different from the issues raised by Lakoff? How would Lakoff feel about the use of the word *girl* in Wong's title? Why?

If Black English Isn't a Language . . . What Is?

James Baldwin

From the 1950s until his death in 1988, James Baldwin was one of the most eloquent voices on the subject of race relations. He made important contributions in fiction and essay-writing, including Gio-vanni's Room (1956) and The Fire Next Time (1963). In this essay, he defends the status of black English, maintaining that it is more than simply a dialect of standard English.

KEY WORDS

diaspora (par. 7)   group migration
chattel (par. 7)   disposable property
tabernacle (par. 7)   a place of worship

THE ARGUMENT CONCERNING THE use, or the status, or the reality, of black English is rooted in American history and has absolutely nothing to do with the question the argument supposes itself to be posing. The argument has nothing to do with language itself but with the *role* of language. Language, incontestably, reveals the speaker. Language, also, far more dubiously, is meant to define the other—and, in this case, the other is refusing to be defined by a language that has never been able to recognize him.

2   People evolve a language in order to describe and thus control their circumstances, or in order not to be submerged by a reality that they cannot articulate. (And, if they cannot articulate it, they *are* submerged.) A Frenchman living in Paris speaks a subtly and crucially different language from that of the man living in Marseilles; neither sounds very much like a man living in Quebec; and they would all have great difficulty in apprehending what the man from Guadeloupe, or Martinique, is saying, to say nothing of the man from Senegal—although the "common" language of all these

areas is French. But each has paid, and is paying, a different price for this "common" language, in which, as it turns out, they are not saying, and cannot be saying, the same things: They each have very different realities to articulate or control.

3   What joins all languages, and all men, is the necessity to confront life, in order, not inconceivably, to outwit death: The price for this is the acceptance, and achievement, of one's temporal identity. So that, for example, though it is not taught in the schools (and this has the potential of becoming a political issue) the south of France still clings to its ancient and musical Provençal, which resists being described as a "dialect." And much of the tension in the Basque countries, and in Wales, is due to the Basque and Welsh determination not to allow their languages to be destroyed. This determination also feeds the flames in Ireland, for among the many indignities the Irish have been forced to undergo at English hands is the English contempt for their language.

4   It goes without saying, then, that language is also a political instrument, means, and proof of power. It is the most vivid and crucial key to identity: It reveals the private identity, and connects one with, or divorces one from, the larger public, or communal identity. There have been, and are, times, and places, when to speak a certain language could be dangerous, even fatal. Or, one may speak the same language, but in such a way that one's antecedents are revealed, or (one hopes) hidden. This is true in France and is absolutely true in England: The range (and reign) of accents on that damp little island make England coherent for the English and totally incomprehensible for everyone else. To open your mouth in England is (if I may use black English) to "put your business in the street": You have confessed your parents, your youth, your school, your salary, your self-esteem, and, alas, your future.

5   Now, I do not know what white Americans would sound like if there had never been any black people in the United States, but they would not sound the way they sound. *Jazz*, for example, is a very specific sexual term, as in *jazz me, baby*, but white people purified it into the Jazz Age. *Sock it to me*, which means, roughly, the same thing, has been adopted by Nathaniel Hawthorne's descendants with no qualms or hesitations at all, along with *let it all hang out* and *right on! Beat to his socks*, which was once the black's most total and despairing image of poverty, was transformed into a thing called the Beat Generation, which phenomenon was, largely, composed of *uptight*, middle-class white people, imitating poverty, trying to *get down*, to get *with it*, doing their *thing*, doing their

despairing best to be *funky,* which we, the blacks, never dreamed of doing—we *were* funky, baby, like *funk* was going out of style.

6   Now, no one can eat his cake and have it, too, and it is late in the day to attempt to penalize black people for having created a language that permits the nation its only glimpse of reality, a language without which the nation would be even more *whipped* than it is.

7   I say that this present skirmish is rooted in American history, and it is. Black English is the creation of the black diaspora. Blacks came to the United States chained to each other, but from different tribes: Neither could speak the other's language. If two black people, at that bitter hour of the world's history, had been able to speak to each other, the institution of chattel slavery could never have lasted as long as it did. Subsequently, the slave was given, under the eye, and the gun, of his master, Congo Square, and the Bible— or, in other words, and under these conditions, the slave began the formation of the black church, and it is within this unprecedented tabernacle that black English began to be formed. This was not, merely, as in the European example, the adoption of a foreign tongue, but an alchemy that transformed ancient elements into new language: *A language comes into existence by means of brutal necessity, and the rules of the language are dictated by what the language must convey.*

8   There was a moment, in time, and in this place, when my brother, or my mother, or my father, or my sister, had to convey to me, for example, the danger in which I was standing from the white man standing just behind me, and to convey this with a speed, and in a language, that the white man could not possibly understand, and that, indeed, he cannot understand, until today. He cannot afford to understand it. This understanding would reveal to him too much about himself, and smash that mirror before which he has been frozen for so long.

9   Now, if this passion, this skill, this (to quote Toni Morrison) "sheer intelligence," this incredible music, the mighty achievement of having brought a people utterly unknown to, or despised by "history"—to have brought this people to their present, troubled, troubling, and unassailable and unanswerable place—if this absolutely unprecedented journey does not indicate that black English is a language, I am curious to know what definition of language is to be trusted.

10   A people at the center of the Western world, and in the midst of so hostile a population, has not endured and transcended by means of what is patronizingly called a "dialect." We, the blacks,

are in trouble, certainly, but we are not doomed, and we are not inarticulate because we are not compelled to defend a morality that we know to be a lie.

11   The brutal truth is that the bulk of the white people in America never had any interest in educating black people, except as this could serve white purposes. It is not the black child's language that is in question, it is not his language that is despised: It is his experience. A child cannot be taught by anyone who despises him, and a child cannot afford to be fooled. A child cannot be taught by anyone whose demand, essentially, is that the child repudiate his experience, and all that gives him sustenance, and enter a limbo in which he will no longer be black, and in which he knows that he can never become white. Black people have lost too many black children that way.

12   And, after all, finally, in a country with standards so untrustworthy, a country that makes heroes of so many criminal mediocrities, a country unable to face why so many of the nonwhite are in prison, or on the needle, or standing, futureless, in the streets—it may very well be that both the child, and his elder, have concluded that they have nothing whatever to learn from the people of a country that has managed to learn so little.

EXERCISES

Details and Their Meanings

1. Give some examples of languages that have the same name but are nevertheless distinct.
2. In paragraph 3, what does Baldwin say is the true purpose of language? In what way is language political?
3. What do *Jazz* and *sock it to me* refer to in black English? How did white America modify their meaning?
4. Why didn't Africans speak their own language when they were brought to America?
5. Where did black English begin? What institution is responsible for originating it? What purpose was served by the development of a separate tongue understood by black Americans but not by white people?

6. What does Baldwin say black children will lose if they are cut off from their language?

Reading and Critical Thinking

1. Who says Provençal is a dialect of French? Who says it is not? How does this discussion relate to black American English?
2. What do you infer is the result of speaking improper English in England?
3. Who is Nathaniel Hawthorne? Why does Baldwin refer to him in paragraph 5? What is Baldwin implying?
4. What is the Beat Generation? What were the beatniks pretending to be, according to Baldwin? What were they really? How is the Beat Generation similar to its 1990s counterpart?
5. Why does Baldwin suggest that black people with a common language would not have tolerated slavery for long? How might a common language unify people against oppression?
6. What is a dialect? Why does Baldwin consider the description of black English as a dialect to be patronizing? Do you agree or disagree? Why?
7. What does Baldwin mean by "we are not compelled to defend a morality that we know to be a lie" (paragraph 10)? Do you agree? Why or why not?
8. How does the concluding paragraph turn the question of language and truth around? What implied challenge to education do you see in paragraph 12? How might this challenge be met?

The Writer's Strategies

1. What is Baldwin's thesis? Where does he state it?
2. In which paragraph does Baldwin give examples of dialects that are really distinct languages?
3. What is Baldwin's purpose in including many examples of black English? How does the use of these terms strengthen his argument?
4. What is Baldwin assuming that his audience knows about the black English debate? Is his assumption justified in your case?
5. Why does Baldwin put the last sentence of paragraph 7 in italics?
6. Why does Baldwin include a quotation from Toni Morrison in paragraph 9? Who is she?

7. Why is "dialect" put in quotation marks in paragraph 10? What emotion is Baldwin conveying by the use of this punctuation?

Thinking Together

Break into groups and brainstorm to produce a list of qualities of the language "white English." What linguistic elements define "white English"? How do these elements compare and contrast to the qualities of black English?

Vocabulary

James Baldwin uses the following italicized words in this selection. Write a definition of each one, using clues from the context of the sentence in which the word appears below.

1. We asked the dean to *articulate* her position on off-campus housing more clearly.
2. The continental United States is divided into four *temporal* zones: Eastern, Central, Mountain, and Pacific.
3. Our professor told us that the adding machine and the calculator were *antecedents* of the computer.
4. Although Martin was nervous about many things, he had no *qualms* about skydiving.
5. The Chicago Bulls *transcended* many problems this season and won the championship.
6. By giving us study guides that included every exam question, the professor made the test *patronizingly* simple.
7. Sunlight is essential to the *sustenance* of most plant life.
8. The gangster decided to *repudiate* his criminal past and join a monastery.
9. After auditioning dozens of *mediocrities,* the director decided to hold another day of tryouts for talent night.

WRITER'S WORKSHOP ▬▬▬▬▬▬▬

Critical Thinking in Writing

1. Write an essay describing the qualities of the English you use. How does your language reveal social and cultural factors in your life? How does it reveal political factors?

2. Although Baldwin doesn't address this point directly, implied in his essay is the suggestion that black students should be taught in their own language in schools. If this were done, how would it change the nature of education? Take a position on this issue, and write an essay supporting your argument.

3. As Baldwin says, language divides as much as it unites. Should we retain our current concept of standard English, or should each segment of American culture teach and write in its own idiom? Can the same argument Baldwin makes for black English be applied to Spanglish, American Sign Language, and Cajun as well? Or do you see merit in elements of the "English only" argument—English should be the exclusive language of discourse in America, particularly its schools and courts?

Connecting Ideas

Read Stephen Carter's "I Am an Affirmative Action Baby" (page 132). How do you think Carter would respond to Baldwin's contention that a black child who does not understand black English "will no longer be black"?

On Being a Cripple

Nancy Mairs

Nancy Mairs, a writer and college teacher, gives a first-person account of what it is like to live with a chronic, debilitating disease.

KEY WORDS

chagrin (par. 1)   embarrassment, humiliation
euphemism (par. 4)   a more polite renaming
calamitous (par. 5)   devastating
circumscribed (par. 9)   limited, confined
venerability (par. 10)   impressiveness due to age or tradition
predilections (par. 11)   preferences, inclinations
sedentary (par. 11)   inactive, sitting
insinuate (par. 16)   hint, suggest
recriminations (par. 19)   blaming
depredations (par. 22)   destructions
decrepitude (par. 25)   wasting away, weakening
foray (par. 27)   attack, raid
intransigence (par. 34)   refusal to compromise, stubbornness
deprecate (par. 35)   condemn, put down

To escape is nothing. Not to escape is nothing.

—Louise Bogan

THE OTHER DAY I was thinking of writing an essay on being a cripple. I was thinking hard in one of the stalls of the women's room in my office building, as I was shoving my shirt into my jeans and tugging up my zipper. Preoccupied, I flushed, picked up my book bag, took my cane down from the hook, and unlatched the door. So many movements unbalanced me, and as I pulled the door open

215

I fell over backward, landing fully clothed on the toilet seat with my legs splayed in front of me: the old beetle-on-its-back routine. Saturday afternoon, the building deserted, I was free to laugh aloud as I wriggled back to my feet, my voice bouncing off the yellowish tiles from all directions. Had anyone been there with me, I'd have been still and faint and hot with chagrin.

2   I decided that it was high time to write the essay.

3   First, the matter of semantics. I am a cripple. I choose this word to name me. I choose from among several possibilities, the most common of which are *handicapped* and *disabled*. I made the choice a number of years ago, without thinking, unaware of my motives for doing so. Even now, I'm not sure what those motives are, but I recognize that they are complex and not entirely flattering. People—crippled or not—wince at the word *cripple*, as they do not at *handicapped* or *disabled*. Perhaps I want them to wince. I want them to see me as a tough customer, one to whom the fates/gods/viruses have not been kind, but who can face the brutal truth of her existence squarely. As a cripple, I swagger.

4   But, to be fair to myself, a certain amount of honesty underlies my choice. *Cripple* seems to me a clean word, straightforward and precise. It has an honorable history, having made its first appearance in the Lindisfarne Gospel in the tenth century. As a lover of words, I like the accuracy with which it describes my condition: I have lost the full use of my limbs. *Disabled*, by contrast, suggests any incapacity, physical or mental. And I certainly don't like *handicapped*, which implies that I have deliberately been put at a disadvantage, by whom I can't imagine (my God is not a Handicapper General), in order to equalize chances in the great race of life. These words seem to me to be moving away from my condition, to be widening the gap between word and reality. Most remote is the recently coined euphemism *differently abled*, which partakes of the same semantic hopefulness that transformed countries from *undeveloped* to *underdeveloped*, then to *less developed*, and finally to *developing* nations. People have continued to starve in those countries during the shift. Some realities do not obey the dictates of language.

5   Mine is one of them. Whatever you call me, I remain crippled. But I don't care what I am called, as long as it isn't *differently abled*, which strikes me as pure verbal garbage designed, by its ability to describe anyone, to describe no one. I subscribe to George Orwell's thesis that "the sloppiness of our language makes it easier for us to have foolish thoughts." And I refuse to participate in the degen-

eration of the language to the extent that I deny that I have lost anything in the course of this calamitous disease; I refuse to pretend that the only differences between you and me are the various ordinary ones that distinguish any one person from another. But call me *disabled* or *handicapped* if you like. I have long since grown accustomed to them; and if they are vague, at least they hint at the truth. Moreover, I use them myself. Society is no readier to accept crippledness than to accept death, war, sex, sweat, or wrinkles. I would never refer to another person as a cripple. It is the word I use to name only myself.

6   I haven't always been crippled, a fact for which I am soundly grateful. To be whole of limb is, I know from experience, infinitely more pleasant and useful than to be crippled; and if that knowledge leaves me open to bitterness at my loss, the physical soundness I once enjoyed (though I did not enjoy it half enough) is well worth the occasional stab of regret. Though never any good at sports, I was a normally active child and young adult. I climbed trees, played hopscotch, jumped rope, skated, swam, rode my bicycle, sailed. I despised team sports, spending some of the most wretched afternoons of my life, sweaty and humiliated, behind a field-hockey stick and under a basketball hoop. I tramped alone for miles along the bridle paths that webbed the woods behind the house I grew up in. I swayed through countless dim hours in the arms of one man or another under the scattered shot of light from mirrored balls, and gyrated through countless more as Tab Hunter and Johnny Mathis gave way to the Rolling Stones, Creedence Clearwater Revival, Cream. I walked down the aisle. I pushed baby carriages, changed tires in the rain, marched for peace.

7   When I was twenty-nine, I started to trip and drop things. What at first seemed my natural clumsiness soon became too pronounced to shrug off. I consulted a neurologist, who told me that I had a brain tumor. A battery of tests, increasingly disagreeable, revealed no tumor. About a year and a half later I developed a blurred spot in one eye. I had, at last, the episodes "disseminated in space and time" requisite for a diagnosis: multiple sclerosis. I have never been sorry for the doctor's initial misdiagnosis, however. For almost a week, until the negative results of the tests were in, I thought that I was going to die right away. Every day for the past nearly ten years, then, has been a kind of gift. I accept all gifts.

8   Multiple sclerosis is a chronic degenerative disease of the central nervous system, in which the myelin that sheathes the nerves is somehow eaten away and scar tissue forms in its place,

interrupting the nerves' signals. During its course, which is unpredictable and uncontrollable, one may lose vision, hearing, speech, the ability to walk, control of bladder and/or bowels, strength in any or all extremities, sensitivity to touch, vibration, and/or pain, potency, coordination of movements—the list of possibilities is lengthy and horrifying. One may also lose one's sense of humor. That's the easiest to lose and the hardest to survive without.

9   In the past ten years, I have sustained some of these losses. Characteristic of MS are sudden attacks, called exacerbations, followed by remissions, and these I have not had. Instead, my disease has been slowly progressive. My left leg is now so weak that I walk with the aid of a brace and a cane; and for distances I use an Amigo, a variation on the electric wheelchair that looks rather like an electrified kiddie car. I no longer have much use of my left hand. Now my right side is weakening as well. I still have the blurred spot in my right eye. Overall, though, I've been lucky so far. My world has, of necessity, been circumscribed by my losses, but the terrain left me has been ample enough for me to continue many of the activities that absorb me: writing, teaching, raising children and cats and plants and snakes, reading, speaking publicly about MS and depression, even playing bridge with people patient and honorable enough to let me scatter cards every which way without sneaking a peek.

10   Lest I begin to sound like Pollyanna, however, let me say that I don't like having MS. I hate it. My life holds realities—harsh ones, some of them—that no right-minded human being ought to accept without grumbling. One of them is fatigue. I know of no one with MS who does not complain of bone-weariness; in a disease that presents an astonishing variety of symptoms, fatigue seems to be a common factor. I wake up in the morning feeling the way most people do at the end of a bad day, and I take it from there. As a result, I spend of a lot of time *in extremis* and, impatient with limitation, I tend to ignore my fatigue until my body breaks down in some way and forces rest. Then I miss picnics, dinner parties, poetry readings, the brief visits of old friends from out of town. The offspring of a puritanical tradition of exceptional venerability, I cannot view these lapses without shame. My life often seems a series of small failures to do as I ought.

11   I lead, on the whole, an ordinary life, probably rather like the one I would have led had I not had MS. I am lucky that my predilections were already solitary, sedentary, and bookish—unlike the world-famous French cellist I have read about, or the young

woman I talked with one long afternoon who wanted only to be a jockey. I had just begun graduate school when I found out something was wrong with me, and I have remained—interminably— a graduate student. Perhaps I would not have if I'd thought I had the stamina to return to a full-time job as a technical editor; but I've enjoyed my studies.

12   In addition to studying, I teach writing courses. I also teach medical students how to give neurological examinations. I pick up free-lance editing jobs here and there. I have raised a foster son and sent him into the world, where he has made me two grandbabies, and I am still escorting my daughter and son through adolescence. I go to mass every Saturday. I am a superb, if messy, cook. I am also an enthusiastic laundress, capable of sorting a hamper full of clothes into five subtly differentiated piles, but a terrible housekeeper. I can do italic writing and, in an emergency, bathe an oil-soaked cat. I play a fiendish game of Scrabble. When I have the time and the money, I like to sit on my front steps with my husband, drinking amaretto and smoking a cigar, as we imagine our counterparts in Leningrad and make sure that the sun gets down once more behind the sharp childish scrawl of the Tucson mountains.

13   This lively plenty has its bleak complement, of course, in all the things I can no longer do. I will never run again, except in dreams, and one day I may have to write that I will never walk again. I like to go camping, but I can't follow George and the children along the trails that wander out of a campsite through the desert or into the mountains. In fact, even on the level I've learned never to check the weather or try to hold a coherent conversation: I need all my attention for my wayward feet. Of late, I have begun to catch myself wondering how people can propel themselves without canes. With only one usable hand, I have to select my clothing with care not so much for style as for ease of ingress and egress, and even so, dressing can be laborious. I can no longer do fine stitchery, pick up babies, play the piano, braid my hair. I am immobilized by acute attacks of depression, which may or may not be physiologically related to MS but are certainly its logical concomitant.

14   These two elements, the plenty and the privation, are never pure, nor are the delight and wretchedness that accompany them. Almost every pickle that I get into as a result of my weakness and clumsiness—and I get into plenty—is funny as well as maddening and sometimes painful. I recall one May afternoon when a friend

and I were going out for a drink after finishing up at school. As we were climbing into opposite sides of my car, chatting, I tripped and fell, flat and hard, onto the asphalt parking lot, my abrupt departure interrupting him in midsentence. "Where'd you go?" he called as he came around the back of the car to find me hauling myself up by the door frame. "Are you all right?" Yes, I told him, I was fine, just a bit rattly, and we drove off to find a shady patio and some beer. When I got home an hour or so later, my daughter greeted me with, "What have you done to yourself?" I looked down. One elbow of my white turtleneck with the green froggies, one knee of my white trousers, one white kneesock were blood-soaked. We peeled off the clothes and inspected the damage, which was nasty enough but not alarming. That part wasn't funny: The abrasions took a long time to heal, and one got a little infected. Even so, when I think of my friend talking earnestly, suddenly, to the hot thin air while I dropped from his view as though through a trap door, I find the image as silly as something from a Marx Brothers movie.

15   I may find it easier than other cripples to amuse myself because I live propped by the acceptance and the assistance and, sometimes, the amusement of those around me. Grocery clerks tear my checks out of my checkbook for me, and sales clerks find chairs to put into dressing rooms when I want to try on clothes. The people I work with make sure I teach at times when I am least likely to be fatigued, in places I can get to, with the materials I need. My students, with one anonymous exception (in an end-of-the-semester evaluation), have been unperturbed by my disability. Some even like it. One was immensely cheered by the information that I paint my own fingernails; she decided, she told me, that if I could go to such trouble over fine details, she could keep on writing essays. I suppose I became some sort of bright-fingered muse. She wrote good essays, too.

16   The most important struts in the framework of my existence, of course, are my husband and children. Dismayingly few marriages survive the MS test, and why should they? Most twenty-two- and nineteen-year-olds, like George and me, can vow in clear conscience, after a childhood of chicken pox and summer colds, to keep one another in sickness and in health so long as they both shall live. Not many are equipped for catastrophe: the dismay, the depression, the extra work, the boredom that a degenerative disease can insinuate into a relationship. And our society, with its empha-

sis on fun and its association of fun with physical performance, offers little encouragement for a whole spouse to stay with a crippled partner. Children experience similar stresses when faced with a crippled parent, and they are more helpless, since parents and children can't usually get divorced. They hate, of course, to be different from their peers, and the child whose mother is tacking down the aisle of a school auditorium packed with proud parents like a Cape Cod dinghy in a stiff breeze jolly well stands out in a crowd. Deprived of legal divorce, the child can at least deny the mother's disability, even her existence, forgetting to tell her about recitals and PTA meetings, refusing to accompany her to stores or church or the movies, never inviting friends to the house. Many do.

17   But I've been limping along for ten years now, and so far George and the children are still at my left elbow, holding tight. Anne and Matthew vacuum floors and dust furniture and haul trash and rake up dog droppings and button my cuffs and bake lasagna and Toll House cookies with just enough grumbling so I know that they don't have brain fever. And far from hiding me, they're forever dragging me by racks of fancy clothes or through teeming school corridors, or welcoming gaggles of friends while I'm wandering through the house in Anne's filmy pink babydoll pajamas. George generally calls before he brings someone home, but he does just as many dumb thankless chores as the children. And they all yell at me, laugh at some of my jokes, write me funny letters when we're apart—in short, treat me as an ordinary human being for whom they have some use. I think they like me. Unless they're faking. . . .

18   Faking. There's the rub. Tugging at the fringes of my consciousness always is the terror that people are kind to me only because I'm a cripple. My mother almost shattered me once, with that instinct mothers have—blind, I think, in this case, but unerring nonetheless—for striking blows along the fault-lines of their children's hearts, by telling me, in an attack on my selfishness, "We all have to make allowances for you, of course, because of the way you are." From the distance of a couple of years, I have to admit that I haven't any idea just what she meant, and I'm not sure that she knew either. She was awfully angry. But at the time, as the words thudded home, I felt my worst fear suddenly realized. I could bear being called selfish: I am. But I couldn't bear the corroboration that those around me were doing in fact what I'd always suspected them of

doing, professing fondness while silently they put up with me because of the way I am. A cripple. I've been a little cracked ever since.

19   Along with this fear that people are secretly accepting shoddy goods comes a relentless pressure to please—to prove myself worth the burdens I impose, I guess, or to build a substantial account of good will against which I may write drafts in times of need. Part of the pressure arises from social expectations. In our society, anyone who deviates from the norm had better find some way to compensate. Like fat people, who are expected to be jolly, cripples must bear their lot meekly and cheerfully. A grumpy cripple isn't playing by the rules. And much of the pressure is self-generated. Early on I vowed that, if I had to have MS, by God I was going to do it well. This is a class act, ladies and gentlemen. No tears, no recriminations, no faintheartedness.

20   One way and another, then, I wind up feeling like Tiny Tim, peering over the edge of the table at the Christmas goose, waving my crutch, piping down God's blessing on us all. Only sometimes I don't want to play Tiny Tim. I'd rather be Caliban, a most scurvy monster. Fortunately, at home no one much cares whether I'm a good cripple or a bad cripple so long as I make vichyssoise with fair regularity. One evening several years ago, Anne was at the dining room table reading while I cooked dinner. As I opened a can of tomatoes, the can slipped in my left hand and juice spattered me and the counter with bloody spots. Fatigued and infuriated, I bellowed, "I'm sick of being crippled. . . ." Anne glanced at me over the top of her book. "There now," she said, "do you feel better?" "Yes," I said, "yes I do." She went back to her reading. I felt better. That's about all the attention my scurviness ever gets.

21   Because I hate being crippled, I sometimes hate myself for being a cripple. Over the years I have come to expect—even accept—attacks of violent self-loathing. Luckily, in general our society no longer connects deformity and disease directly with evil (though a charismatic once told me that I have MS because a devil is in me) and so I am allowed to move largely at will, even among small children. But I'm not sure that this revision of attitude has been particularly helpful. Physical imperfection, even freed of moral disapprobation, still defines and violates the ideal, especially for women, whose confinement in their bodies as objects of desire is far from over. Each age, of course, has its ideal, and I doubt that ours is any better or worse than any other. Today's ideal woman, who lives on the glossy pages of dozens of magazines, seems to

be between the ages of eighteen and twenty-five; her hair has body, her teeth flash white, her breath smells minty, her underarms are dry; she has a career but is still a fabulous cook, especially of meals that take less than twenty minutes to prepare; she does not ordinarily appear to have a husband or children; she is trim and deeply tanned; she jogs, swims, plays tennis, rides a bicycle, sails, but does not bowl; she travels widely, even to out-of-the-way places like Finland and Samoa, always in the company of the ideal man, who possesses a nearly identical set of characteristics. There are a few exceptions. Though usually white and often blonde, she may be black, Hispanic, oriental, or Native American, so long as she is unusually sleek. She may be old, provided she is selling a laxative or is Lauren Bacall. If she is selling a detergent, she may be married and have a flock of strikingly messy children. But she is never a cripple.

22   Like many women I know, I have always had an uneasy relationship with my body. I was not a popular child, largely, I think now, because I was peculiar; intelligent, intense, moody, shy, given to unexpected actions and inexplicable notions and emotions. But as I entered adolescence, I believed myself unpopular because I was homely: my breasts too flat, my mouth too wide, my hips too narrow, my clothing never quite right in fit or style. I was not, in fact, particularly ugly, old photographs inform me, though I was well off the ideal; but I carried this sense of self-alienation with me into adulthood, where it regenerated in response to the depredations of MS. Even with my brace I walk with a limp so pronounced that, seeing myself on the videotape of a television program on the disabled, I couldn't believe that anything but an inchworm could make progress humping along like that. My shoulders droop and my pelvis thrusts forward as I try to balance myself upright, throwing my frame into a bony S. As a result of contractures, one shoulder is higher than the other and I carry one arm bent in front of me, the finger curled into a claw. My left arm and leg have wasted into pipe-stems, and I try always to keep them covered. When I think about how my body must look to others, especially to men, to whom I have been trained to display myself, I feel ludicrous, even loathsome.

23   At my age, however, I don't spend much time thinking about my appearance. The burning egocentricity of adolescence, which assures one that all the world is looking all the time, has passed, thank God, and I'm generally too caught up in what I'm doing to step back, as I used to, and watch myself as though upon a stage.

I'm also too old to believe in the accuracy of self-image. I know that I'm not a hideous crone, that in fact, when I'm rested, well dressed, and well made up, I look fine. The self-loathing I feel is neither physically nor intellectually substantial. What I hate is not me but a disease.

24   I am not a disease.

25   And a disease is not—at least not singlehandedly—going to determine who I am, though at first it seemed to be going to. Adjusting to a chronic incurable illness, I have moved through a process similar to that outlined by Elizabeth Kübler-Ross in *Death and Dying.* The major difference—and it is far more significant than most people recognize—is that I can't be sure of the outcome, as the terminally ill cancer patient can. Research studies indicate that, with proper medical care, I may achieve a "normal" life span. And in our society, with its vision of death as the ultimate evil, worse even than decrepitude, the response to such news is, "Oh, well, at least you're not going to *die."*

26   Are there worse things than dying? I think there may be.

27   I think of two women I know, both with MS, both enough older than I to have served me as models. One took to her bed several years ago and has been there ever since. Although she can sit in a high-backed wheelchair, because she is incontinent she refuses to go out at all, even though incontinence pants, which are readily available at any pharmacy, could protect her from embarrassment. Instead, she stays at home and insists that her husband, a small quiet man, a retired civil servant, stay there with her except for a quick weekly foray to the supermarket. The other woman, whose illness was diagnosed when she was eighteen, a nursing student engaged to a young doctor, finished her training, married her doctor, accompanied him to Germany when he was in the service, bore three sons and a daughter, now grown and gone. When she can, she travels with her husband; she plays bridge, embroiders, swims regularly; she works, like me, as a symptomatic patient instructor of medical students in neurology.

28   Guess which woman I hope to be.

29   At the beginning, I thought about having MS almost incessantly. And because of the unpredictable course of the disease, my thoughts were always terrified. Each night I'd get into bed wondering whether I'd get out again the next morning, whether I'd be able to see, to speak, to hold a pen between my fingers. Knowing that the day might come when I'd be physically incapable of killing myself, I thought perhaps I ought to do so right away, while I still

had the strength. Gradually I came to understand that the Nancy who might one day lie inert under a bedsheet, arms and legs paralyzed, unable to feed or bathe herself, unable to reach out for a gun, a bottle of pills, was not the Nancy I was at present, and that I could not presume to make decisions for that future Nancy, who might well not want in the least to die. Now the only provision I've made for the future Nancy is that when the time comes—and it is likely to come in the form of pneumonia, friend to the weak and the old—I am not to be treated with machines and medications. If she is unable to communicate by then, I hope she will be satisfied with these terms.

30   Thinking all the time about having MS grew tiresome and intrusive, especially in the large and tragic mode in which I was accustomed to considering my plight. Months and even years went by without catastrophe (at least without one related to MS), and really I was awfully busy, what with George and children and snakes and students and poems, and I hadn't the time, let alone the inclination, to devote myself to being a disease. Too, the richer my life became, the funnier it seemed, as though there were some connection between largesse and laughter, and so my tragic stance began to waver until, even with the aid of a brace and a cane, I couldn't hold it for very long at a time.

31   After several years I was satisfied with my adjustment. I had suffered my grief and fury and terror, I thought, but now I was at ease with my lot. Then one summer day I set out with George and the children across the desert for a vacation in California. Part way to Yuma I became aware that my right leg felt funny. "I think I've had an exacerbation," I told George. "What shall we do?" he asked. "I think we'd better get the hell to California," I said, "because I don't know whether I'll ever make it again." So we went on to San Diego and then to Orange, up the Pacific Coast Highway to Santa Cruz, across to Yosemite, down to Sequoia and Joshua Tree, and so back over the desert to home. It was a fine two-week trip, filled with friends and fair weather, and I wouldn't have missed it for the world, though I did in fact make it back to California two years later. Nor would there have been any point in missing it, since in MS, once the symptoms have appeared, the neurological damage has been done, and there's no way to predict or prevent that damage.

32   The incident spoiled my self-satisfaction, however. I renewed my grief and fury and terror, and I learned that one never finishes adjusting to MS. I don't know now why I thought one would. One

does not, after all, finish adjusting to life, and MS is simply a fact of my life—not my favorite fact, of course—but as ordinary as my nose and my tropical fish and my yellow Mazda station wagon. It may at any time get worse, but no amount of worry or anticipation can prepare me for a new loss. My life is a lesson in losses. I learn one at a time.

33   And I had best be patient in the learning, since I'll have to do it like it or not. As any rock fan knows, you can't always get what you want. Particularly when you have MS. You can't, for example, get cured. In recent years researchers and the organizations that fund research have started to pay MS some attention even though it isn't fatal; perhaps they have begun to see that life is something other than a quantitative phenomenon, that one may be very much alive for a very long time in a life that isn't worth living. The researchers have made some progress toward understanding the mechanism of the disease: It may well be an autoimmune reaction triggered by a slow-acting virus. But they are nowhere near its prevention, control, or cure. And most of us want to be cured. Some, unable to accept incurability, grasp at one treatment after another, no matter how bizarre: megavitamin therapy, gluten-free diet, injections of cobra venom, hypothermal suits, lymphocytopharesis, hyperbaric chambers. Many treatments are probably harmless enough, but none are curative.

34   The absence of a cure often makes MS patients bitter toward their doctors. Doctors are, after all, the priests of modern society, the new shamans, whose business is to heal, and many MS patients rove from one to another, searching for the "good" doctor who will make them well. Doctors too think of themselves as healers, and for this reason many have trouble dealing with MS patients, whose disease in its intransigence defeats their aims and mocks their skills. Too few doctors, it is true, treat their patients as whole human beings, but the reverse is also true. I have always tried to be gentle with my doctors, who often have more at stake in terms of ego than I do. I may be frustrated, maddened, depressed by the incurability of my disease, but I am not diminished by it, and they are. When I push myself up from my seat in the waiting room and stumble toward them, I incarnate the limitation of their powers. The least I can do is refuse to press on their tenderest spots.

35   This gentleness is part of the reason that I'm not sorry to be a cripple. I didn't have it before. Perhaps I'd have developed it anyway—how could I know such a thing?—and I wish I had more

of it, but I'm glad of what I have. It has opened and enriched my life enormously, this sense that my frailty and need must be mirrored in others, that in searching for and shaping a stable core in a life wrenched by change and loss, change and loss, I must recognize the same process, under individual conditions, in the lives around me. I do not deprecate such knowledge, however I've come by it.

36   All the same, if a cure were found, would I take it? In a minute. I may be cripple, but I'm only occasionally a loony and never a saint. Anyway, in my brand of theology God doesn't give bonus points for a limp. I'd take a cure; I just don't need one. A friend who also has MS startled me once by asking, "Do you ever say to yourself, 'Why me, Lord?'" "No, Michael, I don't," I told him, "because whenever I try, the only response I can think of is 'Why not?'" If I could make a cosmic deal, who would I put in my place? What in my life would I give up in exchange for sound limbs and a thrilling rush of energy? No one. Nothing. I might as well do the job myself. Now that I'm getting the hang of it.

EXERCISES

Details and Their Meanings

1. What incident makes the writer decide to write an essay "on being a cripple"? Why does she decide to do so?
2. Why does the writer choose to label herself *cripple?* What other words could she have used? Why does she choose the word she does and not one of the others? What effect does she hope this word will have on people? What effect does this word have on you as a reader?
3. How has multiple sclerosis changed Mairs' life? What things can she do and not do? What does she expect to happen next?
4. How have the writer's husband and children responded to her disability? How have their lives changed? How have their lives remained the same?
5. How does Mairs feel about the fact that multiple sclerosis is incurable? If a cure were found, would she take it? What if she had to give something up in exchange for a cure? What do these responses tell you about how she defines or views herself?

Reading and Critical Thinking

1. At the end of paragraph 5, Mairs says, "I would never refer to another person as a cripple." Why is it all right for her to use this name to refer to herself but not to others? Would you ever use this word to refer to someone with a physical disability? Why or why not?

2. What does the writer's discussion of "semantics" in the first five paragraphs suggest about the relation between words and identity? Do names and labels affect the people they refer to? If so, how? If not, why not?

3. How does the way Mairs presents the "facts" of her disease convey how she feels about being "a cripple"? How does having a disability affect her sense of self?

4. In paragraph 24, Mairs states, "I am not a disease." What does she mean by this? From the statement, what inferences can you make about the way people with disabilities are usually viewed and the struggles they have in viewing themselves?

5. In what ways does Mairs describe her disability as socially constructed, that is, as a product of the way she and others react to her physical limitations? In what ways does she describe her disability as an objective fact, as something that exists physically apart from the reactions of herself and others? How does she reconcile these two descriptions?

6. How does this essay challenge stereotypes about people with disabilities?

The Writer's Strategies

1. What is the thesis of this selection? State it in your own words.

2. How does the first incident described in the essay help identify Mairs's attitude toward her disease, herself, and this essay? What personal narratives other than the opening incident does she present? What effect to they have on the reader?

3. Who is the primary audience for this essay? What assumptions does the writer make about her audience? Are those assumptions justified in your case? Why or why not?

4. What is the tone of this essay? Would you call it angry, resigned, funny, or indifferent, or would you use some other term? Does the tone suit the writer's subject, do you think? Explain your opinion.

5. In describing the effects of multiple sclerosis in paragraph 8, Mairs says a sense of humor is the thing that is "the easiest to lose and the hardest to survive without." Where does Mairs use humor in her essay? Where does she use humor in her own life? What effect does this strategy have on you?

6. How does the writer use comparison and contrast in the essay? What effect does this strategy have on your understanding of what "being a cripple" means?

7. How does Mairs end the essay? How does that ending reflect some of the complexity of her feeling about herself and the disease? What is the particular effect of the last sentence?

Thinking Together

In small groups, generate a list of general and specific terms that are used to label people with disabilities or disabilities themselves, beginning with the terms that Mair discusses at the beginning of her essay. Then, as a class, categorize these terms according to their connotations and discuss the advantages and disadvantages of using each term. Discuss how you might respond to these terms if they were used to describe you or if you used the terms to describe a condition you yourself had.

Vocabulary

This essay uses many technical terms referring to medicine, disease, and cures. Define each of the following using context clues from the essay. Consult a dictionary if necessary.

1. neurologist (par. 7)
2. disseminated (par. 7)
3. diagnosis (par. 7)
4. multiple sclerosis (par. 7)
5. myelin (par. 8)
6. exacerbations (par. 9)
7. *in extremis* (par. 10)
8. physiologically (par. 12)
9. abrasions (par. 14)
10. contractures (par. 22)
11. incontinent (par. 27)
12. symptomatic (par. 27)

13. autoimmune (par. 33)
14. gluten-free (par. 33)
15. hypothermal suits (par. 33)
16. lymphocytopharesis (par. 33)
17. hyperbaric chambers (par. 33)

WRITER'S WORKSHOP

Critical Thinking in Writing

1. Select three terms used by Mairs to refer to people with disabilities. Conduct an informal survey of five of your peers to discover their reactions to the words. Then write up the results of your survey in a report of about two pages.
2. Write a one-page journal entry describing what your life would be like if you had a disability like multiple sclerosis. How would your life be different? What things would change? What things would stay the same?
3. Write an essay comparing two terms that refer to the same personal or group trait (for example, physical capacity, ethnicity, gender). Using the opening paragraphs of Mairs's essay as a model, argue for the use of one term over the other.

Connecting Ideas

Read "Making Things Whole," by Joseph Varilla (page 287). Compare and contrast his experience of multiple sclerosis with that of Nancy Mairs. How is his experience of disability similar to hers? How is it different? What factors account for these differences? gender? marital status? occupation? personality?

Of Mice and Men— and Morality

David Gelman

This selection about a minor event in a laboratory seems at first to be about animal rights. But David Gelman is really writing about the power of language to influence how we think about each other and how we act toward each other. Notice how the simple story at the beginning gains more and more meaning and significance and finally raises major moral issues.

KEY WORDS

scrupulous (par. 2)   extremely careful
pathogens (par. 3)   disease-causing organisms
lethal (par. 4)   deadly
subsist (par. 5)   to live off of
predator (par. 5)   a creature that lives by eating another
imbroglio (par. 6)   a confused tangle

IT WON'T SETTLE THE argument—probably nothing could. But it is something to be pondered in the never-ending wrangle over animal rights. It is a story of "good mice" and "bad mice" and how animal researchers make judgments about them.

2   The University of Tennessee's Walters Life Sciences Building is a model animal facility, spotlessly clean, scrupulous in obtaining prior approval for experiments from an animal-care committee. Of the 15,000 mice housed there in a typical year, most give their lives for humanity. These are "good" mice and, as such, warrant the protection of the animal-care committee.

3   At any given time, however, some mice escape and run free. These mice are pests. They can disrupt experiments with the pathogens they carry. They are "bad" mice and must be captured and destroyed. Usually, this is accomplished by means of "sticky"

traps, a kind of flypaper on which they become increasingly stuck. Mice that are not dead by morning are gassed.

4   But the real point of this cautionary tale, says animal behaviorist Harold A. Herzog Jr., writing in the June issue of *American Psychologist,* is that the labels we put on things can skew our moral responses to them. Using sticky traps or the more lethal snap traps would be deemed unacceptable for good mice. Yet the killing of bad mice requires no prior approval. "Once a research animal hits the floor and becomes an escapee," writes Herzog, "its moral standing is instantly diminished."

5   In Herzog's own home, there was a more ironic example. When his young son's pet mouse, Willie, died recently, it was accorded a tearful, ceremonial burial in the garden. Yet even as they mourned Willie, says Herzog, he and his wife were setting snap traps to kill the pest mice in their kitchen. With the bare change in labels from "pet" to "pest," the kitchen mice attained a totally different moral status. Something of the sort happens with so-called feeders—mice raised to be eaten by other animals. At the Walters facility, no approval is needed for feeding mice to laboratory reptiles that subsist on them. But if a researcher wants to film a mouse defending itself against a predator, the animal-care committee must review the experiment, even though the mouse will often survive. The critical factor in the moral regard of the mouse is whether it is labeled "subject" or "food."

6   **Beyond the Laboratory**   Although it is hard to come near the issue without inflaming it, Herzog insists he has no desire to touch off yet another animal-rights imbroglio. In writing about labeling he was also thinking beyond the laboratory: how politicians or governments use labels, for instance. "A contra is a freedom fighter to the Reagan administration," he says, "but in Nicaragua, a contra may be a terrorist." The moral "numbing" that American GIs experienced in Vietnam resulted in part from their calling the enemy "gooks" and "dinks."

7   Labels can be dehumanizing, a way of disposing of things. Calling ghetto minorities the "underclass" helps identify a problem, but also puts it at an impersonal distance. The "Third World" designation reminds us there is more to our world than the Western and Eastern countries, but it lumps the teeming millions of Asia and Africa into a faceless mass. "Labels," says Herzog, "are a fundamental part of how we interact with people." Not to mention mice.

EXERCISES

Details and Their Meanings

1. Where is the laboratory in which the animal experiments are carried out? How does David Gelman describe it? What point is he making by the description? What kinds of mice are in the laboratory? How are they treated?

2. Who is Harold Herzog? What is the importance of his role? What is his interest in how the mice are treated? Where did he publish his article about the mice? Why is his article appropriate for a journal in psychology?

3. In the opening paragraph, what labels are given to two kinds of mice? How does the writer explain and expand on these labels in the following paragraphs? How do the labels influence the treatment received by the mice?

4. How is the concept "escapee" similar to and different from the concept "bad"? What does the term *escapee* imply about a mouse's former condition and about the mouse's desires? In actual practice, is a mouse treated any differently if it is called "bad" or "escapee"? How does the use of the term *escapee* make you rethink the meaning of the categories "good" and "bad"?

5. In what way is the story of the pet mouse and pest mice in Herzog's home ironic?

6. What is the laboratory distinction between feeders and mice used in studies of predators? Is the fate of the mice the same in both cases? For whom is there a difference? What is the meaning of this difference?

7. In the last two paragraphs, the writer mentions labels given to humans. Which labels are paired with their opposites? What is the significance of using these labels or their opposites? Which labels are not paired with an opposite? What do you think their opposite might be?

8. Do any of these labels applied to humans have a positive intention but partly negative result? How?

Reading and Critical Thinking

1. Gelman begins by mentioning the controversy over animal rights. What is the animal-rights issue? Why is it said to be volatile? Why does the writer say that Herzog's article does not

settle the issue? What does Herzog's article contribute to the discussion?

2. Why don't Gelman and Herzog actually state where they stand on the protection of animal rights? What do you think their position is?

3. In what ways are the examples of mice at home or in the laboratory making the same point? In what ways do they develop slightly different aspects of the same idea?

4. How do you evaluate the practice of treating mice in different ways depending on the labels they are given? Is the difference in treatment silly and absurd, or does it make a certain kind of sense? Explain your opinion.

5. How does the need to do good science and the need to create a pleasant family life stand behind the distinctions made between mice? Are the distinctions warranted? Are the distinctive labels given to humans, described in paragraphs 6 and 7, justifiable? Is it fair to label others because of your own needs? How can you express your needs without labeling others?

The Writer's Strategies

1. What issues does Gelman refer to in the opening paragraph? What is this thesis? What issues does he refer to in the closing paragraph? How does he get from the opening issues to the closing issues?

2. In the middle paragraphs, how many incidents does the writer relate? What point does he make with each of these incidents? How do these incidents work together to raise an important issue overall?

3. What phrases does the writer use to highlight the point of each incident? What phrases does he use to tie the ideas of the separate incidents together?

4. How do the points made by the incidents establish an idea that is developed in the last two paragraphs? What phrases tie the discussion about animal rights to the discussion about human relationships?

5. Each paragraph is built around a contrast of labels. In each paragraph what labels are contrasted? What is the final overall contrast or comparison between mice and humans?

6. What is the purpose of this essay? Who is the audience?

Thinking Together

Form a small group and select one member to read aloud the last paragraph of this essay to the rest of the group. Then discuss the validity of the points raised in the last paragraph. Does your group agree with Gelman? Why? What instances in your own experience support or challenge his conclusions? Finally, report back to the class at large on what your group concluded.

Vocabulary

In this selection, several words and phrases gain special meaning from the way the writer uses them. Give the usual meaning of the following words and phrases. Then find where each item appears in the selection, and define the special meaning created by the context.

1. wrangle (par. 1)
2. warrant (par. 2)
3. cautionary (par. 4)
4. behaviorist (par. 4)
5. skew (par. 4)
6. moral responses (par. 4)
7. moral standing (par. 4)
8. feeders (par. 5)
9. moral regard (par. 5)

WRITER'S WORKSHOP ━━━━━━━━━━━━━━

Critical Thinking in Writing

1. Where do you stand on the issues of animal rights? How did Gelman's article influence your thinking on the issue? Write an essay in which you respond to these questions.
2. In one paragraph, describe a positive label that turned out to have negative consequences.
3. Write several paragraphs describing how people use labels to define people they dislike or people who disagree with their beliefs. Include several appropriate examples.

Connecting Ideas

What light do the ideas presented in this selection shed on the problems of prejudice described in "Bias Outside Appalachia," by Judy Pasternak (page 335); and "Crossing a Boundary," by Athlone G. Clarke (page 349). How might the tensions and divisions described in those articles be thought of in a new way, using the insights presented in "Of Mice and Men—and Morality"?

SIDE BY SIDE

1. In the early part of this century, linguists created an artificial language called Esperanto, which they hoped would become the common language of everyone on Earth one day. Esperanto failed to gain widespread acceptance. Today few people remember it, and even fewer can speak it.

   Would the world be a better place if everyone spoke a common language? How would a common language make the world an easier place in which to live? What would people lose by giving up their national languages in favor of a universal language? Write an argumentative essay drawing on the readings in this unit and support or oppose the idea of giving up national languages for an artificial one.

2. Do you think the number of loan words, such as *macho* and *jazz*, in American English is a sign of the language's strength or weakness? What does American English gain by adopting words from other languages? What are some drawbacks from borrowing words? Write a detailed essay in which you consider this issue.

3. The United States Supreme Court recently has ruled that laws aimed to stop hateful speech are unconstitutional and that freedom of speech is an absolute right, not to be restricted even if people say terrible and insulting things. Do you agree with the Supreme Court's position? Why or why not? Which essays in this section would help you support the argument of absolute free speech? Which would help you oppose it?

FOUR

Jobs: Dollars and Dreams

INTRODUCTION

Regardless of our status or origin, nearly all of us share a belief in the American Dream. In a way, the promise of America is that anyone, no matter how humble or poor, anyone who works and studies hard, anyone with talent, skills, or just plain luck can turn ability into financial success and, ultimately, happiness. We all want to be more successful than our parents, and we expect our children's success to succeed ours.

But dreams sometimes come up against the hard realities that not everyone can rise to the heights of his or her talents, that the dreams and aspirations of some people are "deferred" (to use Langston Hughes's word). Not having a job means not having money, not participating in the economy, not swimming in the mainstream of society. Jobs are essential to fulfilling dreams, sharing in the common life, and gaining the money to live. Yet through persistence, hard work at often menial jobs, and spirited responses to seemingly unyielding obstacles, many people succeed and move ahead in American society.

In this unit, writers share experiences about the struggle to survive and succeed in the world of work. Gary Soto, in "Looking for Work," shows how people strive to connect the reality of their own lives with the images presented on television. Douglas Martin, in "Blind Commuter," and Joseph Varilla, in "Making Things Whole," describe how people with disabilities find dignity and fulfillment in productive work despite the enormous obstacles they confront. In "A Cafe Reopens," William E. Schmidt describes the impact a lunchroom has on the workday life of a Minnesota farming town, and in "Reaching for the Dream," William O'Hare reports on recent trends in minority business ownership in the United States as a whole. In "Green Frog Skin," John Lame Deer, a Native American medicine man, challenges the cash values that support the American dream.

What kind of future do you see for yourself as you take your place in the work force after you leave college? These readings will provide a fascinating look at the interconnections among race, gender, ethnicity, jobs, and economic realities and will help place in perspective your personal efforts to unify dollars and dreams.

PREREADING JOURNAL

1. Write about the best and the worst jobs you ever had. What were they? What about them made them good or bad for you? How did those experiences point you toward the career path that you wish to pursue?

2. Describe the experiences you and your family have had working in the American economy. Has the American economy been a friendly place for your family and you? Have you or your family found satisfying work that will provide an income to allow for a decent way of life? What obstacles or frustrations have you and your family encountered as you tried to find a place in the American economy? To what extent have gender, racial, or ethnic factors influenced the work experiences of your family and yourself?

3. Write a journal entry about where you expect to be in twenty years. What sort of career will you have? What steps will you have to take to achieve your career goals? What career ambitions will you have achieved? What kind of lifestyle will your chosen career enable you to have?

Looking for Work

Gary Soto

Gary Soto is an award-winning poet and author who teaches English and Chicano studies at the University of California at Berkeley. An American of Mexican descent, Soto quickly grasped the difference between Anglo and Chicano culture, as this excerpt from his Living Up the Street *(1985) shows.*

KEY WORDS

egg candler (par. 4)   someone who examines chicken eggs
   to determine whether they have been fertilized
muu-muu (par. 5)   a loose-fitting housedress
feigned (par. 12)   pretended
chavalo (par. 25)   an informal Spanish word meaning "boy"

ONE JULY, WHILE KILLING ants on the kitchen sink with a rolled newspaper, I had a nine-year-old's vision of wealth that would save us from ourselves. For weeks I had drunk Kool-Aid and watched morning reruns of *Father Knows Best,* whose family was so uncomplicated in its routine that I very much wanted to imitate it. The first step was to get my brother and sister to wear shoes at dinner.

2   "Come on, Rick—come on, Deb," I whined. But Rick mimicked me, and the same day that I asked him to wear shoes, he came to the dinner table in only his swim trunks. My mother didn't notice, nor did my sister, as we sat to eat our beans and tortillas in the stifling heat of our kitchen. We all gleamed like cellophane, wiping the sweat from our brows with the backs of our hands as we talked about the day: Frankie our neighbor was beat up by Faustino; the swimming pool at the playground would be closed for a day because the pump was broken.

3   Such was our life. So that morning, while doing-in the train of ants which arrived each day, I decided to become wealthy, and right away! After downing a bowl of cereal, I took a rake from the garage and started up the block to look for work.

4   We lived on an ordinary block of mostly working-class people: warehousemen, egg candlers, welders, mechanics, and a union plumber. And there were many retired people who kept their lawns green and the gutters uncluttered of the chewing gum wrappers we dropped as we rode by on our bikes. They bent down to gather our litter, muttering at our evilness.

5   At the corner house I rapped the screen door and a very large woman in a muu-muu answered. She sized me up and then asked what I could do.

6   "Rake leaves," I answered, smiling.

7   "It's summer, and there ain't no leaves," she countered. Her face was pinched with lines; fat jiggled under her chin. She pointed to the lawn, then the flower bed, and said: "You see any leaves there—or there?" I followed her pointing arm, stupidly. But she had a job for me and that was to get her a Coke at the liquor store. She gave me twenty cents, and after ditching my rake in a bush, off I ran. I returned with an unbagged Pepsi, for which she thanked me and gave me a nickel from her apron.

8   I skipped off her porch, fetched my rake, and crossed the street to the next block where Mrs. Moore, mother of Earl the retarded man, let me weed a flower bed. She handed me a trowel and for a good part of the morning my fingers dipped into the moist dirt, ripping up runners of Bermuda grass. Worms surfaced in my search for deep roots, and I cut them in halves, tossing them to Mrs. Moore's cat who pawed them playfully as they dried in the sun. I made out Earl whose face was pressed to the back window of the house, and although he was calling to me I couldn't understand what he was trying to say. Embarrassed, I worked without looking up, but I imagined his contorted mouth and the ring of keys attached to his belt—keys that jingled with each palsied step. He scared me and I worked quickly to finish the flower bed. When I did finish Mrs. Moore gave me a quarter and two peaches from her tree, which I washed there but ate in the alley behind my house.

9   I was sucking on the second one, a bit of juice staining the front of my T-shirt, when Little John, my best friend, came walking down the alley with a baseball bat over his shoulder, knocking over trash cans as he made his way toward me.

10   Little John and I went to St. John's Catholic School, where we sat among the "stupids." Miss Marino, our teacher, alternated the rows of good students with the bad, hoping that by sitting side-by-side with the bright students the stupids might become more intelligent, as though intelligence were contagious. But we didn't

progress as she had hoped. She grew frustrated when one day, while dismissing class for recess, Little John couldn't get up because his arms were stuck in the slats of the chair's backrest. She scolded us with a shaking finger when we knocked over the globe, denting the already troubled Africa. She muttered curses when Leroy White, a real stupid but a great softball player with the gift to hit to all fields, openly chewed his host when he made his First Communion; his hands swung at his sides as he returned to the pew looking around with a big smile.

11   Little John asked what I was doing, and I told him that I was taking a break from work, as I sat comfortably among high weeds. He wanted to join me, but I reminded him that the last time he'd gone door-to-door asking for work his mother had whipped him. I was with him when his mother, a New Jersey Italian who could rise up in anger one moment and love the next, told me in a polite but matter-of-fact voice that I had to leave because she was going to beat her son. She gave me a homemade popsicle, ushered me to the door, and said that I could see Little John the next day. But it was sooner than that. I went around to his bedroom window to suck my popsicle and watch Little John dodge his mother's blows, a few hitting their mark but many whirring air.

12   It was midday when Little John and I converged in the alley, the sun blazing in the high nineties, and he suggested that we go to Roosevelt High School to swim. He needed five cents to make fifteen, the cost of admission, and I lent him a nickel. We ran home for my bike and when my sister found out that we were going swimming she started to cry because she didn't have the fifteen cents but only an empty Coke bottle. I waved for her to come and three of us mounted the bike—Debra on the cross bar, Little John on the handle bars and holding the Coke bottle which we would cash for a nickel and make up the difference that would allow all of us to get in, and me pumping up the crooked streets, dodging cars and pot holes. We spent the day swimming under the afternoon sun, so that when we got home our mom asked us what was darker, the floor or us? She feigned a stern posture, her hands on her hips and her mouth puckered. We played along. Looking down, Debbie and I said in unison, "Us."

13   That evening at dinner we all sat down in our bathing suits to eat our beans, laughing and chewing loudly. Our mom was in a good mood, so I took a risk and asked her if sometime we could have turtle soup. A few days before I had watched a television program in which a Polynesian tribe killed a large turtle, gutted

it, and then stewed it over an open fire. The turtle, basted in a sugary sauce, looked delicious as I ate an afternoon bowl of cereal, but my sister, who was watching the program with a glass of Kool-Aid between her knees, said, "Caca."

14   My mother looked at me in bewilderment. "Boy, are you a crazy Mexican. Where did you get the idea that people eat turtles?"

15   "On television," I said, explaining the program. Then I took it a step further. "Mom, do you think we could get dressed up for dinner one of these days? David King does."

16   "*Ay, Dios,*" my mother laughed. She started collecting the dinner plates, but my brother wouldn't let go of his. He was still drawing a picture in the bean sauce. Giggling, he said it was me, but I didn't want to listen because I wanted an answer from Mom. This was the summer when I spent the mornings in front of the television that showed the comfortable lives of white kids. There were no beatings, no rifts in the family. They wore bright clothes; toys tumbled from their closets. They hopped into bed with kisses and woke to glasses of fresh orange juice and to a father sitting before his morning coffee while the mother buttered his toast. They hurried through the day making friends and gobs of money, returning home to a warmly lit living room, and then dinner. *Leave It to Beaver* was the program I replayed in my mind:

17   "May I have the mashed potatoes?" asks Beaver with a smile.

18   "Sure, Beav," replies Wally as he taps the corners of his mouth with a starched napkin.

19   The father looks on in his suit. The mother, decked out in earrings and a pearl necklace, cuts into her steak and blushes. Their conversation is politely clipped.

20   "Swell," says Beaver, his cheeks puffed with food.

21   Our own talk at dinner was loud with belly laughs and marked by our pointing forks at one another. The subjects were commonplace.

22   "Gary, let's go to the ditch tomorrow," my brother suggests. He explains that he has made a life preserver out of four empty detergent bottles strung together with twine and that he will make me one if I can find more bottles. "No way are we going to drown."

23   "Yeah, then we could have a dirt clod fight," I reply, so happy to be alive.

24   Whereas the Beaver's family enjoyed dessert in dishes at the table, our mom sent us outside, and more often than not I went into the alley to peek over the neighbor's fences and spy out fruit, apricots or peaches.

25   I had asked my mom and again she laughed that I was a crazy *chavalo* as she stood in front of the sink, her arms rising and falling with suds, face glistening from the heat. She sent me outside where my brother and sister were sitting in the shade that the fence threw out like a blanket. They were talking about me when I plopped down next to them. They looked at one another and then Debbie, my eight-year-old sister, started in.

26   "What's this crap about getting dressed up?"

27   She had entered her profanity stage. A year later she would give up such words and slip into her Catholic uniform and into squealing on my brother and me when we "cussed this" and "cussed that."

28   I tried to convince them that if we improved the way we looked we might get along better in life. White people would like us more. They might invite us to places, like their homes or front yards. They might not hate us so much.

29   My sister called me a "craphead" and got up to leave with a stalk of grass dangling from her mouth. "They'll never like us."

30   My brother's mood lightened as he talked about the ditch— the white water, the broken pieces of glass, and the rusted car fenders that awaited our knees. There would be toads, and rocks to smash them.

31   David King, the only person we knew who resembled the middle class, called from over the fence. David was Catholic, of Armenian and French descent, and his closet was filled with toys. A bear-shaped cookie jar, like the ones on television, sat on the kitchen counter. His mother was remarkably kind while she put up with the racket we made on the street. Evenings, she often watered the front yard and it must have upset her to see us—my brother and I and others—jump from trees laughing, the unkillable kids of the very poor, who got up unshaken, brushed off, and climbed into another one to try again.

32   David called again. Rick got up and slapped grass from his pants. When I asked if I could come along he said no. David said no. They were two years older so their affairs were different from mine. They greeted one another with foul names and took off down the alley to look for trouble.

33   I went inside the house, turned on the television, and was about to sit down with a glass of Kool-Aid when Mom shooed me outside.

34   "It's still light," she said. "Later you'll bug me to let you stay out longer. So go on."

35   I downed my Kool-Aid and went outside to the front yard. No one was around. The day had cooled and a breeze rustled the trees. Mr. Jackson, the plumber, was watering his lawn and when he saw me he turned away to wash off his front steps. There was more than an hour of light left, so I took advantage of it and decided to look for work. I felt suddenly alive as I skipped down the block in search of an overgrown flower bed and the dime that would end the day right.

_____

EXERCISES

Details and Their Meanings

1. How old is the narrator? In what decade does this piece take place? What suggests the time frame to you?
2. What kind of neighborhood does the narrator live in? What is its ethnic composition? What details give you clues about the family's economic status?
3. What are some jobs that the narrator does to earn money?
4. Where does the narrator go to school? What group does he belong to? What is his teacher's hope in placing students in class?
5. Who is Little John? Where is he from? Who is David King? Why is he an important figure to the narrator?
6. What does the narrator want his family to do at dinner? Why do they reject this proposal?

Reading and Critical Thinking

1. What evidence is there of the narrator's ethnic identity? How does that identity influence the point of view?
2. How do distinctions between different classes of people show up in this piece?
3. Why is the mother angry when the children come home from the pool? Is she justified? Why or why not?
4. What does the request for turtle soup convey about the differ-

ences between the narrator and the rest of his family? How do
you think these differences might have developed?
5. What attitude toward television is expressed in this narrative?
Do you agree or disagree with it? Why or why not?
6. What does Gary Soto mean when he says that the poor children
in the neighborhood were "unkillable"? In what sense is he
using the word?

The Writer's Strategies

1. What is the main point that Soto is trying to make?
2. Why has the writer chosen to tell this narrative in the first
person?
3. How do details help make this piece effective? Which details
do you find appealing? What kinds of sensory descriptions
does Soto use? Which sense predominates in this narrative?
4. Why is this piece titled "Looking for Work"? Did the title prepare you for the narrative? Why or why not?
5. What ordering or organizing principle keeps the selection moving despite the sidetracks from the main narrative?
6. Why does the selection end the same way it began, with the
narrator looking for work? What effect does this full circle
achieve?
7. Where does this selection reach the climax, the decisive point
of resolution? How has the piece been building toward this
point?
8. Why does Soto refer to profanity without using any? How
would this piece be different if he had used profane language?

Thinking Together

The two television shows referred to in this selection, *Father Knows
Best* and *Leave It to Beaver*, showed idealized suburban families and
in a sense gave people who grew up in the 1950s and 1960s a romantic view of how a normal family behaved. What television
shows represent family life today? Brainstorm in groups about
shows like *Beverly Hills 90210*, *The Simpsons*, *Family Ties*, *Roseanne*,
and any others that deal with family life. What kinds of problems
do the shows address? How do they give a true or false picture of
family life?

Vocabulary

The writer creates some vivid images in this selection. Restate the following images in your own words.

1. gleamed like cellophane (par. 2)
2. the train of ants (par. 3)
3. her face was pinched with lines (par. 4)
4. runners of Bermuda grass (par. 8)
5. palsied step (par. 8)
6. blows . . . whirring air (par. 11)
7. toys tumbled from their closets (par. 16)
8. breeze rustled the trees (par. 35)

WRITER'S WORKSHOP ━━━━━━━━━━━━

Critical Thinking in Writing

1. Write a short essay entitled "Looking for Work."
2. Gary Soto describes himself as the only member of his family who aspired to rise above "the commonplace." Which member of your family or of some family you know has similar aspirations? In what ways does this person try to be different? How do other people in the family treat this person?
3. Write an essay in which you explain some of the special problems facing teenagers who seek to join America's work force. What workplace conditions affect a young worker's attitudes most, do you think?

Connecting Ideas

Read "Kiss of Death," Armando Rendón's account of growing up as a Chicano in a predominantly Anglo environment (page 125). How much of Soto's account agrees with Rendón's? What are some major differences in their experiences? What can you conclude about what life was like for a Chicano growing up in northern California?

Blind Commuter

Douglas Martin

Douglas Martin, a reporter for the metropolitan section of The New York Times, *examines the life of Alberto Torres, an X-ray developer at Bronx Municipal Hospital.*

KEY WORDS

labyrinthine (par. 7)   like a complicated maze
invariably (par. 9)   without fail, always the same way
interminably (par. 9)   endlessly
rehabilitating (par. 11)   repairing, fixing for further use
arduous (par. 12)   extremely difficult
transcends (par. 17)   rises above

YOU COULD FEEL SORRY for Alberto Torres, who is blind. The last thing he remembers seeing was his daughter, Lauren, being born 13 years ago. Then the world went blank; he can only imagine what his only child looks like as a cheerleader and honor student.

2   Total darkness came as a result of an inflammation of his optic nerve—a condition that was unrelated to the retinal disease that had obscured his vision since birth. "I went to sleep and woke up with nothing," he said.

3   Bad luck is no stranger to this warm and thoughtful 37-year-old man. His mother died of cancer when he was 4, and Mr. Torres's ailing father had to give him up to foster care when he was 11. He later worked for 19 years in a workshop assembling mops and other household goods, mind-numbing stuff.

4   Earlier this month, Alberto Torres's wife, Idalia, who had just been laid off from her job as a receptionist, had a radical mastectomy and now faces a year of chemotherapy and radiation treatments. Things seemed always to go from almost unbelievably bad to worse. Even Mr. Torres's good luck has a dark side: Five years ago, his beloved seeing-eye dog, Gambler, got him out of the path of a truck. Mr. Torres was unharmed; Gambler died.

251

5   But know this and know it well: Mr. Torres does not feel sorry for himself. "These are just little bumps you have to go over in your life," he said.

6   At 5 A.M. on a recent morning, we caught up with Mr. Torres at the Nassau Avenue subway stop in Greenpoint, Brooklyn, where he lives in a third-floor walkup. He had been up since 3, feeding Greg, his new dog, making coffee, getting ready. "When you're blind, it takes a little longer to do things," he said.

7   Mr. Torres was beginning the labyrinthine two-hour trip to his job developing film in the X-ray department of the emergency room of the Bronx Municipal Hospital Center. He would take the G train to Queens Plaza where he would walk up a set of stairs and down another to the Manhattan-bound RR train. He would then ride the RR to 59th Street where he would walk upstairs to switch to the No. 6.

8   At one point along the journey, he might chat with a stranger. At another, someone would pat Greg, calling him by name. People offered assistance, even seats.

9   At 125th Street, Mr. Torres would transfer to the No. 4 by crossing the platform. At 149th Street, he would descend to the No. 2. He would take that to East 180th Street where he invariably waits interminably for his final train, the Dyre Avenue shuttle to Pelham Parkway. Then he and Greg would walk 20 minutes to the hospital.

10   "They shouldn't make any special provisions for me," Mr. Torres said. "It's a job, and I should be on time."

11   It was a hard job to come by. Before he got the job, Mr. Torres was determined to escape the workshop run by the Lighthouse, an organization dedicated to rehabilitating the visually impaired, and to try to make it on his own. He wanted a job developing X-ray film, something that everyone must do in the dark. The Lighthouse called many hospitals, to no avail, even though they offered to pay his first three months' salary and provide training.

12   The Lighthouse people would have much preferred something closer to his home. But they believed he could handle the arduous trip, as well as the work. "Our philosophy here is that blind people can do just about anything besides drive buses," said Marianne Melley, who tries to help place blind people in jobs.

13   And that, as it turned out, was also the thinking about disabled people at the Bronx hospital. "We find what a person can do rather than what he can't do," said Noel McFarlane, the hospital's associate executive director.

14   "The point is that it works," Pamela Brier, executive director, said.

15   One day a while ago marked the first anniversary of Mr. Torres's hiring. He will likely develop 150 or so X-rays, his usual output, to celebrate. The cards with names and other data will be folded on the upper right hand corner so he can photograph them right-side-up. That is the only concession to blindness.

16   Mr. Torres works by himself in a small, chemical-scented darkroom. He cannot wear protective gloves because he needs to feel. It is exacting work, and, since this is an emergency room, lives can be at stake. His immediate supervisor, Alcides Santambrosio, says he trusts him 100 percent.

17   Mr. Torres makes $20,000 a year. He could be pocketing more than $12,000 from disability payments. But his motivation transcends money. "If I start feeling like a victim, that makes me bitter," he said. "And why be bitter? That makes you go into a hole and stay there."

18   Just then, a technician rushed in undeveloped X-rays of a teenager who had jumped from a window and was in critical condition.

19   "I'm not doing anything out of the ordinary," insisted Mr. Torres as he briskly completed the task.

EXERCISES

Details and Their Meanings

1. Who is Alberto Torres? How did he go blind? When did it happen? What was the last thing he remembers seeing?
2. What other hardships has Torres overcome? Where does he work now? How long has he been working there?
3. What kind of job did Torres have previously? How long was he there? Why did he want to leave this job?
4. Where does Torres live? How does he get to work? What time does he have to get up every morning in order to be at work on time?
5. What is the Lighthouse? How did the Lighthouse help Torres?

6. In what ways has Torres's job been modified to accommodate his visual impairment?

Reading and Critical Thinking

1. Why does Douglas Martin list all the troubles Alberto Torres has endured? How do you think you would have responded to these troubles? What steps can society take to cut down on problems faced by differently abled people?
2. Why is it so hard for Torres to get to work? Would all of his commuting problems vanish if his vision were normal? Why or why not?
3. Where does the writer criticize the subway system? Are his complaints valid? How can other forms of mass transit—buses, planes, and trains—make it easier for the differently abled to use travel facilities?
4. Why is Torres's job a good one for a blind person? What other kinds of jobs are well suited to visually impaired people?
5. Why does Martin mention how much money Torres could receive in disability payments? Why do you think Torres has not chosen this option? If you could advise Torres about taking disability pay, what would you tell him? Why?
6. How does Martin describe Alberto Torres? How does Torres describe himself? How do the descriptions differ? With which description do you agree? Why?

The Writer's Strategies

1. What is the thesis of this selection? Where is it expressed?
2. Why does Martin take four paragraphs to tell how Torres gets to work?
3. What writing strategies is Martin primarily using—description, narration, example? Support your answer with specific references to the text.
4. Identify a paragraph in which Martin uses details.
5. What is the concluding quotation intended to show?
6. Why does the writer quote both the executive director and the associate executive director of the hospital? Why isn't one quotation enough?

Thinking Together

Imagine how your journey to classes or work would be changed if you lost your sight. What things would you have to do differently? What adjustments would you need to make at school, at work, and at home? In small groups, develop responses to these questions.

Vocabulary

The effective use of adjectives and adverbs can heighten the meaning of sentences. Explain why the italicized adjectives and adverbs from the selection make each phrase more forceful.

1. *unbelievably* bad (par. 4)
2. waits *interminably* (par. 9)
3. *arduous* trip (par. 12)
4. *exacting* work (par. 16)
5. *briskly* completed (par. 19)

WRITER'S WORKSHOP ━━━━━━━━━━

Critical Thinking in Writing

1. Some people argue that providing equal access to differently abled Americans would be too expensive and that the costs of installing ramps, Braille signs and buttons on elevators, and so on are not justified. Do you agree? Present your views in an argumentative essay.
2. *Ableism* is a belief that physically challenged people are in some sense inferior to the majority of people who have no special challenges. Sometimes, ableism takes the form of pity or celebrating the ordinary achievements of differently abled people as if they were heroic deeds. Is Douglas Martin's essay ableist? Should Alberto Torres be seen as a hero or as an average man? Write a paragraph to respond to these questions.
3. Alberto Torres believes that everyone has "bumps" to get over in life, although the word *bump* seems to minimize Torres's physical challenges. What bumps have you overcome? How

do they compare with Torres's? Describe, narrate, and give examples of adversity that you faced and overcame.

Connecting Ideas

Read Nancy Mairs's "On Being a Cripple" (page 215). How are Torres's and Mairs's attitudes toward their conditions similar, and how are they different? With what attitudes do they face their physical challenges? What attitude and emotions do they have toward their disabilities? What do they set as goals for their lives?

Reaching for the Dream

William O'Hare

In this study, William O'Hare, a demographic researcher at the University of Louisville, examines statistics on increased minority business ownership in the United States.

KEY WORDS

decennial (par. 7)   done every decade (ten years)
enclave (par. 19)   a small community isolated from a larger surrounding one
potent (par. 19)   powerful, impressive
incubator (par. 19)   an ideal environment for growth

THE RAPID GROWTH OF minority populations is changing the profile of America's business owners. In 1987, minorities owned nearly one-tenth of the nation's 13.7 million firms. As a result, businesses that sell to entrepreneurs face a rapidly changing market. Minority business owners are also altering the balance of economic and political power.

2   The number of businesses owned by various minority groups in 1982 and 1987 is collected in the Census Bureau's Survey of Minority-Owned Business Enterprises. The data reveal wide variations in rates of business ownership among minority groups.[1]

Good Years

3   The mid-1980s were good years for minority business owners. Every significant minority group experienced an increase in the

---

[1] The types of firms included in this study are restricted to partnerships, individual proprietorships, and Subchapter S corporations. For large corporations with many stockholders, determining the race of the owners is virtually impossible.

Minority Business Owners
Koreans are the minority group most likely to own a business; American Indians are the least likely.

(Minority-owned firms per 1,000 population, for minority groups, and percent change 1982–87.)

	1987	1982	Percent Change 1982–87
BLACKS	14.6	11.3	29.2%
HISPANICS	20.9	14.3	46.2
Mexican	18.8	13.7	37.2
Puerto Rican	10.9	6.3	73.0
Cuban	62.9	41.4	51.9
Other Hispanic	22.9	14.2	61.3
ASIAN*	57.0	43.2	31.9
Asian Indian	75.7	51.3	47.6
Chinese	63.4	49.1	29.1
Japanese	66.1	59.3	11.5
Korean	102.4	68.0	50.6
Vietnamese	49.6	14.6	239.7
Filipino	32.8	25.5	28.6
Hawaiian	21.5	16.6	29.5
AMERICAN INDIAN	11.8	8.8	34.1
Aleut	54.0	58.5	−7.7
Eskimo	44.4	36.8	20.7
Native American	10.3	7.4	39.2
NONMINORITY	67.1	61.9	8.4

* Includes Pacific Islanders.

Source: Bureau of the Census, 1982 and 1987 Economic Censuses and population estimates

number of businesses owned and in rates of business ownership. But some minority groups have much higher rates of business ownership than others, and the increases of the mid-1980s were not evenly shared.

4   The total number of minority-owned firms grew by nearly half a million during the mid-1980s, from 742,000 in 1982 to 1,214,000 in 1987. This is more than four times the rate of growth for all businesses (64 percent versus 14 percent). By 1987, minorities owned about 9 percent of the firms in this country, up from 6 percent in 1982.

5   But these overall rates mask important differences among sub-

Asian Profit Centers

The average Asian-owned business
makes twice as much as the
average black-owned business.

(Total minority-owned businesses, total receipts and receipts
per firm, by minority type, 1987.)

	Number of Firms 1987	Receipts (in $000)	Receipts per Firm
Black	424,200	$19,762,900	$46,600
Hispanic	422,400	24,731,600	58,600
Asian*	355,300	33,124,300	93,200
American Indians**	21,400	911,300	42,600

* *Includes Pacific Islanders.*
** *Includes Eskimos and Aleuts.*

Source: Bureau of the Census, 1987 Economic Census

groups. The number of firms owned by Asians[2] grew by 89 percent during the five-year period, not far behind the rate of Asian population growth. The number of firms owned by Hispanics grew by 81 percent. The number of firms owned by American Indians grew 58 percent, a rate slightly below the overall average for minorities, but far higher than the group's population growth rate. Business growth was weakest among black-owned businesses, at 38 percent. But that was still faster than the 13-percent rate of black population growth between 1980 and 1990.

6   The rapid growth of Hispanic-owned firms has brought them to parity with the number of black-owned firms. Blacks owned 424,000 U.S. businesses in 1987, and Hispanics owned 422,000. Each group accounts for just over one-third of minority-owned businesses. Asians account for 29 percent; American Indians, 2 percent.

Asians Have the Edge

7   The raw numbers don't reveal the relative success of various groups. A better measure of success is the business-ownership rate, or the number of businesses owned by members of a group relative to their population size. We used decennial census data to estimate the midyear population of minority groups in 1982 and 1987.

---

[2] In this article, the term *Asians* includes Pacific Islanders, and the term *American Indians* includes Eskimos and Aleuts.

8   The popular image of Asians as industrious immigrants is true. Asians own 57 businesses for every 1,000 people, by far the highest business ownership rate of the four major groups. Their rate is almost three times as high as the rate for the next-highest minority group (Hispanics), but it is still below the business-ownership rate of nonminorities, which was 67 in 1987. Blacks have a business-ownership rate of 15, slightly higher than the rate for American Indians.

9   The high rate of business ownership among Asians is due to several factors. First is their high level of educational attainment. In 1990, about 40 percent of adult Asian Americans had completed college, compared with only 23 percent of non-Hispanic whites. Asian Americans also have relatively high incomes, which provide them with more capital to launch small businesses.

10   A large share of Asian Americans are recent immigrants, many of whom came to the United States specifically to go into business. Between 1982 and 1989, 38 percent of immigrants from Asia and the Pacific Islands had professional or executive occupations, compared with only 17 percent of immigrants from other parts of the world, according to the U.S. Immigration and Naturalization Service. And Asian Americans are concentrated in Los Angeles, San Francisco, and other large West Coast cities where local economies were booming during the 1980s.

11   Minority groups differ from each other in terms of their rates of business ownership and also in the sizes of the firms they own. Once again, Asians have the edge. The average income of an Asian-owned firm was $93,200 in 1987, significantly higher than the average for any other minority group. Hispanic-owned firms had the next highest average income, at $58,600, followed by firms owned by blacks ($46,600) and by American Indians ($42,600).

12   Asian-owned firms have a higher average income, in part, because of the types of firms Asians own. More than 5 percent of Asian-owned firms are partnerships, which tend to be bigger businesses. Just 2.9 percent of Hispanic-owned businesses are partnerships, compared with 2.7 percent of firms owned by blacks and 2.6 percent by American Indians.

13   The larger size of Asian-owned firms is also reflected in data on the number of firms that have paid employees. Most minority-owned businesses have no paid employees other than the owner (as do nonminority-owned businesses). But 26 percent of Asian-owned businesses had paid employees in 1987, compared with 20 percent for Hispanics, 17 percent for American Indians, and 17 per-

Blacks Move Over

Blacks are losing their status as the largest
group of minority business owners.

(Total minority-owned businesses and share of all minority business,
by minority type, and percent growth in businesses, 1982–87.)

| | 1987 | | 1982 | | Percent |
	Number	Percent of Total	Number	Percent of Total	Change 1982–87
All minorities	1,213,800***	—	741,600	—	63.7%
Black	424,200	34.9%	308,300	41.6%	37.6
Hispanic	422,400	34.8	234,000	31.5	80.5
Asian*	355,300	29.3	187,700	25.3	89.3
American Indian**	21,400	1.8	13,600	1.8	57.5

Includes Pacific Islanders.
**Includes Eskimos and Aleuts.*
***Numbers do not add to total because firms that were owned equally by two or more minorities are included in the data for each minority group.*

Source: Bureau of the Census, Economic Censuses

cent for blacks. Among firms with at least one paid employee, the average number of employees for Asian-owned firms was 3.79, compared with 3.19 for firms owned by Hispanics, 3.11 by blacks, and 2.40 by American Indians.

Koreans Are Doing Better

14   Large differences also exist in the business-ownership rates of Asian and Hispanic subgroups. In some cases, the differences between subgroups are larger than the differences between races. The clear leaders among minority business owners are Koreans.

15   In 1982, Koreans had the highest rate of business ownership of any minority group, with 68 businesses owned for every 1,000 Korean residents. By 1987, that rate had gone sky-high. The most recent data show that more than one of every ten Korean Americans is a business owner.

16   The Korean rate of 102 businesses owned per 1,000 population is higher than the rate of any other racial or ethnic group, including nonminorities. This high rate reflects the selective migration of Koreans to the United States, and their relatively high levels of educational attainment. It may also reflect certain sociological or cultural traits of the Korean population in America. For example, Koreans show a willingness to pool their resources to help other Koreans start or expand a business.

17   Several other Asian groups also have high business-ownership rates. These include Asian Indians (76 businesses per 1,000 population), Japanese (66), and Chinese (63). All three of these groups are well represented in the United States at the beginning of the decade. The 1980 census showed that Asian Indians were 10 percent of all Asians and Pacific Islanders, Japanese were 20 percent, and Chinese were 23 percent.

18   The relatively high business-ownership rates among Eskimos (44 per 1,000) and Aleuts (54 per 1,000) are probably because they live in isolated communities almost totally populated by fellow members of these groups. Business ownership reflects that population distribution.

19   Among Hispanics, Cubans have by far the highest business-ownership rates, at 63 businesses for every 1,000 Cuban Americans. This rate is more than three times that of Mexicans (19) and nearly six times that of Puerto Ricans (11). The high rate of business ownership among Cubans is probably due to the selective migration of former business owners and better-educated adults following Fidel Castro's rise to power in 1959. Another reason is the heavy concentration of Cubans in the Miami area, which had a booming economy during the 1980s. That large, prosperous ethnic enclave provides Miami's Cubans with a potent small-business incubator. And 20 percent of Cuban adults have a college education, compared with 9 percent of all Hispanics.

20   The numbers show that some segments of America's minority population are more likely to own businesses than are non-Hispanic whites. Other groups are catching up fast. Taken together, minorities are rapidly becoming a larger share of America's business owners.

EXERCISES

Details and Their Meanings

1. What percentage of America's businesses were owned by members of minority groups in 1982? in 1987? What factors account for this change?

2. Which minority group experienced the largest increase in business-ownership rates between 1982 and 1987? Which group experienced the smallest increase? Why did some minority groups experience higher growth rates than others?
3. Which minority group is more likely to own a business? Which is least likely? How does the writer account for this difference?
4. Which minority-owned businesses have the most income? Which have the least? How does the writer account for this phenomenon?
5. Which Asian subgroup has the largest percentage per 1,000 population of business owners? Which Hispanic subgroups has the largest percentage per 1,000 population of business owners? What reason is given for these facts?
6. How does the writer account for relatively high business-ownership rates of Eskimos and Aleuts?

Reading and Critical Thinking

1. The first paragraph mentions that "in 1987 minorities owned nearly one-tenth of the nation's 13.7 million firms." How does this percentage compare with overall percentage of minorities in the population? What inferences, if any, can you draw from these figures?
2. At the end of the first paragraph, the writer states that increased rates of minority business ownership are "altering the balance of economic and political power" in the United States. What does he mean by this statement?
3. How much does the economic climate during the mid-1980s help to explain the increases in minority business-ownership rates reported in this selection? Given what you know about the current economic climate, do you think that these increases will continue? Why? What are your predictions for future minority business-ownership rates?
4. How does the writer's points about Asian business ownership either reinforce or challenge stereotypes about Asians and Asian Americans? How do the pictures of the business success of other groups mentioned in the article reinforce or contradict stereotypes?
5. What conclusions can you draw from the data in this article about the way various minorities are participating in the American economy?

6. One of the basic beliefs of American society is that education is the key to success. In what ways does O'Hare's study support this belief?

The Writer's Strategies

1. What is the thesis of the essay? What is the purpose? Are the thesis and purpose stated directly? If so, where?
2. What kinds of statistical data does the writer cite in this selection? What is the source of these data? How does this source give authority to the writer's claims?
3. What statistic does the writer use in the opening paragraph? How does this information provide an effective opening to the essay?
4. What kinds of visual aids does the writer provide in this selection? How do they supplement the information conveyed in the written text?
5. Who is the intended audience for this selection? Why might this audience be interested in the data that the writer reports?

Thinking Together

Find an article on the economy or on minority business ownership from a recent newspaper or news magazine. In class, break into small groups and compare articles. Then present your findings to the class in order to generate a description of the present state of the economy and its effect on minority business ownership.

Vocabulary

Determine the meanings of the following business and economics terms used in this selection by considering the context in which they appear. Write definitions in your own words.

1. firms (par. 1)
2. entrepreneurs (par. 1)
3. market (par. 1)
4. parity (par. 6)
5. capital (par. 9)
6. professional (par. 10)

7. executive (par. 10)
8. local economies (par. 10)
9. booming (par. 10)
10. partnerships (par. 12)
11. selective migration (par. 16)

WRITER'S WORKSHOP

Critical Thinking in Writing

1. Write a one-page summary of the statistical data reported in this selection. Choose only the most important data from the written text and tables.
2. Recent economic hard times have made some people resent recent immigrants who come to the United States, buy businesses, and achieve the American dream. Write an informal journal entry exploring how you feel about this issue. Use both data from the article and your own experience.
3. The title of this selection refers to the American Dream. Write a one-page description of the version of this dream implied by the selection. What are the minority business owners described in this selection reaching for? How is this version of the American Dream similar to or different from your own?

Connecting Ideas

"Like Mother, Like Daughter" on page 271 describes how women are taking over family businesses. In what ways are the factors that lead women to become entrepreneurs similar to and different from the factors that lead members of minorities to become entrepreneurs? Also how can you relate the attitudes toward business of the new entrepreneurs as described in the two selections?

Green Frog Skin

John Lame Deer

John Lame Deer is writer, lecturer, and shaman of the Sioux tribe. In this essay, he critiques the values related to money in white American society.

KEY WORDS

gally-hooting (par. 2)   racing
buffalo chips (par. 3)   dried manure used as fuel

THE GREEN FROG SKIN—that's what I call a dollar bill. In our attitude toward it lies the biggest difference between Indians and whites. My grandparents grew up in an Indian world without money. Just before the Custer battle, the white soldiers had received their pay. Their pockets were full of green paper and they had no place to spend it. What were their last thoughts as an Indian bullet or arrow hit them? I guess they were thinking of all that money going to waste, of not having had a chance to enjoy it, of a bunch of dumb savages getting their paws on that hard-earned pay. That must have hurt them more than the arrow between their ribs.

2   The close hand-to-hand fighting, with a thousand horses gally-hooting all over the place, had covered the battlefield with an enormous cloud of dust, and in it the green frog skins of the soldiers were whirling around like snowflakes in a blizzard. Now, what did the Indians do with all that money? They gave it to their children to play with, to fold those strange bits of colored paper into all kinds of shapes, making them into toy buffalo and horses. Somebody was enjoying that money after all. The books tell of one soldier who survived. He got away, but he went crazy and some women watched him from a distance as he killed himself. The writers always say he must have been afraid of being captured and tortured, but that's all wrong.

3   Can't you see it? There he is, bellied down in a gully, watching

266

what is going on. He sees the kids playing with the money, tearing it up, the women using it to fire up some dried buffalo chips to cook on, the men lighting their pipes with green frog skins, but mostly all those beautiful dollar bills floating away with the dust and the wind. It's this sight that drove that poor soldier crazy. He's clutching his head, hollering, "Goddam, Jesus Christ Almighty, look at them dumb, stupid, red sons of bitches wasting all that dough!" He watches till he can't stand it any longer, and then he blows his brains out with a six-shooter. It would make a great scene in a movie, but it would take an Indian mind to get the point.

4   The green frog skin—that was what the fight was all about. The gold of the Black Hills, the gold in every clump of grass. Each day you can see ranch hands riding over this land. They have a bagful of grain from their saddle horns, and whenever they see a prairie-dog hole they toss a handful of oats in it, like a kind little old lady feeding the pigeons in one of your city parks. Only the oats for the prairie dogs are poisoned with strychnine. What happens to the prairie dog after he has eaten this grain is not a pleasant thing to watch. The prairie dogs are poisoned because they eat grass. A thousand of them eat up as much grass in a year as a cow. So if the rancher can kill that many prairie dogs he can run one more head of cattle, make a little more money. When he looks at a prairie dog he sees only a green frog skin getting away from him.

5   For the white man each blade of grass or spring of water has a price tag on it. And that is the trouble, because look at what happens. The bobcats and coyotes which used to feed on prairie dogs now have to go after a stray lamb or a crippled calf. The rancher calls the pest-control officer to kill these animals. This man shoots some rabbits and puts them out as bait with a piece of wood stuck in them. That stick has an explosive charge which shoots some cyanide into the mouth of the coyote who tugs at it. The officer has been trained to be careful. He puts a printed warning on each stick reading, "Danger, Explosive, Poison!" The trouble is that our dogs can't read, and some of our children can't either.

6   And the prairie becomes a thing without life—no more prairie dogs, no more badgers, foxes, coyotes. The big birds of prey used to feed on prairie dogs, too. So you hardly see an eagle these days. The bald eagle is your symbol. You see him on your money, but your money is killing him. When a people start killing off their own symbols they are in a bad way.

7   The Sioux have a name for white men. They call them *wasi-cun*—fat-takers. It is a good name because you have taken the fat

of the land. But it does not seem to have agreed with you. Right now you don't look so healthy—overweight, yes, but not healthy. Americans are bred like stuffed geese—to be consumers, not human beings. The moment they stop consuming and buying, this frog-skin world has no more use for them. They have become frogs themselves. Some cruel child has stuffed a cigar into their mouths and they have to keep puffing and puffing until they explode. Fat-taking is a bad thing, even for the taker. It is especially bad for Indians who are forced to live in this frog-skin world which they did not make and for which they have no use.

EXERCISES

Details and Their Meanings

1. What term does John Lame Deer use for *dollars?*
2. Why did white people want to possess the Black Hills? What valuable substance was there?
3. What about the Black Hills was valuable to Native Americans?
4. Why do cowboys throw oats into prairie dog holes? Which animals feed on prairie dogs?
5. What does Lame Deer say will eventually happen to the prairie?
6. What do the Sioux call white men? According to Lame Deer, what is the function of white people?

Reading and Critical Thinking

1. Is Lame Deer's description of the aftermath of the Battle of Little Bighorn a matter of fact or an invention? How can you be sure? Why does Lame Deer conclude that the last surviving soldier killed himself over money?
2. What does Lame Deer find especially troubling about the possible extinction of the American eagle? Do you agree with him?
3. Why did the Sioux give money to their children to play with?
4. How can you tell from the piece what tribe John Lame Deer belongs to?

5. Why are prairie dogs considered pests?
6. What do you infer is Lame Deer's attitude toward modern culture? Do you agree or disagree with him? Why?
7. What do you think Lame Deer would like to see happen to Native American peoples?

The Writer's Strategies

1. What do you think is Lame Deer's thesis? Comment on the introduction. Is it effective? Why or why not?
2. How much of this essay is based on opinion? How much is based on direct observation?
3. What emotions does the writer express toward white people? What words best convey these emotions?
4. Where does Lame Deer offer examples in this essay? Where does he offer analysis?
5. Where does Lame Deer use generalizations? How valid are they?
6. Is Lame Deer writing for an audience of Native Americans or others? How can you tell?

Thinking Together

Most of the people who settled the American prairie and displaced the Indians were poor immigrants fleeing from oppression and poverty in Europe. Break into groups to discuss this question: When people's rights are in conflict, how can you decide what decisions are appropriate? Then as a whole class, discuss the findings of the groups.

Vocabulary

Lame Deer uses the following informal words to make his points. Write a definition of each one in your own words.

1. paws (par. 1)
2. bellied (par. 3)
3. gully (par. 3)
4. hollering (par. 3)
5. dough (par. 3)
6. crazy (par. 2)

WRITER'S WORKSHOP ━━━━━━━━━━━

Critical Thinking in Writing

1. Do you think Lame Deer's critique of white society is valid? Are you yourself or are your friends, for instance, motivated in your job goals primarily by the pursuit of money and the consumption of material goods? Write a reply to Lame Deer in which you discuss the validity of his conclusions.
2. Lame Deer raises critical questions about the relation between capitalism and the environment, earning money and its potential dangers to nature. Write a short essay exploring those issues. In the light of human financial need just how much should we put our environment at risk?
3. Suppose you could speak with a Native American who never had experienced contemporary culture as you know it in America today. What would you tell this person about American values—especially money values?

Connecting Ideas

Compare the attitude to economic and business success expressed by John Lame Deer and that expressed by the various people described in "Reaching for the Dream," by William O'Hare (page 257). How would you characterize the values of the various groups of people? Which values seem to you to be preferable? Why?

Like Mother, Like Daughter

Lloyd Gite

Lloyd Gite points to a variation on an old business tradition as women bring their daughters into the family firm. With this new development come new challenges.

ANDREA, CHERYL, AND DERYL McKissack were barely out of diapers when their father started teaching them the family business. William McKissack, the late owner and president of McKissack & McKissack, the nation's oldest black-owned architectural and engineering firm, used to bring his daughters to the company's job sites every Saturday, giving them an "inside look" into how the architecture business works. Moses McKissack II, William's father and the man who founded McKissack & McKissack in 1905, used to give his son that same up-close-and-personal look into the company.

2   Andrea McKissack, now 40, still remembers those Saturdays spent at various job sites. "The three of us started at the architectural drawing board early on," she admits. "I remember going to my father's office when I was 6 years old, and I remember drawing architectural plans for my father when I was 13. By the time I got to high school, all of us were designing our own structures."

3   Today, these "designing women" are doing more than just blueprinting structures in their spare time. In 1983, when a stroke forced William into retirement, his wife, Leatrice, a former high-school math teacher with a master's degree in psychology, took over the Nashville, Tennessee–based firm and became its chairman and CEO. Five years later, when her husband passed away, she asked her daughters to join the company. "I didn't have any fears about bringing my daughters into the firm," recalls the 60-year-old Leatrice, whose company has designed more than 4,000 structures over the past 86 years, including facilities at Howard University and Tennessee State University. "I just decided that this was family. It was a legacy."

4   Cheryl, who at the time was a consultant for Weidlinger Associates, a New York–based engineering consulting firm, vividly remembers how her mother made the offer. "She said, 'I have all this work and I don't know what to do. I need some help.'"

5   Cheryl immediately came to her mother's rescue. For nearly two years, she commuted from New York to Nashville, where she served as the company's vice president of marketing. Cheryl, 30, also opened McKissack & McKissack branch offices in Memphis and New York. (She manages the latter.) In November 1989, Deryl McKissack-Cappell followed in Cheryl's footsteps. The 30-year-old twin sister joined the firm and opened a Washington, D.C., office. Andrea, who has a degree in architectural engineering from Tennessee State University, recently came on board at the New York office where she handles marketing, contract negotiations, and consulting.

6   So far, bringing her daughters into the family business has paid off handsomely for Leatrice—and McKissack & McKissack. When Leatrice took over, McKissack & McKissack was designing projects totaling $30 million. Last year, the 28-employee company handled $75 million worth of projects, 10 percent of which the company received as fees.

7   Since taking over, Leatrice has won over a multitude of fans. "I like the low-key, highly professional way in which Leatrice goes about business," says Benjamin F. Payton, president of Tuskegee University (McKissack & McKissack has designed several of the school's buildings.) "Her husband was a real professional—someone who cared deeply about the work he did. Leatrice is the same. She has demonstrated to us that she can carry out major architectural work."

All In The Family

8   According to the Small Business Administration (SBA), the number of family-owned companies—many of which are run by mothers and daughters—is on the rise. In 1988, of the nearly 19 million companies in the United States, more than 13 million were sole proprietorships. Most of those were described as family-owned businesses with two or more related individuals who were working together. While there are no hard numbers of how many mother-daughter companies exist, experts agree that more mothers and daughters are going into business together.

9   "About 90 percent of American businesses are family-owned and/or controlled," says Marta Vago, Ph.D., a Los Angeles family

business consultant. "People still prefer, whenever possible, to work with people they know."

10　　Experts say that during the go-go 1980s, many children of business owners shied away from working in their parents' companies. Instead, many elected to get their advanced degrees and to cut their teeth in corporate America. But now with the problems in the economy and the realization of the proverbial "glass ceiling," many women are returning to the entrepreneurial fold.

11　　"Family members are going into business together because of their disenchantment with the corporate world," says Dennis T. Jaffe, Ph.D., author of *Working with the Ones You Love: Conflict Resolution & Problem Solving Strategies for a Successful Family Business* (Conari Press: Berkeley, CA), and co-owner with his wife, Cynthia, of The Heartwork Group, a San Francisco consulting firm specializing in family business. "Many women who want to get to the top think, 'Why don't I just join the family business or form a company with my mother?' "

12　　Daughters who become partners with their mothers in business will face many challenges that traditional father-son or father-daughter companies won't. For starters, it's more difficult for women-owned firms to get start-up capital to launch their businesses. And for black women, the chase is even tougher.

13　　Sexism often poses another major hurdle. Says Deryl McKissack: "We only deal with men. Most of the presentations I go to, I'm the only woman in the room and I'll get wisecracks like, 'Deryl, all you have to do is show your legs.' I usually just smile and continue the presentation. It goes with the territory."

14　　Renee Ferrell, president of sales and operations for Bennie Ferrell Catering Co., says that many of the men in her company used to give her, her sister, and her mother a hard time. "Initially, the men in our company—especially some of the white men who worked for us—didn't want to listen to anything that we had to say because we were women," says Renee, who runs the 32-year-old Houston catering company with her mother, Norma, and her sister, Cynthia. "They figured that we didn't know what we were doing. But we had no problems getting rid of those men."

15　　And the Ferrells didn't have any problems deciding that Bennie Ferrell Catering would have to be more aggressive in the 1990s if it was going to remain competitive. In May, the Ferrells opened a new retail outlet in River Oaks, a fashionable upper-middle-class neighborhood in Houston.

16　　"We were dying in the area where we were," says Renee of the company's other location in West Houston, a heavily industrialized area of the city. The move marked a new beginning for the $1.2 million business that was launched in 1959 by the late Bennie Ferrell and his wife, Norma.

17   During the downturn in Houston's oil-based economy in the mid-1980s, Bennie Ferrell Catering, which has 12 full-time employees and 150 part-time workers, took a severe financial beating. In 1982, the company posted sales of $800,000. Three years later, revenues plummeted to $400,000.

18   In an effort to boost sagging sales, the Ferrells opened Catering Supplies, a company that sells such items as tablecloths, linens, silverware, and serving trays. They also teach gourmet cooking classes and sell cooking accessories. The Ferrells believe that diversification will help lift the company's sales to $5 million—an ambitious projection—by 1994. Says Renee of the new thrust, "We needed to breathe new life into our company."

Making It Work

19   Breathing life into a mother-daughter business venture won't be easy. Marta Vago says that if the mother and daughter have had a dysfunctional relationship throughout the years, that kind of relationship will also be taken into the business. She advises that if you're thinking about going into business with your mother, ask yourself the following questions:

- How uncomfortable am I with disagreeing with my mother openly?
- Are we able to respect each other's differences of opinion?
- Can we find common ground even if we don't agree on everything?
- How do we solve problems?
- Will I have a tendency to go along with my mother so I won't hurt her feelings, or am I going to be more outspoken about what I really think and feel?

20   Author Dennis Jaffe suggests that mothers and daughters work together in some informal setting before forming a business partnership. And that's just what Sharon Pryor did before she joined Cluttered Corners, her mother's 16-year-old, Detroit-based antique store. "As a child, I always worked with my mother on projects," says Sharon, the company's 36-year-old marketing and public

relations manager. "We've always had a good working relationship."

What Are the Drawbacks?

21 That old saying, "Mothers will always be mothers," certainly applies here. Many daughters say that one of the major drawbacks to successfully running a mother-daughter company can be the inability of the mother to respect the daughter's professional skills. Some mothers still treat their daughters as "mommy's little girl"—despite the fact that they're adult business owners. That thinking can cripple a mother-daughter operation.

22 "Did I have reservations about working with my mother? Sure I did," says Cheryl McKissack. "Mom still likes to exert a certain amount of control over me. That's the biggest issue. My most difficult challenge is weaning myself from my mother. Her challenge is to look at her children more as trained professionals."

23 As in any company, it's also important to clearly define the roles and responsibilities of each employee. Cheryl McKissack remembers getting upset while she and her mother were making a presentation. "Mom answered a question that I should have answered because it was of a technical nature. Did that bother me? Yes. But, she has the savvy in dealing with people, and nobody seemed concerned about it but me," she says.

24 Objective job performance standards should also be adopted to apply to all employees, including family members. "Everyone in the company, including the daughters, should go through a period of evaluation and performance review," says Vago. "The more objective those standards are, the more objective the judgments can be. Either you performed or you didn't perform. The less objective these job performances are, the greater the likelihood that the mother will either play favorites or will treat the daughter uncommonly harsh."

25 If it's difficult for mothers and daughters to deal with problems, Jaffe recommends using a mediator. "They might need somebody who can help them talk," he says. "It could be another family member involved in the company. But I think the best mediators are people outside the company—somebody they both trust."

26 Mother-daughter businesses can be very rewarding ventures. Just ask the McKissacks, the Ferrells, and the Pryors. "There are many advantages to working with my mother and sisters," says Deryl McKissack. "There are fewer restrictions placed on my

professional growth. And we have strong relationships that make things work."

EXERCISES

Details and Their Meanings

1. Who founded the architectural business of McKissack & McKissack? When? How many generations of the family have been in the family business? Until recently, what was the gender of the principals of the company? Who was the first woman to take a major role in the company? When and why did she do so?

2. How did Andrea, Cheryl, and Deryl first learn about the architectural business? Did they learn in the same way as their father? What training did they receive? Why and when did they return to the family business after having other jobs? Was their professional success dependent on joining the family business? What have been the results of their partnership with their mother?

3. How widespread are family-owned businesses in the United States? How are children's attitudes toward working in family businesses changing? Why are they changing?

4. What special challenges face female-led companies, challenges not faced by companies with males in leadership roles? Are these challenges attributable to the women themselves or to the surrounding society? How does the Ferrell family company illustrate these challenges? How has Bennie Ferrell Catering overcome these and other challenges?

5. What advice do experts give to women thinking of running a business? What does that advice suggest about the problems such companies may have?

Reading and Critical Thinking

1. Of the problems that mother-daughter businesses are likely to face, which ones are father-son or any other family business also likely to face? What problems do you think are peculiar to mother-daughter businesses?

2. Lloyd Gite suggests that good personal relations are important

to the success of any business. In what ways might family businesses have advantages or disadvantages over other small businesses in this respect?

3. How strong a force is sexism in the business world, according to the writer? In what ways does it influence the careers and companies described here? How does sexism draw daughters into family businesses? How do families protect daughters from sexist discrimination? How does sexism present obstacles to company growth? Do you believe that sexism is a stronger or a weaker force in the workplace than is described here?

4. After reading this article, do you think it would be a good idea to go into a family business? In what ways would this article help you to do so?

5. Evaluate the questions that Marta Vago suggests daughters ask themselves if they are thinking about going into business with their mothers. Would the questions really help? Why or why not? Would the questions also serve sons seeking to go into business with their fathers? What questions might you add to the list?

The Writer's Strategies

1. What is the thesis of this selection? In what paragraph is the thesis most directly expressed? Why doesn't the thesis appear at the beginning of the piece? How does the direct presentation of the thesis change the level of discussion?

2. How much of the piece and what part of the piece is devoted to the McKissack family? Do the McKissacks reappear later in the piece? What point is made by their first appearance? by their later appearance? How does the example of this family tie the selection together?

3. What other examples are used beside the McKissacks? What do these additional examples add?

4. How does the focus of the last part of the article change, beginning with paragraph 18? What purpose might this section serve for some readers?

5. How does the last paragraph sum up the main point? What does that ending suggest about the writer's overall purpose?

Thinking Together

In small groups, discuss family-owned businesses that you are familiar with. Discuss the kinds of opportunities, problems, and temptations that are likely to arise in family businesses.

Vocabulary

Embedded in the following words from the selection are root words. Identify each root word, and then define both the root and the larger term.

1. architectural (par. 1)
2. diversification (par. 18)
3. dysfunctional (par. 19)
4. industrialized (par. 16)
5. mediator (par. 25)

WRITER'S WORKSHOP ━━━━━━━━━━

Critical Thinking in Writing

1. In a few paragraphs, describe instances that you have observed or experienced in which sexism in the workplace slowed the careers of women or limited the success of women-led companies.
2. From what you know of relations between mothers and daughters and between fathers and sons, explain the advantages and disadvantages of family business partnerships. Which—father-son or mother-daughter—might be more likely to succeed in what circumstances? You may also consider father-daughter, mother-son, brother-sister, and any other family combination.
3. Choose one activity that you have successfully carried out with a member of your family. Write one page of advice about how to get along and work well with family members in this activity and what to watch out for.

Connecting Ideas

Jesus Sanchez's "Era Passes from the Landscape" (page 299) also describes the career choices of different generations. Write a few paragraphs comparing how and why the choices described by Sanchez differ from the choices described here by Lloyd Gite.

A Cafe Reopens: Lunch Returns to the Prairie

William E. Schmidt

Reporter William E. Schmidt tells about the reopening of a cafe in a small farming town. He also tells about the changing way of life in rural America.

KEY WORDS

refuge (par. 2)   safe place, away from difficulties
progeny (par. 12)   offspring, children, descendants
plight (par. 14)   unhappy fate
facade (par. 21)   front exterior of a building
circuit box (par. 23)   a metal box in which the main electrical line for a house or building is split into separate circuits; often contains fuses or circuit-breakers

WHEN LOUISBURG'S LAST CAFE closed its doors in 1988, Keith Hansen and John Lund and the other men who farm the rich, rolling prairies of western Minnesota found themselves confronting a new and lonely challenge: lunch.

2   Not only had they lost their midday refuge in town, a place to gather over coffee and talk prices and politics, but they had no one back at the house to cook for them either.

3   "My wife's got a job now," Mr. Lund said. "So does Keith Hansen's and Spence's and Elmo's. You want to keep your farm these days, you need two incomes."

4   **$4,500 to Reopen the Doors**   So a few months ago, Mr. Lund and his neighbors near Louisburg did what seemed natural. Nearly 50 of them got together, raised about $4,500 in contributions, and reopened the little cafe that has served this remote town of sixty residents since the turn of the century.

5   For the farmers in Louisburg and other small towns across America, the cafe represents more than just a yearning for hearty home-cooked meals at noon, which the men say they do not have the time or the skills to make for themselves.

6   The campaign to reopen the cafe is a measure of the way in which the rhythms of rural life have changed.

7   More and more farm women now have jobs off the farm, forcing their husbands and their children to adapt to life in families in which both parents are wage-earners just as their counterparts have in the cities.

8   **Creation of the Railroad**   What has happened in Louisburg also reflects the concerns that are shared by residents of many small towns who have watched their communities wither away, bled by declining populations and failing businesses along Main Street.

9   "There is not much left here in Louisburg, but we're not ready just yet to let go of it," said Mr. Hansen, surveying the afternoon crowd in the cafe, where Emily Hansen, who is no relation, and her husband, Harold, were busy filling coffee cups and chatting up the customers. "At least we managed to bring a little bit of action back to town."

10   Like most places in the far reaches of western Minnesota and the Dakotas and Montana, Louisburg was a creation of the railroad, one of hundreds of small towns built at regular intervals along rail lines during the late nineteenth century so that nearby farmers could deliver a horse-drawn wagon of grain to the rail siding and be back home again by nightfall.

11   The grain elevator is still the town's biggest enterprise and its most imposing structure. Its tin-sided towers dominate the long, low prairie horizon, and it is easily seen from several miles away.

12   But Louisburg, almost straight west from Minneapolis and close to the South Dakota border, is not on the railroad's main line. It is not even on some highway maps, since it is several miles from the nearest state road. Although the population nearly reached 100 in the 1950s, mostly the progeny of the Scandinavian and German farmers who first settled the area, it began slipping in the 1960s.

13   In the mid-1970s the farm implement dealership closed, and the town's only gasoline station shut its doors a decade later, along with the last grocery store. Except for two soda machines on the sidewalk in front of empty storefronts, the only retail commerce conducted along the main street these days is at the cafe.

14   Steve Padgitt, a sociologist at Iowa State University who spe-

cializes in rural areas, said residents of Louisburg were confronting a plight common to farm people throughout the region: as small communities and their populations have shrunk, services have been concentrated in fewer and more distant places.

15   "From the house where I was raised, I could always see the smoke from two or three other chimneys," Mr. Padgitt said. "Now the countryside has thinned out so that people have to drive 10 miles to get their mail or 30 miles to find a restaurant."

16   When the old cafe closed in 1988, Mr. Lund said, it meant that he was traveling 10 miles to Madison, the closest town, to buy lunch. It was either that or make do alone at home. "You can only eat Campbell's soup for so long," said Mr. Lund, whose wife, Nancy, works as a bank teller in Appleton, about 12 miles to the east.

17   As farm profits have declined in recent years, particularly among the operators of small family farms, both husbands and wives have been forced to seek work off the farm. A 1988 Agriculture Department survey estimated that 50 percent of all farm households had someone in the family who was working off the farm. As often as not it is the wife, as most farms are operated by men. In farm communities closest to urban areas, Mr. Padgitt said, some studies suggest that more than half the farm wives now hold jobs off the farm. In any case, sociologists say the number has been growing slowly but steadily over the years.

18   **Offer from Former Resident**   The idea of reopening Louisburg's cafe took root last December, when Catherine Wiese, who grew up in Louisburg but now lives in California, came home to visit her father. Since the cafe had closed, her father, Arnold, an elderly widower, had lost a place to go for meals and companionship. She said she would help buy the cafe if others in the town could help fix it up and find someone to run it.

19   Mr. Lund and the men down at the elevator started taking up a collection, asking for donations of $50 or $100. "The names on the list just kept coming and coming," Mr. Lund said. Some nearby banks and businesses contributed, too, and the local power company offered three months of free electricity.

20   Most of the work was done by Harlan Wiese, who is Ms. Wiese's cousin. Along with helpers, he tore out the interior of the old cafe, a one-story storefront, and put up plywood paneling and installed floor tiles and new kitchen equipment. Dining tables were ordered and a new menu board was mounted on the wall for notice

of the dinner special, which costs $3.50 and changes daily. Today it was roast beef with mashed potatoes.

21   Then they painted the facade and put out an American flag and a sign that reads: "Louisburg Cafe: Service with a Friendly Smile." At least that is what it was supposed to say: on one side the painter misspelled *service* as *sevrice*.

22   The restaurant had its formal opening in mid-April. Toby Haug and His Playmores, a polka band from Madison, performed on the street out front, and most of the town turned out to dance and drink a little beer. Radio station KQLP from Madison broadcast live from the scene. So many people showed up to sample Mrs. Hansen's swiss steak that they had to wait in line for tables.

23   Since then, there have been some problems. The roof started leaking, and the farmers had to go $4,000 into debt to replace it. Then the electrical system blew. Now they say they are going to have to install a new circuit box.

24   But Emily Hansen, who was managing a convenience store in Madison when she was asked to take on the cafe, says she and her husband, who had been laid off from his job, will stay on as long as they can. They work every day as it is, including Sunday, when the church crowd comes in for coffee.

25   "Even if we don't get rich, it's such a great feeling just to be here," said Mrs. Hansen, who had just finished baking a fresh batch of homemade doughnuts. "Whatever else, we feel like we're helping to hold this little community together."

EXERCISES

Details and Their Meanings

1. When did the last cafe in Louisburg close? What kind of problem did this closing create for the men of Louisburg? Why do you think that the writer describes lunch as a "new and lonely challenge" (paragraph 1)?
2. Where is Louisburg located? How big is it? How do the location and size of the town affect the significance of the cafe? Who helped pay for the reopening of the cafe? Why did it seem the "natural" thing to do?

3. What forces and events led to the growth of Louisburg over the last century? How is the history of the town related to major landmarks still in the town? Is Louisburg like other neighboring towns in its origin and design? How do you know?
4. What led to the closing of Louisburg's previous cafe? Did other businesses close? How is what happened in Louisburg related to what happened in other farming communities?
5. Where do the residents of Louisburg (and small towns like it) go to shop, do business, and work? How do you think this affects the pace of their lives?
6. Who decided to rebuild the cafe? Which people and organizations got involved and in what ways? Do businesses usually start in that way? What is the significance of such wide involvement?
7. Who has taken over management of the cafe? What were their personal reasons for taking on the job? Did they have any other reasons? What satisfaction do they expect to get from the job? Why do you think it might not matter to Mrs. Hansen or to the town whether the cafe makes a profit?
8. From the information provided by the writer, what future would you predict for the Louisburg cafe? What further information would you need to more accurately predict its future?

Reading and Critical Thinking

1. In what ways do you believe the process of reopening the cafe benefited the community? In what ways do you think the residents of Louisburg will benefit from being able to have lunch together?
2. From the descriptions of Louisburg and the surrounding area, what do you think some of the daily "hardships" faced by the residents might be (besides not having a cafe)?
3. What can you infer from this piece about how settlement patterns in the United States are changing?
4. What can you infer from this selection about the farming industry in general? How do you believe the occupation of farming is changing?
5. Find at least two quotations from the selection that indicate a resident's positive feelings about both the cafe and the town of Louisburg. Speculate about why people might want to live in a place like Louisburg. How does it compare to where you live now?

The Writer's Strategies

1. What issues does William E. Schmidt mention in the first three short paragraphs? From these three paragraphs, what seems to be the main focus of the selection? Do you think that this in fact is the overall idea? If it is not, which paragraph contains the best statement of the main idea?

2. What is the tone of the selection—that is, the writer's attitude toward the topic he is writing about? How does the writer create this tone?

3. Explain the figurative language in this quotation from paragraph 8: "What has happened in Louisburg also reflects the concerns that are shared by residents of many small towns who have watched their communities wither away, bled by declining populations and failing businesses along Main Street." How does the language help create an image in your mind of what is happening to this town? What are some of the images you have as a result of this sentence? Find two more sentences from the piece that contain figurative language. What images do they give you?

4. How does the writer support his claims about changes in rural life? What are the sources of his evidence? Do you find the evidence convincing? Why or why not?

5. What kind of information do paragraphs 8 through 17 give about Louisburg? What pattern does the writer use to present the case of the Louisburg cafe? How does the background information broaden the significance of the cafe's history?

6. In the last four paragraphs, do you think the writer indicates a particular hope for what happens to the cafe? If he does, what is that hope, and how do you think the order of the information at the end affects what you decided?

Thinking Together

Discuss with a small group the popular gathering places in your hometown or on your campus. What do people do in these places, and how are the places important to people's lives? Are they associated with eating, sports, or some other activity? How do these places foster a spirit of community? Each student should write a paragraph description of his or her community's most important meeting place and explain how it serves to bring people together.

Vocabulary

In the space next to each definition, write the letter of the appropriate term from the essay.

_____ 1. strong desire

a. remote (par. 4)

_____ 2. things given

b. sociologist (par. 14)

_____ 3. a coordinated operation, like an army's maneuvers

c. grain elevator (par. 11)

d. contributions (par. 4)

_____ 4. make fit, get used to

e. campaign (par. 6)

_____ 5. storehouse for grain

f. wither (par. 8)

_____ 6. project

g. yearning (par. 5)

_____ 7. rule over, take up a large part

h. adapt (par. 7)

_____ 8. far off

i. enterprise (par. 11)

_____ 9. dry up, lose liveliness

j. dominate (par. 11)

_____ 10. one who studies society and the ways in which people interact in groups

WRITER'S WORKSHOP ━━━━━━━━━━━━

Critical Thinking in Writing

1. Write a brief essay on what your daily life would be like if you lived in Louisburg. Imagine what would be different from your present life and what would be the same. Would you like your new life?
2. Explain in a brief essay some of the changes that the residents of Louisburg, Minnesota, have experienced in the last twenty

years. How do these changes compare and contrast with the changes that residents in your community have experienced? How does community change affect people's lives?

3. Should communities take steps to preserve a known, comfortable way of life in the face of social and technological changes, or is change inevitable and desirable even if old familiar places must vanish? Take a position on these questions in an argumentative essay.

Connecting Ideas

In a few paragraphs, compare the role of the cafe in the town of Louisburg with the role of the family kitchen in Rosemarie Santini's "An American Dream" (page 56) or in Gary Soto's "The Jacket" (page 64). End by thinking about the ways in which food and eating places bring people together.

Making Things Whole

Joseph Varilla

Joseph Varilla, an executive with the Xerox Corporation, describes how two people with different disabilities can combine their abilities for a productive, if unusual, relation.

KEY WORDS

overbearing (par. 7)   bossy, domineering
albeit (par. 8)   although
exacerbated (par. 9)   made worse
relinquished (par. 9)   gave up
managerial (par. 9)   directorial, supervisory
proficient (par. 14)   competent, skillful
intuitively (par. 15)   instinctively, without being taught

I FOUND OUT I had multiple sclerosis when I was about 40 years old. I am now in my mid-50s. Hardly noticeable at first, my M.S. has progressed dramatically.

2   Medically, I am now classified as a functional quadriplegic. I can't walk. I can't shake hands. I can't pick up a pencil. Signing my name is out of the question. It's impossible to feed myself. Brushing my teeth is a job for someone else.

3   I can't get out of bed by myself. I can't shower by myself. I can't go to the bathroom by myself. I can't dress myself. If I slide forward in my wheelchair, I don't have the strength to straighten myself out. I can't even read unless someone turns the pages. I don't drive. I don't visit people. I don't go to the theater. I do watch a lot of mindless television.

4   But I can still work—thanks to an understanding and accommodating employer who believes my brain still functions even if my body does not. While my heart has been broken many times, it has also been warmed. My business associates are particularly helpful. They have done everything from helping me into the

bathroom to setting up a car pool so that I can get between home and office. They have lifted my spirits when I was emotionally down and they have picked me up when I have fallen.

5   Despite all that support and despite all that help, I still could not work without Phil. He is disabled, too, but his is a learning disability. Together, we make one whole person. He has become my arms and legs.

6   The two of us produce a magazine that goes to all Xerox employees in the United States and to many overseas. I do all of the research, interviewing, writing, editing, and production coordination. Phil's arms and legs make it possible. Before an interview, he sets up the tape recorder and then operates it. He turns the pages so that I can read notes and other material. As I dictate the words, he patiently types them at a computer work station.

7   We have a relationship that began by accident and could have unraveled any number of times. I am often impatient with him. He sometimes resents my overbearing attitude. He doesn't like when I yell; it drives me crazy when he simply clams up and says nothing.

8   He began working for me in 1988—a tough time for me and a critical point in his life. My upward mobility had come to a screeching halt as a result of my rapidly deteriorating physical condition. Phil had passed his twenty-fifth birthday and still hadn't found a real job despite years in special education programs for the learning disabled. It was time for him to begin his work life; it was time for me to continue mine, albeit in a different role.

9   I had had an automobile accident in 1985 that exacerbated my M.S. What had been a slow and almost orderly progression of the disease now became a physical nose dive. Before long, I relinquished my managerial responsibilities as director of corporate communications for Xerox and began tailoring a new individual assignment. I had a vague brief to develop a program that would "cross functional and organizational lines and have potential corporatewide impact." Eventually I would take on the responsibility to develop and produce a new publication for employees.

10   While I was trying to define my new role, I was also trying to find a new secretary-administrative assistant. Someone suggested that I should look for a male secretary who, in addition to his normal duties, might be able to give me some physical assistance. With that requirement in mind, we contacted a local rehabilitation agency that we thought would understand my problem and that might know of some candidates. Yes, they knew someone. In fact,

they were working with a young man they would like us to consider. Enter Phil.

11   He wasn't exactly what I had in mind. Phil was learning disabled, had attended special schools, and couldn't come close to passing our typing test. We scheduled an interview anyway. As we talked, I began to envision a different kind of job for Phil. Without managerial responsibility, I really didn't need Super Secretary. What I needed was someone who could compensate for my disabilities. I remembered my two biggest problems—I needed someone to assist me at home in the morning and I needed someone to drive me to and from work. Suppose he could do those two jobs and then spend the rest of the day doing clerical assignments, as well as giving me some physical assistance? He was willing to try.

12   He never had a problem with helping me physically. Office work was something else. The first several months were a trial for both of us. Phil's typing was awful, his spelling was worse, and office routine was a mystery to him. Given my impatience, I was not a very good teacher.

13   This was a young man who was not very happy and was often lonely. He simply felt bad about himself. He had suffered criticism and insults for a long time.

14   He can't work fast and he can't think fast. He learns differently from most, and there is a limit to what he can assimilate. If he is able to do something a number of times, he won't ever forget how. He has become very proficient with an office work station and knows far more about this computer than I do. He rides a motorcycle and does most of the repair himself. No, Phil is not an uncomplicated person.

15   He is totally loyal and helpful to me. As my M.S. progressed, Phil increasingly compensated for my physical inabilities. He has indeed become my arms and legs. We spend at least eight hours a day together. And I have learned to become more even-tempered with him. He understands intuitively that even though I rage at him, I am really expressing anger at my body's inability to function. He knows that within minutes I will apologize.

16   We have traveled together often to gather material for articles. We've been to California several times, as well as to Europe. He gets me onto the plane and off. He gets me into automobiles and out. He wheels me into meetings and is available for errands. Especially on trips, I rely on him totally.

17   But what about tomorrow?

18   Will the M.S. progress to the point where, despite assistance and loyal help, I can no longer work? Can it attack my eyesight, as it has with some? Might it affect my brain, as it has with some? Will I become an unresponsive blob whose only proper place is a nursing home? The unpredictability of the disease is the toughest part.

19   And what about Phil?

20   He will be taking on a new, more conventional clerical job. Four years is long enough in a physically and emotionally exhausting role. He has earned a change. I will miss him. We have demonstrated that, despite inevitable problems of communication, two people with different disabilities can combine their different abilities to do productive work.

21   My new assistant will have big shoes to fill.

EXERCISES

Details and Their Meanings

1. How does the writer's disability restrict his actions? What kinds of abilities does he still have? What is his attitude toward his disability?

2. What does the writer do for a living? How did his disability affect his work and career? How do his employer and associates react to his disability?

3. What kind of disability does Phil, the writer's assistant, have? What does he do for a living? What impact does his disability have on the work he does? What did he do before he came to work for the writer?

4. What can Phil do for the writer that the writer cannot do for himself? What can the writer do that Phil can't do? How do their two sets of abilities fit together? What can they do together with each other's help?

5. What does the writer expect his own future to be like? Phil's future? How does the writer feel about the coming changes? What has he learned from his relation with Phil? What do you think he wants you to learn from it?

Reading and Critical Thinking

1. Compare and contrast the two disabilities described in this selection. In what ways are the experiences of the two men who have them similar? In what ways are these experiences different?

2. At the end of paragraph 14, after he describes Phil's limitations, the writer states, "No, Phil is not an uncomplicated person." What does this statement mean? Why does the writer include it? Who might think that Phil is "an uncomplicated person"?

3. How did the writer's employer "accommodate" his disability? How did the writer "accommodate" Phil's disability? How is this kind of treatment different from the treatment employees usually receive? In what ways do these accommodations benefit Phil, the writer, and the company that employs them? Do you see any negative consequences of the accommodation?

4. How is the relation between Phil and the writer similar to the relation among other employees who work together? In what ways, if any, is it different?

The Writer's Strategies

1. What is the writer's main point in this selection? Where does he state it directly? What is the effect of placing it here and not elsewhere?

2. How does the writer begin the selection? What effect does the beginning have? How do the opening paragraphs help set up the problem the selection deals with?

3. How does the writer describe his disability in paragraphs 2 and 3? How does the way he presents these details reveal his attitude toward his disability?

4. Where does the writer narrate events? Where does he describe himself, Phil, and the work they do? How do the narration and description help build the thesis of the essay?

5. Which paragraphs are devoted mostly to the writer and his situation? Which paragraphs are mostly devoted to Phil and his situation? Which paragraphs are about the both of them together? What differences are there in the tone and attitude of the paragraphs that describe them as individuals and those that describe them together?

6. Why does the writer use a series of questions in paragraphs 17 through 19?

Thinking Together

In small groups, compare experiences in which you had to rely on someone else to help you do something that you could not do yourself. How did you feel about that person? How did you feel about yourself? What kind of connection developed between you over time?

Vocabulary

Write definitions for the following figurative phrases that appear in this selection.

1. "out of the question" (par. 2)
2. "While my heart has been broken, it has also been warmed" (par. 4)
3. "lifted my spirits" (par. 4)
4. "He has become my arms and legs" (par. 5)
5. "could have unraveled" (par. 7)
6. "clams up" (par. 7)
7. "upward mobility" (par. 8)
8. "come to a screeching halt" (par. 8)
9. "a physical nose dive" (par. 9)
10. "an unresponsive blob" (par. 18)
11. "big shoes to fill" (par. 21)

WRITER'S WORKSHOP ━━━━━━━━━━━━━

Critical Thinking in Writing

1. Write an informal journal entry about someone you know or have read about who has had to cope with diminished physical abilities—for example, an aging parent or grandparent or someone who has had an incapacitating illness or injury. How has this person dealt with the change in his or her abilities? How has this change affected that person's sense of self?

2. Explore how accessible and accommodating your campus is to people with disabilities. Are the entries to buildings equipped with ramps? Are hallways and aisles wide enough for wheelchairs to pass through easily? Are crosswalks and bike-path

crossings equipped with rubber signal bumps so that people with visual impairments can cross safely? Does your campus make interpreters available for students who are hearing impaired? What kind of accommodation is provided for students with learning disabilities? for students with temporary physical limitations? Then write a letter to the chancellor or president of your college suggesting changes that might make your campus more accessible and (or) accommodating to students, staff, and faculty with disabilities.

3. Write an essay to analyze a mutual dependency relation that you had with someone or that you witnessed between two other people. What was gained in the relation? What was lost?

Connecting Ideas

Compare the employment experience of Alberto Torres described in "Blind Commuter," by Douglas Martin (page 251), with the experiences of the writer and his assistant described in "Making Things Whole." Is Alberto Torres's experience closer to Varilla's experience or to Phil's? Which do you think is more typical of employment experiences for people with disabilities today? Do you think that this will change in the future? Why or why not?

Easy Job, Good Wages

Jesus Colon

Jesus Colon describes how unpleasant work can be. The disparity between his hopes and the realities of the job he finds raises questions about the promises of the workplace.

KEY WORDS

galvanized (par. 2)   made of sheet metal covered with zinc
mucilage (par. 4)   a type of glue for paper

THIS HAPPENED EARLY IN 1919. We were both out of work, my brother and I. He got up earlier to look for a job. When I woke up, he was already gone. So I dressed, went out and bought a copy of the *New York World*, and turned its pages until I got to the "Help Wanted Unskilled" section of the paper. After much reading and rereading the same columns, my attention was held by a small advertisement. It read: "Easy job. Good wages. No experience necessary." This was followed by a number and street on the west side of lower Manhattan. It sounded like the job I was looking for. Easy job. Good wages. Those four words revolved in my brain as I was traveling toward the address indicated in the advertisement. Easy job. Good wages. Easy job. Good wages. Easy . . .

2   The place consisted of a small front office and a large loft on the floor of which I noticed a series of large galvanized tubs half filled with water out of which I noticed protruding the necks of many bottles of various sizes and shapes. Around these tubs there were a number of workers, male and female, sitting on small wooden benches. All had their hands in the water of the tub, the left hand holding a bottle and with the thumbnail of the right hand scratching the labels.

3   The foreman found a vacant stool for me around one of the tubs of water. I asked why a penknife or a small safety razor could not be used instead of the thumbnail to take off the old labels from

294

the bottles. I was expertly informed that knives or razors would scratch the glass thus depreciating the value of the bottles when they were to be sold.

4   I sat down and started to use my thumbnail on one bottle. The water had somewhat softened the transparent mucilage used to attach the label to the bottle. But the softening did not work out uniformly somehow. There were always pieces of label that for some obscure reason remained affixed to the bottles. It was on those pieces of labels tenaciously fastened to the bottles that my right-hand thumbnail had to work overtime. As the minutes passed I noticed that the coldness of the water started to pass from my hand to my body, giving me intermittent body shivers that I tried to conceal with the greatest of effort from those sitting beside me. My hands became deadly clean and tiny little wrinkles started to show especially at the tip of my fingers. Sometimes I stopped a few seconds from scratching the bottles to open and close my fists in rapid movements in order to bring blood to my hands. But almost as soon as I placed them in the water they became deathly pale again.

5   But these were minor details compared with what was happening to the thumb of my right hand. For a delicate, boyish thumb, it was growing by the minute into a full-blown tomato-colored finger. It was the only part of my right hand remaining blood red. I started to look at the workers' thumbs. I noticed that these particular fingers on their right hands were unusually developed with a thick layer of cornlike surface at the top of their right thumb. The nails on their thumbs looked coarser and smaller than on the other fingers—thumb and nail having become one and the same thing—a primitive unnatural human instrument especially developed to detach hard pieces of labels from wet bottles immersed in galvanized tubs.

6   After a couple of hours I had a feeling that my thumbnail was going to leave my finger and jump into the cold water of the tub. A numb pain imperceptibly began to be felt coming from my right thumb. Then I began to feel such pain as if coming from a finger bigger than all of my body.

7   After three hours of this I decided to quit fast. I told the foreman so, showing him my swollen finger. He figured I had earned 69 cents at 23 cents an hour.

8   Early in the evening I met my brother in our furnished room. We started to exchange experiences of our job hunting for the day. "You know what?" my brother started, "early in the morning I

went to work where they take labels off old bottles—with your right-hand thumbnail. . . . Somewhere on the west side of lower Manhattan. I only stayed a couple of hours. 'Easy job . . . Good wages . . .' they said. The person who wrote that ad must have had a great sense of humor." And we both had a hearty laugh that evening when I told my brother that I also went to work at that same place later in the day.

9   Now when I see ads reading, "Easy job. Good wages," I just smile an ancient, tired, knowing smile.

––––––––––––

EXERCISES

Details and Their Meanings

1. What words in the ad appealed to young Jesus Colon? Why? What was his attitude toward work?
2. What did Colon see at the workplace? What did that indicate about the work?
3. What instructions was Colon given? What did the instructions suggest about the concerns of the employers and their attitude toward the workers?
4. What happened to Colon's right thumb as he worked? What had happened to the thumbs of the other workers? What does the condition of their thumbs suggest about how long they had been employed and what they had been putting up with?
5. How much did Colon earn? What was the year? Did he view his earnings as a decent wage for the time? Do you think he was paid a decent wage?
6. What was Colon's brother's experience? How does it relate to the writer's experience?

Reading and Critical Thinking

1. The incident described by the writer took place over seventy years ago. Do similar work circumstances still exist? With what kinds of jobs and workers?
2. What attitudes about work does the writer develop as a result

of this incident? What does the last paragraph indicate about his new attitude? Does that attitude reflect an appropriate generalization?

3. Do the bosses in this narrative seem to show concern for what happens to the workers? Do you think such an attitude is typical of bosses? Why or why not? How do these employers compare with those you or someone you know has worked for?

4. Do any of the workers seem to have been at the job for a long time? How do you know? Why do you think they stayed? Do you think they liked the work? What do you suspect their attitude was? Would you have stayed? What would have been your attitude?

5. Why does Jesus talk with his brother about his experiences? How does the brother's view reinforce his own? What point is the writer making?

The Writer's Strategies

1. What is the main point of this piece? State it in your own words.
2. What mood does Colon convey at the start of the selection? What details help build that mood?
3. In what order does the writer present the details? Does any idea or perspective build up as the piece continues?
4. How does Colon increase the reader's sense of his pain? What details does he give about his discomfort and that of the other workers? How do the descriptions of hands, fingers, and nails change as the narrative progresses?
5. Where does the title of the narrative come from? Where do the words of the title appear in the selection? Do you think the title is appropriate? Why or why not? How is the title ironic—in other words, is the writer suggesting something opposite to what he says? How do you become aware of the irony? What helps to build the sense of irony?
6. What is the effect of the last sentence? Why does the writer use the words *ancient, tired,* and *knowing* to describe his own smile?

Thinking Together

In small groups, share your experiences of your first days on a recent job. What surprised you? What did you like and dislike? How did you relate to your supervisor?

Vocabulary

Locate the following words in the narrative, and then write a definition that fits the context in which the word is used.

1. loft (par. 2)
2. protruding (par. 2)
3. depreciating (par. 3)
4. uniformly (par. 4)
5. tenaciously (par. 4)
6. intermittent (par. 4)
7. immersed (par. 5)
8. imperceptibly (par. 6)

WRITER'S WORKSHOP ━━━━━━━━━━

Critical Thinking and Writing

1. Write a few paragraphs describing how you came to learn that work is hard.
2. Jobs and careers are rarely what you imagine them to be. Write one page describing how one job you are familiar with is not the same as the employer made it sound or you thought it would be.
3. Write an essay in which you define the perfect job from your point of view. What does the job have to offer? What makes it perfect?

Connecting Ideas

Compare and contrast the realities and expectations about job experiences in this piece and in Gary Soto's "Looking for Work" (page 243). Describe a conversation that might take place between the narrators of these selections.

Era Passes from the Landscape

Jesus Sanchez

Jesus Sanchez considers the passing tradition of Japanese-American gardeners in Southern California, the forces of economics and prejudice that originally led Japanese Americans to take on the job, and the forces that are leading a new ethnic group to take over the work.

KEY WORDS

dormant (par. 3)   asleep
flourished (par. 6)   grew well and thrived
indignity (par. 7)   humiliating experience

UP ALONG WINDING BELFAST Drive, amid a lushly planted terrace in the Hollywood Hills, the last Japanese gardener on the block prepared for a change of seasons.

2   Ted Koseki plopped flower bulbs into freshly dug holes beneath blooming rose bushes that seemed to dance in the stiff breeze on a recent morning.

3   When the bushes lie dormant in late winter, Dutch irises, daffodils, and tulips will bloom in their place, said Koseki.

4   And who will replace the gray-haired Koseki—already semi-retired after more than 45 years in the business—as caretaker of this hillside garden one day? Probably not another Japanese-American gardener.

5   "I used to talk shop with them, and I would see them on the road," the gravelly-voiced Koseki said of his fellow Japanese-American gardeners. "But I don't see them anymore."

6   The former legions of Japanese-American gardeners, whose profession flourished amid prosperity and prejudice in Southern California, are fast disappearing from the suburban landscape they mowed, trimmed, and pruned with renowned skill and pride for nearly a century.

7   Most of the gardeners have reached retirement age and are giving up their routes or selling them—many to Latinos and other recent immigrants. The vast majority of younger Japanese Americans want nothing to do with the physically demanding profession that brought their fathers indignity despite the care they brought to their work.

8   "There is no new blood to follow," said Takeshi Kotow, general manager of the Southern California Gardeners' Federation, whose 3,000 members are predominantly Japanese-American men in their 60s. "The Japanese gardener—their quality, their pride—it's soon going to be lost. Most of today's gardening is just cut and blow."

9   The end of an era—when a Japanese gardener attired in khaki work clothes and pith helmet was a suburban status symbol—meets with mixed emotions among Japanese Americans, who recall the racism that forced so many men to labor under the sun six days a week.

10   Japanese began gardening in California at the turn of the century, another ethnic minority for whom manual labor was the entry point into the U.S. economy.

11   Though gardening offered a decent living to men who couldn't speak English—about $2 a day—there were other, less benign reasons why so many immigrants entered the trade. California's Alien Land Laws forced many Japanese farmers to abandon their property; widespread discrimination severely limited job opportunities.

12   "Somehow, the public has a romantic notion that the Asian immigrant has a special skill that makes them gravitate to agriculture or horticulture," said Ronald Tadao Tsukashima, a sociology professor at Cal State Los Angeles and the son of a gardener. "That's not necessarily true. It was not their first choice. It was more of a matter of necessity, because of the barriers erected around them."

13   Still, it was not till after World War II—after thousands of Japanese Americans were stripped of their livelihoods and herded into relocation camps—that they came to dominate the gardening trade.

14   Leaving the camps with little money and few opportunities, the Japanese Americans found a refuge in gardening, where they still were held in high esteem by West Coast homeowners, and it did not take a lot of cash to get started. As a result, college graduates and former businessmen turned to the skin-toughening work, making as little as $5 a month per customer for once-a-week service.

15   In the Japanese-American neighborhoods of Los Angeles, it seemed as if everyone's father was a gardener. A study shortly after the war estimated that seven of ten adult Japanese-American males in West Los Angeles worked as gardeners.

16   "When we came out of the camps, we were all in the same boat—we had to make a living," said James Kawaguchi, who scrapped his prewar plans to attend college to take up gardening. "I had other dreams. But I had to be realistic."

17   The gardeners played a major role in rebuilding Japanese-American communities from San Diego to Seattle that were uprooted during the war, and they paved the way for the next generation to enter the professional class. Even as late as 1970, about 8,000 gardeners supported an estimated 20 percent of Japanese-American households in Southern California, according to an analysis of U.S. Census statistics by historian Nobuya Tsuchida.

18   "The Japanese gardener is the unsung or unrecognized hero of the Japanese ethnic community," said Tsukashima. "After the war, they represented the economic backbone of the Japanese community."

19   Despite their hard work, many skilled gardeners felt their profession never got the respect it deserved. One gardener recalled the formation of a Japanese-American service club for professionals. There were doctors and lawyers, but no gardeners—even though some made it big, earning $250,000 a year and directing groups of ten or more helpers.

20   For most, though, the rewards were more modest—enough to buy homes and raise children.

21   "When Japanese Americans are asked about a prominent individual or occupation, Japanese gardeners are often left out," said Tsukashima. "It was hard work that did not confer very much status in the larger community of things."

22   The children of the gardeners grew up with mixed feelings about their fathers' profession.

23   "Most of my friends growing up had fathers who were gardeners," said John Tateishi, now a 52-year-old public affairs consultant in Los Angeles. "We sort of compared notes on whose father had what movie stars. My dad was the gardener for Marilyn Monroe. He was the gardener when she died."

24   But Tateishi has other childhood memories—like spending long, weary Saturdays helping his father at Bel-Air and Brentwood homes so big it took hours just to hand mow the lawns.

25   "You looked at some of your Caucasian friends, they went out on Saturday and played," said Tateishi. "That gave you a notion that there were other ways to make a living. I don't think any kid whose father was a gardener ever considered it as a career option."

26   Bryan Yamasaki is one of the rare young Japanese Americans who has followed his father into gardening.

27   As a teenager, the 29-year-old Yamasaki, a third-generation gardener, said he viewed the work as tedious and dirty when he would help his father on weekends.

28   But when the Los Angeles man started college, he began working a gardening route to finance his studies in landscape architecture. Eventually, his plan is to offer his clients landscape design, construction, and maintenance all from one source.

29   "I'm very picky about who my clients are," said Yamasaki, who charges at least $150 a month. "To be my client, one has to listen to my suggestions to improve the yard. The customers look to me for input as to how to solve landscape problems."

30   Yamasaki is the exception. Most gardeners these days are young Latinos, not young Japanese Americans.

31   Mas Nishikawa, 70, who began gardening in 1950 and is now semiretired, has passed along some of his former clients to an apprentice, Antonio Betancourt. "They will ask for a Japanese gardener," said Nishikawa. "But I tell them I know a Latino fellow that is just as good."

32   Betancourt performed house and yard work for a Los Feliz homeowner who also employed Nishikawa as gardener. After a while, Nishikawa began to entrust his gardening know-how—as well as customers—to Betancourt.

33   While the work is hard and the competition stiff, Betancourt enjoys working outdoors, and his route generates a sufficient income to support his wife and two daughters. But Betancourt—like the Japanese Americans before him—vows no child of his will ever work as a gardener.

34   "If I had a son, I don't think I would want him to have a job like this," said Betancourt, who added he had never even thought of his daughters as future gardeners. "I believe they could get a better education and a better job."

35   These days, Latino gardeners tend to most of the yards along Belfast Avenue where Ted Koseki has worked for nearly 25 years. Like most other Japanese-American gardeners, Koseki never encouraged his only child, Calvin, to enter the field. And his son never showed any interest.

36   "When he saw me doing this kind of work, he said, 'I want to be something else,' " Koseki recalled.

37   "He wanted me to go to college," said Calvin Koseki, a 44-year-old father of two young children. "When you go to college, you start to see how other kids' parents make a living."

38   Comparing his own generation to that of his father, Koseki said: "We just had more opportunity than they did."

39   Calvin Koseki is an optometrist in San Diego. He takes care of his own yard, sometimes with the help of his father.

EXERCISES

Details and Their Meanings

1. What is Ted Koseki's ethnic background? What is his work? For whom does he work? At what point is he in his career? In what way is he typical of a group of people?

2. What is the primary ethnicity and average age of members of the Southern California Gardeners' Federation? Why don't younger Japanese Americans want to enter the business? Who is taking over from the Japanese Americans?

3. Why and when did Japanese Americans first turn to gardening as a career? What happened during World War II that led to Japanese-American domination of the gardening trade? How widespread was Japanese-American participation in gardening at its height? What was the effect of this group of workers on the Japanese-American community as a whole?

4. Were gardeners given much respect in the Japanese-American community? Were they considered professionals? Was the Japanese-American view of them fair? Explain your answers.

5. What relation did the gardeners have with clients? What was the effect of the fathers' work on their children? Were the children's feelings simply positive or negative? Why?

6. Who is Bryan Yamasaki? What does he do for a living? In what way is he unusual? How does his special way of doing business set him apart from the traditional Japanese-American

gardener? What does he demand from clients that his parents' generation wasn't in a position to demand?

7. Who is taking over the gardening routes? Why? In what ways are the new gardeners like the previous generation of Japanese-American gardeners? Do you think their children will follow in their footsteps? Why or why not?

Reading and Critical Thinking

1. Why do you think gardening flourished as a career for Japanese Americans? How did the Japanese workers bring dignity, quality, and pride to hard manual labor? In what ways do first generation laborers pave the way for a different kind of work for their second generation offspring?
2. In what ways, all other things being equal, was gardening a good career choice and in what ways a bad one? Consider the particular circumstances of Japanese Americans earlier in this century. In what ways was the choice good or bad in that light?
3. What does the Yamasaki story reveal about what was missing in the experience of the previous generation? What does it say about the lives of current Hispanic-American gardeners?
4. Is it better to adopt a lesser job and survive or to fight against unfair conditions? Explain your response.
5. In what ways does the writer look back nostalgically at the experience of the Japanese-American gardeners? In what way might the memories be fond ones for the employers? for the gardeners? Who do you think is more likely to be nostalgic? Why?
6. What idea and attitude does the title of the selection reflect? Is it good or bad that the era is passing away? Will the new era be any different? For whom?

The Writer's Strategies

1. What is the thesis of the selection? How do the introductory paragraphs help set the stage for the thesis?
2. Where and with whom does the selection end in the last paragraph? How does the discussion of Ted Koseki at the end con-

trast with the opening? What points are made by the contrast? How does the last anecdote tie the themes of the piece together?

3. Who is the audience for this piece? How can you tell? How might the various ethnic groups represented here react to Jesus Sanchez's point?

4. What are the various ways in which the writer shows that there was another, less pleasant, side to the job? How is the comparison with the children's career choices used to highlight the shortcomings of a career in gardening? How are the children's choices related to the passing of the era?

5. What specific connections are made between the Japanese-American and the Hispanic-American gardeners? How do these connections shed light on the conditions of the new generation of gardeners, and how do they predict the future? What does the writer's name suggest about his ethnicity? What do you think his interest in the issues might be?

6. Explain the introduction in this piece. How is it related to the closing? How do they both relate to the title?

Thinking Together

In small groups, discuss the ways in which the experience of the Japanese-American gardeners may or may not be similar to the work experience of other immigrant groups in the United States. Compare the experiences described here with what you know of your own family's history. Also consider the effect of the United States being at war with the country of origin. Do you think German Americans suffered similar difficulties in entering the American economy? Why or why not?

Vocabulary

Write definitions for the following words, which appear in the selection.

1. lushly (par. 1)
2. caretaker (par. 4)
3. pruned (par. 6)
4. gravitate (par. 12)
5. horticulture (par. 12)

WRITER'S WORKSHOP ━━━━━━━━━━

Critical Thinking in Writing

1. Describe a time when you made the best of a bad situation and were able to feel a sense of achievement and take some pleasure in your handling of some painful choices.
2. Write a paragraph describing whether and in what ways your career goals and choices parallel or differ from those of your parents. Explain why you think they do or do not do so.
3. Are you familiar with any immigrant or ethnic group that has been limited to a narrow range of careers or has found its best opportunities within a single career? Write a few paragraphs describing the career experience of this group and the forces that directed group members toward their careers.

Connecting Ideas

In what ways might the gardeners presented here agree or disagree with Jesus Colon's feelings about his work experience in "Easy Job, Good Wages" (page 294)?

SIDE BY SIDE

1. Drawing on the information and examples presented in the selections in this chapter, write an essay evaluating whether America is the land of opportunity.

2. Recalling what you have learned from the selections in this chapter, write a letter to a college-age student from any country and of any ethnic background. This student is thinking of emigrating to the United States and has asked for your advice about where and how he or she might successfully enter the American economy. Before writing the letter, write a brief paragraph describing the background of the student you are writing to.

3. Write an essay about how the different people described in the selections of this chapter confront the obstacles and frustrations they find in the workplace and economy. What traits of character help them deal with difficulties? What strategies do they use to gain some place in the economy? What attitudes do they develop to deal with their situations?

FIVE

Prejudices:
Tears in the Rainbow Fabric

INTRODUCTION ━━━━━━━━━━━━━━━━━

No one can make a special claim for his or her group as the "true" Americans because, in fact, no human beings are indigenous to this continent. Everyone, even the intrepid Native Americans who first discovered this land thousands of years ago, came from somewhere else. Some people who came to North America chose to leave their homes in search of better lives; others were brought as prisoners or slaves. But each wave of immigrants has come to view the next group as outsiders. Fear and competition for land, jobs, and spouses often breed conditions in which newcomers are excluded and considered dangerous. In this way prejudices develop, grow, and overwhelm.

In this unit you will read about the experiences of people who come up squarely against discrimination, either because of their race or because of their heritage. In "Zoot Suit Riots," Albert Camarillo examines the anger and violence that erupt when people find themselves excluded from the benefits of American life. Hisaye Yamamoto, in "Wilshire Bus," looks at the hurt of modern-day prejudices in Los Angeles. Judy Pasternak, in "Bias Outside Appalachia," describes the prejudices and social ills that families face decades after they left the mountains looking for a better life in Cincinnati. In "A Hanging," the only selection in this book to show a clash of cultures outside America, George Orwell takes us to the execution of a Burmese man during the British occupation of the man's country. In "Against the Great Divide," Brian Jarvis describes the subtle racial tension that exists at his high school and offers suggestions for increasing understanding between students of different races. Ellen Goodman in "The Great Divide" and Marcus Mabry in "Confronting Campus Racism" explore growing concerns about racism on college campuses and the incidents of bias that sometimes arise in the shadow of the ivory tower.

A fundamental element in the promise of America is both its open invitation to immigrants of all lands and its support for assimilation into the American way. Nevertheless, human behavior has many dark sides, and none perhaps is so unreasonable and without validity as prejudging other human beings because of how they look or what they believe. Prejudice tears at the rainbow fabric

310

of equity and fairness that should tie together the people of a nation.

PREREADING JOURNAL

1. Write a journal entry about an experience in which you or someone you know was the victim of discrimination. When did it take place? What were the circumstances? What characteristic of you or the other person—appearance, sex, age, race, or something else—made you or that person a victim? What was the outcome of this event? How did it change you or the other person?
2. How do you think prejudices develop? Do you think people learn prejudices or are prejudices innate? If your parents or neighbors harbor prejudices against some group, do you think you will inevitably develop the same beliefs?
3. Imagine you are a stranger to this country. You do not speak the language or know the customs. The food is strange, and many people seem unfriendly. Write a journal entry in which you describe how you would feel in these circumstances. What steps will you take to become comfortable in your new surroundings? How will you work to overcome the potential or apparent hostility of people toward you?

Against the Great Divide

Brian Jarvis

Brian Jarvis is a high school junior in St. Louis. In this selection, he describes the subtle racial tension that exists in his school and offers suggestions for teaching students of different races how to get along.

KEY WORDS

African nationalist (par. 1)   one who feels African identity to be most important
desegregation (par. 7)   the elimination of the separation of people according to race
multicultural (par. 12)   combining people of diverse backgrounds

I ALWAYS NOTICE ONE thing when I walk through the commons at my high school: the whites are on one side of the room and the blacks are on the other. When I enter the room, I think I'm at an African nationalist meeting. The atmosphere is lively, the clothes are colorful, the voices are loud, the students are up and about, the language is different, and there's not a white face to be seen. But the moment I cross the invisible line to the other side, I feel I've moved to another country. There are three times as many people, the voices are softer, the clothes more subdued. Everyone's sitting or lying down, and one has as much chance of seeing a black student as a Martian.

2   The commons is a gathering spot where students relax on benches and talk with friends. They also buy candy and soda, watch TV, and make phone calls. It's a place where all sorts of things happen. But you'll never find a white student and a black student talking to each other.

3   After three years, I still feel uncomfortable when I have to walk through the "black" side to get to class. It's not that any black stu-

313

dents threaten or harass me. They just quietly ignore me and look in the other direction, and I do the same. But there's one who sometimes catches my eye, and I can't help feeling awkward when I see him. He was a close friend from childhood.

4   Ten years ago, we played catch in our backyards, went bike riding, and slept over at one another's houses. By the fifth grade, we went to movies and amusement parks and bunked together at the same summer camps. We met while playing on the same Little League team, though we attended different grade schools. We're both juniors now at the same high school. We usually don't say anything when we see each other, except maybe a polite "Hi" or "Hey." I can't remember the last time we talked on the phone, much less got together outside of school.

5   Since entering high school, we haven't shared a single class or sport. He plays football, a black-dominated sport, while I play tennis, which is, with rare exception, an all-white team. It's as if fate has kept us apart; though, more likely, it's peer pressure.

6   In the lunchroom, I sit with my white friends and my childhood friend sits with his black ones. It's the same when we walk through the hallways or sit in the library. If Michael Jackson thinks, "It don't matter if you're black or white," he should visit my high school.

7   I wonder if proponents of desegregation realized that even if schools were integrated, students would choose to remain apart. It wasn't until 1983 that St. Louis's voluntary city-suburban desegregation program was approved. Today, my school has 25 percent black students. While this has given many young people the chance for a better education, it hasn't brought the two races closer together.

8   In high school, I've become friends with Vietnamese Americans, Korean Americans, Iranian Americans, Indian Americans, Russian Americans, and exchange students from France and Sweden. The only group that remains at a distance is the African Americans. I've had only a handful of black students in all my classes and only one black teacher (from Haiti).

9   In its effort to put students through as many academic classes as possible and prepare them for college, my school seems to have overlooked one crucial course: teaching black and white students how to get along, which in my opinion, would be more valuable than all the others. It's not that there haven't been efforts to improve race relations. Last fall, a group of black and white students established a program called Students Organized Against Racism. But at a recent meeting, SOAR members decided that the separation of blacks and whites was largely voluntary and there was little

they could do about it. Another youth group tried to help by moving the soda machine from the "white" side of the commons to the "black" side, so that white students would have to cross the line to get a Coke. But all that's happened is that students buy their sodas, then return to their own territory.

10   Last summer, at a youth camp called Miniwanca in Michigan, I did see black and white teens get along. I don't mean just tolerate one another. I mean play sports together, dance together, walk on the beach together, and become friends. The students came from all races and backgrounds, as well as from overseas. Camp organizers purposely placed me in a cabin and activity group that included whites, blacks, Southerners, Northerners, and foreigners, none of whom I'd met before.

11   For 10 days, I became great friends with a group of strangers, at least half of whom were black. One wouldn't know that racism existed at that idyllic place, where we told stories around campfires, acted in plays, and shared our deepest thoughts about AIDS, parents, abortion, and dating. Everyone got along so well there that it was depressing for me to return to high school. But at the same time, it made me hopeful. If black and white teenagers could be friends at leadership camp, couldn't they mix in school as well?

12   Schools need to make it a real priority to involve whites and blacks together as much as possible. This would mean more multicultural activities, mandatory classes that teach black history, and discussions of today's racial controversies. Teachers should mix whites and blacks more in study groups so they *have* to work together in and out of school. (Students won't do it on their own.) And most important, all students should get a chance to attend a camp like Miniwanca. Maybe the Clinton administration could find a way to help finance other camps like it.

13   As it is now, black and white teenagers just don't know one another. I think a lot about my friend from childhood—what he does on weekends, what he thinks about college, what he wants to do with his life. I have no answers, and it saddens me.

EXERCISES

Details and Their Meanings

1. What is "the commons"? Who are the groups of people there? Why are they there? How do they behave and interact?

How does the writer feel about being in various parts of the commons?

2. Where is the writer's childhood friend now? How has their relation changed over ten years' time? How does the writer account for this change? How does the writer's relations with students of other racial and ethnic groups compare to his relations with African-American students?

3. When were the schools in St. Louis desegregated? What have been the effects of desegregation?

4. What is SOAR? What are its goals? What methods does it use to achieve these goals? How effective are these methods?

5. What experiences did the writer have at Miniwanca? How do they compare to his experiences at school? What is the cause of the difference in the experiences?

6. What does the writer say is the root of the problem he describes in this selection? What solutions does he offer? How do these solutions follow from the writer's causal analysis of the problem?

Reading and Critical Thinking

1. Some critics of desegregation have argued that you can't change people's minds by changing the law and that legislating tolerance and acceptance between races can make people even less tolerant and accepting. Does the writer agree with this view? Find evidence in the essay to support your opinion.

2. The writer cites historical facts and recent statistics about desegregation in his city. Why do you think that St. Louis's voluntary city-suburban desegregation program was not approved until 1983? Why do you think the movement toward integrating schools was voluntary rather than mandatory?

3. How does the writer account for the fact that desegregation has not brought people of different races together? What other factors might help to explain this fact?

4. Why was the writer unable to remain close to his childhood friend? What conclusions can you draw about how young children of different races relate to each other? teenagers? adults? What do your conclusions suggest about some of the causes of racism?

5. How do the writer's experiences at Camp Minawanca relate to the general solutions he offers to racial separation? Do you think these solutions will work outside the camp setting? Why or why not?

The Writer's Strategies

1. What is the writer's thesis? In what paragraphs does the writer identify most directly the problem he raises in the essay? In what paragraphs does he illustrate and elaborate on the problem and its causes? In what paragraphs does he provide solutions to this problem? How does the organization contribute to the writer's main point in this selection?
2. Where does the writer present narratives of his own experience? How do these narratives help develop his argument?
3. Where does the writer use comparison and contrast in this selection? How does this rhetorical strategy reinforce the writer's main point?
4. How does the essay end? How does this ending bring together the themes of this essay?
5. Why does the writer use the words *black* and *white* to describe race in this selection? What other terms does he use to describe other groups of students? What are the differences in using the various kinds of terms?

Thinking Together

Brainstorm in small groups about the kind of racial segregation that you think exists in the United States today in housing, education, industry, entertainment, and so forth. How do you account for these instances of segregation? To what extent are these instances of segregation voluntary? How might desegregation be implemented in these areas? Ought we try to eliminate all instances of segregation or should people be allowed to engage in certain kinds of voluntary segregation?

Vocabulary

Use context to define the following italicized words found in this selection.

1. walk through the *commons* at my high school (par. 1)
2. more likely, it's *peer* pressure (par. 5)
3. the *proponents* of desegregation (par. 7)
4. that *idyllic* place (par. 11)
5. a real *priority* (par. 12)
6. *mandatory* classes (par. 12)

WRITER'S WORKSHOP ────────────

Critical Thinking in Writing

1. Write an informal journal entry in which you imagine that you are a member of a different racial group from the one to which you belong. How would your friends treat you? Would race affect the relation you have with them? If so, how? If not, explain why.
2. Write a letter to Brian Jarvis in which you express your support for or opposition to his solution to the problem described in this selection. Draw on your own experiences and observations to illustrate why you feel the way you do.
3. In paragraph 12, the writer makes some recommendations for curricula and teaching strategies that he believes will help students of different races interact more positively. Consider whether or not you believe that these strategies would work at your former high school or your current college. Then write a proposal of a couple of pages addressed to the principal of the high school or the president of your college outlining your own recommendations.

Connecting Ideas

Read "The Great Divide," by Ellen Goodman (page 344). How does her description of segregation on college campuses compare to Jarvis's description of segregation at his high school? How do you think Goodman would respond to Jarvis's recommendations for improving race relations in educational institutions? Would she think that his solutions would work? Why or why not? Does Jarvis's experience undercut the hope for the future that Goodman expresses in her essay? If so, how?

Wilshire Bus

Hisaye Yamamoto

In this selection, a Japanese-American woman riding on a bus witnesses a racist incident and realizes something disturbing about herself and society as a whole.

KEY WORDS

somatotonic (par. 5)   aggressive, physical personality type
   associated with a muscular body
metaphor (par. 8)   word or phrase that compares two things
diatribe (par. 9)   abusive speech
coolies (par. 12)   unskilled, poorly paid Chinese laborers
gloating (par. 15)   delighting in someone else's misfortune
desolate (par. 17)   deserted, joyless
craw (par. 22)   stomach

WILSHIRE BOULEVARD BEGINS SOMEWHERE near the heart of downtown Los Angeles and, except for a few digressions scarcely worth mentioning, goes straight out to the edge of the Pacific Ocean. It is a wide boulevard and traffic on it is fairly fast. For the most part, it is bordered on either side with examples of the recent stark architecture which favors a great deal of glass. As the boulevard approaches the sea, however, the landscape becomes a bit more pastoral, so that the university and the soldiers' home there give the appearance of being huge country estates.

2   Esther Kuroiwa got to know this stretch of territory quite well while her husband Buro was in one of the hospitals at the soldiers' home. They had been married less than a year when his back, injured in the war, began troubling him again, and he was forced to take three months of treatments at Sawtelle before he was able to go back to work. During this time, Esther was permitted to visit him twice a week and she usually took the yellow bus out on Wednesdays because she did not know the first thing about driving

and because her friends were not able to take her except on Sundays. She always enjoyed the long bus ride very much because her seat companions usually turned out to be amiable, and if they did not, she took vicarious pleasure in gazing out at the almost unmitigated elegance along the fabulous street.

3   It was on one of these Wednesday trips that Esther committed a grave sin of omission which caused her later to burst into tears and which caused her acute discomfort for a long time afterwards whenever something reminded her of it.

4   The man came on the bus quite early and Esther noticed him briefly as he entered because he said gaily to the driver, "You robber. All you guys do is take money from me every day, just for giving me a short lift!"

5   Handsome in a red-faced way, greying, medium of height, and dressed in a dark grey sport suit with a yellow-and-black flowered shirt, he said this in a nice, resonant, carrying voice which got the response of a scattering of titters from the bus. Esther, somewhat amused and classifying him as a somatotonic, promptly forgot about him. And since she was sitting alone in the first regular seat, facing the back of the driver and the two front benches facing each other, she returned to looking out the window.

6   At the next stop, a considerable mass of people piled on and the last two climbing up were an elderly Oriental man and his wife. Both were neatly and somberly clothed and the woman, who wore her hair in a bun and carried a bunch of yellow and dark red chrysanthemums, came to sit with Esther. Esther turned her head to smile a greeting (well, here we are, Orientals together on a bus), but the woman was watching, with some concern, her husband who was asking directions of the driver.

7   His faint English was inflected in such a way as to make Esther decide he was probably Chinese, and she noted that he had to repeat his question several times before the driver could answer it. Then he came to sit in the seat across the aisle from his wife. It was about then that a man's voice, which Esther recognized soon as belonging to the somatotonic, began a loud monologue in the seat just behind her. It was not really a monologue, since he seemed to be addressing his seat companion, but this person was not heard to give a single answer. The man's subject was a figure in the local sporting world who had a nice fortune invested in several of the shining buildings the bus was just passing.

8   "He's as tight-fisted as they make them, as tight-fisted as they come," the man said. "Why, he wouldn't give you the sweat off

his . . ." He paused here to rephrase his metaphor, ". . . wouldn't give you the sweat off his palm!"

9   And he continued in this vein, discussing the private life of the famous man so frankly that Esther knew he must be quite drunk. But she listened with interest, wondering how much of this diatribe was true because the public legend about the famous man was emphatic about his charity. Suddenly, the woman with the chrysanthemums jerked around to get a look at the speaker and Esther felt her giving him a quick but thorough examination before she turned back around.

10   "So you don't like it?" the man inquired, and it was a moment before Esther realized that he was now directing his attention to her seat neighbor.

11   "Well, if you don't like it," he continued, "why don't you get off this bus, why don't you go back where you came from? Why don't you go back to China?"

12   Then, his voice growing jovial, as though he were certain of the support of the bus in this at least, he embroidered on this theme with a new eloquence, "Why don't you go back to China, where you can be coolies working in your bare feet out in the rice fields? You can let your pigtails grow and grow in China. Alla samee, mama, no tickee no shirtee. Ha, pretty good, no tickee no shirtee!"

13   He chortled with delight and seemed to be looking around the bus for approval. Then some memory caused him to launch on a new idea. "Or why don't you go back to Trinidad? They got Chinks running the whole she-bang in Trinidad. Every place you go in Trinidad . . . "

14   As he talked on, Esther, pretending to look out the window, felt the tenseness in the body of the woman beside her. The only movement from her was the trembling of the chrysanthemums with the motion of the bus. Without turning her head, Esther was also aware that a man, a mild-looking man with thinning hair and glasses, on one of the front benches, was smiling at the woman and shaking his head mournfully in sympathy, but she doubted whether the woman saw.

15   Esther herself, while believing herself properly annoyed with the speaker and sorry for the old couple, felt quite detached. She found herself wondering whether the man meant her in his exclusion order or whether she was identifiably Japanese. Of course, he was not sober enough to be interested in such fine distinctions, but it did matter, she decided, because she was Japanese, not Chinese, and therefore in the present case immune. Then she was startled to realize that

what she was actually doing was gloating over the fact that the drunken man had specified the Chinese as the unwanted.

16   Briefly, there bobbled on her memory the face of an elderly Oriental man whom she had once seen from a streetcar on her way home from work. (This was not long after she had returned to Los Angeles from the concentration camp in Arkansas and been lucky enough to get a clerical job with the Community Chest.) The old man was on a concrete island at Seventh and Broadway, waiting for his streetcar. She had looked down on him benignly as a fellow Oriental, from her seat by the window, then been suddenly thrown for a loop by the legend on a large lapel button on his jacket. I AM KOREAN, said the button.

17   Heat suddenly rising to her throat, she had felt angry, then desolate and betrayed. True, reason had returned to ask whether she might not, under the circumstances, have worn such a button herself. She had heard rumors of I AM CHINESE buttons. So it was true then; why not I AM KOREAN buttons, too? Wryly, she wished for an I AM JAPANESE button, just to be able to call the man's attention to it, "Look at me!" But perhaps the man didn't even read English, perhaps he had been actually threatened, perhaps it was not his doing—his solicitous children perhaps had urged him to wear the badge.

18   Trying now to make up for her moral shabbiness, she turned toward the little woman and smiled at her across the chrysanthemums, shaking her head a little to get across her message (don't pay any attention to that stupid old drunk, he doesn't know what he's saying, let's take things like this in our stride). But the woman, in turn looking at her, presented a face so impassive yet cold, and eyes so expressionless yet hostile, that Esther's overture fell quite flat.

19   Okay, okay, if that's the way you feel about it, she thought to herself. Then the bus made another stop and she heard the man proclaim ringingly, "So clear out, all of you, and remember to take every last one of your slant-eyed pickaninnies with you!" This was his final advice as he stepped down from the middle door. The bus remained at the stop long enough for Esther to watch the man cross the street with a slightly exploring step. Then, as it started up again, the bespectacled man in front stood up to go and made a clumsy speech to the Chinese couple and possibly to Esther. "I want you to know," he said, "that we aren't all like that man. We don't all feel the way he does. We believe in an America that is a melting pot of all sorts of people. I'm originally Scotch and French myself." With that, he came over and shook the hand of the Chinese man.

20 "And you, young lady," he said to the girl behind Esther, "you deserve a Purple Heart or something for having to put up with that sitting beside you."

21 Then he, too, got off.

22 The rest of the ride was uneventful and Esther stared out the window with eyes that did not see. Getting off at last at the soldiers' home, she was aware of the Chinese couple getting off after her, but she avoided looking at them. Then, while she was walking toward Buro's hospital very quickly, there arose in her mind some words she had once read and let stick in her craw: People say, do not regard what he says, now he is in liquor. Perhaps it is the only time he ought to be regarded.

23 These words repeated themselves until her saving detachment was gone every bit and she was filled once again in her life with the infuriatingly helpless, insidiously sickening sensation of there being in the world nothing solid she could put her finger on, nothing solid she could come to grips with, nothing solid she could sink her teeth into, nothing solid.

24 When she reached Buro's room and caught sight of his welcoming face, she ran to his bed and broke into sobs that she could not control. Buro was amazed because it was hardly her first visit and she had never shown such weakness before, but solving the mystery handily, he patted her head, looked around smugly at his roommates, and asked tenderly, "What's the matter? You've been missing me a whole lot, huh?" And she, finally drying her eyes, sniffed and nodded and bravely smiled and answered him with the question, yes, weren't women silly?

―――――

EXERCISES

Details and Their Meanings

1. During what years do you assume the selection is taking place? What important events occurred in this time period? In general, why do you think it might be important to know the time period reflected in a written selection?

2. How is Wilshire Boulevard described by the narrator? What is her usual experience of the bus ride to see her husband? What

does this information have to do with what happens to Esther
Kuroiwa?

3. Identify the ethnic origins of Esther Kuroiwa, the elderly woman
   who is holding a bunch of chrysanthemums, the drunk somatotonic man on the bus, and the sympathetic man who speaks to
   the elderly woman after the drunk man gets off the bus. Why do
   you think the writer mentions all these different ethnic groups?
4. What do you know about Esther Kuroiwa's husband, Buro?
   How does his role in World War II contribute to what you think
   the overall point of the selection might be? Where was Esther
   Kuroiwa during World War II? What does this detail have to
   do with the other bus ride that she remembers?
5. How does Esther feel at first about the drunk man's comments?
   By the time she gets to her husband's room, how does she feel?
   How have Esther's attitudes about racial issues changed by the
   end of the piece?
6. Is Esther's reaction to the drunk man's racism clearly known
   to the other riders? Why do you think her reaction upsets her
   so much?

Reading and Critical Thinking

1. What is the significance of the "I am Korean" button? Why do
   you think Esther remembers it on this particular bus ride? How
   did Esther's racism differ from that of the man she observed
   wearing the "I am Korean" button? What kind of racism has
   Esther experienced?
2. In what ways did Esther's and Buro's experience during World
   War II contrast? How does the contrast contribute to the overall
   meaning of the narrative?
3. Why do you think Esther repeats the saying: "do not regard
   what he says, now he is in liquor" and then thinks to herself,
   "Perhaps it is the only time he ought to be regarded"? What
   does her analysis have to do with the feeling that she has committed a grave sin of omission?
4. In what ways does this selection intend to change stereotypic
   expectations of what racism is? Has the piece helped you see
   racism in a new light? How?
5. Do you think "grave sin of omission" describes what Esther
   "did"? What did she omit? How might you word what she
   "did" in a different way?

6. How do you think your knowledge of history or different cultures affects your reading of this piece?

The Writer's Strategies

1. How does Yamamoto open the selection? What do the first two paragraphs have to do with the event that the narrative discloses?
2. From whose point of view are the events told? In what ways could the narrative be different if told from another character's perspective? Discuss several different possibilities.
3. The point of the selection is announced in paragraph 3, but it is not really understood until approximately paragraph 15. What effect does this have on the reader? What is the purpose of the second half of the story after Esther's realization?
4. Pick out several descriptions, lines of dialogue, or thoughts that give you an idea of what Esther is feeling. How does the writer make Esther's thoughts and feelings real to you?
5. Why do you think the writer included the man of Scotch and French background? If this character were not present, how would the meaning of the selection change?

Thinking Together

In small groups, discuss whether you or someone you know has been in a situation similar to that of any of the people in the selection. Discuss what you did in the situation and how you felt. Then discuss with the group if you wish you had responded differently. If you do, think about how you could respond differently in the future in a similar situation. As a group, discuss what sort of thinking has to change for the Wilshire bus "scene" to disappear.

Vocabulary

The following adjectives and adverbs describe characters, places, objects, and ideas mentioned in the selection. Define each word.

1. stark (par. 1)
2. pastoral (par. 1)
3. amiable (par. 2)

 4. vicarious (par. 2)
 5. unmitigated (par. 2)
 6. grave (par. 3)
 7. acute (par. 3)
 8. resonant (par. 5)
 9. jovial (par. 12)
10. detached (par. 15)
11. benignly (par. 16)
12. solicitous (par. 17)
13. infuriatingly (par. 23)
14. insidiously (par. 23)

WRITER'S WORKSHOP

Critical Thinking in Writing

1. Suppose you are invited to speak to a group of third grade children about racist attitudes. What would you tell the children about how to develop positive relations with people no matter what their backgrounds? What would you say about the causes of racism and how to avoid it?
2. What effects do you think racism has on people to whom it is directed? Write a short essay on this question. If you want, use this selection or other selections, as well as your own experiences and knowledge, as evidence to support your main point.
3. Write a short piece about the different forms of racism that exist in your community. Like Hisaye Yamamoto does in this piece, use scenes of people and places to illustrate the kinds of racism that you identify.

Connecting Ideas

In this piece, the narrator at first distances herself from the fate of other people being discriminated against but then makes an imaginative leap to understand sympathetically how another person's situation might be just as real as hers.

Compare that process of sympathetic imagination to the one that occurs in George Orwell's "A Hanging" (page 327) or to one occurring in any other selection in this anthology.

A Hanging

George Orwell

George Orwell, author of Animal Farm *(1945) and* Nineteen
Eighty-four *(1949), was one of England's most important writers
in the middle of the twentieth century. In this essay, he describes an
experience he had while serving as a police officer in Burma. Orwell
was not American, nor does he write here of America; yet he is to
this day one of the best chroniclers of social and cultural issues.*

KEY WORDS

sodden (par. 1)   soaked with water
pariah (par. 6)   an outcast
timorously (par. 15)   timidly, fearfully
refractory (par. 22)   stubborn

IT WAS IN BURMA, a sodden morning of the rains. A sickly light, like
yellow tinfoil, was slanting over the high walls into the jail yard.
We were waiting outside the condemned cells, a row of sheds
fronted with double bars, like small animal cages. Each cell measured about ten feet by ten and was quite bare within except for a
plank bed and a pot of drinking water. In some of them brown
silent men were squatting at the inner bars, with their blankets
draped round them. These were the condemned men, due to be
hanged within the next week or two.

2   One prisoner had been brought out of his cell. He was a Hindu,
a puny wisp of a man, with a shaven head and vague liquid eyes.
He had a thick, sprouting moustache, absurdly too big for his body,
rather like the moustache of a comic man on the films. Six tall Indian warders were guarding him and getting him ready for the
gallows. Two of them stood by with rifles with fixed bayonets,
while the others handcuffed him, passed a chain through his hand-
cuffs and fixed it to their belts, and lashed his arms tight to his
sides. They crowded very close about him with their hands always

on him in a careful, caressing grip, as though all the while feeling him to make sure he was there. It was like men handling a fish which is still alive and may jump back into the water. But he stood quite unresisting, yielding his arms limply to the ropes, as though he hardly noticed what was happening.

3   Eight o'clock struck and a bugle call, desolately thin in the wet air, floated from the distant barracks. The superintendent of the jail, who was standing apart from the rest of us, moodily prodding the gravel with his stick, raised his head at the sound. He was an army doctor, with a grey toothbrush moustache and a gruff voice. "For God's sake hurry up, Francis," he said irritably. "The man ought to have been dead by this time. Aren't you ready yet?"

4   Francis, the head jailer, a fat Dravidian in a white drill suit and gold spectacles, waved his black hand. "Yes sir, yes sir," he bubbled. "All iss satisfactorily prepared. The hangman iss waiting. We shall proceed."

5   "Well, quick march, then. The prisoners can't get their breakfast till this job's over."

6   We set out for the gallows. Two warders marched on either side of the prisoner, with their files at the slope; two others marched close against him, gripping him by arm and shoulder, as though at once pushing and supporting him. The rest of us, magistrates and the like, followed behind. Suddenly, when we had gone ten yards, the procession stopped short without any order or warning. A dreadful thing had happened—a dog, come goodness knows whence, had appeared in the yard. It came bounding among us with a loud volley of barks and leapt round us wagging its whole body, wild with glee at finding so many human beings together. It was a large woolly dog, half Airedale, half pariah. For a moment it pranced round us and then, before anyone could stop it, it had made a dash for the prisoner, and jumping up tried to lick his face. Everyone stood aghast, too taken aback even to grab at the dog.

7   "Who let that bloody brute in here?" said the superintendent angrily. "Catch it, someone!"

8   A warder, detached from the escort, charged clumsily after the dog, but it danced and gambolled just out of his reach, taking everything as part of the game. A young Eurasian jailer picked up a handful of gravel and tried to stone the dog away, but it dodged the stones and came after us again. Its yaps echoed from the jail walls. The prisoner, in the grasp of the two warders, looked on incuriously, as though this was another formality of the hanging. It was several minutes before someone managed to catch the dog.

Then we put my handkerchief through its collar and moved off once more, with the dog still straining and whimpering.

9   It was about forty yards to the gallows. I watched the bare brown back of the prisoner marching in front of me. He walked clumsily with his bound arms, but quite steadily, with that bobbing gait of the Indian who never straightens his knees. At each step his muscles slid neatly into place, the lock of hair on his scalp danced up and down, his feet printed themselves on the wet gravel. And once, in spite of the men who gripped him by each shoulder, he stepped slightly aside to avoid a puddle on the path.

10   It is curious, but till that moment I had never realised what it means to destroy a healthy, conscious man. When I saw the prisoner step aside to avoid the puddle, I saw the mystery, the unspeakable wrongness, of cutting a life short when it is in full tide. This man was not dying, he was alive just as we were alive. All the organs of his body were working—bowels digesting food, skin renewing itself, nails growing, tissues forming—all toiling away in solemn foolery. His nails would still be growing when he stood on the drop, when he was falling through the air with a tenth of a second to live. His eyes saw the yellow gravel and the grey walls, and his brain still remembered, foresaw, reasoned—reasoned even about puddles. He and we were a party of men walking together, seeing, hearing, feeling, understanding the same world; and in two minutes, with a sudden snap, one of us would be gone—one mind less, one world less.

11   The gallows stood in a small yard, separate from the main grounds of the prison, and overgrown with tall prickly weeds. It was a brick erection like three sides of a shed, with planking on top, and above that two beams and a crossbar with the rope dangling. The hangman, a grey-haired convict in the white uniform of the prison, was waiting beside his machine. He greeted us with a servile crouch as we entered. At a word from Francis the two warders, gripping the prisoner more closely than ever, half led, half pushed him to the gallows and helped him clumsily up the ladder. Then the hangman climbed up and fixed the rope round the prisoner's neck.

12   We stood waiting, five yards away. The warders had formed in a rough circle round the gallows. And then, when the noose was fixed, the prisoner began crying out on his god. It was a high, reiterated cry of "Ram! Ram! Ram! Ram!", not urgent and fearful like a prayer or a cry for help, but steady, rhythmical, almost like the tolling of a bell. The dog answered the sound with a whine. The hangman, still standing on the gallows, produced a small cotton bag like a flour bag and drew it down over the prisoner's face.

But the sound, muffled by the cloth, still persisted, over and over again: "Ram! Ram! Ram! Ram! Ram!"

13   The hangman climbed down and stood ready, holding the lever. Minutes seemed to pass. The steady, muffled crying from the prisoner went on and on, "Ram! Ram! Ram!" never faltering for an instant. The superintendent, his head on his chest, was slowly poking the ground with his stick; perhaps he was counting the cries, allowing the prisoner a fixed number—fifty, perhaps, or a hundred. Everyone had changed colour. The Indians had gone grey like bad coffee, and one or two of the bayonets were wavering. We looked at the lashed, hooded man on the drop, and listened to his cries—each cry another second of life; the same thought was in all our minds: oh, kill him quickly, get it over, stop that abominable noise!

14   Suddenly the superintendent made up his mind. Throwing up his head he made a swift motion with his stick. "Chalo!" he shouted almost fiercely.

15   There was a clanking noise and then dead silence. The prisoner had vanished, and the rope was twisting on itself. I let go of the dog, and it galloped immediately to the back of the gallows; but when it got there it stopped short, barked, and then retreated into a corner of the yard, where it stood among the weeds, looking timorously out at us. We went round the gallows to inspect the prisoner's body. He was dangling with his toes pointed straight downwards, very slowly revolving, as dead as a stone.

16   The superintendent reached out with his stick and poked the bare body; it oscillated, slightly. *"He's* all right," said the superintendent. He backed out from under the gallows and blew out a deep breath. The moody look had gone out of his face quite suddenly. He glanced at his wristwatch. "Eight minutes past eight. Well, that's all for this morning, thank God."

17   The warders unfixed bayonets and marched away. The dog, sobered and conscious of having misbehaved itself, slipped after them. We walked out of the gallows yard, past the condemned cells with their waiting prisoners, into the big central yard of the prison. The convicts, under the command of warders armed with lathis, were already receiving their breakfast. They squatted in long rows, each man holding a tin pannikin, while two warders with buckets marched round ladling out rice; it seemed quite a homely, jolly scene, after the hanging. An enormous relief had come upon us now that the job was done. One felt an impulse to sing, to break into a run, to snigger. All at once everyone began chattering gaily.

18   The Eurasian boy walking beside me nodded toward the way

we had come, with a knowing smile: "Do you know, sir, our friend (he meant the dead man), when he heard his appeal had been dismissed, he pissed on the floor of his cell. From fright—Kindly take one of my cigarettes, sir. Do you not admire my new silver case, sir? From the boxwallah, two rupees eight annas. Classy European style."

19   Several people laughed—at what, nobody seemed certain.

20   Francis was walking by the superintendent, talking garrulously: "Well, sir, all hass passed off with the utmost satisfactoriness. It wass all finished—flick! like that. It iss not always so—oah, no! I have known cases where the doctor wass obliged to go beneath the gallows and pull the prisoner's legs to ensure decease. Most disagreeable!"

21   "Wriggling about, eh? That's bad," said the superintendent.

22   "Ach, sir, it iss worse when they become refractory! One man, I recall, clung to the bars of hiss cage when we went to take him out. You will scarcely credit, sir, that it took six warders to dislodge him, three pulling at each leg. We reasoned with him. 'My dear fellow,' we said, 'think of all the pain and trouble you are causing to us!' But no, he would not listen! Ach, he wass very troublesome!"

23   I found that I was laughing quite loudly. Everyone was laughing. Even the superintendent grinned in a tolerant way. "You'd better all come out and have a drink," he said quite genially. "I've got a bottle of whisky in the car. We could do with it."

24   We went through the big double gates of the prison, into the road. "Pulling at his legs!" exclaimed a Burmese magistrate suddenly, and burst into a loud chuckling. We all began laughing again. At the moment Francis's anecdote seemed extraordinarily funny. We all had a drink together, native and European alike, quite amicably. The dead man was a hundred yards away.

—————

EXERCISES

Details and Their Meanings

1. What is the setting for this essay? What sort of day is it? What time of day is it? Why is the time unusual?

2. Who is about to be hanged? What crime is he convicted of?
3. What is George Orwell's function at the prison? Why is he there?
4. Whose dog wanders into the action? Why is the dog tolerated?
5. Why are the other prisoners eager to see the man hanged?
6. What event makes Orwell realize the absurdity of this situation?

Reading and Critical Thinking

1. What is Orwell's attitude toward the Burmese? toward the British? Where does this attitude become clear? What significance do you see in the fact that the British, in a country not their own, are executing an Indian Hindu?
2. Why are so many people needed to execute one man? What other function do they serve?
3. Why does the condemned man step around the puddle? Why is this detail so important for explaining Orwell's position on what is about to take place?
4. What quality do human beings have that lower animals do not have? How does your answer reveal an irony about capital punishment?
5. Why are the witnesses so tense? How would their answer to that question differ from Orwell's? Why does everyone laugh at the end? What are they laughing about?

The Writer's Strategies

1. What is the main point of the essay? Which paragraph best suggests Orwell's thesis?
2. What kinds of details does Orwell use to make this writing effective? What mood do these details create?
3. Where does Orwell use comparison and contrast as a development strategy? What other rhetorical strategies does he use?
4. Does this piece appeal more to reason or to emotion? What helps you to answer this question?
5. What is the function of the dog? Why does Orwell include him?
6. Who is the audience for this essay? What action does Orwell wish his readers to take?
7. Which paragraphs represent the introduction, body, and conclusion? What is the purpose of the last sentence?

Thinking Together

Supporters of capital punishment say it deters murderers in society. In an almanac, look up the American states that have reinstated capital punishment since the 1970s. How many people are on death row? How many have actually been executed? In the same book, you can also look up the number of murders each year in the United States. Does what you find surprise you? Discuss in class your interpretation of the data—the relation between homicide and capital punishment.

Vocabulary

Use context clues to determine the meaning of the following italicized words from the selection, and then write a definition of each.

1. a bugle call, *desolately* thin in the wet air (par. 3)
2. moodily *prodding* the gravel with his stick (par. 3)
3. Everyone stood *aghast,* too taken aback even to grab at the dog. (par. 6)
4. the dog . . . danced and *gambolled* just out of his reach (par. 8)
5. He greeted us with a *servile* crouch as we entered. (par. 11)
6. It was a high, *reiterated* cry of "Ram! Ram! Ram! Ram!" (par. 12)
7. stop that *abominable* noise! (par. 13)
8. the bare body . . . *oscillated,* slightly. (par. 16)
9. Francis was walking by the superintendent, talking *garrulously.* (par. 20)
10. We all had a drink together . . . quite *amicably.* (par. 24)

WRITER'S WORKSHOP ━━━━━━━━━━━━

Critical Thinking in Writing

1. According to surveys, most Americans favor capital punishment. Why? Are you personally in favor of it? On what grounds? Write an argument to defend your views.
2. It is possible to exercise control without violence? Must a society discipline and punish its citizens in order to ensure law and order? What alternatives can you suggest?

3. Some people argue that life in prison is actually a worse punishment than death. If you were forced to choose between these
   alternatives for yourself, which one would you pick and why?

Connecting Ideas

Read Douglas Martin's "Blind Commuter" (page 251). What support do you find there for Orwell's views on the sanctity of life,
on the connection between life and hope, and on the human capacity to cling to life in difficult circumstances?

Bias Outside Appalachia

Judy Pasternak

Judy Pasternak reports on the prejudice and social ills faced by Appalachian immigrants to Cincinnati.

KEY WORDS

sermonize (par. 3)   preach
automation (par. 9)   work done by machines
emigration (par. 9)   moving away
diaspora (par. 11)   time away from a homeland
mainstream (par. 11)   part of the dominant culture
lineage (par. 12)   family history
adage (par. 12)   saying
prestigious (par. 27)   highly regarded
clientele (par. 36)   group of people served by an organization

---

FOR NEARLY 30 YEARS after World War II, the mountain children of eastern Kentucky were said to learn three lessons early in life: reading, writing, and Route 25, the old road to the factory jobs in this Ohio River city.

2   Newcomers here no more, the urban Appalachians are set apart, even in the second and third generations. "Turns out that old highway could lead to a world of misery," country-music star Dwight Yoakam sings in a plaintive lyric dedicated to his Appalachian-born family.

3   In neighborhoods of shabby row houses and cramped bungalows, where preachers sermonize in storefronts and laundry dries on lines, tens of thousands of coal miners' descendants make up a lasting white underclass plagued by high unemployment, horrendous dropout rates, and drug and alcohol addiction. About 44 per-

cent of the area's residents of mountain stock are either poor or at serious risk of falling into poverty, sociologists have found; virtually all of them live within city limits.

4   A major reason for the troubles, community activists believe, is lingering prejudice and ignorance of mountain culture. "Did you ever see the *Beverly Hillbillies*?" asked Pauletta Hansel, an assistant director of the Urban Appalachian Council here. "Snuffy Smith. *The Dukes of Hazzard.* That's the stereotype."

5   The caricatures can make the basics—schooling, housing, jobs—hard to come by or to keep. A twang in the voice, a quirky expression like "I reckon," a taste for banjo music, all passed on to children and grandchildren raised here, can lead to many other assumptions: This person is not smart, this person won't show up on time, this person's temper is likely to be quick. "Hillbilly" jokes and quips are not uncommon.

6   Sixteen months ago, Cincinnati responded by adopting the nation's only human rights ordinance banning discrimination against Appalachians.

7   With an estimated 20 percent to 30 percent of the city's residents of Appalachian stock, the mountain folk are the second-largest distinct group in town, behind the 40 percent of the population that is black. The city schools have designated May as "Appalachian Month," and a political action committee, AppalPAC, supports sympathetic candidates, albeit with a mixed record of success. An advocacy group, the Urban Appalachian Council, provides social services and works to instill pride.

8   But problems persist. "The fair housing department has not been oriented to helping Appalachians," said City Councilwoman Bobbie Sterne. "We had to fight for youth jobs. They said Appalachians weren't applying." She sighed. "I don't know."

9   Appalachian activists say similar troubles have surfaced in Columbus, Dayton, and Akron, Ohio, in Indianapolis, and in other cities that lured more than 3 million people from Appalachia over three decades. Many of them were forced to leave home as automation in the coal mines took away their work. During a second mountain emigration in the 1980s, 45,000 people headed mostly to boom towns in the Carolinas and Georgia.

10   "If the numbers continue, those areas [in the Southeast] are going to face many of the same problems down the road that the Midwest cities face today," said Ronald D. Eller, director of the University of Kentucky's Appalachian Center. His own memories as a child of Appalachian parents in Akron—the "capital of West Virginia" was its nickname at the time—are more than tinged with bitterness.

11   The diaspora has resulted in mountain people becoming "an invisible minority," in their new homes, said Phillip J. Obermiller, a sociologist who has written extensively about them. On paper, they couldn't be more mainstream: white, English-speaking, Protestant.

12   Though some blacks also live in the Appalachians, the majority of the residents trace their lineage to settlers from England, Ireland, and Scotland who rejected the coastal cities of America in favor of frontier freedoms, beginning in the late 1700s. If a man heard a rifle shot, the adage went, he packed up and left to escape overcrowding.

13   Over the years, as farming and hunting gave way to coal mining, the isolated gaps and hollows nurtured a distinctive way of life, based on helping kin and neighbors while staying independent and wary of outsiders. The emphasis on clan traditions meant that the taking of sides during the Civil War could lead to feuds lasting well into this century. It also resulted in the custom of decorating family graveyards once a year while telling old tales, a practice that is still observed.

14   The culture has demonstrated remarkable staying power in the cities, in part because so many Appalachians moved together and in part because their old homes were so close by. The first generation of urban Appalachians could drive or take a bus back each weekend, carrying the children along. Now, that second generation brings the grandchildren back on special occasions.

15   At the same time, however, "it's hard to get ahead if you don't feel part of something," said Larry Redden, an organizer with the Urban Appalachian Council.

16   Here in Cincinnati, it is clear that those who retain traces of the hills in their lives can be made to feel different, indeed. Others may make sport of dulcimer music, or of a popular custom of sending a funeral arrangement in the shape of a phone off the hook, with the sign declaring "Jesus Has Called." This is a city where some liberal middle-class whites recall that, during childhood, *hillbilly* was a term used at home, while racial epithets were strictly forbidden.

17   Whether such separateness deserves legal protection is a matter of local debate, especially among Cincinnati's African Americans, who tend to fare slightly worse than Appalachians, statistics show. "They have a lot of the same kinds of problems [as blacks]," said Sheila Adams, president of the city's chapter of the Urban League. "But do I think it's easier for them in the long run? Probably."

18   Councilman Dwight Tillery, who is black, said he found it "interesting" when he noticed that Appalachians were included in the human rights ordinance. He voted for it, figuring, "What harm

could it do?" The measure also banned bias on the basis of gender, age, race, religion, disability, or sexual orientation.

19   Then, last month, Tillery held hearings on unemployment and poverty in Cincinnati. "I got an education from the Appalachian community," he said. "I can see very well the real possibility of other whites discriminating against them. They've been through a lot of pain."

20   June Smith Tyler moved to the Cincinnati area from Harlan County, Kentucky, in 1966. Now 51 and a partner at a prominent law firm, she tells of a job interview elsewhere in the city a decade ago, when she had just graduated from night school. Working days as a nurse, she had still managed to earn a place on the law review. After a pleasant lunch with several attorneys, a senior partner told her in the privacy of his office that he had to "be careful" about hiring anyone with a mountain accent.

21   Even now, she winces at thoughtless one-liners tossed off by would-be wits. She lives south of the Ohio River, which is the Kentucky boundary, and has lost count of the times she's been asked if she kicks off her shoes as soon as she crosses the bridge.

22   Today, Amy Morgan, 22 and Cincinnati-born, is frequently asked where she's from. The question is based on the soft twang acquired from her mother, aunt, and grandparents. "I just tell them, Kentucky,'" she said and shrugged. "I was brought up like I was in Kentucky."

23   Growing up, if she and her siblings weren't home by dark, "we'd be getting a switching," said Morgan, now separated from her husband and the mother of two toddlers. She is taking a high school refresher class and hopes to study to become a veterinarian technician. Her cousins, high school seniors, still have to be in bed by 9 on school nights.

24   Morgan cherishes her family, but she did get teased. Once, a high school classmate had a thing or two to say about Morgan living next door to her aunt. Her zoology teacher overheard, and asked: "Your family lived all together in a holler, didn't they?" It was true, actually; they had. Why was his tone so condescending?

25   Such tales of slights at school are not unusual. Mike Overbey, 39, who works for the Urban Appalachian Council, remembers getting suspended when he was 17 for slapping a teacher who'd called him a "backward hillbilly."

26   More recently, another teacher read a list of Appalachian jokes to a class of young teenagers. He included this description of a "hillbilly seven-course dinner": A six-pack and a bag of potato chips.

27   Just weeks ago, at a prestigious magnet school for the performing arts, tenth-graders discussed the play *Antigone*.

28   A student described the incest in the drama as "confusing."

"Not if you're from Kentucky," teacher Matthew Rabold answered.

29   Later, Rabold, 30, called the remark "thoughtless." Puzzling over why the offending words slipped out, he finally decided: "It's just the perceptions I've gotten from the popular media, even cartoons: the shoeless, toothless backwoodsman. I've never seen a positive portrayal." A five-year veteran of public school faculties, he could not remember any special activities for "Appalachian Month."

30   The verbal slaps help explain why 17 percent of Appalachians and their descendants over age 18 in Greater Cincinnati never finished high school, said Michael Maloney, who runs mountain culture workshops for teachers and social workers around the Midwest. Dropout rates in several city neighborhoods run closer to 80 percent, he said—worse than in eastern Kentucky itself, where the figures are in the 40 percent to 50 percent range.

31   "Dignity and respect are more important than education," said Maloney, who grew up in Lee County, Kentucky. "Parents will yank their kids out of school" because of insults.

32   That argument, however, fails to persuade everyone. "It's a copout," said Don Bearghman, principal of a grade school in Lower Price Hill, a part of town where virtually everyone has Appalachian roots.

33   The student body at Bearghman's Oyler Elementary School is almost evenly divided between bussed-in blacks and the white children and grandchildren of Kentucky immigrants. "An Appalachian being called a hillbilly is like a black child being called the 'n-word,'" the principal said. "It's no reason to drop out of school. I don't buy that."

34   Certainly other factors are involved. Money, for one. Obermiller, who surveyed Appalachians in Greater Cincinnati in 1980 and 1989, said that many families achieve working-class status by making everyone, including teens, get jobs.

35   It was a job at a turkey farm near Cincinnati that pulled Danny Courtney from school when he was 17. But economics can also be an effective argument in favor of education. Now 32, Courtney and his wife are on welfare while they attend classes to prepare for the General Equivalency Diploma test. They need, he says, to boost their earning power for the sake of their four-year-old son.

36   Returning to studies, though, is far from easy and the vast majority of dropouts never do. "It would help if they know there are

good things in their culture, things to be valued," said Larry Hol-
comb, coordinator of the Northside Community School, a continuing education center with an Appalachian clientele. "Then they
could envision themselves going to college."

37   Matthew Rabold, repentant, wants to do his part. He met with
members of the Urban Appalachian Council following complaints
about the *Antigone* incident and ever since, he has been searching
out mountain writers for his students to read. He hopes that a local
poet, Brenda Saylor, will speak to his class.

38   He has been touched by her words about "my people," the
ones she describes as "the men, tall stiffbacked; the women with
their long hair/and unpainted smiles." She writes of self-denial
and of embracing the past:

> *"Their kids will laugh at their dreams*
> *and shy from their songs*
> *but when the fiddle plays*
> *the young will pick up their feet,*
> *move to an ancient rhythm*
> *and ask for the stories*
> *of their grandmothers.*
> *Faraway, a mountain will sigh, knowing it has not been forgotten."*

EXERCISES

Details and Their Meanings

1. Where does Route 25 lead? Where, according to the writer,
   does it lead figuratively? How do lyrics from a country song
   by Dwight Yoakam help explain the meaning of Route 25?
2. When did the emigration of Appalachians to Cincinnati take
   place? Why did they leave Appalachia? What did they hope to
   find in the city? Have they realized their hopes?
3. To what economic class does a large percentage of urban Appalachians belong? What social problems do they face? According
   to the writer, what has caused these problems?
4. What is the commonly held stereotype of the Appalachian?
   Where does this stereotype come from? How is it reinforced

through popular culture? How does this stereotype affect the way urban Appalachians are perceived and treated by others? How does it affect the way they view themselves?

5. What percentage of Cincinnati's population is of Appalachian stock? African American? What do these two groups have in common? To what extent do they work together, and to what extent do they see their interests as separate?

6. What are the elements of Appalachian culture that distinguish it from mainstream American culture? How do the differences between Appalachian and mainstream American culture help to explain the problems experienced by urban Appalachians?

7. How have Appalachian-born students been treated in schools? How have urban Appalachians been treated in the workplace? According to the writer, what broader impact does this treatment have on the Appalachian community? What steps has the city of Cincinnati taken to combat the prejudice and discrimination experienced by urban Appalachians? To what extent have these steps been effective?

Reading and Critical Thinking

1. The writer cites sociologist Phillip J. Obermiller who claims that urban Appalachians have become "an invisible minority." What does he mean by this? What makes urban Appalachians "invisible"? What are the effects of being "invisible"?

2. How does language—the language used by urban Appalachians as well as the language used to describe them—contribute to stereotyping and discrimination?

3. What causes does the writer present for the problems that urban Appalachians face? Do you think that she has provided an adequate explanation? Why or why not? Do the solutions she presents make sense? Why or why not? What other solutions would you suggest?

4. At various times, America has enacted laws, like the one passed in Cincinnati, that prohibit discrimination against various groups who do not conform to mainstream American society. To what extent and in what ways has this legal solution worked in the past? Do you think it will work in the particular instance described in this selection? How much can laws change the way people act, think, and feel about others?

5. Based on the information reported in this selection, what can you predict for the future of urban Appalachians? Will things get better or worse? Why do you think so?

The Writer's Strategies

1. What is the writer's main point in this selection? Where is this point stated?
2. Which paragraphs describe the problems faced by Appalachians and the causes of the problems? Which paragraphs describe the background, experience, and heritage of the Appalachians? Which paragraphs describe attempted solutions and programs? How are these various parts organized to form a coherent essay?
3. Where does the writer draw on statistical evidence? Where does she cite first-person accounts? Where does she cite authorities? What effect does each kind of evidence have on the reader?
4. Why does the writer repeat the stereotypes, insults, and jokes about Appalachians? What is the effect of their retelling? Does the retelling just continue the prejudice, or does it help people overcome the prejudices? Why do you think so?
5. What are the various terms used in this selection to refer to people of Appalachian descent? Who uses these different terms, and what attitudes do the people display in using the terms? Which terms does the writer use when she is not presenting other people's attitudes? Why do you think she chooses these terms and not the others?
6. Why does the writer conclude with a quotation from an Appalachian poet? What points does this excerpt reinforce?

Thinking Together

Brainstorm as a class to generate a list of the characteristics of some culture about which you have no personal knowledge but which has been portrayed on television or in movies. Do you think this list is accurate or are the characteristics that you listed stereotypical? Discuss how the media images of this culture affect the way you feel about the culture and how they might affect your reaction to people of that culture whom you might meet.

Vocabulary

Define the following terms, which refer to negative aspects of the experience of Appalachian emigrants to urban areas.

1. plaintive (par. 2)
2. underclass (par. 3)
3. horrendous (par. 3)
4. caricatures (par. 5)
5. quirky (par. 5)
6. epithets (par. 16)
7. condescending (par. 24)
8. slights (par. 25)

WRITER'S WORKSHOP ━━━━━━━━

Critical Thinking in Writing

1. Research the origins of the word *hillbilly*, and write a one-paragraph summary of your findings. What does it mean? What are its origins? How was it used in the past? How is it used today?
2. Write a two-page essay comparing the discrimination and prejudice faced by urban Appalachians to the problems of discrimination and prejudice faced by a different minority group.
3. Write one page to analyze the feelings and ideas represented in the poem at the end of this selection by local poet Brenda Saylor. What does the poem suggest about the conflict between the desire to assimilate and the desire to maintain a distinct cultural heritage?

Connecting Ideas

Read "Teaching Young Fathers the Ropes," by Sophfronia Scott Gregory (page 432). What do the young African-American fathers described in this selection have in common with urban Appalachians? How is the prejudice and discrimination they both experience similar? How is it different? In what ways are both "invisible"?

The Great Divide

Ellen Goodman

Ellen Goodman is a syndicated newspaper columnist whose work is seen by millions of readers. In this essay, she discusses segregation on American college campuses.

KEY WORDS

apartheid (par. 1)   racial separation
camaraderie (par. 3)   friendship
shantytown (par. 4)   a neighborhood of shacks and hovels
transversed (par. 5)   moved across at an angle
volatile (par. 9)   likely to blow up

THE MAN WAS TALKING about what he called the "resegregation" of American life. He was a veteran of the civil-rights movement and went South as a student in the 1960s when whites and blacks fought American apartheid together.

2   The man went on to make his life in a Midwestern university, where he was my guide one spring day. Indeed he taught about race in America until he felt discredited on account of his skin color—white—and went into administration.

3   Walking me into the student union, he said: "Look." The tables were nearly as segregated as a lunch counter in the Alabama of the 1960s. There was just one table where black and white undergraduates ate in noisy camaraderie. They, my guide explained, were members of the varsity team.

4   Pausing, he counted on one hand the number of places where blacks and whites interact on his campus these days: in sports, the arts, or, he added ironically, in race-relations class. A few years back there was a shantytown on campus, a makeshift protest against investing in South Africa. Now he was almost sorry the university divested because it had been one of the few actions that brought students together.

---

5   I brought this story home to a woman who disputed only one phrase: resegregation. We never desegregated, she says. An academic and black, she knows few people who ever had social lives that easily transversed the color lines.

6   As a mother, she sees her grade-school kids with friends of all hues, but her college students subdivided by skin color. So she also wonders when it happens and why. Many of her black students believe they can only integrate on white terms and turf. Many of her white students feel unwelcome by blacks. Many feel unwelcoming.

7   Who was defensive and who was racist and who was just uncomfortable? And why this great silence today between blacks and whites about race relations in America?

8   Both of these academics, now enjoying the summer that is their chief professional perk, can cite incidents over the past year. Graffiti, hostility, tension. Yet they would agree that these are by no means the worst days on campus or the worst years. They remember the KKK, Mississippi, legal segregation.

9   But they also know that nearly every campus holds a volatile mix of attitudes that in no way resembles a melting pot. In some places, whites believe that their black classmates were admitted because of their race. In others, blacks believe that whites believe that.

10   On many universities, the black search for identity—their own place on a white campus—can end up fusing blackness with victimization. In many universities, white classmates resent the racist label brushing them indiscriminately.

11   There is today a high degree of racial consciousness and a sorry lack of a language, of a forum, of a common ground where people can talk honestly about race. These two facts have given many campuses the look and sound of two cultures. And in these segregated places, there may not even be faith anymore in the value of integration.

12   Neither of my guides believes that campuses are unique in their sharp segregations. Quite the opposite is true, they say. Look around the office. Look around town.

13   In Washington, it is still almost impossible for blacks and whites to talk about the trial of Mayor Barry. To most whites in the nation's capital, the case was "about" the mayor and his alleged use of drugs. To most blacks the case was "about" the entrapment of a black leader. Across the great divide of race, the words defied interpretation.

14   Even in journalism, bylines often come color-coded. White journalists are awkward writing about blacks as if race were a qual-

ification. Black journalists are often both required and discredited for writing about "their own."

15   And in our cities, there are neighborhoods as separated by race as ever in our history. There are people who speak for the "black community" and the "white community" as if their apartness was an accepted and permanent reality.

16   But universities have often thought of themselves as models, communities of scholars. At best, they are expected to uphold their own values. At a minimum, they are places where we are to think and talk deeply about what troubles the "real world."

17   The universities are reopening. They start each new year with a fresh curriculum. But what troubles the real world as much as anything these days is race relations. It's a problem that exists on a scale as large as a city. But it can also be seen—and changed— on a scale as small as a dining-room table.

_____

EXERCISES

Details and Their Meanings

1. What signs of racism on campus does Ellen Goodman report?
2. What is the KKK? Why is it mentioned in this essay?
3. Who is Marion Barry? Why is his case a good barometer of race relations in the United States?
4. In what places on campus do blacks and whites interact? What grounds are there for mistrust between blacks and whites on campus?
5. What future hope does Goodman hold out in paragraph 6? What other paragraph is hopeful?
6. How are lunch counters in Alabama in the 1960s relevant to this selection?

Reading and Critical Thinking

1. How in paragraphs 1 through 4 does Goodman establish the administrator's right to speak?
2. What made Goodman choose college campuses as the focus of this essay? Are college campuses more segregated than other areas of American life? How are race relations on your campus?

3. What forums for dialogue between and among races are there in American society? What would you propose to improve communication?

4. How does Goodman define the word *resegregation*? Is it a real word?

5. What does Goodman mean in paragraph 14 when she says that journalism is "color-coded"? Do you agree or disagree? Why?

6. What can you infer from the author's statement that blacks and whites interpret the Marion Barry case differently?

7. Goodman suggests that blacks on campus fuse blackness with victimization. What support does she give for this observation? Do you agree with her? Why or why not?

8. Why is this article titled "The Great Divide"?

The Writer's Strategies

1. Where does the writer state her main idea? Why does it come so late in the essay?

2. What is the connection between the title and the main idea?

3. Why are the paragraphs so short, often only one or two sentences long?

4. Why is this essay based more on facts than on opinions?

5. What is the primary writing strategy that the writer uses to develop this essay?

6. Why doesn't Goodman mention the names of the administrator and the black academic?

Thinking Together

Conduct a survey in your class. How many people have good friends who are from different races? How many have acquaintances, people they interact with on a daily basis, from other races? How many live in racially mixed neighborhoods? From the results, is it fair to conclude that you and your classmates live in a segregated or in an integrated society?

Vocabulary

The following words have prefixes. Separate each prefix from its root word, and write a definition.

1. resegregation (par. 1)
2. discredited (par. 2)
3. interact (par. 4)
4. divested (par. 4)
5. disputed (par. 5)
6. desegregated (par. 5)
7. integrate (par. 6)
8. unwelcome (par. 6)
9. indiscriminately (par. 10)
10. entrapment (par. 13)

WRITER'S WORKSHOP ━━━━━━━━━━

Critical Thinking in Writing

1. Write an essay about befriending someone from a racial or ethnic group different from your own. What steps would you take to establish and nurture the friendship? Would you have to take any special steps? Which? Why?
2. Do colleges have a responsibility to talk deeply about the problems of the real world? Is college supposed to be a place where people receive training for future employment, or is it supposed to be a model community intended to address social ills? Explain your position.
3. Write an essay in which you suggest how you could create "a forum, . . . a common ground where people can talk honestly about race," as Goodman suggests.

Connecting Ideas

Goodman writes, "And in our cities, there are neighborhoods as separated by race as ever in our history." How do Athlone G. Clarke's "Crossing a Boundary" (page 349), Humberto Cintrón's "Across Third Avenue: Freedom" (page 384), and Hisaye Yamamoto's "Wilshire Bus" (page 319) support Goodman's remark? How do you account for racially separated neighborhoods?

Crossing a Boundary

Athlone G. Clarke

*Athlone G. Clarke describes how racial barriers are subtly maintained
even when nobody seems to be taking an openly racist position. Notice
how the writer, a middle-class and moderate African American, gradually comes to feel like an outsider.*

KEY WORD

Bensonhurst (par. 6)   a neighborhood in Brooklyn where a
well-known racial incident occurred

THERE WAS A BIG sign that warned of a NEIGHBORHOOD WATCH
IN PROGRESS and then there were the less obvious ones. Placed
strategically at the entrances of mile-long driveways bordering
multiacre lawns were smaller signs emblazoned with the names of
some of America's finest security companies. Something told me
I had strayed from the beaten path.

2   Being a creature of habit, I have always jogged a path that takes
me under a certain bridge into a recreational park for a breathtak-
ing three-mile run. I've stuck to this path like a bus route. This
particular evening, I accepted the challenge of trying a new route.
Brad, a white middle-aged jogging acquaintance with the stamina
and speed of a Derby winner, thought it would break the monot-
ony. As usual, ten minutes into the run he chose to quicken his
pace, while I chose to continue living. It wasn't long before he disappeared. I remembered his directions and instead of going under
the bridge, I crossed over it and made a few extra turns. Twilight
Zone it must have been because within minutes, I was in unfamiliar
territory where homes boasted titles like "chateau," "estate" and
"villa." The vegetation was orderly and even the light breeze
seemed to cooperate. There were signs with pictures of dogs baring
their fangs and words like *patrol and protection.*

3   The way I figured it, the warnings were meant for those harbor-

ing criminal motives or acting suspiciously. Being a clean-shaven black male in broad daylight, wearing no bulky attire to hide weapons, no suspicious bag, no dark glasses (and not being in South Africa where they have the Group Areas Act), I had nothing to worry about. Wrong! I started to get an eerie feeling. A lot of expensive cars were suddenly slowing down, almost as if there were a visibility problem. I assumed I was it. A silver-haired old lady, who oozed power from every pore, abruptly halted her Jaguar and sweetly inquired whether I worked for the McArthurs. On hearing ''No,'' she sped off in apparent concern. Still, I reassured myself that this was America. I would not retreat, even while drowning in sweat and adrenaline.

4   I thought back to the media depiction of a white middle-class suburbanite who gets lost in the heart of a tough inner-city neighborhood and takes leave of his nerves. At that moment if I could have had my choice, I would have chosen the inner city. It wasn't long before a police car cruised by and I noticed the driver adjusting his rear-view mirror. As he didn't stop I knew trouble was stalking me.

5   I saw a few other blacks in the neighborhood but they wore the working clothes of gardeners, nannies, and utility technicians. I wore a spandex running outfit, headphones, and an ingratiating smile. The teeth of the black man have been known to get him out of some tight spots, and my father did not raise a fool. There were a few fellow joggers and some walkers who moved with impressive alacrity as they crossed the street and responded to my nervous nod with furtive glances. It was not hard to imagine that to come face to face with a stranger the same color as Willie Horton must have been, for them, a terrifying experience.

6   I tried to quicken my pace, hoping that through some miracle I could catch up with Brad or at least keep him in sight. Experience has taught me that a little ethnic buffering serves the politics of acceptance and at the very least lessens the shock factor. However, it seemed decreed that I would do this journey alone. I kept reminding myself that this was not Bensonhurst and there was little chance of a mob-induced fracas. These people obviously had class and believed in maintaining secure borders.

7   I sensed I was being followed and looked around. My fears were confirmed. Driving about 150 yards behind me at funeral-procession speed was a lone police car. As it pulled alongside my flank, a portly white police officer in the trademark sunglasses ordered me to pull over. ''Do you live around here, sir?'' he asked.

"May I see some kind of ID?" As I never go jogging with my driver's license, or my wallet for that matter, I knew this would make "Bull Connor" a little upset. I explained my predicament. He then said something I was not ready to hear. "That's OK, sir," he said, "I've been watching you for the last 15 minutes and you do seem like a runner going about his business. The problem I'm having, and I hope you'll try to understand, is that some of these people think their snot can make cole slaw; fact is, I still have to do my job." He went on to explain that the police had gotten a flood of phone calls about a suspicious black man roaming the area.

8   We spoke for another two minutes. I went on to point out that in my own neighborhood, I had witnessed a few white strangers running by in the name of exercise and wondered if maybe I ought to start calling the police. As he got back into his car he removed his glasses. His weary eyes appeared to plead for some kind of tacit understanding: in the future, he would be counting on me not to make his life more difficult by running through this forbidden stretch. I sensed a conspiracy to cooperate with the forces of bigotry.

9   Later I recounted my journey to Brad and wasn't surprised when he said the only problem he'd had was his hamstring acting up again. He also thought I was being a little sensitive. On reflection, I think I can see Brad's point. Yet where would we be today if Rosa Parks's "sensitivity" hadn't gotten her into all that mess in Montgomery 35 years ago?

EXERCISES

Details and Their Meanings

1. What signs did Athlone G. Clarke notice in the neighborhood he was passing through? Whom did he think the signs were for? What message did he get from the signs? In light of what happened later, what further meanings do the signs convey?
2. What activity and sequence of events brought the writer to this neighborhood? How was he dressed? Was it unusual for someone dressed as he was to go jogging in this neighborhood? Did

he think he looked dangerous? Did others think he looked dangerous? Why or why not?

3. Who stopped the writer or otherwise took notice of him? What were their reactions? Who did they think he might be? How did these responses to his presence make him feel?

4. Did Clarke see any other blacks in the neighborhood? Who were they, and what were they doing? Would passers-by think he was one of them? Which would, and which would not?

5. What questions did a police officer ask Clarke? What attitude did the officer have? Did he think Clarke was dangerous? Why was the officer following him? What was the effect of the police officer's stopping him? Did the officer's attitude influence the consequences of the writer's being stopped?

6. What happened to Brad, the friend Clarke was jogging with, once he and Clarke were separated? Why did Clarke think that rejoining Brad would be a good idea? Did Brad undergo experiences similar to Clarke's? How did Brad react when he heard Clarke's story?

7. Who was Rosa Parks? Why is she mentioned? In what way did Clarke act like Rosa Parks? In what ways did he not act like her? What meaning does the writer wish to convey by making the comparison to Rosa Parks?

Reading and Critical Thinking

1. What was the attitude of the neighborhood residents to Clarke? Why were they upset at Clarke's presence? Is their reaction a form of racism? How would members of your community react to an informal visitor from a racial group different from those groups represented in your neighborhood?

2. Why does Clarke say that the police were part of a conspiracy? Did the policeman treat him badly or think poorly of him? Whom did the officer think more poorly of? What should have been the policeman's attitude?

3. How did Clarke feel in this neighborhood? How do his feelings of anger and injustice build throughout the narrative? Why did Brad think Clarke was being too sensitive? Did you think he was being too sensitive? Why or why not?

4. What other blacks does Clarke mention? What roles does he suggest are available to blacks who wish to move freely about all neighborhoods?

5. Do you think the white people described in this piece consider themselves racists? Do you consider them racists? Why or why not?

The Writer's Strategies

1. What is the writer's thesis? How do the introduction and conclusion support the thesis? the title?
2. Why does Clarke begin the essay by describing the signs in the neighborhood? What is he trying to convey about the messages sent from the neighborhood to people who pass through?
3. Why does the writer compare his feelings to those of a white suburbanite lost in an inner-city neighborhood? What various meanings can you take from this comparison? How is the comparison-contrast strategy particularly useful here?
4. The narrative ends with a discussion of the writer's sensitivity and a comparison to Rosa Parks. How does this ending contrast with the opening no-trespassing signs? What attitude is the writer expressing by this shift?
5. Who is the audience for this piece? How can you tell?

Thinking Together

In small groups, discuss a time that you felt out of place and other people viewed you suspiciously. What did you think they were thinking about you? What category were they putting you in? Is there anything you could have done to change their minds? How did their categorization influence your behavior?

Vocabulary

Find words in the selection with the following meanings. The definitions are listed in the order in which the words appear in Clarke's essay.

1. in a planned, goal-directed manner
2. written in bold letters
3. three fancy names for home
4. carefully hiding
5. a bodily chemical that heightens emotions

6. designed to appear friendly
7. secret
8. fight or riot
9. a shared plan to do wrong
10. a muscle in the lower leg

WRITER'S WORKSHOP ━━━━━━━━━

Critical Thinking in Writing

1. Write an essay describing how racist actions can result from subtle suspicions and quiet signals as well as from overt hostile behavior.
2. Describe how a group or neighborhood that you belong to takes notice of and views someone from outside. Which kinds of outsiders (if any) are welcomed with wholehearted gestures? Which kinds of outsiders are treated more cautiously?
3. Write an essay in which you analyze the title "Crossing a Boundary." What are the various boundaries being crossed here? Include your own definition of the word *boundary*.

Connecting Ideas

In one paragraph, compare the subtle racism presented by Athlone G. Clarke with the subtle racism presented by Hisaye Yamamoto in "Wilshire Bus" (page 319).

Confronting Campus Racism

Marcus Mabry

Marcus Mabry, an associate editor of Newsweek, *lives and works in Washington, D.C. In this piece, he discloses the tense racial climate on college campuses and describes a few attempts to increase understanding.*

KEY WORDS

blatant (par. 3) obvious
deluge (par. 3) flood
epithets (par. 7) names
egregious (par. 7) glaringly bad
explicitly (par. 8) with clarity and precision
abridgements (par. 10) shortenings, contractions

IT WAS SUPPOSED TO be a day for "Bridging the Gap," a program on interracial understanding sponsored by African-American and white fraternities at George Mason University. But instead of building bridges, they were being burned, as African-American students and whites clashed over one of the most recent racial incidents on America's college campuses. The women of Gamma Phi Beta sorority had decided it would be funny to put a wig and charcoal black face on a Sigma Chi man during an "ugliest girl" contest, sponsored by the fraternity. Not surprisingly, African-American students (and a lot of whites) were not amused. The black face incident touched off a wave of racial tensions that left one fraternity suspended and most students hurt and angry. The Virginia college is not alone: from anti-Black and anti-Jewish graffiti to hate notes slipped under students' doors, racial episodes are as much a part of college life these days as fraternity parties and football.

2   Timothy Maguire, a third-year student at Georgetown Law

Center, set off another racial tempest with an article saying African Americans didn't belong at Georgetown. In an opinion piece titled "Admissions Apartheid," Maguire used LSAT test scores and grade point averages to argue that lesser qualified African Americans are admitted. Although Maguire used hard data on grades and test scores, he wrapped them in racist rhetoric. For instance, he argues that on one African-American student's transcript: "There alongside a C+ in Shakespeare, C in Macroeconomics, and F in Calculus were 8 A's in African-American courses," leaving the implications unstated. At one point he concludes, "The biggest problem is that in every area and at every level of postsecondary education, Black achievements are inferior to those of whites." Really? And, if so, Therefore? Maguire later apologized for much of the article, not only to the Georgetown Law community but to the press as well when reporters asked him to clarify or prove many of his points.

3   Although no one keeps hard statistics on racial incidents on college campuses (the FBI only this year started doing it for the nation), the National Institute Against Prejudice & Violence at the University of Maryland–Baltimore County says racial episodes have been reported at over 300 colleges and universities over the past five years. Moreover, "Surveys indicate that one in five minority (students) have been victimized. We have seen an increase in the number of reports of racial incidents—and only the most blatant get reported," says Adele Terrell, program director. When the incidents of tense race relations are added to the recent deluge of articles and broadcasts condemning colleges' efforts to confront these problems as "political correctness" or a "tyranny of minorities," an African-American student victimized by racism might ask, "Is there nowhere to turn?"

4   Actually, there is. An increasing number of African-American students are deciding that an education at a predominantly white school isn't worth the racial hassle, and they're heading for historically Black colleges where the atmosphere isn't hostile. The United Negro College Fund's member schools reported 1990–91 enrollment was up 21 percent over the previous school year to 49,397— and applications were up 39 percent. But African-American students don't have to flee predominantly white schools. Most colleges and universities recognize racial harassment as a serious breach of student conduct and offer a range of options for students who have been harassed.

5   A simple first step for an offended student is to let the victimizer know that you're hurt. That might sound close to sophomoric

once you have been slighted through an off-hand comment about how Blacks don't do this . . . or Blacks always do that . . . but based on the philosophy (not always true) that hurtful or offensive acts of prejudice are often committed out of ignorance, communication can be your most effective weapon.

6   Nichet Smith and three other African-American women at Arizona State University took this approach last year. They were walking through a dorm when they saw a leaflet posted on a door with the heading "Simplified Form of a job application. Form for minority applicants." The flier went on to insult people of color by asking "Sources of income: (1) theft, (2) welfare, (3) unemployment"; "Marital Status: (1) common law, (2) shacked up, (3) other," and "Number of legitimate children (if any)." The women were angry, so they knocked on the door. They explained how they felt about the poster and one of the roommates (not the one who put it up apparently) took it down. The women then organized dorm meetings to discuss the poster and its underlying assumptions. From there, feelings and suspicions that had been stewing under the surface at Arizona State were brought into the open where they could be dismissed or discussed and wounds could be healed, or at least exposed to the fresh air. John Singsank, the president of Sigma Chi fraternity at George Mason, says the university never tried to educate Sigma Chi; instead they placed the group on probation for two years, dictating that they cannot meet or socialize as a chapter.

7   Clearly, just talking is not always the solution to a racial confrontation, even though it is likely to be a good step. Although ignorance can be a root cause of much unconscious prejudice, it cannot explain many of the grotesquely offensive actions that have recently plagued college campuses. Students at the University of Texas surely knew that the epithets spray-painted on a car in front of the fraternity were racist. Likewise, whoever scribbled "NIGGERS" across the poster advertising a Black Greek party at Stanford knew exactly what he was doing. In cases of egregious racism or when you feel your own safety might be threatened by trying to talk to the offender, you can usually turn to the college or university for help.

8   Almost all colleges and universities have student codes of conduct or a "fundamental standard" that requires students to behave themselves with a basic sense of civility at all times. Cheating, stealing, and harassing others generally fall under these age-old codes. But many schools, including the University of Georgia, finding that these codes did not condemn racist actions explicitly enough, now

have speech codes that forbid students from using racially offensive language. At Stanford University, students and faculty can say whatever they please in a public forum or a classroom. But they are not allowed to address a racial or ethnic epithet to a specific individual. So while a white student could give a speech in the middle of the Quadrangle arguing that Blacks are inferior, he is not allowed to come up to an African-American student and call him "nigger."

9   If you are offended and your school has a speech code like Stanford's—and more and more colleges do—you generally file a complaint with a student-faculty judiciary board that oversees violations of the student code of conduct, including offenses like plagiarism. The committee will listen to both sides of the story, assess whether one party broke the school's rules and if so, how he should be punished. Penalties can run the gamut, from attending a racial-sensitivity seminar to suspension from university housing (where people from all different backgrounds have to live in close proximity to one another) to expulsion from school. At the University of Texas's Austin campus an offended student and the offending party hash out their differences before any disciplinary process goes into motion. "It's a two-tier system," says Curtis Polk, race relations counselor at U.T. Austin. "The first part is education and mediation. The second part is penalties. Often the offended party doesn't want anything more than the offender to be more racially sensitive."

10   Some speech codes, like the University of Wisconsin's and the University of Connecticut's, are being challenged in court as unconstitutional abridgements of students' First Amendment rights to free speech. The University of Michigan was forced to modify its code when it was ruled unconstitutional. But universities are in a bind. They have to strike a balance between all students' right to free speech and the rights of students of color to an equal education under the Fourteenth Amendment.

11   While these codes and standards are useful if you have been racially harassed by another student, most schools have Affirmative Action Equal Education Opportunity programs that cover faculty and staff as employees of the university. These codes are meant to guide the university in hiring and promotion, and to prevent discrimination against people of color, but they also demand that discrimination be brought up before a school administrator whenever a faculty or staff member has launched a racial incident.

12   This impressive body of regulation, for all its might, is reactive—it only springs into effect after much of the damage has been

done. A lot of schools—and many students—are deciding that they can't wait until the dam breaks to address racial tensions. They are going after the problems before they erupt through seminars, courses, and workshops aimed at helping us to better understand our differences and to talk about them.

13   The most common university practice is to have programs in the dorm that address racial differences. Student resident assistants, or R.A.s, often lead the sessions which can include films like "Still Burning . . . Confronting Ethnoviolence on Campus," distributed by the University of Maryland–Baltimore County, or workshop materials from the International Committee Against Racism, a New York City group. In a common version of a dorm racial-sensitivity seminar, all residents are lined up on one side of a room, a facilitator (often an R.A.) calls out a category like "Black or African American" or even "tall." All the people who place themselves in that group walk to the other side of the room. Then they look back at the students they are separated from, usually the "majority"—and tell them "all the things I never want to hear again," that they have heard people say about their group. The majority is not allowed to ask why or to criticize. Later all the individuals come back into one group and talk about how each of them is, in some way or another, a member of a group discriminated against—and how each of them has been told things they don't want to be told again.

14   Another method of achieving racial sensitivity is through curricular coursework. Many colleges are redesigning their required curricula and including more works from people of color and women. Educators have argued that teaching African Americans and whites, for instance, about the contributions of people of color to human civilization and to the United States will foster greater respect of people of color today, as well as present a more accurate picture of human endeavor and achievement.

15   Other colleges, like Cornell University, offer specific racial-sensitivity courses. James Turner, associate professor of Africana Studies and founder of the Africana Studies and Research Center, has taught "Racism in American Society" for four years. For the first three years, student enrollment tripled each year. In this course, students from different races confront their fellow students' prejudices and their own. "Our job in the classrooms is to provide an analysis of the historical sociology, the development of racism," says Turner. "We show how patterns of relationships have developed along racial lines . . . individual attitudes and ideas derive

from the historical development of racism in society." As individual students learn about the perspectives in our society that are subtly racist, they can identify the subtle racism in their own thoughts and behavior. And they can work to alleviate it or at least be more sensitive to it.

16   And what if you don't feel it's your job to educate others—all you want to do is get an education? That's all right, too. If you are victimized in a racial incident and you just seek healing from the pain, there are usually many resources on campus that can help. Student counseling or psychological services usually have at least one counselor who can aid racial harassment victims. His goal is usually to remind you of your own self-worth. In addition to your friends, the Black student union is often a valuable support network as well.

17   Even though African-American students should not feel obligated to instruct their white peers in how to care about the feelings of others, every community member has an obligation to work for greater understanding. That means talking to students of other races in and out of class in your dorm. Students who want to decrease racial tensions on campus can have a positive effect by getting involved before the problems surface. You can take the initiative by organizing workshops in your dorm, sponsoring films aimed at stimulating cross-cultural discussion, or sponsoring inter-Greek activities between Black and white fraternities and sororities. Before things get to the raw level of insults and slurs, try to personally (and in the African-American organizations you're a part of) foster interaction with different kinds of students and create an atmosphere of mutual education rather than mutual suspicion. Students of color have more to gain than anyone else from greater sensitivity on campus. There are many Americans who would like to see the world's grandest experiment in multiculturalism fail. If we give them victory, then we lose.

EXERCISES

Details and Their Meanings

1. What happened at George Mason University on "Bridging the Gap" day? What incident sparked the trouble? What punishment did the offending group receive?

2. Who is Timothy Maguire? What did he write that caused a stir at Georgetown?
3. How many colleges have reported racial incidents over the past five years? What proportion of minority students has been victimized? When did the FBI start keeping records?
4. What impact are racial incidents having on enrollment at predominantly black schools?
5. How are some colleges trying to increase dialogue between the races? Which schools have adopted speech codes to suppress racist epithets?
6. Which colleges are offering courses to promote understanding? What kinds of courses are they offering?

Reading and Critical Thinking

1. What conclusion can you draw from the enrollment changes in historically black colleges?
2. Where in the selection does Marcus Mabry suggest that racial incidents stem from ignorance? Where does he suggest other causes? Which causes do you find most valid? Why?
3. What distinction is Stanford University making about the difference between classroom speech and personal attacks? Do you believe this distinction is valid? Why or why not?
4. Why are colleges in a bind when it comes to outlawing racist speech?
5. What does the writer criticize about the new body of regulations? Do you support his criticism? Why or why not?
6. What does Mabry suggest is at stake if campus racism cannot be overcome? What other consequences can you see?

The Writer's Strategies

1. Where does the main point of this essay appear? What is it? Who is the audience for this piece? Is Mabry writing primarily for a black audience? How can you tell?
2. What is Mabry's purpose in writing this essay?
3. Why do you think the writer encloses the phrases "political correctness" and "tyranny of minorities" in quotation marks in paragraph 3?
4. What is your reaction to the lengths of the paragraphs? Why do you think they are so long?

5. What words does Mabry use to make transitions from one paragraph to another?
6. In what sense is this a how-to essay? What process does Mabry explain?

Thinking Together

Divide up your class according to height. Have all the tall people go to one side of the room and the short people go to the other side. If everyone is nearly the same height, pick some other superficial physical attribute as a means of separation—eye or hair color, for example. Once the class has separated, seach group brainstorms to produce a list of annoying things that the other group might do to you, say about you, or assume about you. The groups then compare lists. What did you discover?

Vocabulary

The following terms are relatively new and are the subject of discussion on college campuses and in the media. Write an appropriate definition of each.

1. political correctness (par. 3)
2. ethnoviolence (par. 13)
3. racial-sensitivity courses (par. 15)
4. multiculturalism (par. 17)

WRITER'S WORKSHOP ⎯⎯⎯⎯⎯⎯⎯⎯⎯⎯⎯

Critical Thinking in Writing

1. Write a narrative about an experience you have had with a member of another racial group. What did you expect beforehand? What did your experience teach you?
2. When the rights of free speech and equal opportunity are in conflict, which right should be upheld? Which right is more important to the well-being of society? Write an essay in which you compare and contrast the two rights.
3. Write an essay called "How to Create Interracial Understand-

ing." In it, explain the process that you would put into place to address racism on your own campus or other campuses that you know.

Connecting Ideas

Read Ellen Goodman's "The Great Divide" (page 344). What in Mabry's piece confirms Goodman's observations? How does the Mabry selection suggest a solution to the problems that Goodman sees?

Zoot Suit Riots

Albert Camarillo

Albert Camarillo is a historian. In this selection from his book Chicanos in California: A History of Mexican Americans in California, *he highlights an overlooked episode in Los Angeles history during World War II.*

KEY WORDS

pompadoured (par. 2)   a style in which the hair is brushed up high from the forehead and held in place with pomade
disdain (par. 2)   reject, disregard
stigmas (par. 2)   marks of shame or dishonor
internment camps (par. 3)   in this selection, places in California where thousands of Japanese Americans were held during World War II
xenophobic (par. 3)   afraid of strangers
quelled (par. 6)   put to an end

NOTHING HAS COME TO symbolize more dramatically the racial hostility encountered by Chicanos during the 1930s and 1940s than the Sleepy Lagoon case and the Zoot Suit Riots. Both involved Chicano youth in Los Angeles city and county, local police departments, and the judicial system.

2   At the heart of these conflicts was the growing attention paid to Chicano youth by the local media. The press focused on *pachucos*, members of local clubs or neighborhood gangs of teenagers (both male and female). They separated themselves from other barrio youth by their appearance—high-pompadoured ducktail haircuts, tattoos, and baggy zoot suits for boys; short skirts, bobby sox, and heavy make-up for girls—and by their use of *caló*, a mixture of Spanish and English. Their characteristics, according to the press, included unflinching allegiance to neighborhood territories, clannishness, and bravado. Though other teenagers in cities such as

364

Detroit, Chicago, and New York dressed like their counterparts in wartime Los Angeles, *pachuquismo* became popularly identified with Chicano youth who came of age during the 1930s and 1940s in the Los Angeles area. Predominantly children of immigrant parents, these youths matured in an environment in which they saw themselves as neither fully Mexican nor American. Raised in impoverished barrios and alienated from a society that discriminated against Mexicans, they identified only with others of their age and experience. Pachucos constituted a minority among Chicano youth, and they set themselves apart by their disdain of the public schools, skipping classes and drawing together into neighborhood gangs where they found companionship and camaraderie. To outsiders who relied on the local media for their information, pachucos were perceived not only as marijuana-smoking hoodlums and violence-prone deviants, but also as un-American. These stigmas during the early 1940s, particularly during the first two years of a frustrating war for Americans, helped create a climate of repression for pachucos and, by extension, to others in the Chicano community.

3   In the hot summer days of August 1942, most Los Angeles residents had wearied of newspaper reports of setbacks against the Japanese forces in the Pacific. Japanese Americans on the home front had already been relocated to internment camps, thereby temporarily silencing Californians embittered by Pearl Harbor. Many xenophobic citizens also did not like Mexicans, especially the "foreign, different-looking" pachucos arrested following an incident at Sleepy Lagoon.

4   Sleepy Lagoon, a swimming hole frequented by Chicano youth of east Los Angeles, soon became the symbol of both popular outrage and repression. At a home near the lagoon, where the night before two rival gangs had confronted one another, the body of a young Chicano was discovered. Though no evidence indicated murder, the Los Angeles Police Department summarily arrested members of the 38th Street Club, the teenage group that had crashed a party the prior evening and precipitated the fighting.

5   The grand jury indicted twenty-two members of the club for murder and, according to Carey McWilliams, "to fantastic orchestration of 'crime' and 'mystery' provided by the Los Angeles press seventeen of the youngsters were convicted in what was, up to that time, the largest mass trial for murder ever held in the country."

Reflecting on the treatment of the Sleepy Lagoon defendants, the aroused McWilliams stated:

> For years, Mexicans had been pushed around by the Los Angeles police and given a very rough time in the courts, but the Sleepy Lagoon prosecution capped the climax. It took place before a biased and prejudiced judge (found to be such by an appellate court); it was conducted by a prosecutor who pointed to the clothes and the style of haircut of the defendants as evidence of guilt; and was staged in an atmosphere of intense community-wide prejudice which had been whipped up and artfully sustained by the entire press of Los Angeles. . . . From the beginning the proceedings savored more of a ceremonial lynching than a trial in a court of justice.

Concerned Anglo and Chicano citizens, headed by McWilliams, sharply criticized violations of the defendants' constitutional and human rights (such as beatings by police while the youths were being held incommunicado and the courtroom improprieties indicated above by McWilliams). They organized the Sleepy Lagoon Defense Committee and, with the support of such groups as the Congreso and UCAPAWA, faced down intimidation by the media and accusations of being "reds" by state senator Jack Tenney and his Committee on Un-American Activities. In 1944 they succeeded in persuading the District Court of Appeals to reverse the convictions, declare a mistrial, and release the defendants from San Quentin prison.

6   The Sleepy Lagoon case served as a prelude to an even more discriminatory episode in wartime Los Angeles—the so-called Zoot Suit Riots of 1943. Racial tensions intensified after the Sleepy Lagoon case as police continued to arrest large numbers of Chicano youth on a variety of charges. Adding to the unrest were confrontations between military servicemen and Chicano zoot suiters on city streets. Then on June 3, 1943, rumors circulated that Chicanos had beaten sailors over an incident involving some young Mexican women. The newspapers seized on the rumor and soon sailors and marines from nearby bases converged on the downtown area and on Chicano neighborhoods. There they attacked Chicano youth, regardless of whether they wore zoot suits, beat them, stripped off their clothes, and left them to be arrested by the police who did nothing to interfere with the "military operations." A virtual state of siege existed for Chicanos in Los Angeles as hundreds of ser-

vicemen in "taxicab brigades" looked for Mexicans on whom to vent their anger. "I never believed that I could see a thing like that," recalled Josephine Fierro de Bright.

> I went downtown and my husband and I were standing there and we saw all these policemen hanging around . . . and hundreds of taxis with sailors hanging on with clubs in their hands, bullies just beating Mexicans on Main Street. And we went up and asked a cop to stop it: he says, "You better shut up or I'll do the same to you." You can't do a thing when you see people and the ambulances coming to pick them up and nobody is stopping the slaughter. It's a nightmare. It's a terrible thing to see.

The local press continued to feed the hysteria with headlines announcing the sailors' "war" against zoot-suited pachucos. After five days of beatings, mass arrests, and rampant fear in Chicano communities, military authorities—ordered by federal officials at the request of the Mexican consulate—quelled the riots by declaring downtown Los Angeles off limits to all naval personnel.

7   In the wake of the riots, which also occurred in San Diego and several other communities but with much less violence than in Los Angeles, the Chicano community remained paralyzed with fear of another occurrence. The Mexican government and many local citizens protested the outrages, and Governor Earl Warren appointed a committee composed of clergy, public officials, and other well-known citizens to investigate the incident. Even so, Chicano relations with the police remained tense for many years. Jesse Saldana, a Los Angeles resident who witnessed the riots, articulated the sentiment of many Chicanos: "Justice is blind; she can't see the Mexicans."

8   The Zoot Suit Riots climaxed an era of overt hostility against Chicanos in California. Beginning with mass deportations during the early years of the depression and the violent suppression of unionization efforts, the 1930s and early 1940s witnessed much sadness and frustration for Chicanos who struggled to keep family and neighborhood from moral and physical deterioration. The irony was that tens of thousands of Mexican fathers and sons were fighting overseas with the U.S. armed forces as their families on the home front were experiencing bigotry and persecution. But this period of depression and repression also aroused in Chicanos a desire to gain the equality that eluded them. The post–World War

II decades witnessed a new upsurge of activity and a sense of hope within the Mexican community.

EXERCISES

Details and Their Meanings

1. What time period is Albert Camarillo examining? What event of national importance was also taking place? In which state, city, and neighborhood did the Zoot Suit Riots take place?
2. Why did some young Chicanos separate themselves from mainstream society? In what ways did they make themselves distinct?
3. Who is Carey McWilliams? Why does he play an important role in this selection?
4. Why were twenty-two Chicanos arrested for murder? Why were they convicted? What eventually happened to them?
5. What event touched off the Zoot Suit Riots? How long did the riots last? When did they end? Why did they end?
6. What was the long-term political result of the Zoot Suit Riots?

Reading and Critical Thinking

1. What does the writer suggest is the relation between the barrio and the *pachucos*? Is his point well made? Do you agree or disagree with him? Why or why not?
2. What kinds of people do you think wore zoot suits in other American cities? How were the zoot suits a kind of costume or emblem?
3. How would you characterize the court's treatment of the 38th Street Club?
4. Why do you think that sailors indiscriminately attacked young Chicanos? Do indiscriminate attacks on ethnic groups take place today? Where?
5. What can you conclude is the reason that the police didn't en-

force the law? How do you think the police today would react
to the events presented in this selection?

6. Which group does the writer suggest is responsible for pro-
longing the conflict between Chicanos and sailors? Do you
agree? Why or why not?

7. What is a fair inference to draw about the Anglo community
in Los Angeles at the time of the Zoot Suit Riots? How would
you characterize that community today?

8. Why might you consider the conclusion of this piece ironic?

The Writer's Strategies

1. What is Camarillo's thesis? How does the introduction contribute to his main point?

2. What is Camarillo's purpose in writing this piece? Who is his
audience?

3. With which group does the writer sympathize? What clues give
away his position?

4. Why does Camarillo mention the internment of the Japanese
Americans in California at a similar period? Is the introduction
of this issue a good rhetorical strategy? Why or why not?

5. What is the tone of this selection?

6. How much of this selection is the result of Camarillo's direct
experience? In which paragraphs does the writer express his
own opinion? Where does he quote the opinions of others?

7. Was this piece written during the 1940s, shortly after, or long
after? What clues tell you the answer to this question?

Thinking Together

Many people believe that relations between law enforcement offi-
cers and minority youths have improved in the last fifty years. Can
you support this conclusion from your own experience, the experience of your friends, or information you've read or heard about?
Are there gangs in your town? What kinds of youngsters join
gangs? Are there still gangs in Los Angeles and other large cities?
How do young people get along with the police in large cities?
Make an outline of the steps to take in order to investigate these

questions. Working in small groups try to get some answers. After your research is finished, make a group report to the class.

Vocabulary

Items 1 through 5 are period or historical references. Look them up in a dictionary or an encyclopedia. Items 6 through 12 are Spanish or Chicano in origin. Look them up in a Spanish/English dictionary. Write definitions of all twelve items in your own words.

1. zoot suit (par. 2)
2. ducktail haircuts (par. 2)
3. bobby sox (par. 2)
4. internment of Japanese Americans (par. 3)
5. Pearl Harbor (par. 3)
6. Chicano (par. 1)
7. *pachucos* (par. 2)
8. barrio (par. 2)
9. *caló* (par. 2)
10. incommunicado (par. 5)
11. camaraderie (par. 2)
12. Congreso (par. 5)

WRITER'S WORKSHOP ━━━━━━━━━━━━━

Critical Thinking in Writing

1. Prepare a brief—that is, a lawyer's argument—summarizing the reasons Camarillo gives for granting the 38th Street gang a new trial.
2. Each generation chooses its own fashions and hairstyles to show alienation and rebellion. Today, teenagers do not wear bobby sox, zoot suits, or ducktail haircuts. Write an essay to describe how a rebellious teenager today is likely to dress, wear his or her hair, and behave in order to show disaffection. Draw an illustration if you'd like.
3. The Los Angeles riots of 1992, which produced scorching fires in some areas of the city, in large part resulted from simmering tensions between minorities and the police. What steps can ur-

ban communities take to reduce those tensions? Write an essay to explain the process you would put in place if you could.

Connecting Ideas

Gary Soto, in "Looking for Work" (page 243), and Armando Rendón, in "Kiss of Death" (page 125), are the sons of Chicanos who experienced discrimination during the 1930s and 1940s. Look at the parents and other grown-ups in Soto's and Rendón's pieces to see what you can discover about those adults' attitudes and expectations. Would they probably agree with the remark made by Jesse Saldana in paragraph 7 of the Camarillo selection: "Justice is blind; she can't see the Mexicans"?

SIDE BY SIDE

1. Drawing on the incidents and issues described in this chapter, write an essay evaluating the state of race relations in the United States and discussing what can be done to create a better future.
2. Write an essay examining what you have learned about prejudice from the selections in this chapter. Are there any activities or attitudes that you now, for the first time, understand are prejudicial? Have any of your attitudes changed? Do you now better understand the behaviors and attitudes of any other people? Is there anything you will do or say in a different way? In each instance of change that you can identify, specify exactly what in the readings led to this new thought.
3. One of the root causes of prejudice is the competition between groups for limited resources. Does society as a whole have a responsibility to remedy the unequal distribution of resources? What new policies, if any, would you adopt to help groups that have suffered from discrimination and exclusion? Argue your position in a well-detailed essay.

SIX

Side by Side:
The Sum of the Parts

INTRODUCTION

Many of the innovations that Americans have helped develop—
the telephone, air travel, the mass-produced automobile, television,
recorded music, the computer—have changed the nature of this
country and the rest of the world. Physical distances between people are no longer significant. Information moves so quickly that
local and even regional differences shrivel and fade. So powerful
is the electronic image and so immediate its visual record that during the Persian Gulf War, Saddam Hussein watched Cable News
Network (CNN), not direct field action, to learn how his own
troops were doing. In a world where nearly everyone listens to
rock music and eats at McDonald's the things that make individuals unique are difficult to identify.

Being part of a diverse society with a shared identity has many
rewards: we learn from each other; we adopt notable behaviors
and attitudes from the many cultures around us; we connect
broadly and deeply with groups different from our own. Indeed,
what makes our country great is that so many varied racial, religious, and ethnic groups can live side by side in relative harmony,
interacting, sharing, expanding our visions.

Yet, many feel an inevitable trade-off in the leveling of people
and communities is the erosion of group-based cultural identity.
Certainly, much of who Americans are is the result of where we
come from or the feelings we have for a particular place, a heritage,
a family background. When one voice rolls into everyone's living
room from the television, when one town's mall looks the same as
another's, when millions of adolescents around the world dress
every day in the required jeans and T-shirt costume, it is easy to
forget cultural connections and past history, to lose the sense of
what made each of us unique and special.

The selections in this unit explore the ways people balance the
struggle to maintain a unique identity with compelling demands
of a dynamic American culture. Alex Haley searches for his roots,
and Kathleen Teltsch, in "Scholars and Descendants," describes a
group of people who have forgotten theirs. In "Teaching Young
Fathers the Ropes," Sophfronia Scott Gregory describes how young
unwed fathers are learning how to cope with adult life and becom-

ing responsive and responsible men and fathers. David Masello, in "In My Father's House," describes a visit with his father in which they came to terms with the unspoken differences—and the similarities—between the two worlds in which they live. In "Five New Words at a Time," Yu-Lan Ying describes her own feelings of being a stranger in a new land and pays tribute to her mother, who gave her confidence, determination, and a strong sense of who she is.

Together the writers of these selections ask what we lose and gain by becoming part of this country. They are living testimony to how varied perspectives contribute to American culture and to how much we can learn from each other. But even more, the selections say that we are here, together, and they consider how we can live here, together, peacefully, successfully, with lives richly lived and powerfully intertwined.

PREREADING JOURNAL

1. Describe some aspect of a culture other than your own that appeals to you. Why does it appeal to you? From what cultural community does it come? What values are represented by this cultural practice? How might this practice be related to the entire way of life of that culture? How has your appreciation of this aspect opened your eyes not only to another culture but also to another side of yourself?

2. Write a journal entry in the form of a top-ten list entitled "The Top Ten Most Essential Aspects of American Culture." The items in the list should be the characteristics that you feel best describe America, its culture, its values, and its way of life.

3. Psychologists sometimes describe the human personality by comparing it to an onion with many layers separating the surface from the core. When you look at your own personality or the personality of a friend or family member in this way, what does each level of identity contain? Write a journal entry in which you discuss each level of personality, identifying the levels that are most apparent and closest to the surface and the levels that are deeper. Where does ethnic identity fit in? How apparent is regional or local identity? How has experience added to or modified early layers of personality?

Five New Words at a Time

Yu-Lan (Mary) Ying

In this selection, Yu-Lan (Mary) Ying, a student at the renowned Bronx High School of Science in New York, describes how learning English changed her view of her mother—and of herself.

KEY WORDS

fatigue (par. 2)   weariness, exhaustion
aura (par. 4)   radiant light
solely (par. 6)   only, totally

MY FAMILY CAME TO America in 1985. No one spoke a word of English. In school, I was in an English as a Second Language class with other foreign-born children. My class was so overcrowded that it was impossible for the teacher to teach English properly. I dreaded going to school each morning because of the fear of not understanding what people were saying and the fear of being laughed at.

2   At that time, my mother, Tai-Chih, worked part time in a Chinese restaurant from late afternoon till late in the night. It was her unfamiliarity with the English language that forced her to work in a Chinese-speaking environment. Although her job exhausted her, my mother still woke up early in the morning to cook breakfast for my brother and me. Like a hen guarding her chicks, she never neglected us because of her fatigue.

3   So it was not surprising that very soon my mother noticed something was troubling me. When I said nothing was wrong, my mother answered: "You are my daughter. When something is bothering you, I feel it too." The pain and care I saw in her moon-shaped eyes made me burst into the tears I had held back for so long. I explained to her the fear I had of going to school. "Learning

379

English is not impossible," my mother said. She cheerfully suggested that the two of us work together to learn the language at home with books. The confidence and determination my mother had were admirable because English was as new to her as it was to me.

4   That afternoon I saw my mother in a different light as she waited for me by the school fence. Although she was the shortest of all the mothers there, her face with her welcoming smile and big, black eyes was the most promising. The afternoon sun shone brightly on her long, black hair creating an aura that distinguished her from others.

5   My mother and I immediately began reading together and memorizing five new words a day. My mother with her encouraging attitude made the routine fun and interesting. The fact that she was sacrificing her resting time before going to work so that I could learn English made me see the strength she possessed. It made me admire my mother even more.

6   Very soon, I began to comprehend what everyone was saying and people could understand me. The person solely responsible for my accomplishment and happiness was my mother. The reading also helped my mother learn English so that she was able to pass the postal entrance exam.

7   It has been seven years since that reading experience with my mother. She is now 43 and in her second year at college. My brother and I have a strong sense of who we are because of the strong values my mother established for herself and her children. My admiration and gratitude for her are endless. That is why my mother is truly the guiding light of my life.

EXERCISES

Details and Their Meanings

1. When did the writer and her family emigrate to the United States? What is their country of origin? How do you know? Is this fact important? Why or why not?
2. How does the writer describe her initial experiences in school?

What classroom environment does she face? How does this environment affect her ability to learn English? her self-esteem?

3. Describe the writer's mother. Where does she work? What hours does she work? Why does she do this and not something else? How does her work affect her family? How does the writer describe her mother in paragraph 4? How is this description different from her earlier description? What has caused the change?

4. How did the writer and her mother learn English? How does learning English affect their lives? What lesson has Tai-Chih Ying taught her children by example, and what has been the effect of that lesson?

Reading and Critical Thinking

1. From the information about the writer's family included in this essay, what can you infer about their socioeconomic class? What can you infer about their definition of *the American Dream?*

2. To what degree do the experiences of the writer and her family affirm the widespread belief that education is the key to opportunity? What role does education play in their assimilation to American culture?

3. From reading this selection, what can you infer about the role that the older generation plays in passing down a heritage to the younger generation? In this particular case, what is the nature of the heritage that passes from mother to daughter?

4. In the final paragraph of this selection, the writer states, "My brother and I have a strong sense of who we are because of the strong values my mother established for herself and her children." What are these values? To what degree are they "American" values? To what degree are they Chinese values?

5. The writer of this selection is a high school student. To what extent might her age account for the attitudes she expresses? How might her feelings change over time?

The Writer's Strategies

1. What is the thesis of this short essay? What method does the

writer use to develop her essay? How does she organize the material?

2. What attitude does the writer have toward her mother? What are some words and phrases that help reveal that attitude?

3. Where does the writer use dialogue? Do you think that the writer quotes this conversation directly, or do you think that she translates it into English? What is the effect of including the quotations from her mother?

4. Why does the writer use Yu-Lan (Mary) Ying as her name? What does the use of *Yu-Lan* and *Mary* reveal about her sense of identity? How does that sense of identity fit with the attitudes presented in the essay?

Thinking Together

Brainstorm in small groups to consider the impact that limited knowledge of the English language has on the daily lives of recent immigrants. What can recent immigrants do to cope with the obstacles that they face? What is being done to help them? What else needs to be done?

Vocabulary

Explain the meanings of the following figurative phrases that appear in this selection.

1. "like a hen guarding her chicks" (par. 2)
2. "moon-shaped" (par. 3)
3. "in a different light" (par. 4)
4. "guiding light" (par. 7)

WRITER'S WORKSHOP ━━━━━━━━━━

Critical Thinking in Writing

1. Write a journal entry describing a time that you dreaded going to school. How was this experience similar to or different from the experience the writer describes? To what extent did you overcome that fear and how?

2. Interview a friend or classmate for whom English is a second language in order to find out how he or she learned English. Then write a brief essay comparing and contrasting the experiences of this student and the experiences that the writer describes in this selection.
3. Write a two-page essay exploring the tension between assimilation and maintaining a sense of cultural identity. To what degree does the writer's experience illustrate that it is possible to assimilate into American culture without losing a sense of who you are and where you come from?

Connecting Ideas

Read "Classrooms of Babel," by Connie Leslie, with Daniel Glick and Jeanne Gordon (page 179). How does the background provided in this essay help to explain the difficulties that Yu-Lan Ying experienced in school? Which approach to learning English—bilingualism, ESL, or immersion—does Ying's family take and why?

Across Third Avenue: Freedom

Humberto Cintrón

Humberto Cintrón, a writer and television producer, describes child-hood attitudes that taught him not to venture forth far into the world but to protect himself.

KEY WORDS

Third Avenue El (par. 1)   an elevated train that ran on
   tracks above Third Avenue in Manhattan
oblivious (par. 3)   not aware
vicarious (par. 3)   experienced imaginatively through the experience of others
meanderings (par. 3)   wanderings
P. F.'s (par. 3)   a brand of sneakers

THIRD AVENUE. AS FAR as the eye could see, the cobblestone street was saddled by a great, black, spiderlike iron monster called the "Third Ave. El." It cast a checkerboard shadow, alternating with shafts of sunlight like a huge web draped across the wide boule-vard waiting for unsuspecting victims. I remember sitting on the curb, staring across to the east side of the street, the ominous, fore-boding presence of the "El" weighing on my 8-year-old mind and giving more substance to the taboo that Third Avenue was for the Puerto Rican kid in East Harlem.

2   Across that no man's land was an unknown world filled with exotic delights and adventures not accessible to me except through hearsay. Somewhere beyond was Jefferson Park and an Olympic-sized swimming pool; the Italian festival of Our Lady of Mt. Carmel, complete with Ferris wheel, merry-go-round, pizza pies, cotton candy, multiflavored ices, and fireworks; there were a live market, fishing piers that extended into the East River, and the

Boys Club. That I knew of for certain. The things I didn't know about were endless. My imagination soared as I sat watching the red and gold trolleys rattle along on the shiny silver tracks embedded in the cobblestones and listened to the roar and clatter of the iron horse overhead, spattering sparks into the air.

3   The traffic wasn't so heavy, and the traffic light was no different from any other. Red meant "stop," green meant "go." And there wasn't any barbed wire or solid wall or alligator-filled moat or any other physical obstacle to keep me sitting on the curb daydreaming while other people came and went, oblivious to my vicarious meanderings. None of that. The fact is, with my P. F.'s I could probably beat nearly anyone across and back.

4   No, the barrier wasn't one my wiry body couldn't run under, over, or through. The barrier was inside my head. Not that it wasn't real. It was real. But it had gotten inside my head the same way the knowledge of Jefferson Pool and the Boys Club had gotten there— through hearsay: stories, rumors, and countless tales that fill the ether, the "stuff" of which tradition is made, transmitted from one person to another over time and distance. It was accepted fact without ever having been experienced. It was self-fulfilling.

5   Puerto Ricans were not to cross Third Avenue; that was Italian territory. Period.

6   Even Danny—"Italian Junior" we called him then—to this day among my closest and most trusted friends, more a brother than a friend, could not offer a solution.

7   Beyond Third Avenue you risked your life. It was a challenge I grew up with. Over the years the Third Avenue "barrier" appears to have crumbled under the steady flow of Puerto Ricans into "El Barrio" and Italians out of East Harlem. Not without a good measure of violence and heartache and bloodshed. Yet although the "Third Avenue El" and the trolleys no longer run on Third Avenue, and although the movement of Puerto Ricans in and around New York seems, on the surface, to have overcome the "barrier," no such thing has ever happened. The wall of "unwelcome" flourishes. As always it is invisible. It came to us through tradition, through institutional behavior—it is the lifestyle of America. It can be traced back through the various ebbs and flows of waves and waves of immigrants who were nursed on an institutional inferiority syndrome which required them to cast away their cultural values in order to assume the American identity.

8   Nor am I suggesting that this behavior was peculiar to Italians in East Harlem. No such luck—had it been that way it would be

easy to deal with. No, they learned it here, as a result of their experience as newcomers. And others had learned it before them, and they in turn learned from their predecessors. That's what tradition is. That's how social institutions are built.

9   In those days I never questioned the pennies dropped into the church basket or the coins for the poor box that mom gave us ritually on Sunday, though our table seldom saw a chicken or a pork chop. That too was tradition.

10   In the midst of the roar of bricks launched from a rooftop and zip-gun blasts in the night, we were learning in school that George Washington never told a lie; Abraham Lincoln freed slaves; and every child in America could grow up to be president. We learned it all by rote ("Four score and seven years ago our forefathers brought forth upon this continent a new nation conceived in liberty and dedicated to the proposition that all men are created equal . . . "). Those words reverberated through my mind on many occasions; while I heaved a garbage can down hard and heavy on some bastard who I'd knocked to the ground before he got to me; and when I rolled in the gutter tasting blood and dirt while someone's booted foot dug deep into my ribs and spine.

11   But I never grew up bitter.

12   I grew up hauling blocks of ice up five flights for the little old Italian lady who lived next door; and running every conceivable kind of errand for anybody who needed it; and translating for Mrs. Rivera and Mr. Gonzalez to the teacher, insurance agent, welfare investigator, cop, landlord, nurse, truant officer, etc., etc., etc. "What a good boy you have, Maria," all the neighbors said. And I was.

13   And I grew up getting my ass kicked and kicking the next guy's ass up and down the streets of El Barrio.

14   "That's a bad dude, Chino," the reputation went. And I was.

15   I grew up knowing that cruelty and violence and deceit were all part of the personal repertoire of social tools that I needed to be armed with to fend off the merchants of hypocrisy that rule and govern and perpetuate the "traditions" that make America "great." In the vernacular of contemporary American thought it all comes under the category of "being realistic."

16   The idea was never to unleash your weapons until the showdown came. The "good guy," after all, never drew his gun first in the movies. But when he did, look out.

17   A strange ethic when you look at it. In order to be the "good guy" you have to be able to do all the things that characterized the

"bad guy" better than they did. Simplistic? Probably so—it's also what the Watergate mess appears to be about. A self-righteous hypocrisy that led some people to think that they, being the "good guys," could use any means necessary to insure that they could continue to be the "good guys."

18   Bullshit.

19   But it's the American way and it's the system that has been perpetuated in institution after institution, from the church to the Mafia; from government to revolutionary movements; from the suburbs to the central city. From corporations to united funds.

20   I'm not going to judge it. After all, even the "Watergate" came to light; and there may be a remedy for that mess; and someone may say, "It was that same system that weeded out the imperfections and developed a solution"; and certainly the traditions and institutions in America seek to resolve the problems they confront.

21   I won't disagree with that.

22   But history has taught me that the institution which is a solution to one problem quickly becomes, itself, the next problem for which a solution must be found. So it is with churches and armies and police and museums and corporations and labor unions and newspapers and commissions.

23   "Third Avenue" has been with me all my life and I suspect it will be with all Puerto Ricans all of their lives, in one form or another. And it affected and will continue to affect every experience of any significance in my lifetime.

24   It was there in the military when, after four years as an instructor and "Guided Missiles Expert," I was discharged A/2C.

25   It was there in college, which required seven years and three dropouts to complete.

26   It was there in Mississippi when we started "freedom schools" to achieve "equal" education.

27   It was still there in "El Barrio" during the rent strike days and community action days when the antipoverty program raised hopes and generated dreams of self-help, only to be ground into the dust of yesterday's rhetoric.

28   And it lived on with the experimental school districts and the struggles for "community control" and the vain attempts to wrest control in a neighborhood shared politically by legislators from other communities but served by none.

29   It was there when the publishers sent rejection slip after rejection slip and I finally had to raise the bucks to publish my book myself.

30   It's still there now, when every instrument of mass communica-

tions—print and electronic—chooses to ignore the Puerto Rican editorially; or carefully selects the images it presents, thus helping to perpetuate stereotypical negativism or promote a token Puerto Rican personality while systematically denying employment and opportunities to Puerto Ricans exclusive of the mail room. In New York City today you can count on the fingers of your hands the number of Puerto Ricans employed in a professional capacity in all the major television, radio, and print media combined.

31   I suppose I'll always sit on the curb somewhere, staring in the Third Avenues of the world, wanting to belong. And I suppose too that I'll venture forth into that unknown, seeking and probing and discovering. And I expect too that I'll always have my pennies for the poor box, eager to serve and be "good" in what is likely to be a quixotic adventure. But one thing you can count on as absolutely certain:

32   "Third Avenue" was not and will not be a deterrent to joining the struggle and doing the things that need to be done—or, better said, trying to do what needs to be done. It certainly cannot deter me from choosing to put on my P. F.'s and running under, over, or through it.

EXERCISES

Details and Their Meanings

1. Why did Third Avenue seem like a barrier? Was it a real barrier? How did Humberto Cintrón come to treat it as a barrier?
2. Does the barrier still exist? for whom? How has it become an institution?
3. What were some of the elements to be found on the other side of Third Avenue? How did Cintrón find out about them? Who lived on the other side of Third Avenue? Did Cintrón know any people from that group? Did he have real reasons to fear those people?
4. What did Cintrón learn in school? How did he behave in school and with adults? How did he behave on the streets? How did those two different places affect who he became? What kinds of values did he develop? In what way are they American values?
5. How did Cintrón's feelings about Third Avenue and his street

values carry over to his later life? In which examples is he using Third Avenue thinking? In which cases is it being used against him?

6. How did Cintrón fight prejudices against him? How is he continuing to do so? In what way is his struggle also part of Third Avenue thinking?

Reading and Critical Thinking

1. What was the effect on the writer's growth and attitudes of staying within his own community? Was this pattern of staying among his own inevitable for him? Is this a common pattern in neighborhoods? Why or why not?

2. What does the writer mean in paragraph 22 when he says, "the institution which is a solution to one problem quickly becomes, itself, the next problem for which a solution must be found"? What example does he use to support this point? What other examples can you think of?

3. Do you think the writer has left Third Avenue? In what ways has he not? In what ways is it still a struggle for him to cross over from his home territory?

4. What is the meaning of the title? Do you observe any ironies in it?

The Writer's Strategies

1. What overall point is Humberto Cintrón making? Does he ever argue it directly? How does he use the narrative about his own development to make this point? What audience does he have in mind—that is, whom do you think he is trying to reach with this selection?

2. Where does the narrative start? Where does it end? How do the locale and the ideas change from beginning to end? How are they linked?

3. What rhetorical strategies other than narrative does the writer use?

4. How does the writer relate personal local experiences to general American patterns? Why does he do so? What is he showing about the way he must act in wider American society?

5. What transitions help the writer connect ideas between paragraphs? within paragraphs?

6. Comment on the writer's style. Is it formal or informal? How do the sensory details contribute to the style? How do the short, simple sentences contribute to the style?

Thinking Together

In small groups, compare your experiences of places that were off limits to you as a child. To what places were you not supposed to go? Who established this prohibition? How did you learn you weren't supposed to go to a specific place? What did you think would happen if you went there? Did you accept the limitations to your freedom? When (if ever) did you step beyond the boundaries? Why did you do so, and what was the effect? What do you think now about those limitations?

Vocabulary

Find the context in the selection for the following words. Then define each word as it is used there.

1. boulevard (par. 1)
2. ominous (par. 1)
3. foreboding (par. 1)
4. inferiority syndrome (par. 7)
5. predecessors (par. 8)
6. reverberated (par. 10)
7. repertoire (par. 15)
8. hypocrisy (par. 15)
9. perpetuate (par. 15)
10. vernacular (par. 15)
11. ethic (par. 17)
12. wrest (par. 28)

WRITER'S WORKSHOP ━━━━━━━━━━

Critical Thinking in Writing

1. Describe the values you learned in school, church, or some other adult-led institution; then describe the values you learned

in your neighborhood or on the street. Finally, compare the two sets of values, explaining how well they fit together and how you reconciled them.

2. Write a narrative essay to show how you moved beyond some restrictions of your childhood to discover a bigger world.

3. Write a short essay about some value you learned in childhood that has stayed with you or that you changed as you grew older.

Connecting Ideas

Compare Humberto Cintrón's way of dealing with the many cultures in his world with Elizabeth Wong's way of dealing with the many worlds she describes in "The Struggle to Be an All-American Girl" (page 39).

The Business of Selling Mail-Order Brides

Venny Villapando

This selection is a sociological description of an unusual practice: men selecting wives through the mail. The men are usually white, and the women are usually poor Asians from underdeveloped countries.

KEY WORDS

intimidating (par. 6)   frightening
resurgence (par. 6)   a return to activity or importance
exploitation (par. 25)   unjust use of another person for advantage
unabashedly (par. 30)   without disguise or embarrassment
prevail (par. 38)   to continue, survive

THE PHENOMENON IS FAR from new. Certainly in the Old West and in other frontier situations such as the labor camps at the sugar farms in Hawaii, the colonization of Australia, or even in the early Irish settlements of New York, there were always lonely men who would write to their homeland for a bride. These women would come on the next train or on the next boat to meet their husbands for the very first time.

2   For Japanese immigrants traditional marriages were arranged in Japan between relatives of the man and the prospective bride. Information was exchanged between the two families about the potential union, and photographs were exchanged between the couple. If both parties agreed, then the marriage was legalized in the home country, and the bride came to America.

3   While these marriages occurred in less than ideal situations, a number of them were successful. For example the Japanese sugar worker who once waited on the Honolulu pier for the arrival of his picture bride today enjoys the company of a family clan that

spans at least two generations. That is indeed an achievement considering the picture bride of yesteryear, just like the contemporary mail-order bride, has always been at a disadvantage. She comes to the marriage from far away, without the nearby support of her family or a familiar culture. The distance that she has traveled is measured not so much in nautical as in emotional miles. She is not quite the happy bride who has been courted and wooed, freely choosing her groom and her destiny.

4   Today's mail-order brides are products of a very complex set of situations and contradictions. They are confronted by far more complicated conditions than the picture brides of years past. They do not quite fit the simple pattern of a marriage between a lonely man stranded in a foreign land and a woman who accepts him sight unseen.

5   In the present matches brides-to-be are generally Asian and husbands-to-be are Caucasians, mostly American, Australian, and Canadian. A majority of the women are poor and because of economic desperation become mail-order brides. Racial, as well as economic, factors define the marriage however. The new wife is relegated to a more inferior position than her picture bride counterpart. Plus the inequity of the partnership is further complicated by the mail-order bride's immigrant status. Consequently she is a foreigner not only to the culture, language, and society, but to her husband's race and nationality as well.

6   **Why Men Choose Mail-Order Brides**   "These men want women who will feel totally dependent on them," writes Dr. Gladys L. Symons of the University of Calgary. "They want women who are submissive and less intimidating." Aged between thirty and forty, these men grew up most likely before the rise of the feminist movement, adds Symons. She partially attributes the resurgence of the mail-order bride to a backlash against the 1980s high-pressure style of dating.

7   Dr. Davor Jedlicka, a sociology professor from the University of Texas, notes in his study of 265 subscribers of mail-order bride catalogues that "very many of them had extremely bitter experiences with divorce or breakups or engagements." His research also shows the median income of these men to be higher than average— 65 percent of them had incomes of over $20,000. According to Jedlicka, the average age was thirty-seven, average height five feet seven inches, and most were college educated. Only 5 percent never finished high school.

8   The Japanese American Citizens League, a national civil rights group, confirms this general profile of the typical male client and adds other findings. According to its recent position paper on mail-order brides, the group found that the men tend to be white, much older than the bride they choose, politically conservative, frustrated by the women's movement, and socially alienated. They experience feelings of personal inadequacy and find the traditional Asian value of deference to men reassuring.

9   In her interview in the Alberta Report, Symons points out that the men are also attracted to the idea of buying a wife, since all immigration, transportation, and other costs run to only about two thousand dollars. "We're a consumer society," says Symons. "People become translated into commodities easily." And commodities they are.

10   **Gold at the End of the Rainbow**   Contemporary traders in the Asian bride business publish lists sold for twenty dollars for a catalogue order form to twenty thousand dollars for a deluxe video-taped presentation. Perhaps the most successful company is Rainbow Ridge Consultants run by John Broussard and his wife Kelly Pomeroy. They use a post office box in Honakaa, Hawaii. Explains Broussard:

> Basically, we just sell addresses. . . . We operate as a pen pal club, not a front for the slave trade, although some people get the wrong idea. We're not a Sears catalogue from which you buy a wife. You have to write and win the heart of the woman you desire.

For providing this service, Broussard and Pomeroy reported a net profit in 1983 of twenty-five thousand dollars, which catapulted to sixty-five thousand in 1984.

11   Rainbow Ridge Consultants distributes three different publications, of which the top two are *Cherry Blossoms* and *Lotus Blossoms*. These differ from the Sears catalogue only because an issue is only twenty-eight pages long, not several hundred, and photos are black and white, not glossy color. A typical entry reads: "If you like 'em tall, Alice is 5'9", Filipina, social work grad, average looks, wants to hear from men 25–40. $4." For the stated dollar amount, interested men can procure an address and a copy of her biographical data.

12   Broussard and Pomeroy's sister publication *Lotus Blossoms* has twice the number of names, but Broussard admits that *Lotus* is a

"second string" brochure, offering pictures of women who do not have the same looks as those in *Cherry Blossoms*.

13   Six months of subscription to the complete catalogues of Rainbow Ridge will cost the wife-seeker $250. A special service will engage Broussard and Pomeroy in a wife hunt at the rate of $50 per hour and includes handling all details, even writing letters and purchasing gifts when necessary. Should the match succeed, the business pockets another fee of $1,000.

14   Kurt Kirstein of Blanca, Colorado, runs Philippine-American Life Partners, which offers one thousand pictures of Filipino women looking for American men. Louis Florence of the American Asian Worldwide Service in Orcutt, California, provides men with a similar catalogue for $25; another $630 will permit the bride-seeker to correspond with twenty-four women, of whom any fifteen will be thoroughly investigated by the service. The California business reports an annual gross income of $250,000.

15   Selling Asian women is a thriving enterprise because the number of American men who seek Asian brides continues to grow. Broussard estimates the total number of daily inquiries is five hundred. In 1984 the Gannett News Service reported that seven thousand Filipino women married Australians, Europeans, and Americans. The *Wall Street Journal* noted that in 1970, only 34 Asians were issued fiancée-petitioned visas; while in 1983, the figure jumped dramatically to 3,428.

16   Broussard says that he receives one hundred letters a day from Asian and other women. He publishes about seven hundred pictures every other month in his catalogues. Still, Broussard reports that the chances of a man finding a wife through his service are only about one in twenty.

17   When he receives a letter and the appropriate fees from a prospective groom, Broussard sends off a catalogue. One of his correspondents describes the process: "I selected fourteen ladies to send introductory letters to. To my amazement, I received fourteen replies and am still corresponding with twelve of them." One of the reasons why letters so often succeed is the detailed coaching both parties receive. For instance Broussard and Pomeroy publish a 130-page pamphlet entitled "How to Write to Oriental Ladies." There is also one for women called "The Way to an American Male's Heart."

18   The Japanese American Citizens League points out the disadvantage to women in these arrangements because of the inequality of information disseminated. Under the traditional arranged

marriage system, family investigation and involvement insured equal access to information and mutual consent. Now only the women must fill out a personality evaluation which asks very intimate details about their life style and history and is then shared with the men. Prospective grooms do not have to submit similar information about themselves. Some companies, in fact, even discourage their male clients from disclosing certain types of personal facts in their correspondence, including such potentially negative characteristics as being black or having physical disabilities.

19   **The Economics of Romance**   Coaching or no coaching, the mail-order brides business succeeds partly because it takes advantage of the economic deprivation faced by women in underdeveloped Asian countries. The Broussard brochure categorically states:

> We hear lots of stories about dishonest, selfish, and immature women on both sides of the Pacific. Perhaps women raised in poverty will have lower material expectations and will be grateful to whoever rescues them and offers a better life.

20   One Caucasian man who met his wife through the mail says: "They don't have a whole lot of things, so what they do have they appreciate very much. They appreciate things more than what the average American woman would." In other words, they are properly grateful for whatever the superior male partner bestows on them.

21   "Filipinas come because their standard of living is so low," asserts Pomeroy. In 1984 the per capita income in the Philippines was $640. "Most of the women make no secret of why they want to marry an American: money." An Australian reporter who has studied the influx of Filipino mail-order brides to her country agrees: "Most Filipinas are escaping from grinding poverty." Indeed, most Asian governments that are saddled with chronic unemployment, spiraling cost of living, malnutrition, and political turmoil are faced with the problem of emigration and a diminishing labor force. In contrast, Japan, the economic and technological leader of Asia, has very few women listed in mail-order catalogues.

22   The *Chicago Sun-Times* describes Bruce Moore's visit to the family home of his mail-order bride, Rosie, in Cebu, Philippines:

> "All of a sudden, we were driving through the jungle. There was nothing but little huts. I really started worrying about what I got myself into." . . . The house turned out to be an unpainted

concrete building with no doors, plumbing, or electricity. . . . Rosie had worked in a factory, eight hours a day, making 75 to 80 cents a day.

23   Because the Filipinas who avail themselves of mail-order bride service may not have much, Broussard's instructional brochures advise men to use caution in describing their financial status. The woman may turn out to be "a con artist after your money or easy entry into the United States." Despite the poverty, though, many of the women are truly sincere in their responses. The Broussard customer who is still writing to twelve of the fourteen women who wrote him notes:

> They all appeared genuine, and not one has asked me for money or anything else. In fact, in two instances, I offered to help with postage, and in both cases, it was declined. One of the ladies said she could not accept postal assistance, as that would lessen the pleasure she felt in the correspondence.

24   Regardless of the sincerity of the parties involved, one women's rights group in the Philippines has denounced the promotion of relationships through "commerce, industry, negotiation, or investment." Their protests, however, do not seem to affect the business.

25   **Racial Images and Romance**   Added to economic exploitation, a major cornerstone of the mail-order bride business, is the prevalence of racial stereotypes. They have a widespread effect on the treatment of women and influence why so many men are attracted to mail-order romance. "These men believe the stereotypes that describe Oriental women as docile, compliant, and submissive," says Jedlicka. His 1983 survey showed that 80 percent of the respondents accept this image as true.

26   One Canadian male, who asked not to be identified, was quoted as saying: "Asian girls are not as liberated as North American or Canadian girls. They're more family-oriented and less interested in working. They're old-fashioned. I like that."

27   The California-based American Asian Worldwide Service perpetuates the stereotypes when it says in its brochure: "Asian ladies are faithful and devoted to their husbands. When it comes to sex, they are not demonstrative; however, they are inhibited. They love to do things to make their husbands happy."

28   This company began after owner Louis Florence began his

search for a second wife. He says that friends had touted how their Asian wives "love to make their men happy" and finally convinced him to find a wife from Asia.

29   Another mail-order pitch describes Asian women as "faithful, devoted, unspoiled, and loving." Broussard confirms this popular misconception by saying these women are "raised to be servants for men in many Oriental countries." Referring to the Malaysian and Indonesian women who have recently joined his list of registrants, Broussard insists: "Like the Filipinas, they are raised to respect and defer to the male. . . . The young Oriental woman . . . derives her basic satisfaction from serving and pleasing her husband."

30   Virginity is a highly sought virtue in women. Tom Fletcher, a night worker in Ottawa, Canada, who dislikes North American women because they "want to get out [of the house] and work and that leads to break-ups," is especially appreciative of this sign of purity. "These women's virginity was a gift to their husbands and a sign of faithfulness and trust." One mail-order service unabashedly advertises virginity in a brochure with photos, home addresses, and descriptions of Filipino women, some of whom are as young as seventeen. "Most, if not all, are very feminine, loyal, loving . . . and virgins!" its literature reads.

31   Many of the Asian countries affected by the revived mail-order bride business have a history of U.S. military involvement. Troops have either fought battles or been stationed in Korea, the Philippines, and countries in Southeast Asia. During their stays, the soldiers have often developed strong perceptions of Asian women as prostitutes, bargirls, and geishas. Then they erroneously conclude that Asian-American women must fit those images, too. Consequently, the stereotype of women servicing and serving men is perpetuated.

32   The Japanese American Citizens League objects to the mail-order bride trade for that very reason. "The marketing techniques used by the catalogue bride companies reinforce negative sexual and racial stereotypes of Asian women in the U.S. The negative attitude toward Asian women affects all Asians in the country." Further, the treatment of women as "commodities" adds to the "nonhuman and negative perception of all Asians."

33   **Romance on the Rocks**   A marriage made via the mail-order bride system is naturally beset by a whole range of problems. In her testimony before the U.S. Commission on Civil Rights, profes-

sor Bok-Lim Kim, then with the University of Illinois, noted that negative reactions and attitudes toward foreign Asian wives "exacerbate marital problems," which result in incidences of spouse abuse, desertion, separation, and divorce. In addition, writes an Australian journalist, most of the men they marry are social misfits. "Many of them drink too much; some beat their wives and treat them little better than slaves."

34   The Japanese American Citizens League asserts:

> Individually, there may be many cases of couples meeting and marrying through these arrangements with positive results. We believe, however, that for the women, there are many more instances in which the impetus for leaving their home countries and families, and the resulting marriage relationships, have roots and end results which are less than positive.

35   Many of the Caucasian men who marry what they believe are stereotypical women may be in for some surprises. Psychiatry professor Joe Yamamoto of the University of California at Los Angeles says: "I've found many Asian women acculturate rather quickly. These American men may get a surprise in a few years if their wives pick up liberated ways."

36   One legally blind and hard-of-hearing American, married to a Korean woman, was eventually bothered by the same problems that plague other couples: in-laws and lack of money. "She gets frustrated because I don't hear her," complains the man about his soft-spoken Asian wife. In response, she says, "The main problem is [his] parents. I can't adapt to American culture. I was going to devote my life for him, but I can't."

37   Another area which specifically affects foreign-born brides is their immigrant status. According to the Japanese American Citizens League, "these foreign women are at a disadvantage." This civil rights group targets the women's unfamiliarity with the U.S. immigration laws as one of the most disturbing aspects of the business. "As a result [of the ignorance], they may miss an opportunity to become a naturalized citizen, forfeit rights as a legal spouse, or live under an unwarranted fear of deportation which may be fostered by their spouse as a means of control."

38   **Conclusion**   Despite the constant stream of criticism, the mail-order bride system will prevail as long as there are consumers and profit, and as long as underdeveloped countries continue failing

to meet the economic, political, and social needs of their people. Indications show the business is not about to collapse now.

39   Erroneous ideas continue to thrive. An Asian woman dreams she will meet and marry someone rich and powerful, someone to rescue her and free her from poverty-stricken bondage. She hopes to live the rest of her life in a land of plenty. An American man dreams he will meet and marry someone passive, obedient, non-threatening, and virginal, someone to devote her entire life to him, serving him and making no demands. Only a strong women's movement, one tied to the exploited underdeveloped country's struggle for liberation and independence, can challenge these ideas and channel the aspirations and ambitions of both men and women in a more positive and realistic direction.

EXERCISES

Details and Their Meanings

1. What information do Dr. Symons, Dr. Jedlicka, and the Japanese American Citizens League give about the men who use the mail-order service? How does this profile help you understand why these men use the service?
2. What is the profile of the women who use the mail-order service? According to the writer, what is the primary reason they use the service? Do the men and women have equal power in the exchange? Explain.
3. Where do most of the men who use the service come from? Where are most of the women from? What does the economic situation of a man's or woman's country have to do with a person's participation in the mail-order-bride business?
4. How do modern-day mail-order brides compare to the mail-order brides of the past?
5. How is the mail-order-bride business conducted? Describe the differences between the two catalogues, *Cherry Blossoms* and *Lotus Blossoms*. How do the differences highlight some of the sexism involved in this business? How are Asian women described in other brochures and catalogues mentioned in the selection? In what ways do you consider these descriptions sexist and racist?

6. What problems do mail-order marriages have? How do some of these problems reflect an overall problem of racial stereotyping?

Reading and Critical Thinking

1. Why do you think that the men who use the mail-order service believe they will be happy with an Asian woman as a wife? To what extent do the men get what they hope for? In what ways do they get results that they did not expect?
2. Why do you think the "matching" services do not give the women detailed information about the men they are writing to even though the men have detailed information about them? What do you think this difference has to do with Dr. Symons's observation, quoted in paragraph 9: "We're a consumer society. People become translated into commodities easily."
3. What do the Asian women participating expect to gain from the transaction? What do they actually get? What are some of the consequences that they do not expect?
4. In paragraph 10, John Broussard, who runs Rainbow Ridge with his wife, is quoted as saying "Basically, we just sell addresses. . . . We operate as a pen pal club, not a front for the slave trade, although some people get the wrong idea. We're not a Sears catalogue from which you buy a wife. You have to write and win the heart of the woman you desire." Do you agree with this statement? Or do you find the statement contradicted by other facts given about the company and its procedures and services? Explain.
5. Why do you think the writer suggests in her conclusion that "only a strong women's movement, . . . tied to the exploited underdeveloped country's struggle for liberation and independence, can challenge" the mail-order-bride business? Do you agree with her observations? Why or why not?
6. Why do you think the Japanese American Citizens League believes the mail-order-bride system affects all Asians in America?

The Writer's Strategies

1. In the first five paragraphs how does the information about past and present mail-order brides compare? From the compar-

ison, how does the writer seem to want you to feel about present-day mail-order brides? Where in the essay does the main idea first appear? How is the location of this idea related to the comparison?

2. Throughout the piece, the writer uses a variety of language to refer to the practice of selecting wives through the mail. Find as many different words and phrases used as possible. What do they have in common? What is the overall tone that the language conveys about the practice?

3. What kinds of people and organizations does the writer quote? What sorts of patterns do you notice in the kinds of people quoted? For instance, how many professors are quoted? How many mail-order brides are quoted? From the quoted sources, what kind of information do you receive? Is the picture presented balanced? Is it in any way only a partial picture?

4. How do the details from the catalogues and brochures support the writer's thesis?

5. In what different ways do the quotes from the men who were using the mail-order-bride service advance the writer's main point?

Thinking Together

In small groups, discuss whether the mail-order-bride business bears any similarity to other current social practices concerning relations between the sexes or economic relations between rich and poor nations.

Vocabulary

The words in each of the following groups have similar meanings. Define the words to distinguish their different shades of meaning.

1. submissive (par. 6), deference (par. 8), docile (par. 25), compliant (par. 25)
2. perpetuates (par. 27), reinforce (par. 32), exacerbate (par. 33)

Define the following words, using clues from the context of the passage.

1. prospective (par. 2)
2. procure (par. 11)

3. disseminated (par. 18)
4. deprivation (par. 19)
5. prevalence (par. 25)
6. acculturate (par. 35)
7. naturalized (par. 37)
8. deportation (par. 37)

WRITER'S WORKSHOP ━━━━━━━━━━

Critical Thinking in Writing

1. How do you feel about the existence of a mail-order-bride business in today's world? Would you ban it if you had the opportunity, or would you help it to thrive? Explain your opinion in a short essay.
2. The existence of a mail-order-bride business is directly related to society's view of marriage. What elements in this view of marriage contribute to the success of the mail-order-bride business? How are minority women seen in marriage roles? minority men and majority men? Explore your views in a short essay.
3. Write one page about how this selection changed or reinforced your ideas about romance and marriage, racial stereotypes, and stereotypes of men's and women's roles in society.

Connecting Ideas

Compare the experiences of the women described in this essay with the experience of Jesus Colon and his brother described in "Easy Job, Good Wages" (page 294). In what ways were both exploited and lured into unpleasant situations by false promises and hopes? Why do you think Colon and his brother were able to escape exploitation easily while these women for the most part could not? Why could Colon and his brother treat their experience with humor, while it is not a laughing matter for these women?

In My Father's House

David Masello

David Masello is a writer and magazine editor. In this selection he describes a visit with his father in which they both come to terms with a long-kept secret.

KEY WORDS

ludicrous (par. 2)   absurd, ridiculous
wince (par. 3)   shudder
litany (par. 4)   repetitive, rhythmic chant
rhetorical question (par. 4)   question asked for the effect
  with no answer expected
rootedness (par. 5)   a sense of place, a feeling of belonging
exquisitely (par. 7)   beautifully, perfectly
evasive (par. 9)   vague, indirect

WHENEVER I VISIT MY father in Florida I surprise him. It means one less flight for him to worry about, and it also gives him a pure rush of joy that he rarely feels in days that can be filled with weather-channel reports, clipping coupons, and driving to the convenience store for lottery tickets.

2   I am always near giddy with the anticipation of his surprise and often have to fight the impulse to let him know in advance that I am coming. This last trip I could hardly wait to drive up to the small town house he has shared for many years with his girl-friend (something of a ludicrous term, since they are both over 70) in a typical Florida development. I called him from the airport when I landed, having practiced my lines. As soon as he picked up the phone I asked, "So what do you want to do today—do we go to the beach or miniature golfing?"

3   "I hate to ask, but when do you have to leave?" my dad says within minutes of my arrival at his house, as he always does, and with a certain dread. His face registers a slight wince as he awaits

my response. Already I could picture exactly how the final night of my stay would be. The three of us would be watching television, and at a certain point I would stand up to go back to the motel and pack for an early-morning flight. My dad would rise from his chair and retreat to the bathroom, where he would close the door and cry. His girlfriend would gently try to coax him out. As we walked to the car in the driveway he would slip me a $20 bill and begin to cry again, as would I. And so after days of constant activity and conversation, the final minutes of my visit would be in complete silence, neither of us able to compose ourselves sufficiently to utter any words.

4 Certain words, however, recited in a kind of litany, virtually always occur during each visit—the names of Civil War sites, with an occasional World War I battle thrown in. Since my dad's house is so small, I usually stay at a Howard Johnson motel on the beach. On the drive to the motel along a stretch of Florida gulf coast lined with vintage 1950s motels, the names spelled out in neon, I began the process of conversation that has become a routine with my father and me. Asking the rhetorical question, "You're still interested in the Civil War, right?" launches a topic he knows thoroughly and is eager to relate. "There's something about the names of the battle sites that haunts me," he says, as he has many times before. So we recite, in a kind of alternating joint mantra, the names— Shiloh, Chickamauga, Appomattox, the Wilderness, Gettysburg, Manassas. We say each name with a careful emphasis and clarity, even a poetic hush for full effect. In some ways it is our secret language, these battle site names.

5 From my motel balcony there was a view of a narrow, curving waterway that eventually led to the gulf and across which were small, appealing houses. Each was fitted with a tiny wooden dock at which a sailboat or a motorboat was moored. People could be seen hosing down their boats, sweeping patios, or reclining in lawn chairs while reading newspapers. It was the kind of view that pleased my father. It was accessible, animated and reflected a certain rootedness that he has yet to feel in Florida; people lived in these houses, and collectively they became a neighborhood.

6 As I unpacked I put a Frank Sinatra tape into my Walkman and placed the earphones over my dad's ears. He moved a chair toward the view and began the newspaper crossword puzzle. For the first time in many months, I knew that my dad was content, that he wasn't worrying about the peculiar pain in his leg or about

filling another blank day. On this visit especially, I realized how easy it was to give my father moments of real happiness.

7   It was also the first time in a long while that I, too, had come to Florida during a period of great happiness and change in my own life. I was beginning to fall in love with someone back in New York. It was a feeling that I must have had before. I had been in a relationship for eight years, but it had been unwinding for so long that it was difficult to recall the waves of affection and longing I now felt. A bouquet of flowers was on the dresser when I arrived in the motel room, sent by the person. So within minutes I managed to make my father exquisitely happy by simply being with him in the place where he lived. Realizing this, and knowing that I had secured love in New York where I lived, I, too, was happy.

8   My father has worried for years about my being alone. "Everybody gets rejected sometimes," he often says to me. He thinks that's the reason why at 35 I still don't have a girlfriend or a wife or ever talk about one. "You know I'm just kidding when I say it," my dad began what I knew how to finish, "but you'd make me the happiest man in the world if you found a nice Italian girl." I wanted to tell him so badly, right there in the motel room, with the dull clang of boat lines hitting their masts just beyond, squawking sea gulls and the occasional plop of big silver fish leaping in the waterway below, that I was in love and happy. But I couldn't, because it was another man that I loved.

9   I don't fault my dad for the fact that this news would trouble him deeply; there is no reason to try to radicalize him with this knowledge. The news, no matter how I presented it or whom I introduced as the man I love, would not be welcome. But I also won't lie and say that I am in love with a woman or that I'm sure I'll get married someday. I remain evasive only to the point of deceit. With the faintest strains of Sinatra's "Summer Wind" coming from the earphones my father has on and the quiet scrawl of his pencil filling in the crossword boxes, I read and reread the simple note of coded affection that came with the flowers. So much happiness was taking place in the motel room. As dusk approached, my dad and I remarked almost simultaneously on the oval-shape silver fish that would fling themselves out of the water below, one eye, unlidded, wholly visible to us from our third-floor perch. I knew that detail would be a forever-memorable image that my dad and I would cite over and over again on each visit.

10   In the middle of my stay he overheard a phone conversation I was having in his kitchen and confronted me the next morning.

Detecting a certain tenderness in my voice during the call, he asked with sudden rage, "What is there between you and that friend? Tell me, is he straight?" He began to form another question, but he was unable to complete the sentence.

11   In the trembling, awkward silence that followed, all had been asked and answered. My father's questions were, in fact, statements of his knowledge. We had played out our own peculiar battle and soon, while touring the sites we had mapped out that day, were back to reciting those of the Civil War.

EXERCISES

Details and Their Meanings

1. Why does the writer always arrive unannounced when he goes to visit his father? What does this detail reveal about the writer? What does it reveal about his father? What does it reveal about the relation between the two men?
2. Where does the writer's father live? Where does the writer live? What do the two men have in common? What do they do whenever they are together?
3. What questions does his father always ask soon after the son's arrival? What do the question and events reveal about the father and the son and their relationship?
4. What actions of the son make the father happy? What does the son think about those actions?
5. What does the father believe about the son's reasons for not being married? Why doesn't the writer tell his father that he is in love and happy? How does he think his father will react? How does his father find out? How does this knowledge affect their relationship?

Reading and Critical Thinking

1. In this selection, the writer's relation with his father consists of familiar patterns or routines. How does the writer feel about these routines? Does he see them as something positive or neg-

ative? What do you think is gained and (or) lost as a result of these routines?

2. From the father-son relation presented here, what can you infer about the differences in values between the two generations? Is there a generation gap? If so, is this gap bridgeable? Why or why not?

3. What do you think of the reasons that the writer gives for not sharing parts of his life with his father? Are these reasons valid? Why do you think so? Do the advantages of not telling outweigh the disadvantages? Why?

4. The writer, in explaining his decision not to share certain parts of his life with his father, states, "I . . . won't lie . . . I remain evasive to the point of deceit." What does the statement mean? Is "being evasive to the point of deceit" different from lying? Why might the writer feel that this distinction is important?

The Writer's Strategies

1. The title reveals very little about the subject matter of this essay. What do you think the title means? Where do you think it comes from? How does it reflect, indirectly, the central point that the writer is trying to convey?

2. What is the central point the writer is trying to make? Does he ever state it directly? How does he use narrative to make that point? Are there any other points he makes indirectly through story-telling?

3. When does the writer reveal the gender of the person he is in love with? Why does he withhold the detail until this point? Were you surprised? Why or why not?

4. In the final paragraph, the writer uses a metaphor of battle to describe what has taken place during his visit with his father. How does this metaphor help to unify the essay? At the end of this selection, how do you think the writer wants you to feel about his subject? Is the conclusion satisfying? Why or why not?

5. How has the writer used transitions in this essay to advance its coherence?

Thinking Together

In small groups, discuss the difference between "lying" and "not telling the truth." Have you ever lied to or been "evasive to the point of deceit" with a parent or a close friend? How did you justify this deception to yourself? How did your deceit affect your relation with that person? Did you ever "come clean" and tell the truth? If so, what happened?

Vocabulary

Write a brief explanation for each of the following references to American popular culture or history. Consult a dictionary or an encyclopedia if necessary.

1. weather-channel (par. 1)
2. Howard Johnson motel (par. 4)
3. Shiloh (par. 4)
4. Chickamauga (par. 4)
5. Appomattox (par. 4)
6. the Wilderness (par. 4)
7. Gettysburg (par. 4)
8. Manassas (par. 4)
9. Frank Sinatra (par. 6)
10. Walkman (par. 6)

WRITER'S WORKSHOP ━━━━━━━━━━━

Critical Thinking in Writing

1. Write a one- or two-page essay about stereotypes of gay men. What characteristics—physical, behavioral, and so on—do people ascribe to them? Then discuss how this selection challenges these stereotypes.
2. Write a one-page informal journal entry imagining yourself in the position in which the writer finds himself. If you were Masello, what would you do and why? Would you tell your father the truth? Would you lie, or would you be "evasive to the point of deception"?
3. Recently we have heard much debate over the "don't ask, don't tell" policy for gays in the military. Write an essay arguing for or against the use of this policy with family, friends, employers, and so on. What is gained and lost by telling? What is gained and lost by not telling?

Connecting Ideas

Compare the experience Langston Hughes describes in "Salvation" (page 27) to the experience Masello describes in "In My Father's House." How does love for another person make an individual "lie" to make that person happy? How does denial of self in order to conform to what others expect affect the individual?

Scholars and Descendants

Kathleen Teltsch

Kathleen Teltsch is a journalist who writes for The New York Times. *In this selection, she reports on the discovery of a group of people who have been in hiding in New Mexico for five hundred years.*

KEY WORDS

expulsion (par. 1)   exiling, throwing out
obscurity (par. 1)   the condition of being unknown or unidentified
cognizance (par. 10)   awareness, recognition
genealogy (par. 22)   a list of the ancestors who make up one's family tree
exhilarated (par. 27)   excited, gladdened
validation (par. 31)   verification, certification

AFTER SEVERAL CENTURIES, SCHOLARS are uncovering the history of Spanish Jews who converted to Catholicism under threat of expulsion by Spain's monarchs in 1492 and then found refuge and obscurity in the mountains of New Mexico.

2   Although most of these early colonizers lived as practicing Catholics, a significant number, often called *conversos*, continued to cling secretly to Jewish traditions, lighting candles on Fridays, reciting Hebrew prayers, circumcising baby boys, baking unleavened bread, keeping the Sabbath.

3   Researchers are now finding evidence that some nominally Christian families have handed down Jewish traditions, and have done it amid a fear-inspired secrecy that seems hardly to have lessened over five centuries.

4   In the past two or three years, in remote areas of the Southwest, hundreds of gravestones have been found in old Christian

cemeteries with Hebrew inscriptions or Jewish symbols often combined with the cross.

5   Stimulated by the scholarly inquiries, or on their own, young descendants of converso families are searching to find their roots, Jewish and Christian, and comparing their findings.

6   A few of these descendants have returned to Judaism. Others are slowly establishing fragile ties to mainstream Jewish congregations.

7   "I've been here 20 years, and only in the last two or three, after observing me carefully, a handful of these people have made contact with me," said Rabbi Isaac Celnik of Congregation B'nai Israel in Albuquerque.

8   Some come to services, always sitting by themselves, he said. He has been invited five or six times to their homes to lead prayers, often because an elderly relative wants to renew ties to the ancient faith.

9   Still, distrust toward outsiders lingers. "These people lived in fear of persecution for so long, they still look over their shoulders," Rabbi Celnik said. "They are historically conditioned over centuries to be suspicious and alert."

10   **Heritage of Secrecy Is Handed Down**   There are perhaps fifteen hundred families in New Mexico who have some cognizance of their Jewish heritage, said Frances Hernandez, a professor of comparative literature at the University of Texas at El Paso. "They range from those with only blurred memories of Jewish customs or family legends to others who really are aware of their Judaic background and know what it means," she said. "We're talking of people who survived 200 generations of stress and secrecy, and it's a wonder anything survives."

11   In pursuing the conversos' saga, historians are interviewing families and using data in church records in Mexico City and New Mexico on baptisms, weddings, and burials. They have also examined Spanish shipping manifests dating from the 1490s.

12   A few months before Columbus's voyage in 1492, Spain enacted the Edict of Expulsion, compelling Jews to leave or convert to Catholicism under threat of death. Perhaps half of the estimated 200,000 Jews in Spain began an exodus to Portugal, other European countries, and North Africa. Others became "New Christians."

13   But even New Christians who prospered found themselves still persecuted, possibly out of envy. And some only pretended to convert. Under continuing pressure from the Inquisition, which began

to be felt in Portugal as well, some of the persecuted seized opportunities to come to the New World.

14   When the Inquisition stretched its reach to Mexico, they fled
again, crossing deserts and hostile Indian country to the frontier
of what is now New Mexico. There they found a measure of safety
and obscurity.

15   "We only have started to scrape the surface," said Dr. Stanley
Hordes, co-director of a research project on the secret Jews, or
"Crypto-Jews," at the University of New Mexico's Latin American
Institute.

16   Dr. Hordes, who spoke at the recent third annual meeting of
the New Mexico Jewish Historical Society, believes that converso
families who fled to remote areas like New Mexico's Mora,
Charma, and Rio Grande valleys could have settled the first Jewish
community in what is now the United States.

17   But other historians and Jewish scholars dispute Dr. Hordes's
conclusion, saying Christian families carrying on some Jewish
practices or dietary laws do not constitute a Jewish community.
Shearith Israel, the Spanish and Portuguese Synagogue established
in New Amsterdam in 1654, is considered the first Jewish congregation in North America.

18   Rabbi Marc D. Angel of Shearith Israel said the remnants of
Crypto-Jews in New Mexico was a tribute to the human spirit, but
he questioned the claim to an early community.

19   "What concerns me is that because of their dramatic story with
a movielike quality, there will be an eagerness to receive them into
Judaism and forget there is a formal procedure for reentry after
separation that requires instruction, patience, and sincerity," he
said. "There are no short-cuts."

20   **Getting to Know Distant Relatives**   Dr. Hordes's own inquiry be-
gan in 1981 soon after he became New Mexico state historian.
His doctoral dissertation at Tulane University was about Crypto-
Judaism in Mexico in the seventeenth century.

21   "People began dropping into my office, leaning across my desk
and whispering, 'You know, so-and-so lights candles and does not
eat pork.'" Repeated such visits led him to undertake the research
project, together with Dr. Tomas C. Atencio, a sociologist at the
University of New Mexico.

22   Since 1988, they have interviewed almost 50 converso families,
including many who practiced Jewish customs without understanding them, because their families had done so. In the process,

the researchers introduced descendants who did not know they were related and who now are comparing their own genealogy searches.

23   Daniel Yocum, a 23-year-old engineering student, suspected he had Jewish roots on his mother's side. He discovered a wedding photograph of his late grandfather wearing a fringed prayer shawl. He has boyhood memories of him baking round, unleavened bread at certain seasons and butchering livestock in the traditional Jewish way.

24   Nora Garcia Herrera, his mother, elaborates on her son's recollections, recalling that her father and mother disagreed about the family's religious practices. "He said it was all right not to kneel to the saints because you don't need an intermediary to talk to God," she recalled. She objected and called him "Judio," Spanish for "Jew," which her children guessed was a bad word. Her father and grandfather were circumcised by an old man in their community. When he died, her father carved a gravemarker with a Star of David.

25   Ramon Salas, 26, a manufacturing analyst at Digital Equipment in Albuquerque, discovered that he was related to Daniel Yocum after tracing his own lineage seventeen generations. He computerized his findings and says he has found evidence that Crypto-Jewish families, who often intermarried, used code names so they would recognize each other.

26   Mr. Salas said that, when he asked another cousin if they shared Jewish roots, she shot back, "Use your good Jewish head and you'll come to the realization you have Jewish blood."

27   "I remember I was exhilarated; it knocked my head off," Mr. Salas said. But as one who was raised as a Catholic, and in the eyes of his church will always be a Catholic, he is torn about making a choice. Judaism has an appeal—he lights sabbath candles—but he does not want to lose his attachment to the Catholic community.

28   **Memory and Myth Are Intertwined**   Dennis Duran, a corporate official who lives in Santa Fe, came to the historical society meeting with a copy of his family tree going back fourteen generations and showing his kinship to the Salas family. He has collected data suggesting their ancestors were among the Jews who came with Don Juan de Oñate in 1598 to colonize New Mexico. Mr. Duran, who is 36, formally converted to Judaism even before beginning his search for his Jewish heritage.

29   He has recollections of his grandfather secretly praying daily

at sundown in a cellar where the family kept fruit and wine, and of playing games as a child with tops, similar to the dreidel of Jewish origin.

30   Paul Marez, a 24-year-old graduate student, is the only one in his family who attends temple services. Family members are practicing Catholics, but he recalls his grandmother preparing for the Sabbath and, after a relative's death, observing a period of mourning and turning mirrors to the wall, as in the Jewish custom.

31   A number of the young adults are counseled about Judaism by Loggie Carrasco, a teacher with a magnetic style. Rabbi Celnik calls her Mama Loggie. "Young people look to her for validation because she is so knowledgeable," he said. "She is their rabbi."

32   Ms. Carrasco said she has traced her family to Seville and Madrid in the early 1600s. She said one ancestor, Manuel Carrasco, was tried in Mexico City by the Inquisition in 1648 for carrying matzo under his hat, which he tried to explain was a remedy for headache. His sugar plantations were confiscated and he disappeared.

33   While protectively withholding the names of conversos, Rabbi Celnik said that for many months he gave religious instruction to an artist from Taos who came weekly, arising at 4 A.M. to travel here. The rabbi also prayed with a dying elderly woman who lived as a Catholic but cherished her Jewish roots.

34   "I went to see her in the hospital," he said. "Her eyes brightened when I came into the room, and she recognized me. It happened to be Passover, and I placed a morsel of matzo on her lip. It meant a lot to her."

35   **Starting to Reconcile Two Disparate Faiths**   Rabbi Celnik said that, among the conversos who go to church, there is a segment that very much wants to return to Judaism. An equally small segment wants to be Catholic and Jewish; they are comfortable in both traditions. "But there also is a very small group committed to vengeance against those who return to Judaism, and this is regarded as a genuine threat," the rabbi said. "They are afraid of their own cousins."

36   Rabbi Celnik said this may be the opportune moment for Crypto-Jews to embrace their heritage openly because 1992 marks the 500th anniversary of both Columbus's voyage and the Expulsion Edict.

37   The International Jewish Committee, Sepharad '92, formed to commemorate the anniversary of the expulsion, would welcome

the support of the New Mexicans, said Andre Sassoon, the committee vice president.

38   Would they be regarded as genuinely Jewish? "We're a tolerant
people," Mr. Sassoon said.

39   "Personally, whether someone is truly a Jew or not, only God
can judge, and not mortals."

EXERCISES

Details and Their Meanings

1. What two important historical events occurred in 1492?
2. How many Jews were living in Spain in the fifteenth century?
   Why did many Jews convert to Catholicism? What happened
   to those who did not?
3. What is a converso? How many converso families live in New
   Mexico? What is the relation between conversos and Crypto-
   Jews?
4. In what ways were some New Mexicans able to uncover their
   Jewish ancestry?
5. What kinds of rituals have conversos maintained? How has
   their long exile changed their rituals?
6. Who is Stanley Hordes? Why is he important to conversos?
7. Who is Daniel Yocum? How did he find his cousin?
8. What special significance did the year 1992 have for conversos?

Reading and Critical Thinking

1. Why did Spanish Catholics force Jews to abandon their faith?
   Why would this be unlikely to happen today? How do you
   think you would feel if a religious group in power forced you
   to abandon your faith?
2. What can you infer is one reason that America appealed to
   Spanish Jews? Was their belief justified?
3. Why does the congregation of Shearith Israel question the
   claims of Crypto-Jews in New Mexico? Are their questions
   valid, do you think? Why or why not?

4. What would explain the tendency of converso families to inter-marry? How does American society feel about intermarriage? What is your view on this issue?
5. Why are some conversos reluctant to abandon Catholicism? How does their refusal present a problem for their community?
6. What attitude do conversos have toward religion in general? How do you explain their attitude?
7. How can you explain the deterioration of religious tradition among the Crypto-Jews?

The Writer's Strategies

1. What is Kathleen Teltsch's attitude toward her subject? How does she feel about conversos?
2. Who is the original audience for this selection? How can you tell?
3. What is Teltsch's purpose in writing this piece? Is she writing primarily to convey facts or express opinions? How can you decide?
4. What ordering principle does Teltsch use?
5. Why does the writer use subheadings?
6. Where does the writer make use of quotations? Why are quotations important to this essay?
7. What emotion is expressed in the conclusion? Would you call the conclusion powerful, negative, hopeful, or tentative?

Thinking Together

One of the people cited in the selection says that Jews have survived "200 generations of stress and secrecy," which is roughly six thousand years. In small groups, brainstorm to develop a list of reasons you feel that Jews have endured despite centuries of oppression and a list of lessons that contemporary American minorities can learn from the experience of the Jews.

Vocabulary

The following religious or cultural terms are important in the context of the selection. You can determine the meaning of some from their context, but others you will need to look up. Write a definition of each in your own words.

1. conversos (par. 2)
2. unleavened bread (par. 2)
3. exodus (par. 12)
4. Inquisition (par. 13)
5. dreidel (par. 29)
6. Passover (par. 34)

WRITER'S WORKSHOP ━━━━━━━━━━━━━━━

Critical Thinking in Writing

1. Suppose you were faced with a dilemma similar to the one faced by fifteenth-century Spanish Jews: you must abandon your identity or else face exile and possibly death. Which alternative would you choose? Write an essay that explains your choice.
2. Some conversos are still afraid of persecution. Do you think this fear is justified? Write a letter to a converso in which you support his or her decision to remain hidden or argue that the time for hiding is at an end.
3. People sometimes choose to hide their religious, racial, or ethnic background in an attempt to assimilate into a dominant culture. Write an essay called "The Crypto-___" (fill in the blank with your own word).

Connecting Ideas

Read Richard T. Schaefer's "Minority, Racial, and Ethnic Groups" (page 187). Do the conversos fit Schaefer's definition of *minority*? Are they truly distinct enough from Jews and Catholics to be considered unique? Make your points with direct references to Kathleen Teltsch's essay.

Roots

Alex Haley

This selection comes from a shortened version of Roots *(1974), Haley's enormously successful novel about his family from the time of his ancestors' capture in Africa until the present day. Haley, who died in 1992, was the ghostwriter of* The Autobiography of Malcolm X *(1964).*

KEY WORDS

saga (par. 4)   an epic story, usually one that covers a great
   deal of time and has many characters
lineage (par. 15)   the line of descent from one's ancestors
profusion (par. 15)   abundant supply
staccato (par. 20)   composed of abrupt percussive sounds
din (par. 20)   a great noise
welled (par. 20)   issued forth like water

MY EARLIEST MEMORY IS of Grandma, Cousin Georgia, Aunt Plus, Aunt Liz, and Aunt Till talking on our front porch in Henning, Tennessee. At dusk, these wrinkled, graying old ladies would sit in rocking chairs and talk, about slaves and massas and plantations— pieces and patches of family history, passed down across the generations by word of mouth. "Old-timey stuff," Mama would exclaim. She wanted no part of it.

2   The furthest-back person Grandma and the others ever mentioned was "the African." They would tell how he was brought here on a ship to a place called "Naplis" and sold as a slave in Virginia. There he mated with another slave and had a little girl named Kizzy.

3   When Kizzy became four or five, the old ladies said, her father would point out to her various objects and name them in his native tongue. For example, he would point to a guitar and make a single-syllable sound, *ko*. Pointing to a river that ran near the plantation, he'd say "Kamby Bolongo." And when other slaves addressed him

as Toby—the name given him by his massa—the African would strenuously reject it, insisting that his name was "Kin-tay."

4   Kin-tay often told Kizzy stories about himself. He said that he had been near his village in Africa, chopping wood to make a drum, when he had been set upon by four men, overwhelmed, and kidnaped into slavery. When Kizzy grew up and became a mother, she told her son these stories, and he in turn would tell *his* children. His granddaughter became my grandmother, and she pumped that saga into me as if it were plasma, until I knew by rote the story of the African, and the subsequent generational wending of our family through cotton and tobacco plantations into the Civil War and then freedom.

5   At 17, during World War II, I enlisted in the Coast Guard, and found myself a messboy on a ship in the Southwest Pacific. To fight boredom, I began to teach myself to become a writer. I stayed on in the service after the war, writing every single night, seven nights a week, for eight years before I sold a story to a magazine. My first story in the *Digest* was published in June 1954: "The Harlem Nobody Knows." At age 37, I retired from military service, determined to be a full-time writer. Working with the famous Black Muslim spokesman, I did the actual writing for the book *The Autobiography of Malcolm X*.

6   I remembered still the vivid highlights of my family's story. Could this account possibly be documented for a book? During 1962, between other assignments, I began following the story's trail. In plantation records, wills, census records, I documented bits here, shreds there. By now, Grandma was dead; repeatedly I visited other close sources, most notably our encyclopedic matriarch, "Cousin Georgia" Anderson in Kansas City, Kansas. I went as often as I could to the National Archives in Washington, and the Library of Congress, and the Daughters of the American Revolution Library.

7   By 1967, I felt I had the seven generations of the U.S. side documented. But the unknown quotient in the riddle of the past continued to be those strange, sharp, angular sounds spoken by the African himself. Since I lived in New York City, I began going to the United Nations lobby, stopping Africans and asking if they recognized the sounds. Every one of them listened to me, then quickly took off. I can well understand: me with a Tennessee accent, trying to imitate African sounds!

8   Finally, I sought out a linguistics expert who specialized in African languages. To him I repeated the phrases. The sound "Kin-

tay," he said, was a Mandinka tribe surname. And "Kamby Bolongo" was probably the Gambia River in Mandinka dialect. Three
days later, I was in Africa.

9   In Banjul, the capital of Gambia, I met with a group of Gambians. They told be how for centuries the history of Africa has been
preserved. In the other villages of the back country there are old
men, called *griots,* who are in effect living archives. Such men
know, and, on special occasions, tell the cumulative histories of
clans, or families, or villages, as those histories have long been told.
Since my forefather had said his name was Kin-tay (properly
spelled *Kinte*), and since the Kinte clan was known in Gambia, they
would see what they could do to help me.

10   I was back in New York when a registered letter came from
Gambia. Word had been passed in the back country, and a *griot* of
the Kinte clan had, indeed, been found. His name, the letter said,
was Kebba Kanga Fofana. I returned to Gambia and organized a
safari to locate him.

11   There is an expression called "the peak experience," a moment
which, emotionally, can never again be equaled in your life. I had
mine, that first day in the village of Juffure, in the back country in
black West Africa.

12   When our 14-man safari arrived within sight of the village, the
people came flocking out of their circular mud huts. From a distance I could see a small, old man with a pillbox hat, an off-white
robe and an aura of "somebodiness" about him. The people
quickly gathered around me in a kind of horseshoe pattern. The old
man looked piercingly into my eyes, and he spoke in Mandinka.
Translation came from the interpreters I had brought with me.

13   "Yes, we have been told by the forefathers that there are
many of us from this place who are in exile in that place called
America."

14   Then the old man, who was 73 rains of age—the Gambian way
of saying 73 years old, based upon the one rainy season per year—
began to tell me the lengthy ancestral history of the Kinte clan. It
was clearly a formal occasion for the villagers. They had grown
mouse-quiet, and stood rigidly.

15   Out of the *griot's* head came spilling lineage details incredible
to hear. He recited who married whom, two or even three centuries
back. I was struck not only by the profusion of details, but also by
the Biblical pattern of the way he was speaking. It was something
like, "—and so-and-so took as a wife so-and-so, and begat so-
and-so. . . . "

16   The *griot* had talked for some hours and had got to about 1750 in our calendar. Now he said, through an interpreter, "About the time the king's soldiers came, the eldest of Omoro's four sons, Kunta, went away from this village to chop wood—and he was never seen again. . . ."

17   Goose pimples came out on me the size of marbles. He just had no way in the world of knowing that what he told me meshed with what I'd heard from the old ladies on the front porch in Henning, Tennessee. I got out my notebook, which had in it what Grandma had said about the African. One of the interpreters showed it to the others, and they went to the *griot*, and they all got agitated. Then the *griot* went to the people, and *they* all got agitated.

18   I don't remember anyone giving an order, but those 70-odd people formed a ring around me, moving counterclockwise, chanting, their bodies close together. I can't begin to describe how I felt. A woman broke from the circle, a scowl on her jet-black face, and came charging toward me. She took her baby and almost roughly thrust it out at me. The gesture meant "Take it!" and I did, clasping the baby to me. Whereupon the woman all but snatched the baby away. Another woman did the same with her baby, then another, and another.

19   A year later, a famous professor at Harvard would tell me: "You were participating in one of the oldest ceremonies of humankind, called 'the laying on of hands.' In their way these tribespeople were saying to you, 'Through this flesh, which is us, we are you and you are us.' "

20   Later, as we drove out over the back-country road, I heard the staccato sound of drums. When we approached the next village, people were packed alongside the dusty road, waving, and the din from them welled louder as we came closer. As I stood up in the Land Rover, I finally realized what it was they were all shouting: "Meester Kinte! Meester Kinte!" In their eyes I was the symbol of all black people in the United States whose forefathers had been torn out of Africa while theirs remained.

21   Hands before my face, I began crying—crying as I have never cried in my life. Right at that time, crying was all I could do.

22   I went then to London. I searched and searched, and finally in the British Parliamentary records I found that the "king's soldiers" mentioned by the *griot* referred to a group called "Colonel O'Hare's forces," which had been sent up the Gambia River in 1767 to guard the then British-operated James Fort, a slave fort.

23   I next went to Lloyds of London, where doors were opened for

me to research among all kinds of old maritime records. I pored through the records of slave ships that had sailed from Africa. Volumes upon volumes of these records exist. One afternoon about 2:30, during the seventh week of searching, I was going through my 1,023rd set of ship records. I picked up a sheet that had on it the reported movements of 30 slave ships, my eyes stopped at No. 18, and my glance swept across the column entries. This vessel had sailed directly from the Gambia River to America in 1767; her name was the *Lord Ligonier;* and she had arrived at Annapolis (Naplis) the morning of September 29, 1767.

24   Exactly 200 years later, on September 29, 1967, there was nowhere in the world for me to be except standing on a pier at Annapolis, staring seaward across those waters over which my great-great-great-great-grandfather had been brought. And there in Annapolis I inspected the microfilmed records of the *Maryland Gazette.* In the issue of October 1, 1767, on page 3, I found an advertisement informing readers that the *Lord Ligonier* had just arrived from the River Gambia, with "a cargo of choice, healthy SLAVES" to be sold at auction the following Wednesday.

25   In the years since, I have done extensive research in 50 or so libraries, archives, and repositories on three continents. I spent a year combing through countless documents to learn about the culture of Gambia's villages in the eighteenth and nineteenth centuries. Desiring to sail over the same waters navigated by the *Lord Ligonier*, I flew to Africa and boarded the freighter *African Star.* I forced myself to spend the ten nights of the crossing in the cold, dark cargo hold, stripped to my underwear, lying on my back on a rough, bare plank. But this was sheer luxury compared to the inhuman ordeal suffered by those millions who, chained and shackled, lay in terror and in their own filth in the stinking darkness through voyages averaging sixty to seventy days.

EXERCISES

Details and Their Meanings

1. Where did Alex Haley learn to write? How old was he when he began writing for a living?

2. How old was Haley when he first heard about "the African"? Who told the writer about his heritage?
3. In what year did Haley's search to document his family's story begin? How long did it take him to document the American side of his family? How long did it take him to find "the African"?
4. What documentary resources did Haley use? Which ones could other African Americans also use?
5. Who is Kunta Kinte? How was Kinte captured?
6. Who is Kebba Kanga Fofana? Why is he essential to Haley's family history?
7. How many libraries did Haley consult? How many continents did Haley visit to research his story?
8. What was the *Lord Ligonier*? Where did it come from? How does it figure in Haley's story?

Reading and Critical Thinking

1. Why did Kinte teach his daughter African words? How would this piece be different if he had not done so?
2. Why is it essential to the selection that Haley learned his family story through his grandmother? How would this piece be different if Haley's primary source of information had been his mother? What details of your own family history did you learn from your grandparents? from your parents?
3. What clues enabled Haley to begin his search? Why were these resources unlikely to be available to most African Americans?
4. How did Haley's career enable him to conduct his search relatively easily? Why did Haley go to Gambia? What essential resource was available only there?
5. Why did the Gambian women make Haley touch their babies? How long did it take Haley to figure out the reason? Why did the Gambians call Haley "Meester Kinte"?
6. Why do you think that Haley doesn't mention his father's side of the family?
7. Why did Haley travel to America aboard the *African Star*? What were his accommodations like?

The Writer's Strategies

1. What is the thesis of this selection?
2. What rhetorical strategies does Haley use?

3. Why are names, dates, and other specific details so important? How would the selection be less effective without them?
4. Why is the use of first person essential to this selection? How would the piece be less effective if told in third person?
5. Which paragraphs represent the introduction?
6. What is Haley's opinion of slavery? Where does Haley express it?
7. What paragraph is the conclusion? What new emotion is introduced there?

Thinking Together

In small groups discuss the importance of names in maintaining cultural identity. In an attempt to mask their cultural identities and to assimilate easily into their surrounding culture many people choose, for example, to "Americanize" their given names or surnames. Other people choose to herald their ethnic background by returning to names identified with their particular heritage. How do you account for the differences in approach? Why do we as a society infuse names with as much meaning as we do?

Vocabulary

The following words are part of Alex Haley's African heritage. Some of them are defined in the text. Write a definition of each one.

1. *ko* (par. 3)
2. Kamby Bolongo (par. 3)
3. Mandinka (par. 8)
4. Gambia (par. 9)
5. *griots* (par. 9)

WRITER'S WORKSHOP ━━━━━━━━━

Critical Thinking in Writing

1. How much of your family's history do you know? Write an essay entitled "Roots" in which you trace your family's history through as many generations as you can.

2. Imagine that you, like Kunta Kinte, suddenly are stolen from your home and family. Write a detailed essay about what steps you will take to teach your heritage to your children. What do you think it will be important to preserve? How will you make sure that your descendants remember where you were from?

3. Haley writes, "There is an expression called the 'peak experience,' a moment which, emotionally, can never again be equaled in your life." Have you or someone close to you had a "peak experience"? Write an essay to describe and explain it.

Connecting Ideas

Read "Scholars and Descendants," by Kathleen Teltsch (page 411). What major differences can you find between the elders in that piece and Haley's relatives in Henning, Tennessee? How did the manner in which those groups became exiles dictate their relations to past history? What do you think Alex Haley would tell the conversos about the need to discover and embrace their heritage?

The Return of the Melting Pot

Alan Wolfe

Alan Wolfe is a professor of sociology and political science. In this essay, he compares earlier views of ethnic diversity in the United States with current views.

KEY WORDS

nativist (par. 2)   favoring native-born inhabitants over immigrants
entrepreneurial (par. 5)   taking risks in business ventures

I RECALL FROM MY childhood in Philadelphia that no discussion of ethnicity could begin without two rituals: a quiz and a story.

2   The quiz was designed to convey how truly diverse the American population had become. It generally took the following form: What is the second-largest Irish (or Jewish or Italian or Polish) city in the world? The story, on the other hand, went like this: once upon a time America was an empty land settled, except for Native Americans, mostly by folk from the British Isles. When immigrants began to arrive from the poorer countries of Europe, nativist sentiment and racial prejudice kept them in second-class jobs and ethnic ghettos. But the immigrants were a determined lot—how else to explain the risks they took in coming?—and they worked hard to provide opportunities for their children. The second generation, bilingual and able to keep the old rituals even while adopting new customs, succeeded economically, moving out of ethnic enclaves and up the job ladder. Their children, in turn, assimilated, but at the same time they retained an ethnic identity. America is thus defined, as Lawrence Fuchs puts it, by both the *pluribus* and the *unum*. We are similar because we are different.

3   Since the passage of an immigration reform law in 1965, a new wave of immigration has begun once again to alter the ethnic and

racial composition of the American population. In 1980, 6.2 percent of the American population was foreign born, nowhere near the 13.2 percent of 1930, but far higher than it had been for the previous thirty years. Moreover, the bulk of this new immigration has come not from Europe, but from Third World countries, especially Mexico, the Dominican Republic, India, China, the Philippines, Cuba, and Vietnam.

4   There is, consequently, enough material for a new generation of quizzes. How much higher is the minimum wage in the United States than the average wage in Mexico? (Six times). Which city receives the most Chinese immigrants: New York, San Francisco, or Los Angeles? (Twice as many come to New York as to San Francisco, two-and-a-half times more to New York than Los Angeles.) What country provides the single largest source of Chicago's new immigrants? (Mexico.) Does Canada or Cambodia send more immigrants to the state of Iowa? (Cambodia.) Where, outside of Samoa, can one find an entire city softball league reserved for Samoans? (San Francisco.) For the following countries, are the educational attainments of the immigrants higher than, similar to, or lower than the American average: Nigeria, Peru, Egypt, England, Canada, the Netherlands, Germany, the Soviet Union, Portugal, and Italy? (The first three are higher, the next four are about the same, and the last three are lower.) From what country came the 12-year-old girl who placed second in a spelling bee in Chattanooga because she could not spell *enchilada?* (Cambodia.) How many new immigrants come each year to live in Oklahoma? (More than a thousand.)

5   Not surprisingly, the new quiz is also accompanied by a follow-up to the story, which in its most recent retellings incorporates these newer groups. It is true, the saga continues, that these immigrants are not primarily Europeans; and because of their race and their foreignness, American nativists are already active, insisting on English as an official language, closing union doors to new workers, and, on extreme occasions, engaging in physical violence. But this will pass, as the earlier nativism passed. For the new immigrants, too, are unusually entrepreneurial, and they, too, are determined for their children to succeed. We should keep our borders open, welcome the new immigrants, allow them to keep their language and culture, and enrich ourselves in the process, since diversity and pluralism will not only generate new sources of economic growth, but they will also contribute to the social mosaic that makes our country distinct.

EXERCISES

Details and Their Meanings

1. What question does the writer recall from his childhood? What point is made by this question?
2. What story was typically told in the writer's childhood? What was the point of the story?
3. In 1965, what happened to change immigration patterns? What was the specific effect of that event? In what ways was immigration after 1965 similar to earlier patterns of immigration? In what ways was it different?
4. What are some of the questions to be asked for a new quiz? What is the point made by these questions? How similar to or different from the earlier quiz questions are they?
5. What is the new story? How is it similar to or different from the old story?
6. How did nativist feeling influence earlier immigrants? How does it influence current immigrants? How permanent was the effect then, and how permanent does the writer think it will be now?
7. What characteristics of the immigrants allowed them to succeed in the past and will allow them to succeed now?
8. What conclusions does Wolfe draw from the comparison of earlier and current discussions of ethnicity? What sentence best sums up the main point of this selection?

Reading and Critical Thinking

1. What do the older quiz and story tell you about the way people used to think about diversity in America? How much does retelling certain facts determine the conclusions we can draw? What issues get left out once we grant the quiz and story as starting points?
2. Are the new questions that the writer lists really the first thing you think of when you discuss diversity in the United States now? Why or why not? Where have you seen these questions in evidence? What other questions have you also heard? Where? How do the other questions differ from the ones Wolfe poses?
3. What are the implications of the modern retelling of the assimilation story? What less optimistic stories have you heard?

4. Do you agree that the image of the melting pot is still appropriate? Why or why not?
5. Do you agree that "We should keep our borders open"? Why or why not? Are your reasons similar to or different from the reason Wolfe provides in the last paragraph?
6. In paragraph 2, what does the writer mean when he restates Fuchs's point that "America is thus defined . . . by both the *pluribus* and the *unum*"? Where do these Latin words come from? Do you agree that "We are similar because we are different"? What does that paradoxical statement mean?

The Writer's Strategies

1. Comment on the introductory paragraph. Is it effective? Does it capture and hold your attention? Why or why not?
2. What is the point of starting out by recalling the old quiz and story? How does the theme of quiz and story hold the selection together?
3. How surprising are the facts referred to in the answers to the new quiz? In what ways does Alan Wolfe use both surprise and lack of surprise to make the point about America's diversity?
4. How does the writer compare the period of his childhood to the present? What point is made by the comparison? Why is comparison such a useful rhetorical strategy in this piece?
5. Does the writer ever state his own position on whether the quizzes and stories represent the truth of immigration to this country? What do you think his position is? How does he let the comparisons and assumptions make his point?

Thinking Together

Use the last sentence of this selection as the basis of a discussion in groups. Do you agree that the United States should (1) keep its borders open, (2) welcome new immigrants, (3) and allow new immigrants to keep their language and culture? Report back to the class at large on your group's responses.

Vocabulary

Define the following italicized words, using the essay context.

1. no discussion of *ethnicity* could begin without two *rituals* (par. 1)

2. moving out of ethnic *enclaves* (par. 2)
3. America is thus defined . . . by both the *pluribus* and the *unum* (par. 2)
4. the educational *attainments* of the immigrants (par. 4)
5. she could not spell *enchilada* (par. 4)
6. *diversity* and *pluralism* will not only generate new sources of economic growth (par. 5)
7. the social *mosaic* that makes our country *distinct* (par. 5)

WRITER'S WORKSHOP

Critical Thinking in Writing

1. Write a list of questions that you think reveal your assumptions about success in America.
2. Write a one-page essay evaluating whether the melting pot is a useful or an appropriate metaphor for thinking about diversity in America.
3. Is America as a society pulling apart into separate groups or moving together, or is something more complicated happening? Write a brief essay expressing your thoughts on the direction in which group relations and national identity are moving in this country.

Connecting Ideas

Reread the last two sentences of Wolfe's essay. Then consider them in light of Sam Moses' "A New Dawn" (page 32), Rosemarie Santini's "An American Dream" (page 56), or Elizabeth Wong's "The Struggle to Be an All-American Girl" (page 39). In what ways do the experiences recorded in those selections support Wolfe's assertions at the end of his essay?

Teaching Young Fathers the Ropes

Sophfronia Scott Gregory

In this selection, Sophfronia Scott Gregory, a reporter for Time, *writes of recent attempts to help young unwed fathers learn how to be more responsive and responsible fathers—and men.*

KEY WORDS

inadequacy (par. 2)   not being able
referral (par. 4)   recommendation, direction
bureaucracy (par. 4)   governmental agencies
focal point (par. 8)   center
deterioration (par. 8)   breakdown

———

TWO YEARS AGO, PAUL SMALLEY found himself getting sucked into a stereotype. At 21 he returned home from military prison a frustrated, unemployed young black man who also happened to be a brand-new unmarried father. His son and namesake was already four months old, and Smalley was so unfamiliar with his new role that he thought he could not touch the baby without permission. "I was asking if I could pick him up," he says. "I just didn't feel like a father."

2   Smalley worried because he could see a familiar pattern forming, born of his shame over not being able to support his child, the feeling of inadequacy and the strain of his relationship with the baby's mother. He resisted joining the ranks of young black fathers who cut out on their kids because they will not face the pressures of parenthood, but he could not see how to break the cycle—until he learned from a friend about the Responsive Fathers Program at the Philadelphia Children's Network.

3   While social-assistance programs have long been available to teenage mothers, little effort has gone into helping young fathers.

The Responsive Fathers Program is one of a growing number of groups across the United States seeking to fill the vacuum. The programs try to help young unmarried men become better fathers, providers, and mates through counseling services, particularly assistance in a job search. The sixty-one participants in the Philadelphia program, who range in age from 16 to 26, meet in group sessions once a week and discuss child rearing, self-esteem, male-female relationships, and the job market. "The program helped me to open up," says Smalley. "It gave me the drive to want to do things. I've learned how anger affects my child and about how he needs both parents."

4   Fathers come to the program either by referral from a hospital, community center, or probation office or, like Smalley, by word of mouth from a friend. Thomas J. Henry, 47, the program's director, says that many young fathers just need help cutting through the bureaucracy: filling out forms, standing in the correct lines for public assistance, and dealing with unresponsive bureaucrats. "This system encourages fathers not to be there," he says. "You have many fathers declared absent when they are actually present. People think they're just making babies and don't have any feelings attached to that act. Everyone says, 'We want you to be a responsible father,' but we give them nothing to be responsible with."

5   The Responsive Fathers Program is part of a study being conducted by Public/Private Ventures, a nonprofit public-policy research organization that focuses on youth development. Using five other similar programs from across the country, PPV launched the study last year to try to discover whether it could get young unwed fathers to come forward and seek help, identify their needs, and direct them to the services they require. The group aims to provide information to policymakers responsible for family welfare programs so that as they debate decisions concerning young mothers, they will keep young fathers in mind as well.

6   "It is important for families that we begin to consider the role of fathers," says Bernadine Watson, director of individual and family support at PPV. "Our work has shown that these men, even though they are young and do not have the educational background or employment skills, are very interested in being good parents."

7   Henry believes the Philadelphia program will make a difference because it is willing to take the three to six years needed to "put things right" in a young man's life. Such a philosophy and

time frame contrast with government programs offering quick-fix solutions, but Henry believes in taking a pay-now-or-pay-later approach. His goal for the fathers is true self-sufficiency, by training them for jobs in areas such as printing, building maintenance, and computer programming. This is no easy trick; the program has a hard time persuading employers to give the young men a chance. "We go along begging, pleading to anybody to give us jobs," says Henry. The program currently has fathers who have been on the job waiting list for six months. Still, the dads attend the sessions, even though the only thing Henry and his colleagues can give them is carfare home.

8   The young men say they enjoy the sessions because they can vent their feelings of frustration, often born of their sense that society perceives them as bad parents. The black male has become the focal point of blame for the deterioration of the African-American family. But in many cases such blame is misdirected. Devon Shaw, 24, whose three children range in age from six months to four years, was just out of high school when his first child was born. He doesn't like the way the system "lets you know what we're doing wrong, not what they're doing wrong." Smalley, who now works as an animal-care technician and goes to school at night, admits that many of his friends simply cannot function as fathers: "Some don't even try. Some don't care. They just turn to drugs or drug dealing as their way out." But he stresses that there are many more who are trying to be responsible, who want their kids to have two parents, a good education, and a safe place to live. "It's just we have so many obstacles to becoming decent men," he says. "But it is inside of us. It's in the black men out there."

———

EXERCISES

Details and Their Meanings

1. What situation did Paul Smalley find himself in? What was the pattern he saw forming? What caused that pattern?
2. How are the difficulties that unwed fathers face different from those faced by unwed mothers? How does the writer account for these differences?

3. How does the Responsive Fathers Program attempt to help young fathers? What are the program's goals and philosophy? How has it helped Paul Smalley? To what degree has this program been successful?
4. What do young fathers get out of the Responsive Fathers program sessions?

Reading and Critical Thinking

1. How does Smalley's experience illustrate the difficulties that other unwed fathers face? What factors other than youth contribute to these difficulties?
2. This selection reports on the stigma unwed fathers experience. What assumptions do many people make about unwed fathers and, in particular, about African-American unwed fathers? According to the author, where do these assumptions come from? How does this stigma compare to the stigma unwed mothers face?
3. The name of the program designed to help young fathers described in this selection is the *Responsive Fathers Program*. Why do you think this name was chosen? What does the term *responsive* suggest about the goals of the program? Why might the founders of this program have decided against naming the program the *Responsible* Fathers Program?
4. Bernadine Watson, a policy analyst, suggests here that "It is important for families that we begin to consider the roles of fathers." What according to the writer should be the father's role within the family? Why does she think this role is important? Do you think her view of this role reinforces gender stereotypes? Why or why not?
5. Thomas J. Henry, director of the Responsive Fathers Program, takes a "pay-now-or-pay-later" approach. What does he mean? Who will have to "pay later" if the choice is made not to "pay now"? What forms might this "payment" take now? What forms might this "payment" take in the future?

The Writer's Strategies

1. What is the thesis of this essay? State it in your own words.
2. What does the title of this selection refer to? What does it mean

to teach someone "the ropes"? Where does this figure of speech come from? What "ropes" do young fathers need to learn? Who will teach them?

3. Who do you think is the intended audience for this selection? What assumptions does the writer make about this audience? Are these assumptions valid in your case?

4. Paragraphs 1 and 2 relate Paul Smalley's personal history. Why do you think the writer begins the essay in this way? What other similar personal histories unfold in this selection?

5. What authorities does the writer cite in this selection? Why do you think that she does not cite government studies and statistics? Does the lack of this kind of evidence make her main point less convincing? Why or why not?

6. How does the writer conclude this selection? What is the effect of ending it in this way? Who gets the final word?

Thinking Together

Brainstorm as a class about the way that gender roles influence parental roles. What is the role of the mother? What is the role of the father? What roles are shared? How have these roles changed since your parents were children? How have they changed since your grandparents were children? To what degree do gender stereotypes contribute to the way parental roles are defined today?

Vocabulary

For each of the following compound words that appear in the selection, first define the parts of each term and then define the entire word.

1. namesake (par. 1)
2. social-assistance (par. 3)
3. self-esteem (par. 3)
4. policymakers (par. 5)
5. self-sufficiency (par. 7)
6. quick-fix (par. 7)
7. carfare (par. 7)

WRITER'S WORKSHOP

Critical Thinking in Writing

1. What roles should fathers play in families? Draw both on the experience of your own family and the plans you may have for raising children.
2. In the last thirty years, the rates of "children having children" have increased dramatically. What do you think should be done to address the problem of teenage parenthood in the United States? Write a letter to a state official (governor or member of the legislature) detailing specific recommendations for resolving this problem.
3. Write a two-page essay about why you think so little public attention has turned to the difficulties faced by young unwed fathers. Why do people in general and social-assistance programs in particular focus on the problems faced by young unwed mothers instead? What has been the effect of not supporting young fathers? Draw on your own observations as well as what you learned from reading this selection.

Connecting Ideas

Read "Bias Outside Appalachia," by Judy Pasternak (page 335). Compare the effect of negative stereotyping on urban Appalachians and young African-American unwed fathers. How do the lack of expectations and (or) expectations of failure become self-fulfilling prophecies for both groups? How are the problems that the two groups face similar? What do the programs that have been implemented to address these problems have in common?

SIDE BY SIDE

1. Drawing on the ideas and information presented in the selections in this chapter, write an essay arguing for the way you think the future of this country ought to be envisioned—as a melting pot, a collection of separate cultures, a diverse mosaic, a shared modern culture, or any other description you would propose.
2. Do you personally identify more with your roots or with some newer version of evolving American culture? Recalling the selections in this unit and the rest of the book, write an essay describing the culture that you feel part of or want to be part of.
3. Imagine that you are given the assignment of filling a time capsule with objects that will not be seen for thousands of years, long after all of the works of modern civilization are gone. What will you include to present a cross section of items that will best describe Americans, in all their diversity, to those people of the future?

PART TWO

Writing Skills Handbook

INTRODUCTION ━━━━━━━━━━━━━━━

We provide this concise writing-skills handbook as a useful reference for the various writing activities throughout this book and your writing course in general.

As you work your way through various drafts of an essay, you'll want to consult these pages for assistance in producing a grammatically sound sentence, in phrasing a passage clearly, and in selecting the right form of a word, spelling a word accurately, or punctuating a sentence correctly. When your instructor returns your papers, indicating the need for revisions in language and sentence structure, use the handbook to understand corrections you may have to make. We do not expect you to work your way through these pages from start to finish; use them only as you need to improve your skills.

Aiming for clarity and ease of use, we provide compact rules and advice, drawing as much as we can on handy word charts and numerous examples to illustrate basic writing principles. We have arranged the information so that you can find what you need quickly as you write, revise, or edit your papers and as you review your teacher's comments and suggestions. The contents list identifies each subject covered. In the handbook itself, we have used a system of numbered and lettered topics that you can locate swiftly. The headings that run along the top of each page also allow you to find material easily. On the inside back cover of the book, the correction chart draws on conventional marking symbols that many teachers use and targets common writing errors in student papers. Use the correction chart to help you find appropriate numbered sections linked to problem areas identified on your drafts.

Overall, we have attempted to create a handbook that you can use independently as your needs dictate. You will be able to understand necessary rules of grammar, usage, and mechanics on your own.

UNIT ONE

The Sentence

1

Sentence Form

1a   THE BASIC SENTENCE

In English, words are put together in units called sentences. Sentences can range from simple statements of only a few words to complex messages made up of many parts. However, unless you write long combinations of words carefully and correctly, complicated sentences can be very confusing. In order to write clear, long sentences you must first master basic, simple sentences. Simple and direct sentences can, in fact, express most of the things that you have to say.

The basic English sentence has a subject and a verb: that is, the sentence mentions some person, place, thing, or idea (the **subject**) and tells what that person, place, thing, or idea does (the **verb**).

Subject	Verb
Jerilyn	thinks.
Jerilyn	is thinking.
Jerilyn	should have thought.

Remember: verbs may be made up of more than one word: *is thinking* and *should have thought* are complete verbs.

Sometimes words must be added to the subject and verb to give more information about the action. If someone or something receives the action, we add a word or group of words called the **object.**

Subject	Verb	Object
Kai	considers	the options.

Some verbs need other words to complete their meaning.

Subject	Verb	Verb completer
Oranges	taste	sour.
Metals	are	conductors.

447

Finding Sentence Parts

▶ *Look for the verb first.* Find the word or words that show action. Then test the word: use *I, we, you, she, he,* or *it* in front of the word you've picked as a verb to see if it makes sense.

In the sentence *Kai considers the options,* the word *considers* shows action. Then you test it: "She considers." It sounds right. The word *considers* is the verb.

If you thought *options* was the verb, as soon as you tested it, you'd reject that idea. "I option?" "She options?" (See **2a** for more help on finding verbs.)

▶ *Look for the subject next.* Ask *who* or *what* is doing the action of the verb. For the sentence *Kai considers the options,* ask, "Who considers?" Kai considers. Kai is the subject. For the sentence *A truck roared,* ask, "What roared?" A truck roared. *Truck* is the subject.

▶ *Look for the object last.* The object receives the action of the verb. Ask *who* or *what* after you say the verb. For the sentence *Kai considers the options,* ask, "Kai considers what?" The answer is the options. The object of the sentence is *options.*

▶ *Look for verb completers after certain verbs.* Words that complete the verb by describing or naming the subject often come after these verbs:

am	was	feel(s)
is	were	look(s)
are	will be	smell(s)
		seem(s)
		appear(s)
		taste(s)

Oranges taste *sour.*

Metals are *conductors.*

The word *sour* completes the verb *taste* by describing the subject, *oranges.* The word *conductors* completes the verb *are* by giving an additional name to the subject, *metals.*

The basic sentence pattern is:

Subject—Verb—Object or **Verb Completer**

We can add other words and phrases telling more about the subject, verb, object, and verb completer, but the basic pattern stays the same. Notice in the following examples that no matter how many words and phrases we add to give more information, the basic pattern remains the same:

> *Kai* [**subject**], confronted with a decision about what to do this summer *considers* [**verb**] the options of working, traveling, going to school, and just taking it easy.

> Containing citric acid, an ingredient in all citrus fruits, even ripe *oranges* [**subject**] *taste* [**verb**] to some degree *sour* [**verb completer**], although not usually as sour as lemons or grapefruit.

1b   SENTENCE FRAGMENTS

A fragment is a broken-off part. A sentence fragment is a broken-off part of a sentence.

A sentence fragment is missing words that would turn it into a complete sentence. Sometimes a fragment has a subject with no verb; sometimes it has a verb with no subject. Sometimes a fragment is only a group of describing words without either subject or verb. Sometimes a sentence fragment is simply a broken-off part of the sentence that came before, needing only to be attached where it belongs.

Finding Fragments

▶ Does the sentence have a subject? See **1b(3).**

▶ Does the sentence have a verb? See **1b(2).**

▶ Is the verb complete or is it only *part* of a two- or three-word verb? See **1b(4)** and **1b(5).**

▶ Does the verb need a completer or an object? See **1a.**

▶ Is there a word group that should be linked to another sentence? See **1b(6).**

1b(1)   Descriptive Word Groups as Fragments

> The troubled mayor consulted Professor Kona. *An expert on community relations.*

> Some days nothing can make me move. *On hot and sunny days.*

To correct: The descriptive words usually refer to a person, thing, or action in a nearby sentence. Attach the fragment to that sentence, or write a new sentence that explains the idea fully.

> The troubled mayor consulted Professor Kona, an expert on community relations.

> Some days nothing can make me move. On hot and sunny days, *I lie on the beach lazily.*

1b(2)   No-Verb Fragments

> A new shopping mall just opened. *Department stores, record shops, and shoe stores.*

To correct: Add a verb and any needed verb completers or attach the fragment to a sentence (you may have to add some words).

> A new shopping mall just opened. Department stores, record shops, and shoe stores *are already crowded.*

> A new shopping mall just opened *with* department stores, record shops, and shoe stores.

1b(3)   No-Subject Fragments

> The drummers finished their song. *Looked up at the audience.*

To correct: Combine the fragment with a nearby sentence. You may have to add words to make the combination make sense.

> The drummers finished their song *and* looked up at the audience.

Or you can make a new sentence by adding a subject to the fragment.

> The drummers finished their song. *They* looked up at the audience.

1b(4)   The *to* Form of the Verb as a Fragment

> The court decided to uphold the fair housing law. To change patterns of discrimination.

To correct: Putting the word *to* in front of a verb changes the verb into an infinitive (see **2c**). An infinitive cannot by itself be the main verb of a sentence. In our example, *to change* cannot be the main verb. Further, there is no subject in the fragment. You must add a subject and full verb to make this kind of fragment a complete sentence.

> The court decided to uphold the fair housing law. *The judges wanted to change patterns of discrimination.*

Or you can add the fragment to a nearby sentence, as long as it makes sense. You may have to add joining words like *and* or *in order to.*

> The court decided to uphold the fair housing law *in order to* change patterns of discrimination.

1b(5) The *ing* Form of the Verb as a Fragment

> The explosion took everyone by surprise. *Bricks flying everywhere.*

To correct: In this fragment the word ending in *ing* (*flying*) is not a verb— it is only part of a verb. But you can add a word such as *is, are, was,* or *were* to make the *ing* form into a verb. (See **2c.**)

> The explosion took everyone by surprise. Bricks *were flying* everywhere.

Or you can add the fragment to a nearby sentence, as long as it makes sense.

> The explosion took everyone by surprise, bricks flying everywhere.

1b(6) Dependent Word Groups as Fragments

> Holidays in my village include storytelling. *When old people tell tales of long ago.*
>
> *Because we slept late.* We missed the first story.
>
> We arrived in time to hear Ramón. *Who tells of adventure in a deep, mysterious voice.*

To correct: A dependent word group (dependent clause) has a subject and a verb (as in all the fragments above); however, to be used correctly, it must link onto another sentence. The words *when, because,* and *who* in the fragments must connect to complete sentences.

> Holidays in my village include storytelling, *when* old people tell tales of long ago.
>
> *Because* we slept late, we missed the first story.

> We arrived in time to hear Ramón, *who* tells of adventure in a deep, mysterious voice.

You could also correct this kind of fragment by leaving out the linking word. (You may have to add some other words to complete the sentence.)

> Holidays in my village include storytelling. Old people tell tales of long ago.

> We slept late. We missed the first story.

> We arrived in time to hear Ramón. *He* tells of adventure in a deep, mysterious voice.

See also **1c(3)**.

1c   COMBINED SENTENCES

To improve your writing, you often need to put together sentences that have related ideas. Two or more simple sentences may be combined to show that the statements fit closely together. The way you combine the sentences shows their relationship.

Here are some ways to combine sentences:

▶ Join two complete sentences together with a semicolon. See **1c(1)**.

▶ Join sentences together equally with the linking words *and, but, or, nor, for, yet, so* (coordinating conjunctions). See **1c(2)**.

▶ Make one sentence a dependent word group (dependent or subordinate clause) by using a dependent linking word (subordinating conjunction). Join the dependent word group to another sentence (independent clause). See **1c(3)**.

Make sure you combine sentences only when you have a good reason; otherwise, you will make sentences that go on and on unnecessarily. Overcombined sentences are rambling and hard to follow, as in this example:

> The watch that I bought downtown when I went to visit my aunt who lives in Chicago has worked very well, and I use it all the time; in fact, I am wearing it right now, and I intend to wear it tonight at a

> formal dinner party, and I will wear it tomorrow on the beach because it is good-looking and sturdy.

A number of smaller sentences would express the same message much more clearly:

> I bought a watch when I visited my aunt, who lives in downtown Chicago. The watch works very well; it is good-looking and sturdy. I wear it all the time. I am wearing it now and will wear it tonight at a formal dinner party and tomorrow at the beach.

See the chart on page 455 for an explanation of how to punctuate combined sentences.

1c(1)   Two Sentences Joined by a Semicolon (coordination)

When two statements are very closely related, a semicolon joins them effectively. Often the two sentences joined by a semicolon have similar sentence structure.

> Kevin couldn't tell a cow from a hog; he had never been out of the city.

> Vera sent her parents in Hong Kong the good news by letter; her sister Irene sent the news by telegram.

You may also use a semicolon to join a sentence to another sentence that starts with a special connecting word like *however, therefore, furthermore, for example, on the other hand, in fact.*

> Marylou ate no popcorn; *however,* she loved gum.

> Children cry easily; *for example,* Marylou screamed because she hated popcorn.

Remember: the semicolon may be used to join two complete sentences only if the ideas of the sentences are connected very closely.

1c(2)   Two Sentences Joined by *and, but, or, nor, for, yet,* or *so* (coordination)

When you combine sentences in this way, each sentence is equally important. Be sure to use a comma after the first sentence and before the connecting word.

Anthony used to own a motorcycle, *but* he sold it to Rosemarie.

Remember: do not string too many sentences together using these linking words. It is better to keep the sentences separate unless you have a good reason for putting them together.

1c(1) and **1c(2)** explain **coordination.** In coordination, you put together ideas that have the same importance. In other words, you join sentences of equal strength and value.

1c(3)   Two Sentences Joined by a Dependent Linking Word (subordination)

Unlike *and, but, or, nor, for, yet, so,* and the semicolon, some words join sentences together so that one sentence needs the other in order to make sense. The part that cannot now stand by itself is called a **dependent clause.** The part that can stand by itself is the **independent clause.** Look at this sentence:

I take care of the car *because* I own it.

The word group *because I own it* cannot be a complete sentence. It depends on the complete thought *I take care of the car* in order to make sense. The word *because* is a dependent linking word; it turns *I own it* into a dependent clause.

Dependent linking words (subordinating conjunctions) begin word groups which, though they contain a subject and a verb, need to be joined to a complete sentence. You should make sure that you do not have a sentence fragment whenever you use one of the linking words.

Dependent Linking Words
▶ To show when: *before, after, while, since, until, once, whenever, when, as long as, as soon as*
▶ To show where: *where, wherever*
▶ To show why: *as, because, in order that, so that, since*
▶ To show how: *how, if*
▶ To show under what condition: *although, though, if, unless, provided, in case, once*
▶ To tell more about someone: *who, whose, that, whom*
▶ To tell more about some place or thing: *which, whose, that*

PUNCTUATING COMBINED SENTENCES

► Two sentences joined by a semicolon:

[Full sentence]; [full sentence].

OR

[Full sentence]; $\left\{ \begin{array}{l} \textit{however} \\ \textit{therefore} \\ \textit{thus} \\ \textit{for example} \\ \textit{in any case} \\ \text{etc.} \end{array} \right\}$, [full sentence].

► Two sentences joined by *and, but, or, nor, for, yet:*

[Full sentence], $\left\{ \begin{array}{l} \textit{and} \\ \textit{but} \\ \textit{or} \\ \textit{nor} \\ \textit{for} \\ \textit{yet} \end{array} \right\}$ [full sentence].

► Two sentences joined by a dependent linking word:

1. Dependent word group at the beginning:

$\left. \begin{array}{l} \textit{Before} \\ \textit{If} \\ \textit{Since} \\ \text{etc.} \end{array} \right\}$ [dependent word group] , [full sentence].

2. Dependent word group in the middle:

[First part of complete sentence], $\left\{ \begin{array}{l} \textit{who} \\ \textit{which} \\ \textit{whom} \\ \textit{whose} \end{array} \right\}$ [dependent word group], [rest of complete sentence].

OR

[First part of complete sentence] $\left\{ \begin{array}{l} \textit{who} \\ \textit{which} \\ \textit{that} \\ \textit{whose} \end{array} \right\}$ [dependent word group] [rest of complete sentence].

Remember: sometimes you need commas around the dependent section appearing within a complete sentence. Other times you do not. See **7b(1).**

3. Dependent word group at the end:

[Full sentence] $\left\{ \begin{array}{l} \textit{because} \\ \textit{when} \\ \textit{which} \\ \text{etc.} \end{array} \right\}$ [dependent word group].

Dependent word groups come at the beginning, in the middle, or at the end of the complete sentence. Look at the following examples.
Dependent word group at the beginning:

> **Unless** *you hand in the final assignment,* you will not pass.
>
> **If** *that instructor threatens me again,* I will speak to the dean.

Dependent word group in the middle:

> The dean, **who** *was always in hiding,* could not be found.

Dependent word group at the end:

> The instructor was strict **when** *she set the deadlines for assignments.*
>
> The student found out **that** *you can't beat the system.*

When you join ideas together so that one depends on another, the process is called **subordination.** In subordination an idea of less importance (the **dependent** section) is connected to a complete thought (the **independent** section), which has more importance.

1d RUN-ON SENTENCES

Run-on sentences are sentences that are not combined correctly. The suggestions in **1c** should help you avoid run-on problems. But here are some specifics about common run-on errors and how to correct them.

1d(1) Fused Sentences

Fused sentences are two sentences put together without any linking words or any punctuation.

> Juan Montez speaks both Spanish and English his family moved to the United States from Mexico eight years ago.

To correct: Either separate the two sentences or add the needed linking words and punctuation.

> Juan Montez speaks both Spanish and English. *His* family moved to the United States from Mexico eight years ago.
>
> Juan Montez speaks both Spanish and English *because* his family moved to the United States from Mexico eight years ago.

1d(2)   Comma Splices

Comma splices are two or more complete sentences put together with just a comma.

> Maria Lonedeer attends tribal meetings, she is proud of her heritage.

To correct: Separate the sentences with a period, replace the comma with a semicolon, or use a joining word.

> Maria Lonedeer attends tribal meetings. She is proud of her heritage.

> Maria Lonedeer attends tribal meetings; she is proud of her heritage.

> Maria Lonedeer attends tribal meetings *because* she is proud of her heritage.

1e   TANGLED SENTENCES

Sentences become tangled when the sentence switches direction in the middle. The switch in direction may happen in a number of different ways. One common way occurs when a single word or group of words is used as part of two separate thoughts.

> Daniel Defoe wrote the novel *Robinson Crusoe* tells the story of a man shipwrecked on a deserted island.

To correct: The words *the novel Robinson Crusoe* serve as both the object of the first part of the tangled sentence and the subject of the second part. Rewrite the tangled sentence as two separate sentences or make one part of the sentence dependent on the other.

> Daniel Defoe wrote the novel *Robinson Crusoe*. **The novel** tells the story of a man shipwrecked on a deserted island.

> Daniel Defoe wrote the novel *Robinson Crusoe*, **which** tells the story of a man shipwrecked on a deserted island.

Sentences also become tangled when two similar phrases are confused.

> Through his adventures, Robinson Crusoe learns that he is capable to take care of himself.

To correct: The sentence confuses the two phrases *capable of taking care* and *able to take care*. Rewrite the sentence to use only one phrase or the other.

Through his adventures, Robinson Crusoe learns that he is *capable of taking care* of himself.

Through his adventures, Robinson Crusoe learns that he is *able to take care* of himself.

Finally, sentences can become tangled when a dependent word group is put at the beginning of the sentence and the writer forgets to include a subject for the independent word group.

Because Crusoe kept a detailed diary, could look back on his accomplishments.

To correct: Add a subject to the independent word group.

Because Crusoe kept a detailed diary, *he* could look back on his accomplishments.

1f   MISPLACED AND DANGLING DESCRIPTIVE WORDS

Watch where you place descriptive words and word groups. They should appear next to the words they describe. Each of the following sentences means something different simply because of the position of the word *only*.

Only the karate champion could smash bricks with her hand. (No other person could do this.)

The *only* karate champion could smash bricks with her hand. (There was no other karate champion.)

The karate champion could *only* smash bricks with her hand. (She had no other skills.)

The karate champion could smash *only* bricks with her hand. (She could not smash other things.)

The karate champion could smash bricks *only* with her hand. (She could not use any other part of her body to do this.)

The karate champion could smash bricks with *only* her hand. (She did not need the help of anything else.)

The karate champion could smash bricks with her *only* hand. (She had just one hand.)

Sentences often change their meaning when a descriptive word group is in the wrong place.

> In the large carton, Sarah found her missing clothes.

This says that Sarah is in the carton. The describing words *in the large carton* are in the wrong place.

> Sarah found **her missing clothes** *in the large carton.*

This sentence is correct: *in the large carton* tells where the clothes were.

Often *ing* and *ed* word groups "dangle" because writers place them next to the wrong word. Dangling words (dangling modifiers) either describe the wrong thing or they describe nothing at all.

> *Weighing ninety-seven pounds,* football was too dangerous for James.

This says that football, the game, weighs ninety-seven pounds.

> *Weighing ninety-seven pounds,* **James** found football too dangerous.

This sentence is correct: it says *James* weighs ninety-seven pounds.

> *Frightened by the police,* the sewer hid the robbers.

This says that the sewer was frightened by the police.

> *Frightened by the police,* **the robbers** hid in the sewer.

Here we see that the *robbers* were frightened. This sentence is correct.

To correct misplaced descriptive words:

▶   Place descriptive words as close as possible to the word they describe.

▶   If the misplaced descriptive word group begins with the *ing* or *ed* form of a verb:

1. Put the word being described right after the descriptive word group.

   > *Weighing ninety-seven pounds,* **James** found football too dangerous.

2. Rewrite the descriptive word group to include the word being described.

   > Because **James** *weighed only ninety-seven pounds*, he found football too dangerous.

1g   SOME POINTERS ON SENTENCE FORM

▶   *Do not leave out needed words.*

WRONG   Officer reported suspect left Empire State Build-
               ing nine o'clock.

RIGHT   *The* officer reported *that the* suspect left *the* Em-
               pire State Building *at* nine o'clock.

▶   *Complete all comparisons.*

WRONG   This year the women's tennis tournament was
               more exciting.

RIGHT   This year the women's tennis tournament was
               more exciting *than the men's tournament.*

▶   *If you list words or phrases in a series, make each item in
     the list similar to the others in grammar and logic* (parallel-
     ism). By keeping the items in the list parallel, you help the
     reader see how the items fit together.

WRONG   For dinner we had French onion soup, thick
               steaks, fresh corn on the cob, giant salads, straw-
               berry shortcake, and soft background music.

RIGHT   For dinner we had French onion soup, thick
               steaks, fresh corn on the cob, giant salads, *and*
               strawberry shortcake; soft background music
               filled the air.

The items you use in a series can be the names of things, as in
the example just above, which lists a series of objects for the
verb *had*. The basic structure of that sentence is:

We [subject] had [verb] ⎧ soup [object]
                        ⎪ steaks [object]
                        ⎨ corn [object]
                        ⎪ salads [object]
                        ⎩ shortcake. [object]

You can also list any other sentence parts such as subjects,
verbs, adjectives, or prepositional phrases. You can even add
whole sentences together in series. However, in each case, you
must make sure the items in the list are parallel. Each item in
the list must be of the same kind. For example, look at the

following sentences. Although the sentence structures vary, the items in each list are parallel.

Presidents Fillmore, Garfield, and *Harding* have little fame.

$$\left.\begin{array}{l}\text{subject}\\\text{subject}\\\text{subject}\end{array}\right\}\text{verb}\quad\text{object}$$

The cheetah *spotted, chased,* and *attacked* its prey.

$$\text{subject}\left\{\begin{array}{l}\text{verb}\\\text{verb}\\\text{verb}\end{array}\right\}\text{object}$$

Because *the temperature is high, humidity is low,* and *winds are heavy,* we may have a dust storm.

$$\begin{array}{c}\text{Dependent}\\\text{linking}\\\text{word}\end{array}\left\{\begin{array}{lll}\text{subject}&\text{verb}&\text{verb completer}\\\text{subject}&\text{verb}&\text{verb completer}\\\text{subject}&\text{verb}&\text{verb completer}\end{array}\right\}\text{subject verb object}$$

Now compare this example of a list in which the items are *not* parallel:

WRONG   The invader from outer space burned down Los Angeles, blew up Houston, destroyed New York, and to annihilate Chicago.

To correct: All the items in the list have verbs that go with the subject *the invader,* except for the last item, which has an infinitive. Change the last item to use a parallel verb form, *annihilated.*

RIGHT   The invader from outer space *burned* down Los Angeles, *blew* up Houston, *destroyed* New York, and *annihilated* Chicago.

Here is another example of an item that does not match the others in the list:

WRONG   During an inflation, prices increase, wages go up, but value of money going down.

To correct: The first two items in the list are independent word groups, but the last is not. Change to make them all independent.

RIGHT   During an inflation, *prices increase, wages go up,* but *the value of money goes down.*

▶ *Vary sentence lengths and types.* If all your sentences follow the same pattern, your readers may find them boring and hard to follow. Try to mix long and short, simple and combined sentences together.

POOR

The first computers used mechanical parts. The next computers used vacuum tubes. The next computers used transistors. The next computers used silicone chips. Computers now use thousands of integrated circuits on a single chip.

BETTER

Although the first computers used only mechanical parts, later models switched to electricity with vacuum tubes and then transistors. The transistors were then miniaturized and combined into integrated circuits on silicone chips. A single silicone chip now can hold thousands of circuits.

2

Verbs

2a WHAT IS A VERB?

The **verb** is the word (or words) that tells what the subject of the sentence does. The verb tells the action of the sentence. Sometimes the action is full of motion, as in this sentence:

The player *cuts, fakes,* and *shoots* a basket.

Sometimes the action only shows how a thing is or exists, as in these examples.

The patient *appears* healthy.

The test results *were* negative.

If you are not sure whether a word is the verb of a sentence, put *I, you,* and *it* in front of the word, one at a time. If any of the resulting word groups makes sense as a sentence, the word is a verb.

tree: I *tree?* You *tree?* (Not a verb)

wrestle: I *wrestle.* You *wrestle.* (Verb)

see: I *see.* You *see.* (Verb)

2b AGREEMENT OF SUBJECT AND VERB

The form of the verb changes in the present tense, depending on who does the action and when the action takes place. When one person or thing does an action, the verb that shows the action must be singular. Most singular verbs in the present tense end in *s.*

The boy *sings.*

He *laughs.*

When more than one person or thing does an action, the verb that shows the action must be plural. Plural verbs in the present tense do not end in *s*.

> Boys *sing*.
>
> They *laugh*.

There are some exceptions to this rule. In the present tense, the words *I* and *you* always work with a verb without an *s* ending.

> I *sing*.   You *sing*.
>
> I *laugh*.   You *laugh*.

When you use the helping verb *do* in front of another verb, only this helping verb changes form with different subjects (*do, does*). The second, main verb does not add an *s* for the singular.

> He *agrees*.   He *does agree*.   They *do agree*.

The helping verb *do* is used for emphasis, for negatives, and for questions.

> I *do agree*.   He *does agree*.
>
> I *do* not *agree*.   He *does* not *agree*.
>
> *Do* I *agree?*   *Does* he *agree?*

Some verbs have the same form for singular and plural in the present tense. These verbs include *can, may, must, ought,* and *will*.

> I *must*.   We *must*.
>
> He *must*.   They *must*.

These verbs (modal verbs) are often used as helping verbs. In such verb combinations, as with *do* above, the verbs appearing after the first helping verb do not change form for singular or plural.

> He *must go*.   They *must go*.
>
> He *can be going*.   They *can be going*.

Here are a few more examples of subject-verb agreement in the present tense:

> I *go*.   I *do go*.   I *can go*.
>
> You *go*.   You *do go*.   You *can go*.
>
> She, he, it *goes*.   She, he, it *does go*.   She, he, it *can go*.

| We *go*. | We *do go*. | We *can go*. |
| They *go*. | They *do go*. | They *can go*. |

Remember: in tenses other than the present, the verb usually does not change form with different subjects. The verb *to be* is an exception to these rules of agreement, however. It has its own set of singular and plural forms, which are given in the chart below.

FORMS OF THE VERB *TO BE*

The verb *to be* has many different forms and causes agreement problems in the past tense as well as the present. You must learn these forms:

Present

I *am*	I *am* hungry.
you *are*	You *are* friendly.
he *is*, she *is*, it *is*	She *is* happy.
we *are*	We *are* finished.
they *are*	They *are* late.

Past

I *was*	I *was* here.
you *were*	You *were* right.
he *was*, she *was*, it *was*	He *was* tense.
we *were*	We *were* in agreement.
they *were*	They *were* crazy.

In the perfect tenses use the form *been* with the correct helping verbs *has*, *have*, or *had*.

John *has been* angry for an hour.

They *have been* away for a week.

Regina *had been* arrested before then.

Warning: *be* cannot by itself be used as a verb. A sentence like *He be here* is not correct. Use *be* only with other verbs or with the word *to*.

The toy *can be* fixed.

I plan *to be* at the park.

Singular or Plural?

In some cases it isn't easy to tell whether a verb should be singular or plural. The following rules can help you to make up your mind.

▶ If two or more subjects are added together, use the plural verb.

Basketball and hockey **attract** large crowds.

▶ If you have a choice of subjects in an *either . . . or* (or *neither . . . nor*) word group, use a verb that works with the subject nearest the verb.

Either *five pieces* of gum or one coconut *bar* **costs** a quarter.

▶ To decide whether to use *there is* or *there are* (or *here is* or *here are*), check the subject that comes after the verb.

There **is** one *can* of beans on the shelf.

There **are** twelve *cans* of soup.

▶ In a dependent word group beginning with *who, which,* or *that,* check the word that *who, which,* or *that* refers to and make the verb agree with it.

The sewing *machine, which* still **works,** now sits in the closet.

The *marbles, which* **are** Alice's prize possession, fall out of the drawer and roll into the corners of the room.

▶ Don't be confused by word groups that come between the subject and the verb. The verb must agree with the subject, not with the extra words that come between the subject and the verb.

The *child* on roller skates ***falls*** on the pavement.

The *books* given to the library ***sit*** in the storage room.

▶ *Anyone, anybody, anything, everyone, everybody, everything, nobody, nothing, someone, somebody,* and *something* used as subjects take singular verbs.

Something *happens.*

Everyone *knows.*

Nobody *cares.*

► Group words (like *class, team, family,* and *army*) usually take singular verbs because each group is one unit.

The *class **votes*** to take the day off.

The *team **leaves*** tomorrow.

2c VERB TENSES

The ability of the verb to show time is called **tense.** We generally show tense by changing the form of the basic verb word.

The basic verb word is called an **infinitive** when it has a *to* in front of it; for example, *to walk* and *to climb* are the infinitives of the basic verb words *walk* and *climb.* The infinitive never changes form. The infinitive cannot by itself be the main verb in a sentence. Each of the following sentences uses the infinitive *to go,* but it is not the main verb.

They *want* to go.

They *wanted* to go.

The form of the verb can tell the reader whether the action takes place in the past, the present, or the future. Other verb tenses can show more precise time ideas, as the table on pp. 468–469 shows. Look at the table before you go on.

To make the past tense, you usually add *d* or *ed* to the verb. To make the perfect tenses, you usually use *have, has,* or *had* with the form of the verb that ends in *d* or *ed.*

Remember: when you have verb phrases made up of several verbs, only the first verb changes form with tense.

She *has* been writing.

She *had* been writing.

FORMATION OF VERB TENSES

	Use	*How to Form*
Present	to show what happens now or can happen at any time	the present form of the verb (add *s* or *es* for all singular subjects except *I* and *you:* see **2b**)
Past	to show what happened at a fixed time in the past	the verb + *d* or *ed* (see list on pages 470–472 for irregular forms)
Future	to show what will happen in the future	*will* + present form of the verb
Present Perfect	to show what has happened in the past and continues in the present; to show what happened in the past, but at no particular time	*have* (or *has* for all singular subjects except *I* and *you*) + *d* or *ed* form of the verb (see list on pages 470–472 for irregular forms)
Past Perfect	to show an action in the past that happened even before another event in the past	*had* + *d* or *ed* form of verb (see list on pages 470–472 for irregular forms)
Future Perfect	to show something that has not yet been done but that will be done before a set time in the future	*will have* + *d* or *ed* form of verb (see list on pages 470–472 for irregular forms)
Present Continuous	to show an event that is going on right now	*am, is* (for singular subjects) or *are* (for plural subjects and *you*) + verb with *ing* ending
Past Continuous	to show an event that was going on when something else happened	*was* (for singular subjects) or *were* (for plural subjects and *you*) + verb with *ing* ending
Future Continuous	to show an event that will be going on when something else happens	*will be* + *ing* form of verb

FORMATION OF VERB TENSES (*cont.*)

Example	Sentence Example
sleep *works*	Now I **sleep.** The washer **works.** We **work** as mail carriers.
talked	Yesterday Lenora **talked** with Harold.
will fly	In the future rockets **will fly** to Mars every week.
have lived *has moaned*	I **have lived** in this house for seven years. The cat **has moaned** for ten minutes in the rain.
had stopped	The car **had stopped** before the truck hit it.
will have completed	By tomorrow Steve **will have completed** the term paper.
am building *is building* *are building*	I **am building** a table. Luisa **is building** a robot in the garage. She and her sister **are building** a model plane.
was rowing *were rowing*	I **was rowing** on Massapequa Lake when it began to rain. Sarah and Maxine **were rowing** swiftly when their oars broke.
will be reading	The guard **will be reading** a newspaper when we sneak up on him.

Many verbs work in special ways. They do not follow the usual rules when they change tense. For the irregular verbs in the list below,

▶ use the verb form from column A to make the present and future tenses.
▶ use the verb form from column B to make the past tense.
▶ use the verb form from column C to make the perfect tenses— and be sure to use *have, has,* or *had* with it.

Common Irregular Verb Forms

A	B	C
Present	*Past*	*Perfect*
awake	awoke	awaked
beat	beat	beaten
become	became	become
begin	began	begun
bend	bent	bent
bet	bet	bet
bite	bit	bitten
bleed	bled	bled
blow	blew	blown
bring	brought	brought
burst	burst	burst
buy	bought	bought
catch	caught	caught
choose	chose	chosen
come	came	come
cost	cost	cost
cut	cut	cut
dig	dug	dug
do	did	done
draw	drew	drawn
drink	drank	drunk
drive	drove	driven
eat	ate	eaten
fall	fell	fallen
feed	fed	fed
feel	felt	felt
fight	fought	fought
find	found	found
fly	flew	flown
forget	forgot	forgotten
freeze	froze	frozen
get	got	gotten, got

Common Irregular Verb Forms (*cont.*)

A *Present*	B *Past*	C *Perfect*
give	gave	given
go	went	gone
grow	grew	grown
hang	hung	hung
have	had	had
hide	hid	hidden
hit	hit	hit
hold	held	held
hurt	hurt	hurt
keep	kept	kept
know	knew	known
lay	laid	laid
lead	led	led
leave	left	left
lend	lent	lent
let	let	let
lie	lay	lain
light	lighted, lit	lighted, lit
lose	lost	lost
make	made	made
mean	meant	meant
meet	met	met
put	put	put
quit	quit	quit
read	read	read
ride	rode	ridden
ring	rang	rung
rise	rose	risen
run	ran	run
see	saw	seen
sell	sold	sold
send	sent	sent
shake	shook	shaken
shine	shone	shone
shoot	shot	shot
show	showed	shown
shrink	shrank	shrunk
shut	shut	shut
sing	sang	sung
sink	sank	sunk
sit	sat	sat
sleep	slept	slept
slide	slid	slid

Common Irregular Verb Forms (*cont.*)

A	B	C
Present	*Past*	*Perfect*
speak	spoke	spoken
speed	sped	sped
spend	spent	spent
spin	spun	spun
spring	sprang	sprung
stand	stood	stood
steal	stole	stolen
stick	stuck	stuck
sting	stung	stung
strike	struck	struck
swear	swore	sworn
sweep	swept	swept
swim	swam	swum
swing	swung	swung
take	took	taken
teach	taught	taught
tear	tore	torn
tell	told	told
think	thought	thought
throw	threw	thrown
wear	wore	worn
weave	wove	woven
weep	wept	wept
win	won	won
wind	wound	wound
wring	wrung	wrung
write	wrote	written

2d   ACTIVE AND PASSIVE VERBS

For **active** verbs the doer of the action is the subject of the sentence.

*Harriet **uses** the drill.*

Passive, on the other hand, means "quietly receiving." With passive verbs the receiver of the action is the subject of the sentence.

*The drill **is used** by Harriet.*

The passive form of a verb includes part of the verb *to be* (*am, is, are, was, were, will be*) and the form of the verb used in perfect tenses. (For irregular verbs see column C in the list on pages 470–472.)

Generally, passive verbs are less direct and are wordier than active verbs. In most cases you should write active, rather than passive, sentences.

PASSIVE	*receiver* The extra furniture *is stored* in the attic by the *doer* Brown family.
ACTIVE	*doer* *receiver* The Brown family *stores* extra furniture in the attic.
PASSIVE	*receiver* The car *was driven* over thirty thousand miles last *doer* year by the traveling salesperson.
ACTIVE	*doer* *receiver* The traveling salesperson *drove* the car over thirty thousand miles last year.

2e   NEEDLESS SHIFTS IN TENSE

Sometimes you need to shift one tense to another in a sentence or in a paragraph. But you can confuse readers if you shift tense without any real reason. Look at this example:

> (1) Tony *stormed* into the room and he *looks* at nobody. (2) His mouth *twitches* in anger. (3) Finally he *spoke*. (4) He *asks*, "Who *wants* to tell me what *happened* to my car?"

These sentences shift tense without any reason. In sentence 1 *stormed* is a past tense verb—but *looks* is in the present tense. Why? In sentence 2 *twitches* is a present tense verb; but in sentence 3 *spoke* is in the past. In sentence 4 the writer uses *asks*, present tense again. Look at the sentences correctly written:

> (1) Tony *stormed* into the room and he *looked at* nobody. (2) His mouth *twitched* in anger. (3) Finally he *spoke*. (4) He *asked*, "Who *wants* to tell me what *happened* to my car?"

WATCH YOUR VERB ENDINGS: A REVIEW CHART

▶ Use an *s* or *es* at the end of almost all verbs in the present tense that go with *he, she, it,* one person's name, or the name of one thing.

He *goes* away.   (NOT He go away.)

John *runs* from his aunt.   (NOT John run from his aunt.)

The book *sits* on the chair.   (NOT The book sit on the chair.)

▶ Do not use *s* at the end of verbs that go with *I, you, we, they,* more than one person's name, or the names of more than one thing.

I *go* away.   (NOT I goes away.)

We *run* from Aunt Jane.   (NOT We runs from Aunt Jane.)

Roberta and Mark *sit* on the chair.   (NOT Roberta and Mark sits on the chair.)

▶ Put a *d* or *ed* at the end of a verb to form the past tense of all regular verbs used with any subject.

I *dressed* quickly.

He *dressed* quickly.

We *dressed* quickly.

▶ Put a *d* or *ed* at the end of a verb to form the perfect tenses of all regular verbs used with any subject.

Roberta and Mark have *dressed*.

Jane has *dressed*.

We all had *dressed* by then.

▶ Put a *d* or an *ed* at the end of a verb to make the passive form of all regular verbs used with a form of the verb *to be*.

The baby *was dressed* by her father.

▶ Put a *d* an *ed*, or an *ing* at the end of all regular verbs used as adjectives (see page 483).

the *called* number	the *calling* person
the *disconnected* telephone	the *disconnecting* operator

▶ Use the forms of irregular verbs according to the explanation on pages 470–472.

▶ Use the forms of the verb *to be* according to the explanation on page 465.

Notice that the present tense verbs were changed to the past tense. In the statement Tony makes in sentence 4, however, the tense shift is all right. First, Tony's words are quoted exactly. Next, he asks a question in the present tense ("Who *wants*") about an event that occurred in the past ("what *happened*"). There is a reason to shift tenses.

3

Pronouns

Pronouns are words that take the place of names of persons or objects.

> Psychology is the study of human minds. *It* is a social science.
>
> Mary likes chocolate mints. *She* eats *them* every night.

In the first sentence *it* is a pronoun; it takes the place of *psychology.*

In the second sentence *she* takes the place of *Mary,* and *them* takes the place of *chocolate mints.* Both *she* and *them* are pronouns.

3a PRONOUN REFERENCES

Use the name of a person or an object at least once before you use a pronoun because it must always be clear which word the pronoun replaces. In the following example, the pronouns *she* and *her* refer to *Jane Austen. Them* refers to her novels.

> Jane Austen wrote *her* novels in the early nineteenth century. In *them, she* described middle- and upper-class British life at that time.

If there is any chance the reader will get confused, either because the pronoun is too far away from the word it replaces or because the pronoun might refer to a word it is not meant to replace, you should not use a pronoun. In the following example, the reader does not know who enjoyed the experience: the boys, the girls, or both.

> UNCLEAR   The boys kissed the girls; they liked it.
> BETTER   The boys kissed the girls; they all liked it.

Make sure you use the right pronoun for the persons or things you are describing. If you shift pronouns, it may seem as if you are writing about something new.

WEAK
College students have difficult lives. *I* have to work hard. *You* have to be motivated.

IMPROVED
College students have difficult lives. *They* have to work hard. *They* have to be motivated.

3b   PRONOUNS AND GENDER

Be sure not to use the male pronouns *he, him,* and *his* when the individual described may be either male or female. You may use the phrases *he or she, him or her, his or her.* You may make the whole sentence plural and use *they, them, their.* Or you may rewrite the sentence to avoid the pronoun. Do not, however, use a plural pronoun if the rest of the sentence remains singular.

WRONG
If *a student* wishes to apply for a loan, *he* should complete an application.

WRONG
If *a student* wishes to apply for a loan, *they* should complete an application.

RIGHT
If *a student* wishes to apply for a loan, *he or she* should complete an application.

RIGHT
If *students wish* to apply for *loans, they* should complete *applications.*

RIGHT
A student who wishes to apply for a loan should complete an application.

3c   PRONOUNS AS SUBJECTS AND OBJECTS

A pronoun can be *singular* or *plural:* it can take the place of one thing or it can take the place of many things. Certain pronouns, however, are always singular: *anyone, everyone, someone, no one, none, anybody, everybody, nobody,* and *somebody.*

Most pronouns change form depending on their place in the sentence, as described on page 478.

As a subject	As an object
I	me
we	us
you	you
he	him
she	her
it	it
they	them
who	whom

Use the **subject form** of the pronoun when:

▶   the pronoun is the subject of the sentence.

She eats lunch.

They screamed.

The pronoun may be part of a double subject, so be careful.

Annette and *she* eat lunch.

▶   the pronoun comes after a form of the verb *to be* (see **2c**).

The winner was *she*.

It was *I* who spoke.

▶   the pronoun is part of a comparison sentence and is parallel to the subject of the sentence.

Francine programs computers better than *I*.

Use the **object form** of the pronoun when:

▶   the pronoun is an object of the sentence (see **1a**).

Antoine pushed *him*.

▶   the pronoun comes after a word that shows direction or relationship like *behind, to, from, in, on, above, below, near, with,* and *beside*. (See Chapter 5 for more on prepositions.)

Bring the book to *me*.

He sang with *her*.

The dog sat beside *him*.

Remember: even if the pronoun is part of a double object, you still use the object form.

> Fran stood between Fred and *me*.

Students often have problems in deciding which pronoun to use when a double subject or a double object appears in a sentence. To avoid such problems, take one word in the double subject or object at a time.

> Stella and _____ drove to school yesterday.

If you do not know, for example, whether to use *him* or *he* in the blank, first think, "*Stella* drove to school." Then think, "*Him* drove to school." That doesn't sound right. Only "*He* drove to school" sounds right. Now return to the sentence with the blank and fill in the correct word:

> Stella and *he* drove to school yesterday.

If you do not know whether to use *him* or *he* in the following blank, take one word at a time:

> They drove to school with Stella and _____.

First think, "They drove to school with *Stella*." Then think, "They drove to school with *he*." That doesn't sound right. Only "They drove to school with *him*" sounds right. Now return to the sentence with the blank and fill in the correct word:

> They drove to school with Stella and *him*.

3d   PRONOUNS THAT SHOW OWNERSHIP

The following possessive forms of the pronouns show that the person or thing replaced by the pronoun owns something:

> my, mine
> our, ours
> your, yours
> his
> her, hers
> its
> their, theirs

his cat	*her* dog	The hat is *yours*.
my goldfish	*their* monkey	The coat is *mine*.

Remember: do not use an apostrophe with a pronoun that shows ownership. If you write *it's,* you mean "it is." However, an apostrophe is required to show ownership with words such as *anyone's, everyone's, somebody's, nobody's.*

── GUIDE TO USING PRONOUNS ──

▶ Make sure it is clear to which word the pronoun refers.

▶ Use the form of the pronoun (singular or plural; male, female, or neuter) that agrees with the noun referred to.

▶ Avoid using only a male pronoun when referring to a person who could be male or female. Use *he or she,* change the whole sentence to plural, or select a genderless alternative like *person.*

▶ Use the subject, object, or ownership form depending on the pronoun's role in the sentence.

4

Adjectives and Adverbs

Adjectives are words that give more information about nouns (that is, about names of persons, places, or things); **adverbs** are words that tell more about verbs and adjectives. Look at this example:

An honest politician never lies.

The words *an* and *honest* are adjectives. They let you know how many politicians (*an*) and what kind of politician (*honest*). Adjectives usually tell *what kind, what size, what color, how many,* or *which one.* The word *never* is an adverb. It lets you know when the action of the verb (*lies*) takes place (*never*). Adverbs usually tell *when, how, where,* or *to what extent.*

Do not confuse adjectives and adverbs. Use only adjectives to describe nouns and only adverbs to describe verbs and adjectives. Adjectives almost never end in *ly,* but most adverbs do end in *ly.* In fact, many adjectives can be changed into adverbs simply by adding *ly* (for example, *kind, kindly; slow, slowly; easy, easily*). Study the following examples:

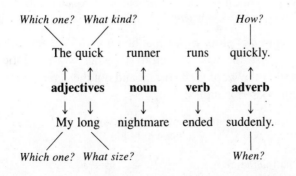

481

Be especially careful in using the adjectives *good* and *bad* and the adverbs *well* and *badly* (see pages 495, 498).

The main purpose of some sentences is to tell you more about the noun that is the subject of the sentence. Such sentences usually have verbs such as *is, looks, feels, seems, becomes,* or *smells.* Use an adjective after these verbs to complete the information about the noun, as in these examples:

> The cheese looks *green.* (What color?)
>
> The meat smells *rotten.* (What kind?)
>
> The mess becomes *enormous.* (What size?)

In each case the adjective describes the noun that stands before the verb.

4a   SINGULAR AND PLURAL ADJECTIVES

Adjectives such as *a, an, this, that, one, any, every, each, another,* and *much* describe only one thing. The noun that follows must be singular. In addition, when you use a singular noun, you usually must use one of these singular adjectives, the word *the,* or a word showing ownership (such as *my* or *John's*) in front of the singular noun. For example:

> *a* party, *this* party, *each* party, *another* party, *the* party, *Carol's* party

The only singular nouns that do not need a singular or ownership adjective in front of them are proper names (that is, the names of specific people, places, or things; for example, *Melinda Jones* or *Michigan State University*) and some collective nouns (words that describe a mass or a collection, such as *rice, beer,* or *school;* see p. 467). For example:

> We grew much *rice* and *wheat,* but after expanding the farm we grew more *rice* and less *wheat.*

Use the word *an* before words that begin with the sound of the letters *a, e, i, o,* or *u.* Use the word *a* before all other words. Notice that the beginning sound of the word is important and not the actual letter that starts the word. Study these examples:

> *a* coconut   *an* excellent coconut
> *an* avocado   *a* green avocado
> *an* F   *a* B
> *a* half *an* hour

Adjectives such as *these, those, all, several, many, two,* and *three* describe more than one thing. The noun that follows them must be plural, but plural nouns do not have to have an adjective in front of them. Use an adjective with a plural noun only to give more information.

> *Pencils* always break.
>
> *Cheap pencils* always break.
>
> *These cheap pencils* always break.

4b   ADJECTIVES MADE FROM VERBS

The *ing* and *ed* forms of verbs are often used as adjectives. Compare the phrases *the depressing news* and *the depressed man, the exciting game* and *the excited crowd.* Be sure not to confuse the meanings of the *ing* and the *ed* forms. The *ing* form lets you know that the noun is actively doing what the adjective describes. The *ed* form usually means the action is being done to the noun (see **2d**). See how the two forms develop in the following examples.

> The news depressed the man.
> > The news was *depressing.* The *depressing* news came as a surprise.
> > The man was *depressed.* The *depressed* man cried.
>
> The game excites the crowd.
> > The game is *exciting.* The *exciting* game ends.
> > The crowd is *excited.* The *excited* crowd cheers.

Whenever you use verb forms as adjectives be sure to use the correct endings. See pages 470–472 for the forms of irregular verbs.

4c   COMPARISONS USING ADJECTIVES
          AND ADVERBS

Adjectives and adverbs can be used to compare two or more things or actions.

> The Hancock Tower is *taller* than the World Trade Center.
>
> Jan eats *more* hungrily than John.

When comparing two items add either an *er* at the end of the adjective or adverb or the word *more* before the adjective or adverb. Do not use both at the same time. Use the *er* ending when the word is short; use the word *more* when the word is long or harder to pronounce.

When comparing three or more items either add an *est* to the end of the adjective or adverb or put the word *most* before the adjective or adverb, depending on the length of the word. Do not use both *est* and *most*.

Look at the following examples:

happy	happier	happiest
happily	more happily	most happily
excited	more excited	most excited
excitedly	more excitedly	most excitedly
early	earlier	earliest

A few words have unusual forms for comparison:

good	better	best
well	better	best
bad	worse	worst
badly	worse	worst

When you write comparisons make sure they are complete (see **1g**).

5

Prepositions and Prepositional Phrases

A **preposition** is a word that goes before a noun or pronoun to make a phrase that acts as an adjective or adverb. The preposition shows how the noun or pronoun is related to the rest of the sentence. For example, look at the following sentence:

Marilyn parked the car in the garage.

The word *in* is a preposition; *in the garage* is a prepositional phrase. The word *in* shows the connection between the garage and the main action of the sentence—parking the car. It tells *where* she parked the car and so acts as an adverb. In the following sentence, the same prepositional phrase *in the garage* serves as an adjective.

The car *in the garage* has a flat tire.

This phrase is an adjective because it identifies *which* car is discussed.

Prepositions Used Most Often

about	before	for	out
above	behind	from	over
across	below	in	through
after	between	inside	to
against	beyond	into	toward
along	by	near	under
among	despite	of	upon
as	during	on	with
at			

The main difficulty most people have with prepositions is knowing which one to use. In particular, certain prepositions often combine with other kinds of words to make standard phrases. The following list presents some combinations that often cause trouble. There are many other similar combinations in English. If you are uncertain about which preposition to use in a combination, a dictionary may give you help.

Some Preposition Combinations

according *to*
agree *on* a plan
agree *to* a proposal
agree *with* a person
angry *at* an event
angry *with* a person
break *down* a door
capable *of*
charge *for* a purchase
charge *with* a crime
clean *up* a house
conform *to*
die *of*
differ *about* a question (to disagree)
differ *from* (to be not like)
differ *with* a person (to disagree)
different *from*
except *for*
fight *for* a cause
fight *with* a person
identical *with*
independent *of*
inferior *to*
in search *of*
open *up* a store
prefer one thing *to* another
prior *to*
rewarded *by* a person
rewarded *for* a deed
rewarded *with* a prize
shut *down* a machine
similar *to*
superior *to*
wait *at* a place
wait *for* an arrival or event
wait *on* a customer

6

Style and Usage

6a SPECIFIC AND GENERAL WORDS

Words that name things do not always tell exactly what the writer means because not all words are **specific** enough. Look at these three words:

animal   horse   colt

The word *animal* could be used to refer to many different kinds of animals: dogs, humans, cats, monkeys. Any word that does not limit meaning for us is called **general;** general, of course, is the opposite of **specific.**

The word *horse* is more specific than *animal* because it limits the meaning to a particular kind of animal. The word *colt* is better still because it gives an even more specific meaning: a colt is a young male horse. The more specific a word is, usually the more **concrete** it is. Concrete words give specific names for things and are especially helpful in giving readers exact information.

Abstract words are words for ideas, things that cannot be touched or seen. *Patience, fear, love, communism,* and *suffering* are abstract words.

Often we need words for ideas and so it is important to use abstract terms. But even when writers must use an abstract word, they need one that is the most specific in stating an idea. In these sentences, all the emphasized words are abstract:

He showed *emotion.*

He showed *fear.*

He showed *terror.*

Emotion, fear, and *terror* are all abstract words because they refer to things we cannot touch or hold. But notice how *terror* is the most specific of the abstract words the writer has chosen. *Emotion* is too general: it could mean love, anger, hate, sorrow, or any strong feeling. *Fear* is better because it limits the kind of emotion the writer wants to tell about. But *terror*, meaning extreme fear, tells exactly what the writer has in mind.

To be specific and concrete:

▶ Think about whether or not the word you have chosen is *exactly* the word you want to use. When you say *nice*, do you mean gentle, thoughtful, or friendly?

▶ Use an exact word whenever you can. Say *hamburger* instead of *meat*, *spinach* instead of *vegetables*, *sparrow* instead of *bird*.

▶ Use details of sight, smell, touch, sound, or action.

General	*Specific*
door	creaking wooden door
building	cool, damp church
bird	fluttering brown wren

▶ Use a dictionary (see **14g**) or a thesaurus to check for specific word meanings, synonyms, and antonyms.

6b   REPETITION

Don't use words that repeat each other's meanings.

POOR	the positive advantages and the negative disadvantages
BETTER	the advantages and disadvantages
POOR	I will begin to start to leave.
BETTER	I will start to leave.
BEST	I will leave.
POOR	The reason is because . . .
BETTER	The reason is that . . .
POOR	Where is the book at?
BETTER	Where is the book?

6c · WORDINESS

Avoid wordy expressions such as these:

Wordy	More direct
a great deal of	much, many
at this point in time	now
being as, being that	because, since
bring to your remembrance	remind you
due to the fact that, on account of the fact that, owing to the fact that	because, since
for the purpose of beginning	to begin
He is the kind of person who likes to talk too much.	He talks too much.
in an angry manner, in an angry way	angrily
in between, out behind	between, behind
in order to bring about the desired end of passing	to pass
in reference to, in regard to	about
in the neighborhood of, in the vicinity of	near
of a friendly nature, of a friendly kind	friendly
One of the things that is important to me is my schoolwork.	My schoolwork is important to me.
The question as to whether	whether
The thing which I want to talk about is . . .	I will talk about . . .
The thing is that George will be late.	George will be late.
which is located in	in

6d   CLICHÉS AND SLOGANS

Clichés are tired, old expressions that no longer carry any strong meaning (for example, *as American as apple pie, wise as an owl,* and *it goes without saying*). Slogans are the catch phrases of different political, social, or other group movements. Look at the following recent American slogans:

What goes around, comes around.

Let's look at the bottom line.

Moving right along . . .

ghostbusters, crimebusters, dustbusters, heatbusters, etc.

When you write clichés and slogans, neither you nor your reader has to think about your meaning. You are passing up a chance to say something more original or significant.

In the following passage the specific troubles of the writer are lost in a fog of clichés. All we learn is that the writer seems unhappy.

> The stresses and strains of the modern world are just too much for any person to cope with. No wonder I feel stressed out and burned out.

If the writer had thought a little more closely about what she really wanted to communicate, she could have defined her condition more specifically and graphically:

> Being a full-time parent, worker, and student leaves me no time to be good at or enjoy any of them. I just run to keep from dropping.

Using the same number of words, she has told us much more.

6e   SHADES OF MEANING

Use the right word to express your exact meaning. Some words, although they mean nearly the same thing, actually mean separate, distinct things. *Boat,* for example, refers to a small craft that is usually open at the top; *ship,* on the other hand, refers to a large seagoing craft.

The small differences between words help you describe different types of similar things quickly and clearly. There are, for example, many types of boats and ships, and each type is described by a specific word. Here are a few of them:

barge	a roomy, flat-bottomed boat
battleship	a large, heavily armed warship
destroyer	a small, fast warship
dinghy	a small rowboat
freighter	a ship for carrying freight

schooner	a large sailing ship
scow	a square-ended barge for carrying garbage or gravel

Not only technical words have shades of meaning. Even when you are writing about human feelings, you need to pay attention to exact shades of meaning. The following words, for example, all describe some kind of unpleasant feeling, but notice how different each is.

envy	a painful awareness that somebody has something you want
jealousy	hostility toward a rival
suspicion	distrust
resentment	a feeling that someone has wronged you
grudge	a long-lasting resentment
revenge	desire to hurt someone in return for what he or she has done
malice	desire to do harm for evil pleasure

The best place to find the shades of meaning of any word is in a dictionary (see **14g**).

6f INCLUSIVE LANGUAGE

Make sure your references to people and groups include all people who appropriately should be included and do not exclude anyone on the basis of race, gender, ethnicity, or other group characteristic. Do not use words that show prejudice against people on the basis of race, sex, national origin, or handicap. Such prejudiced language suggests that all people in a certain group are of lower status than other people. You should avoid insulting words for ethnic or racial groups or for people with handicaps. You should use only words showing respect for individuals in these groups.

Sexist words, however, are sometimes more difficult to spot and avoid than other kinds of prejudiced language. Many words in the English language are based on old notions that only men do certain kinds of jobs and fill certain kinds of roles. Words like *chairman, mailman, weatherman, mankind,* and *forefathers* show a sexist prejudice. Wherever possible, find another term that avoids a sexual stereotype, such as *humankind* or *ancestors*. Because newly invented terms such as *chairperson, mailperson*, and *weatherperson*, although acceptable, may seem awkward, older terms such as *chair* or *head, letter carrier* or *postal clerk*, and *meteorologist* are preferred.

When using pronouns, do not use only male pronouns when the person referred to can be either male or female. Using the phrase *he or she* is acceptable, although sometimes awkward. Rewriting the sentence to make all references plural or to avoid the need for pronouns is usually better. When you are writing a long piece with a number of different pronoun references to different people who may be either male or female, you can also make half the references male and half female. See **3b** for some suggested ways of avoiding sexist pronouns.

6g WORDS COMMONLY CONFUSED

A number of words in English cause problems because they are similar to other words. Here is a list of the most common mistakes.

accept, except
Accept means "to receive willingly."
Except means "leave this one out."

▶ Fran *accepts* the gift.
All my friends *except* Jean wished me a good trip.

adapt, adopt
Adapt means "to change to fit the situation."
Adopt means "to take on as part of oneself."

▶ Kheng *adapted* well to her new job.
She *adopted* a new style of thinking.

advice, advise
Advice is a noun that means "an opinion about what to do."
Advise is a verb that means "to recommend."

▶ Kevin's *advice* was good.
Please *advise* me what to do.

affect, effect
Affect is a verb that means "to change."
Effect is a noun that means "result."

▶ Poor sleep *affects* my mood.
The *effect* of generosity is only sometimes gratitude.

Affect is also a noun that means "feeling."
Effect is also a verb that means "to accomplish."

▶ Winning a competition often is accompanied by the *affect* of elation.
Despite much effort, she could not *effect* the organizational changes that she wanted.

allusion, illusion

An *allusion* is an indirect reference to an idea, person, event, or book.
An *illusion* is a mistaken perception of reality.

▶ The poem has an *allusion* to Plato's idea of the soul.
The idea that the stock market will never go down is an *illusion*.

almost, most

Almost means "nearly."
Most means "more than half."

▶ The robber took *most* of my money; I was left *almost* penniless.

a lot, alot, allot

Alot is an incorrect spelling for *a lot*. *A lot* or *a lot of* is an informal way of saying *many* or *much*. When writing, you should use *many* or *much*.
Allot is a totally different word meaning "to give out shares."

▶ At the fair *many* prizes were given out.
The judges *allot* one prize to each child.

already, all ready

Already (one word) means "before a specific time."
All ready (two words) means "entirely prepared."

▶ It is only noon, but I am *already* tired.
The dinner is *all ready* and on the table.

alright, all right

Alright is incorrect; use only *all right.*

▶ The movie was *all right,* but it wasn't great.

altogether,
all together

Altogether (one word) means "entirely."
All together (two words) means "all in one place."

▶ It is *altogether* too hot.
The math teachers sat *all together* at the meeting.

among, between

Among implies three or more people or things.
Between implies only two.

▶ She divided the ice cream *among* the three children.
The alley runs *between* the two houses.

amount, number

Use *amount* for things in bulk.
Use *number* for things that can be counted.
Similarly, use *little, less,* and *much* for bulk; *few, fewer,* and *many* for counting.

▶ A large *amount* of sugar is in the barrel.
A large *number* of people go hungry every day.

anyone, any one

Anyone (one word) means "any person at all."
Any one (two words) means "any person or thing from a specific group."
Everyone and *every one, someone* and *some one* follow the same pattern.

▶ Does *anyone* want to wash the dishes?
Does *any one* of you children want to wash the dishes?

as, like

Use *as* for word groups with verbs.
Use *like* for word groups without verbs.

▶ Frank practices his flute four hours each day *as* he must to be successful.
Sherry rented a small apartment *like* a closet.

assure, ensure, insure

Assure means "to give confidence and remove doubt" to a person.
Ensure means "to make something certain."
Insure means "to guarantee against loss."

▶ The group leader *assured* the scouts that the trip would not be dangerous.
Careful planning *ensured* the success of the trip.
The scouts *insured* the camp by purchasing a policy.

bad, badly

Bad describes nouns; it is also used after verbs of being, such as *feel* and *look*.
Badly describes verbs.

▶ I had a *bad* time.
The patient looks very *bad*.
Karen plays tennis *badly*.

because of, due to

Due to is too informal for most writing; use *because of*.

▶ *Because of* the high humidity, we fought a constant battle against mold and mildew.

beside, besides

Beside means "next to."
Besides means "in addition to."

▶ The motorcycle is parked *beside* the car.
Besides a car Deborah owned a motorcycle.

breath, breathe

Breath is a noun that means "a gulp of air."
Breathe is a verb that means "to take in and blow out air."

▶ The doctor told me to *breathe* deeply, so I took a deep *breath*.

can, may

Can means "to be able."
May means "to be permitted."

▶ *Can* I run a mile in under four minutes?
You *may* leave the room if you wish.

casual, causal

Casual means "informal or unplanned."
Causal means "relating to a cause."

▶ The meeting was relaxed and *casual*.
The detective found a *causal* connection between Sym's actions and Linnerby's death.

cite, sight, site

Cite is a verb that means "to refer to a text."
Sight is a noun that means "the ability to see."
Site is a noun that means "a place where something happens or is located."

▶ The lawyer *cited* a Supreme Court opinion.
His *sight* was failing because of glaucoma.
We will build a recreation center at this *site*.

complement, compliment

Complement means "to fit well with something else."
Compliment means "to praise someone in person."

▶ Martina *complimented* the designer on how well the color of the dress *complemented* its cut.

conscience, conscious

Conscience is the ability to recognize right and wrong.
Conscious means "aware or awake."

▶ Her *conscience* told her to give back the money.
The boxer was knocked down, but he was still *conscious*.

could have, could've, could of

See *of, have*.

data, media, phenomena

Data, media, and *phenomena* are all plural and must use plural verbs. The singular forms are *datum, medium,* and *phenomenon*.

▶ The *data agree* with the theory.
All the various news *media report* that Congress will act.

Electrical *phenomena were* first observed in the eighteenth century.

desert, dessert

A *desert* is a dry region.
A *dessert* is a sweet at the end of a meal.

▶ Cactus grows in the *desert*.
The Smiths served chocolate cake for *dessert*.

DeSERT (with the accent on the second syllable) can also be a verb, meaning "to leave alone," "to abandon."

▶ Will his wife *desert* him?

discover, invent

To *discover* is to learn about something that already exists, but that people did not know about.
To *invent* is to create something new.

▶ Once humans *discovered* that round objects roll easily, they could then *invent* the wheel.

e.g., i.e.

E.g. is an abbreviation for *exempli gratia,* meaning "as an example."
I.e. is an abbreviation for *id est,* meaning "it is" or "that is."

▶ Southeast Asia has many fruits that are not common in the United States (*e.g.,* rambutans, durians, and loquats).
The person who first complained (*i.e.,* George Williamson) should be responsible for taking action.

emigrate, immigrate

Emigrate means "to leave one country to settle in another."
Immigrate means "to enter and settle in a country where you were not born."

▶ My parents *emigrated* from Poland and *immigrated* to the United States.

enthuse, be enthusiastic

Enthuse is not generally accepted; *be enthusiastic* should always be used instead.

▶ I *am enthusiastic* about the music of John Coltrane.

etc., and etc.

Etc. is an abbreviation for *et cetera,* meaning "and others." Because *etc.* already includes *and,* do not put an additional *and* before it.
Etc. tends to be used too often simply to avoid thinking through the end of a list. Use *etc.* only when it has a clear and specific meaning.

▶ Gathered at the meeting were the college president, deans, teachers, students, *etc.*

everyone, every one

See *anyone, any one.*

farther, further

Farther usually refers to an additional physical distance, while *further* usually refers to additional nontangible amounts.

▶ The *farther* Caroline traveled away from her home, the *further* she felt on her own.

few, fewer, little, less

See *amount, number.*

former, latter

Former means "the first of two people or things."
Latter means "the second of two people or things."

▶ Barbara and Tina both passed; the *former* got an A and the *latter,* a C.

go and, go to, try and, try to, be sure and, be sure to

Go and, try and, and *be sure and* are all incorrect. Use *go to, try to,* and *be sure to.*

▶ Sam must *go to* pay his parking ticket.
You must *be sure to* turn out the lights when you leave.

good, well

Good is an adjective; it describes nouns only.
Well is usually an adverb and so describes verbs, but when it refers to health it can be an adjective and describe nouns.

▶ A *good* dinner warms my heart and fills my stomach.
Mr. Phibbs cooks *well.*
She was sick, but now she is *well.*

had ought, ought *Had ought* is incorrect. Use only *ought.*

▶ I *ought* to be careful when I walk home late at night.

healthful, healthy *Healthful* means "full of those things that make people healthy."
Healthy means "having good health."

▶ Despite Kean Hao's *healthful* diet, he did not look or feel *healthy.*

in, into *In* means "entirely within a space."
Into implies entering the space.

▶ Six people were already *in* the small car when Bob, Jack, Jesse, and Mike tried to get *into* it too.

infer, imply *Infer* means "to conclude something from hints or evidence."
Imply means "to state something indirectly by giving hints."

▶ I *infer* from the report that Smith was doing a poor job.
The report *implies* that Smith was doing a poor job.

irregardless, regardless *Irregardless* is wrong; use only *regardless,* which means "despite."

▶ The governor vowed to improve the schools *regardless* of the expense.

its, it's *Its* is the ownership form of *it.*
It's is a short form of *it is.*

▶ The wolf circled around *its* victim.
This hat may be ugly, but *it's* the latest fashion.

lay, lie *Lay* means "to place, put, or prepare."
Lie means "to stretch oneself out flat" or "to be located."

Check the list of irregular verbs on pages 470–472 for past and perfect forms.

▶ Let me *lay* this package on the table.
Let me *lie* down and take a nap.
The town *lies* north of Boston.

learn, teach

Learn means "to gain knowledge."
Teach means "to give knowledge."

▶ Vera *learned* to count to ten, but then she forgot.
Will you *teach* me how to play chess?

leave, let

Leave means "to depart" or "to cause to remain."
Let means "to permit."

▶ The students wanted to *leave*, but the teacher wouldn't *let* them.
Grandpa made us *leave* our boots on the porch; he refused to *let* us track mud in the house.

loose, lose, loss

Loose is an adjective that means "not tight."
Lose is a verb that means "to misplace."
Loss is a noun that means "a thing no longer in one's possession."

▶ My watchband is *loose*.
I hope I don't *lose* the watch because it would be an expensive *loss*.

maybe, may be

Maybe (one word) means "perhaps."
May be (two words) is a verb form.

▶ *Maybe* the dogs will stop barking, but it *may be* that we will have to listen to them all night.

mine, mines

Mines is wrong; use only *mine* to mean "belonging to me."

▶ The truth may be *mine*, but the power to decide is yours.

moral, morale

Moral means "ethical" or "a lesson at the end of a story."

Morale means "the spirit or mood of a person or group of people."

▶ The *moral* of this story is that one should always behave *morally.*
Our team's *morale* was low after we lost the game.

much, many   See *amount, number.*

must have, must of   See *of, have.*

of, have   *Of* is often incorrectly used for *have* with verb forms such as *could, should, must, may,* and *ought.* Use *could have, should have, must have, may have,* and *ought to have* instead.

▶ The store owner *should have* given you your money back.

passed, past   *Passed* is the past tense of the verb "to pass."
Past is what happened before now.

▶ In the *past,* I never could have *passed* a chocolate chip cookie without eating it.

prejudice, prejudiced   *Prejudice* is a noun that means "the holding of negative preconceived judgments about people."
Prejudiced is an adjective that describes people or groups holding this attitude.

▶ *Prejudice* will exist as long as some people remain *prejudiced.*

principal, principle   *Principal* means "first" or "person with highest rank."
Principle means "a basic truth or assumption."

▶ The *principal* of the school spoke to Jason.
We must follow the *principle* that all men and women are born free.

quiet, quit, quite	*Quiet* is an adjective that means "without a sound."
	Quit is a verb that means "to stop doing something."
	Quite is an adverb that means "very."
	► *Quite* politely our neighbor asked us to be *quiet* and *quit* making noise.
raise, rise	*Raise* means "to lift."
	Rise means "to go up."
	► Ms. Ramirez *raises* her eyebrows.
	Ms. Ramirez' eyebrows *rise* when she is angry.
respectfully, respectively	*Respectfully* means "with great respect."
	Respectively means "in the same order."
	► The private spoke to the general *respectfully*.
	Paula, Diana, and David are twelve, seven, and five years old, *respectively*.
set, sit	*Set* means "to put."
	Sit means "to be seated."
	► Have you *set* the clock ahead for daylight-saving time?
	All the speakers will *sit* on the stage.
should have, should've, should of	See *of, have*.
someone, some one	See *anyone, any one*.
sometime, some time, sometimes	*Sometime* (one word) means "at an unspecified time."
	Some time (two words) is an amount of time.
	Sometimes means "now and then."
	► The plumbers will finish the job *sometime*, but I don't know when.
	Last summer I spent *some time* in Arkansas.
	Sometimes James laughs so loudly the neighbors upstairs complain.

than, then	*Than* is used for comparisons. *Then* is used to show the order of events in time.

▶ Oranges are sweeter *than* lemons.
First make your bed; *then* throw out the garbage.

their, there, they're	*Their* is the ownership form of *they*. *There* means "not here." *They're* is short for *they are*.

▶ They gave *their* promise that the work would be done.
Put the package down over *there*.
They're packing the suitcases right now.

threw, through	*Threw* is the past tense of the verb "to throw." *Through* means "between" or "down the middle."

▶ Pacho *threw* the football *through* the open window.

to, too, two	*To* means "in the direction of." *Too* means "also" and "excessively." *Two* is a number.

▶ Take these letters *to* the post office.
There are *too* many cars on the highway.
The boy sold only *two* bottles of soda.

want, won't	*Want* is a verb that means "to desire." *Won't* is short for "will not."

▶ I *won't* think about what you *want* until you consider the consequences of your actions.

were, we're, where	*Were* is a past tense form of the verb "to be." *We're* is a contraction for "we are." *Where* signifies a place.

▶ The pieces *were* all assembled.
We're going to solve this mystery.
We must know *where* you have been.

who, which, that

Who, which, and *that* are pronouns (see **3**)
used to combine sentences (see **1c**).
Who refers to people only.
Which refers to things and events, but not
to people.
That can refer to either.

▶ The children *who* (or *that*) visited the zoo brought
back balloons.
The balloons *which* (or *that*) they brought back
were soon broken.

who's, whose

Who's is short for "who is."
Whose is the ownership form of *who* and is
usually followed by a noun.

▶ *Who's* in charge here?
Whose bicycle is this?

would have,
would've, would of

See *of, have.*

your, you're

Your means "belonging to you."
You're is short for "you are."

▶ *You're* certain that a balanced diet will improve
your health.

UNIT TWO

Mechanics

7

Punctuation

Marks of punctuation help make sentence meanings clearer.

7a   STOPS AT THE END OF THE SENTENCE

7a(1)   Exclamation Points

Use an exclamation point ! to end an expression of strong feeling.

> Ah! I am in love! I am in love! I am in love!
> Don't you dare say that!
> I never want to see you again!

7a(2)   Question Marks

Use a question mark ? at the end of a direct question.

> When will I ever see you again?
> Why don't you leave me alone?
> Can this be love?

Do not use a question mark at the end of an indirect question.

> He asked if I was sick.

7a(3)   Periods

Use a period . to end any sentence other than a direct question or an expression of strong feeling.

> I first saw her when she stepped onto the subway at Flatbush Avenue and Avenue K.

> She asked me how she could get to the Staten Island Ferry.
>
> I'll show you the way.
>
> Come with me.

Periods are also used to show words left out of quotations. Use three periods **. . .** to show words or sentences left out of the middle of a quotation. Use four periods **. . . .** to show words left out at the end of a quotation.

> We, the people of the United States, in order to form a more perfect Union **. . .** do ordain and establish this Constitution. **. . . .**
> —Preamble to the Constitution

Periods are used after most abbreviations.

> Dr.   Jr.   B.A.   A.M.

7b   BREAKS IN THE MIDDLE OF THE SENTENCE

7b(1)   Commas

▶ Use a comma **,** to separate two sentences joined by *and, but, or, nor, for, so,* or *yet.* (See p. 453.)

> I would have called, *but* I lost your phone number.

▶ Use a comma to separate items in a list.

> Myra packed her bags, said goodbye to her friends, bought an airplane ticket, and left for India.
>
> The tall, dark, handsome stranger wore boots, spurs, black pants, a black shirt, a red kerchief, and a black hat.

▶ Use a comma to set off long groups of words at the beginning of a sentence, particularly prepositional phrases (see p. 485) and descriptive phrases (see p. 455).

> Without money to buy a saddle, the stranger had to ride bareback.

▶ Use a comma to set off a dependent word group at the beginning (but not at the end) of a sentence. (See p. 458.)

> *Because he wore tight boots,* the stranger had blisters.
>
> The stranger had blisters *because he wore tight boots.*

▶ Use commas to separate added-in words and phrases that are not part of the main idea of a sentence.

The stranger, *however,* used Band-Aids to lessen the pain.

▶ Use commas to separate out a descriptive dependent word group that is not needed to identify the person or thing described.

Sam Jones, *who knew the stranger from high school days,* opened the first drugstore west of the Mississippi. (You don't need the words *who knew the stranger . . .* to identify Sam Jones.)

Don't use a comma if the descriptive word group is needed to identify the person or thing.

The man *who knew the stranger from high school days* opened the first drugstore west of the Mississippi.

Here the words *who knew the stranger . . .* identify the man. (Which man? The man who knew the stranger from high school days.) Without those words, we don't know which man the writer is talking about. The phrase restricts the meaning of *man.*

▶ Use commas to set off the name of a person addressed.

Sam, is that you? I haven't seen you for years, *Sam.*

▶ Use a comma to separate phrases that might be confused.

Sam introduced the stranger to the saloonkeeper and the sheriff, and offered to give the stranger a room. (The comma clarifies that *and offered* goes with *introduced* rather than *saloonkeeper* and *sheriff.*)

▶ Use commas in titles, addresses, and dates.

Abdul Ali, M.D.
23 Walker Road, Toledo, Ohio
November 24, 1977

▶ Use commas with quotation marks (see pages 514, 515).

"Tell me what I should do," he said.

"Tell me," he said, "what I should do."

7b(2)   Dashes

Use a dash —— to interrupt a sentence dramatically and to put stress on words you've added. If you continue the main idea of the sentence after the interrupting phrase, use a second dash. A dash is longer than a hyphen; show it by typing two hyphens next to each other: --.

> He shot the gun, and then——

> Afterwards——*yes, he was a real criminal*——he didn't even bat an eyelash!

7b(3)   Parentheses

Use parentheses ( ) to separate out material that breaks up the main idea of a sentence. Parentheses provide a stronger break than commas, but not as strong a break as dashes.

> John Smith (*also known as the Silver Straight-Arrow*) keeps watch over the city.

7b(4)   Brackets

Use brackets [ ] to add your own words within a quotation.

> Ask not what your country can do for you; ask what you [*JFK was speaking to all Americans*] can do for your country.

7b(5)   Colons

► The colon : means "as follows." Use a colon to introduce a long list.

> There are many comic book superheroes: *Superman, Batman, Wonder Woman, Green Arrow, Supergirl, Elastic Man, Captain Marvel, and others.*

> Remember: the words before the colon should be a complete sentence. If the list completes the sentence, the colon is probably not needed.

> WRONG   Two animal superheroes are: Mighty Mouse and Manfred the Wonder Dog.
>
> RIGHT   Two animal superheroes are Mighty Mouse and Manfred the Wonder Dog.

RIGHT   There are two animal superheroes: Mighty Mouse and Manfred the Wonder Dog.

▶ Use a colon to introduce a final word, phrase, or example that shows the meaning or result of the sentence.

Superheroes always manage to save themselves: *all superheroes are immortal.*

▶ Use a colon in the greeting of a formal business letter and in separating hours, minutes, and seconds.

Dear Ms. Bulbenkian:

The time is exactly 7:36 A.M.

7b(6)   Semicolons

▶ Use a semicolon ; to separate two sentences joined together without any linking words. (See p. 453.)

Baseball used to be the national sport of the United States; football has now replaced it.

▶ Use a semicolon to separate two sentences joined by the linking words *therefore, however, thus, moreover,* or the linking phrases *for example, in fact, in any case, on the other hand.*

I can afford the new car; *on the other hand,* I don't really need it.

▶ Use a semicolon instead of a comma to separate items in a list when there are commas within the items. The semicolon will make the separations clearer and prevent confusion.

We invited Harold, the butcher; Maxine, the dentist; Greg, the teacher; Joe, the construction worker; Violet, the factory owner; and Debbie, the landlord.

7c   OTHER PUNCTUATION

7c(1)   Apostrophes

▶ Use an apostrophe ' followed by an *s* to show ownership in words that do not end in *s* or *z*. It makes no difference whether the words are singular or plural.

Bill's house, Gloria's camera, the children's games, the man's car, the women's movement

▶ Use only the apostrophe when the word already ends in *s* or *z*.

Iris' temper, the ladies' magazine, the Joneses' house, Mrs. Ramirez' car

Do not use an apostrophe to make the plural of any word except for the special cases discussed below. *Spoon's* means "belonging to the spoon" and not "more than one spoon."

Do not use apostrophes with pronouns that show ownership (see **3d**). *It's* means "it is," not "belonging to it." Use *its* to show ownership.

▶ Use an apostrophe to show missing letters in contractions.

don't (short for *do not*)
I'd (short for *I would* or *I had*)

▶ Use an apostrophe to make the plural of letters, numbers, abbreviations, and signs.

In advanced math there were two A's, eight B's, fifteen C's, six D's, and three F's.

7c(2)   Hyphens

▶ Use a hyphen - to join some compound words together.

a three-month-old baby   a cross-reference

Check a dictionary to find which words should be written with hyphens.

▶ Use a hyphen to separate starting and ending numbers, dates, and scores.

pages 37-52   1974-1976   The Mets beat the
                                Dodgers 4-3.

▶ Use a hyphen to break a long word at the end of a line. Be sure to break the word only between syllables. Check the dictionary to find the exact syllables of any word.

             poly-   choles-
unsaturated   terol

PUNCTUATION REVIEW

.   To end sentences and abbreviations:

> Dr. Smith called.

?   To end direct questions:

> What time is it?

!   To show surprise or strong emotion:

> I don't believe it!

,   To separate words, phrases, and sentences in a series:

> apples, oranges, pineapples, and bananas
>
> They ate, they drank, and they danced.

To set off opening phrases and dependent word groups:

> *While he was angry,* he was difficult to talk to.

To separate out words and phrases not part of the main idea of the sentence:

> Gene, *on the other hand,* got all the laughs.

To separate out phrases that do not restrict the meaning of nouns:

> Fran, *the teacher's pet,* got all the answers right.

To set off the name of a person you are addressing:

> *Mary,* how have you been?

To use in titles, dates, addresses:

> Allen Schwartz, M.D.   June 30, 1945
> Elk, California

—   To interrupt a sentence and to emphasize added-in phrases:

> Phil—*our last hope*—came to bat.

( )   To separate interrupting material:

> Candy Jones (*of the prominent Jones family*) invited me to a party.

[ ]   To add your own words in a quotation:

> "Four score [*that means eighty*] and seven years ago. . . ."

:   To introduce a long list:

> There are five people here: *Joyce, Tom, Roz, Dom, and Joan.*

;   To join two complete sentences together without using a connecting word:

> Jack went to the theater; Rachel went to the ball game.

'   To show ownership:

> Karen's shoes

To show contractions:

> don't

-    To join words together:

> a six-year-old child

To break words into syllables at the end of a line:

>   ampli-
> fication

_____   To show that titles of long works, foreign words, emphasized words, and words discussed as words should be in italics (see Chapter 13):

> Love Story (printed as *Love Story*)

" "   To show exact quotations (see **8a**):

> "Never," I said.

To show titles of short works (see **8d**):

> "Sweet Little Sixteen"

8

Quotation Marks

8a   DIRECT QUOTATIONS

Enclose the exact words of a speaker or writer within double quotation marks " ". If you use a phrase such as *he says* with a quotation, use the following models for punctuation:

> He said, " I want two pounds of thick, sirloin steak."
>
> "I want," he said, "two pounds of thick, sirloin steak."
>
> "I want two pounds of thick, sirloin steak," he said.

Quotation marks always come in pairs; make sure every time you open a quotation with quotation marks, you close it with quotation marks at the end. If a direct quotation is more than a paragraph long, put quotation marks only at the beginning of each paragraph to remind the reader that the quotation is continuing. Do not use closing quotation marks until the end of the last paragraph of the quotation. If you are writing dialogue, you must start a new paragraph each time a different person speaks.

8b   LONG DIRECT QUOTATIONS

In a research paper, do not use quotation marks for a quotation longer than fifty words. Instead, skip a line, indent each line of the quotation five typewriter spaces, or one-half inch, and single-space the quotation.

> Ernest Hemingway writes in a language that is very
>
> simple; yet, at the same time, it captures the reader's
>
> attention by always stating less than the writer really

means. Here, from "On the Quai at Smyrna," is an

example of such understatement:

> The strange thing was, he said, how they screamed
> at midnight. I do not know why they screamed at
> that time. We were in the harbor and they were all
> on the pier and at midnight they started screaming.
> We used to turn the searchlight on them to quiet
> them. That always did the trick.

8c   QUOTATIONS WITHIN QUOTATIONS

Use single quotation marks ' ' to show a quotation within a quotation.

Jean said, "Eric said to me, 'You'd better not be late to class!' "

8d   TITLES OF SHORT WORKS

Use quotation marks for titles of short works, such as poems, short stories, songs, and television and radio programs.

"The Lady with a Lap Dog"   "St. Louis Blues"

(For titles of major works, see **13a.**)

8e   QUOTATION MARKS WITH OTHER MARKS OF PUNCTUATION

Periods and commas go inside quotation marks.

Abner said, "Hello."

Question marks and exclamation points go inside the quotation marks if they are part of the quotation. If not, they are placed outside the quotation marks.

Sarah asked, "How are you, Abner?"

Abner answered, "I'm angry. Did Jay really say, 'Abner is a turkey'?"

Will Abner beat Jay up for saying "Abner is a turkey"?

Colons and semicolons go outside the quotation marks.

Sarah said, "I really don't know"; she knew better than to get involved in the fight between her two brothers.

9

Documenting Sources

9a WHAT YOU MUST DOCUMENT

Every time you use a quotation, information, or an idea from a book, magazine, or other printed source, you must state where you got the quotation, information, or idea. Even if you paraphrase (change the wording) or summarize (write in brief form) the material in your own words, you must give credit to the source. Quotations must accurately follow the exact wording of the original, and be identified by quotation marks or indentation (see **8a** and **8b**).

You may document your sources using any of a number of different styles, depending on your academic discipline and the preferences of your instructor. Styles of documentation all provide much the same information but differ in format. For the sake of consistency and ease of reference, you should follow precisely the style required by the teacher, profession, or journal for which you are writing. If you don't know what documentation style is required, simply ask. Disciplines in the humanities typically use the Modern Language Association (MLA) style, the social sciences use the American Psychological Association (APA) style, and the sciences use the Council of Biology Editors (CBE) and the American Chemical Society (ACS) styles. Each of these organizations publishes handbooks specifying the details of documentation formats.

This chapter presents the documentation style required by the Modern Language Association (MLA). According to the MLA, you no longer need to use footnotes to document sources. Instead, you should give a **Works Cited** list at the end of your paper. In your paper, whenever you use information, an idea, or a quotation from a work, you refer to that list.

You refer to the Works Cited list by giving the author's last name and the page number of the work from which you got the material. You can give the name and page number in the sentence itself or in parentheses.

518

For example, you could refer to material taken from page 32 of the book *Great Scientific Experiments* by Rom Harre in any one of the following ways:

> "Aristotle must surely be ranked as among the greatest
>
> biologists" (Harre 32).

> Harre comments, "Aristotle must surely be ranked as
>
> among the greatest biologists" (32).

> Harre believes that Aristotle is a top biologist (32).

If you have more than one book by Harre in your Works Cited list, include a short version of the title of the book you are referring to.

> (Harre, Great Experiments 32)

9b   WORKS CITED LIST

The information you must include in your Works Cited list comes from the title and copyright pages of the books you use. If you quote from a magazine article, you will need to look at the first page of the article and the masthead of the magazine. The masthead, which lists publication information, usually appears near the front of the magazine, close to the table of contents.

Here is the basic form for Works Cited listings, showing the elements you must provide, in proper order, for books and articles. Note the style of punctuation.

Book	Author. Title. City of Publication: Publisher, year.
Article	Author. "Article Title." Magazine Titlel Volume number (Date): inclusive pages.

Arrange the items in the list in alphabetical order according to the author's last name. If there is more than one author, the second and third authors should be given first name first. If there is no author, begin with the title.

Sample Items for Works Cited List

Books:

One author	Harre, Rom. Great Scientific Experiments. Oxford: Phaidon, 1981.
Two authors	Glazer, Nathan, and Daniel Patrick Moynihan. Beyond the Melting Pot. Cambridge, Mass.: M.I.T. Press, 1963.
Editor	Kramer, Samuel Noah, ed. Mythologies of the Ancient World. Garden City, N.Y.: Doubleday, 1961.
Essay in a collection	Anthes, Rudolf. "Mythology in Ancient Egypt." Mythologies of the Ancient World. Ed. Samuel Noah Kramer. Garden City, N.Y.: Doubleday, 1961. 15-92.
Encyclopedia article	Kerr, K. Austin. "Lindbergh, Charles A." Academic American Encyclopedia. 1984 ed.

Magazine articles:

Signed	Shapiro, Laura. "Completely Adulterated Seafood." Newsweek 23 Feb. 1987: 64-65.
Unsigned	"Top Dog." Newsweek 23 Feb. 1987: 68.
Scholarly journal	Hashimoto, Irwin. "The Myth of the Attention-Getting Opening." Written Communication 3:1 (1986): 123-132. [3:1 means the first issue of volume 3]

Magazines published weekly (like *Newsweek*) or monthly often do not have volume and issue numbers. Notice, in the examples above, how the dates are treated.

10

Capitals

10a SENTENCES AND QUOTATIONS

Use capitals

▶ for the first word in a sentence.

The child cried. **Her** mother kissed her.

▶ for the first spoken word in a quotation.

Leroy said, "**Let's** go."

10b LETTERS

In a letter, capitalize

▶ the first letter of each word in the salutation.

Dear Sir:
Dear Ms. Stanley:

▶ the first letter of the first word (only) of the complimentary close.

Sincerely yours,
Yours truly,

10c   PROPER NAMES

Capitalize actual names of specific people, places, or things. More general words should not be capitalized even when they identify individual people, places, or things.

10c(1)   Geographical Names

Pike's Peak	that mountain
Rhine River	a river in our state
Portland, Phoenix	our city
Lake Erie	a nearby lake

10c(2)   Streets, Buildings, Businesses, Organizations

Thomson Avenue, Lincoln Road	a wide avenue
East 96 Street, Linden Boulevard	a house on that street
Woolworth Building	that building
Marshall Field's Department Store	a large store
Ford Motor Company	a car company
First Baptist Church	the church

10c(3)   Schools, School Subjects, and Classes

Wichita State College	my college
Seaford High School	this high school
Chinese, English, Spanish	languages
Mathematics 11.1, History 18	mathematics, history
Brewster College Freshman Class	the freshman class

10c(4)   Seasons, Months, Days of the Week, Holidays

April, March, October	winter, spring, summer, fall
Tuesday, Saturday	today
the Fourth of July, Labor Day	my birthday

10c(5)   Directions and Special Regions

Southeast Asia	the northwest corner
She lives in the West.	Walk east on Main Street
I came from the South.	Drive south on the parkway.

10c(6)   Titles of Books, Newspapers, Magazines, Poems, Plays, Movies, TV Shows, Songs, Students' Compositions

Capitalize the first, last, and all other important words.

The Exorcist	a frightening movie
"All in the Family"	my favorite show
"The Raven"	this poem
"An Embarrassment"	the short story

10c(7)   Historical Events

Revolutionary War	a long war
the Boxer Rebellion	a rebellion
the Boston Tea Party	a meeting
the Emancipation Proclamation	a decree, a law

10c(8)   Flowers, Trees, Animals, Games

Do not capitalize the names of flowers, trees, animals, or games.

carnation, maple, horse, soccer

10c(9)   Nationalities, Races, and Religions

Mexican, Chinese	a national holiday
Negro	black, white
Roman Catholic, Lutheran	a church member
Jewish, Protestant	an orthodox believer
God, the Bible	tribal gods, biblical
in His [God's] wisdom	a holy man

10c(10)   People's Names and Titles

Betsy, Charles	the man
Anna Marino	the woman
President Gomez	the president of the college
Dr. Williams	my professor
President Roosevelt	president of the country
Representative Kono	the representative from Oregon

10c(11) Relatives

Capitalize when the word of relation is used as a name.

Aunt Adele	my aunt
Uncle Hy	**Dad**'s brother
I saw **Dad**.	I saw my dad.

11

Numbers

11a FIGURES

In writing sentences that call for figures, spell out the figure if it takes two words or fewer; otherwise, use numerals.

eighty-five tons	687 tons
in *two thousand* years	in 350 years
twenty dollars	$22.15
one-eighth	52⅛

11a(1) Figures in Series

Be consistent if you need to write a series of figures. Use either words *or* numerals, not both together.

two books, *four* pencils, *ten* crayons

218 lbs. of cement, 14 lbs. of nails, 116 bags of sand

11a(2) Figures at the Beginning of the Sentence

Spell out any figure that starts a sentence.

Four thousand cattle lay killed.

If you want to use numerals, rewrite the sentence so the figure does not come first.

They killed 4,828 cattle.

11a(3)   Very Large Figures

Spell out large round numbers, unless you want to stress them—then use numerals.

> *eight billion* dollars   OR $8 *billion*   OR $8,000,000,000
> 16.5 *million*   OR   16,500,000

11b   ADDRESSES

Use numerals in addresses.

> 1218 Remsen Avenue
> Massapequa, New York 11758
> Highway 101

If the name of a street is a number, you may spell out the number if it is below ten.

> 168 *Fifth* Avenue   OR   168 5th Avenue

But:

> 218 East 98 Street   OR   218 East 98th Street

11c   TIMES

Use numerals for telling time.

> 6 P.M., 4:30 A.M., 7:00 A.M.

Before the word *o'clock,* write out the figure.

> *ten* o'clock in the morning

11d   PERCENTAGES

Use numerals to show percentages or decimal figures.

> 92%, a 2.7 mile drive, .37 of an inch

11e   DATES

Use numerals with dates.

>   1860–1865
>   June 28, 1973   (NOT June 28th, 1973)

But:

>   the *fifth* of March, October *first,* the *twentieth* century, the *twenties*

11f   FIGURES THAT SHOW ORDER

In general write out numbers that end in *th, nth, st, nd,* and *rd.*

>   their *thirtieth* anniversary   (NOT their 30th anniversary)

11g   PARTS OF A BOOK

Use numerals to show parts of a book.

>   Part II, Chapter 4, page 27, question 5

12

Abbreviations

Usually, people avoid abbreviations in formal writing. Some abbreviations, however, are all right to use. Abbreviations usually need periods after them. The list here will help you decide when and how to abbreviate.

12a TITLES

Abbreviate titles that go before someone's full name. Don't abbreviate titles used without someone's name.

Dr. Rita Stark	I saw the *doctor.*
Mr. Jacob T. Wildwood	He wanted to be called
Ms. Marion Arlin	*mister.*

Abbreviate titles or degrees used after someone's name. Don't abbreviate *professor, senator,* or *general* before last names alone.

Lionel Chase, *A.A., B.A.*	*General* Bradley
Blanche Jones, *Ph.D.*	*Professor* Hoban
Wilbur T. Washington, *Jr., M.D.*	*Senator* Ortiz

12b PARTS OF COMPANY NAMES

Abbreviate words and symbols used as parts of company names.

R&S Davis, *Inc.; P.* Bruce and Sons, *Ltd.*

12c   PEOPLE'S NAMES

Do not abbreviate people's names.

> Thomas (NOT Thos.), Charles (NOT Chas.)

12d   COMPANIES AND GOVERNMENT AGENCIES

Abbreviate the names of companies, government agencies, and other organizations that are well known.

> UNICEF, NATO, NBC, FBI

12e   SCHOOL SUBJECTS

Do not abbreviate names of school subjects.

> economics (NOT econ.), mathematics (NOT math.), psychology (NOT psych.)

12f   LATIN WORDS

Abbreviate certain Latin words used in writing.

> *i.e.* (that is); *e.g.* (for example); *viz.* (namely); *etc.* (and so forth); *re* (concerning)

12g   SYMBOLS USED WITH WORDS

Some symbols are useful in tables or rough notes, but they should not be used with words in formal writing.

> and (NOT &); number (NOT #); without (NOT w/o)

12h ABBREVIATIONS OR SYMBOLS USED WITH NUMBERS

Use abbreviations or symbols for certain words when they appear with numbers.

> A.M. OR a.m. (5:22 A.M.); P.M. OR p.m. (8:00 p.m.)
> A.D., B.C. (A.D. 68; 2000 B.C.)
> No. OR no. (No. 15)
> $, ¢ ($15.27, 32¢)

12i MONTHS AND DAYS

Do not abbreviate the names of months and days.

> My birthday is in *April*.
> On *Tuesday* he arrived.
> *Friday, November 23*

13

Italics

Italics are slanted print. When using a typewriter or writing long-hand, underline words that should be in italics.

13a TITLES OF MAJOR WORKS

Italicize (underline) titles of books, magazines, movies, plays, record albums, works of art, ships, and the like.

> *Moby Dick, Sports Illustrated, The Exorcist, Hamlet, Tommy,* the *Mona Lisa,* the *Titanic*

(For titles of short works, see **8d**.)

13b FOREIGN WORDS

Italicize (underline) foreign words.

> In Spanish *hasta la vista* means the same as *au revoir* in French: "until we see each other again."

Note: Many foreign words have become accepted as English words and do not need italics. For example,

> Eating too many blintzes, tacos, and pizzas will give you indigestion.

Check a dictionary to see whether a foreign word is now accepted as an English word.

13c   WORDS, LETTERS, AND NUMBERS USED AS SUCH

Italicize (underline) words, letters, or numbers when discussing them as words, letters, or numbers.

> The word *grubby* originally came from the name for certain insect larvae, grubs.

13d   WORDS THAT NEED EMPHASIS

Italicize (underline) occasional words that need emphasis.

> That is absolutely *disgusting*.

Remember: do not use italics for emphasis too often. Make sure you have a good reason when you do use them.

14

Spelling

14a WORDS MOST OFTEN MISSPELLED

You are not alone if you misspell one of a large number of confusing words. The only way to learn these words is to go over them again and again. Write them. Say them. Look at them. Use them in sentences.

The most commonly misspelled words are divided into groups below to make them easier for you to study. The trouble spots are printed in darker type. Try learning one group a week.

I	II
a lot	achi**e**vement
a**ll** right	among
believ**e**	beli**ef**
benefit**e**d	conc**ei**vable
describe	cons**ci**ous
forty	exist**e**nce
guarantee	o**cc**asion
license	po**ss**ible
lonely	profe**ss**or
loo**s**e	pursue
o**cc**u**rr**ed	sense
personal	simil**ar**
rhythm	techni**que**
shining	villa**i**n
than	writing

III	IV
acclaim	accommodate
acquire	analysis
coming	become
definitely	before
discipline	disgusted
dropped	enough
embarrass	occurrence
existent	prisoners
familiar	significance
fascinate	source
marriage	strength
medicine	swimming
necessary	thought
preferred	useless
prepare	various
succeed	

V	VI
arguing	apparent
beneficial	article
description	beginning
interest	exaggerate
mere	experience
occurring	height
particular	losing
receive	practical
recognize	precede
separate	privilege
sincerely	repetition
studying	transferred
therefore	vacuum
thorough	weird
tragedy	whose

VII

afraid
already
beautiful
entrance
excitable
hungry
opinion
personnel
playwright
sacrifice
sociology
stubborn
suspense
unnecessary
view

VIII

argument
bargain
cigarette
escape
except
exercise
fourth
genius
hopeless
hoping
huge
ignorant
imagine
jealous
likely

IX

acceptance
across
advertisement
curriculum
during
fulfill
grammar
possession
prejudice
recommend
relieve
seize
sentence
speech
suppose

X

analyze
arise
certainly
environment
excellence
interest
oppose
quiet
referring
remember
surprise
swimmer
together
useful
yield

14b   THE *IE* RULE

▶   *i* usually comes before *e:*

chief, pierce, field

▶   after the letter *c,* the *e* usually comes first:

ceiling, perceive, receive

▶   if the sound of the two letters is ā (to rhyme with *say*), we usually write *ei:*

neighbor, sleigh, weigh, eight, vein

▶   Exceptions (memorize them!):

either, height, neither, seize, their, weird

14c   FINAL *E*

Words that end in *e* sometimes change when a suffix (an ending) is added.

▶   If the suffix begins with a vowel, drop the *e* at the end of the word and add the suffix.

come + ing = coming
excite + able = excitable

▶   Keep the *e* at the end of the word if the suffix starts with a consonant.

hope + less = hopeless
advertise + ment = advertisement

▶   Exceptions:

notice + able = noticeable
courage + ous = courageous
argue + ment = argument
dye + ing = dyeing
true + ly = truly
judge + ment = judgment

14d DOUBLED LETTERS

When a word changes its form (from *run* to *running*, for example), its last letter is sometimes doubled.

▶ If the word is one syllable long, if it ends in a consonant, and if one vowel comes before the consonant, double the last letter before adding the ending.

run + ing = ru**nn**ing
p**lan** + ed = plan**n**ed

▶ If the word ends in two consonants, or if there are two vowels before the final consonant, do not double the last letter before adding the ending.

gra**sp** + ing = gras**p**ing
l**ea**d + ing = lea**d**ing

▶ In two-syllable words, double the last letter if

1. it is a consonant.
2. only one vowel comes before the consonant.
3. you accent the last syllable when you say the word.

For example:

prefer (pronounced *preFER*) + ed = prefe**rr**ed

But:

retail (pronounced *REtail*) + ing = retailing (two vowels, no accent)

14e FINAL Y

Words that end in *y* sometimes change when a suffix is added.

▶ If the letter before the final *y* is a consonant, change the *y* to *i*.

try + es = tr**i**es
rep**ly** + ed = repl**i**ed

▶ If the letter before the final *y* is a vowel, do not change the *y*.

stay + ed = stayed

▶ If the ending you add begins with *i*, do not change the *y*.

reply + ing = replying

14f PLURALS

Plurals are formed in many ways.

14f(1) Regular Plurals

▶ Add *s* to most words.

book, books; dollar, dollars; table, tables

▶ Add *es* to words ending in *ch, sh, ss, x, z.*

ben**ch**, ben**ches**; wi**sh**, wi**shes**; dre**ss**, dre**sses**; bo**x**, bo**xes**

▶ If a word ends in *y* and a consonant comes before the *y*, change *y* to *i* and add *es.*

fl**y**, fl**ies**; count**ry**, count**ries**

▶ If a word ends in *y* and a vowel comes before the *y*, add *s.* Don't change anything.

da**y**, da**ys**; turke**y**, turke**ys**

▶ If a word ends in *o* and the *o* comes after a vowel, most of the time you add an *s.*

rad**io**, rad**ios**; d**uo**, d**uos**

▶ If a word ends in *o* and the *o* comes after a consonant, add *es.*

Neg**ro**, Neg**roes**; toma**to**, toma**toes**

Exceptions:

sopra**no**, sopra**nos**; pia**no**, pia**nos**; au**to**, au**tos**

▶ Some words ending in *f* or *fe* change *f* to *v* before adding *s* or *es*.

elf, elves; knife, knives; half, halves; wife, wives

▶ Some words ending in *f* or *fe* keep the *f* in the plural form.

belief, beliefs

14f(2) Words with Special Changes

Many words form plurals by changing their spelling completely.

tooth, teeth; goose, geese
man, men; woman, women
child, children; ox, oxen
mouse, mice

The dictionary will tell you which spelling to choose for the plural form.

14f(3) Words That Don't Change

Some words are the same whether singular or plural:

sheep   deer   series

Some words are always plural:

people   cattle   rice

14f(4) Words with Special Endings

Some words—especially words that come from foreign languages—form plurals in unusual ways.

curriculum, curricula; medium, media; criterion, criteria
crisis, crises; analysis, analyses
alumna, alumnae

14f(5) Combined Words

Words made by putting together two or more words form plurals by adding *s* to the base word.

mother-in-law, mothers-in-law
editor-in-chief, editors-in-chief

14f(6)   Letters, Numbers, and Abbreviations

Use an apostrophe and *s* ('s) to show the plural of a letter, number, or abbreviation.

There are two *c*'s and two *m*'s in *accommodate*.

Don't use *etc.*'s in your writing.

P.O.W.'s

the 1980's

14g   USING A DICTIONARY FOR SPELLING AND MEANING

A dictionary contains a great deal of information about words—from their correct pronunciation to their history—as you can see in the labeled sample from the *American Heritage Dictionary* on page 541. Most dictionaries provide an introduction that explains the material covered inside. People use dictionaries most often to check the spellings and meanings of words.

14g(1)   Checking Spelling

In each dictionary entry the main word is spelled in large dark type, and other forms of the word are spelled in smaller dark type. Listed on the sample page after the main entry *salesman*, for example, are the forms *salesmanship* and *saleswoman*. For the word *sake*, a second or alternate spelling is given, *saki*. So once you have found the word entry, you have the spelling for the word and any alternate forms.

The problem is finding the entry for a word you don't know how to spell. Words in a dictionary are arranged in alphabetical order. If you know the first few letters of the word you are looking for, you should have little problem finding it. If you are not sure of the first few letters, try the spelling you think most likely. If you still can't locate it, try all other letter combinations that might sound like your word. For example, if you did

Guide words

Main entries

Pronunciation

Part of speech

Special forms and spellings

Meaning

History of the word

Pronunciation key

safeguard / sallent

620

assuring unmolested passage, as through enemy lines.

safe·guard (sāf'gärd') n. A precautionary measure or device. —v. To insure the safety of; protect.

safe·keep·ing (sāf'kē'pĭng) n. Protection; care.

safe·ty (sāf'tē) n., pl. -ties. 1. Freedom from danger or injury. 2. Any of various protective devices. 3. Football. a. A play in which the offensive team downs the ball behind its own goal line. b. A defensive back closest to his own goal line.

safety match. A match that can be lighted only by being struck against a chemically prepared friction surface.

safety pin. A pin in the form of a clasp, having a sheath to cover and hold the point.

saf·fron (sāf'rən) n. 1. The dried orange-yellow stigmas of a kind of crocus, used to color and flavor food and as a dye. 2. Orange-yellow. [< Ar za'farān.] —**saf'fron** adj.

sag (săg) v. sagged, sagging. 1. To sink or bend downward, as from pressure or slackness. 2. To droop. [Perh < Scand.] —**sag** n.

sa·ga (sä'gə) n. 1. An Icelandic prose narrative of the 12th and 13th centuries. 2. A long heroic narrative. [ON, a story, legend.]

sa·ga·cious (sə-gā'shəs) adj. Shrewd and wise. [< L sagāx.] —**sa·gac'i·ty** (-găs'ə-tē) n.

sage[1] (sāj) n. A venerable wise man. —adj. sager, sagest. Judicious; wise. [< L sapere, to be sensible, be wise.] —**sage'ly** adv.

sage[2] (sāj) n. 1. An aromatic plant with gray-ish-green leaves used as seasoning. 2. Sage-brush. [< L salvia, "the healing plant."]

sage·brush (sāj'brŭsh') n. An aromatic shrub of arid regions of W North America.

sag·it·tal (săj'ə-təl) adj. 1. Of or like an arrow or arrowhead. 2. Relating to the suture uniting the two parietal bones of the skull. [< L sagitta, arrow.] —**sag'it·tal·ly** adv.

Sag·it·ta·ri·us (săj'ə-târ'ē-əs) n. 1. A constellation in the S Hemisphere. 2. The 9th sign of the zodiac. [< L sagittārius, an archer, Sagittarius.]

sa·go (sā'gō) n. A powdery starch obtained from the trunks of an Asian palm. [Malay sagu.]

sa·gua·ro (sə-gwär'ō, sə-wär'ō) n., pl. -ros. Also **sa·hua·ro** (sə-wär'ō). A very large branching cactus of SW North America. [Mex Span.]

Sa·har·a (sə-hăr'ə, -hä'rə). A desert of N Africa.

sa·hib (sä'ĭb) n. A title of respect for Europeans in colonial India, equivalent to master or sir. [Hindi sāhib, master, lord.]

said (sĕd). p.t. & p.p. of say. —adj. Aforementioned.

Sai·gon (si-gŏn'). The capital of South Vietnam. Pop. 1,400,000.

sail (sāl) n. 1. A length of shaped fabric that catches the wind and propels or aids in maneuvering a vessel. 2. A sailing ship. 3. A trip in a sailing craft. 4. Something resembling a sail. —v. 1. To move across the surface of water by means of a sail. 2. To travel by water

in a vessel. 3. To start out on a voyage. 4. To operate a sailing craft; navigate or manage (a vessel). 5. To glide through the air; soar. [< OE segl < Gmc *seglam.]

sail·boat (sāl'bōt') n. A small boat propelled by a sail or sails.

sail·fish (sāl'fĭsh') n. A large marine fish with a large dorsal fin and a spearlike projection from the upper jaw.

sail·or (sā'lər) n. 1. One who serves in a navy or earns his living working on a ship. 2. A straw hat with a flat top and brim.

saint (sānt) n. 1. Theol. a. A person officially entitled to public veneration for extreme holiness. b. A human soul inhabiting heaven. 2. A very holy or unselfish person. [< L sanctus, sacred.] —**saint'dom** n. —**saint'hood'** n.

saint·ly (sānt'lē) adj. -lier, -liest. Of or befitting a saint. —**saint'li·ness** n.

Saint-Saëns (săṅ-säṅs'), Camille. 1835–1921. French composer.

saith (sĕth, sā'əth). Archaic. 3rd person sing. present indicative of say.

sake[1] (sāk) n. 1. Purpose; motive: for the sake of argument. 2. Advantage, benefit, or welfare. [< OE sacu, lawsuit. See sāg-.]

sa·ke[2] (sä'kē) n. Also **sa·ki.** A Japanese liquor made from fermented rice.

sa·laam (sə-läm') n. An Oriental obeisance performed by bowing low while placing the right palm on the forehead. [Ar salām, "peace."] —**sa·laam'** v.

sa·la·cious (sə-lā'shəs) adj. Lewd; bawdy. [< L salāx, fond of leaping, lustful.] —**sa·la'cious·ly** adv. —**sa·la'cious·ness, sa·lac'i·ty** (sə-lăs'ə-tē) n.

sal·ad (săl'əd) n. A dish usually consisting of raw green vegetables tossed with a dressing. [< VL *salāre, to salt.]

sal·a·man·der (săl'ə-măn'dər) n. 1. A small, lizardlike amphibian. 2. A portable stove used to heat or dry buildings under construction. [< Gk salamandra.]

sa·la·mi (sə-lä'mē) n. A highly spiced and salted sausage. [< It salame, "salted pork."]

sal·a·ried (săl'ə-rēd) adj. Earning or yielding a regular salary.

sal·a·ry (săl'ə-rē, săl'rē) n., pl. -ries. A fixed compensation for services, paid on a regular basis. [< L salārium, orig "money given to Roman soldiers to buy salt."]

sale (sāl) n. 1. The exchange of property or ownership for money. 2. Demand; ready market. 3. Availability for purchase: on sale. 4. An auction. 5. A special disposal of goods at lowered prices. [< OE sala < ON.] —**sal'a·ble, sale'a·ble** adj.

Sa·lem (sā'ləm). The capital of Oregon. Pop. 68,000.

sales·man (sālz'mən) n. A man employed to sell merchandise, insurance, etc. —**sales'man·ship'** n. —**sales'wom·an** fem.n.

sal·i·cyl·ic acid (săl'ə-sĭl'ĭk). A white crystalline acid, $C_7H_6O_3$, used in making aspirin. [< L salix, willow.]

sa·li·ent (sā'lē-ənt) adj. 1. Projecting or jutting beyond a line. 2. Striking; conspicuous. [< L salīre, to leap, jump.] —**sal'i·ence, sal'i·en·cy** n.

not know how to spell the word *crime,* you might have to check out all these possible spellings before you came to the right one: cryme, kryme, khryme, chryme, krime, creim, crime.

Also notice where dots mark the syllable breaks in the entry words. For example, the word *salamander* is broken into *sal·a·man·der.* Knowing these syllable breaks is important if you need to break a long word at the end of a line. Break words only at the ends of syllables as discussed in **7c(2).**

14g(2)   Checking Word Meanings

Dictionary entries give the most important or most frequent meaning of a word first, with other meanings following in order of decreasing use. Meanings are also grouped according to the way the word is used grammatically. For example, the word *sail* has more than one meaning as both a noun and a verb. The most important meaning for the noun is the piece of cloth used to catch the wind on a boat. The most important meaning for the verb is to move on water using a sail.

Sometimes the dictionary will give a synonym (abbreviated *Syn.*)— that is, a word that has the same meaning as the entry word. You can find many more synonyms in a thesaurus of a dictionary of synonyms. However, be careful when you replace a word with its synonym in your writing, because the two words may have slightly different shades of meaning (see **6e**). If a synonym has the wrong shade of meaning, it will not fit your sentence.

Index

Index for Authors and Titles